Financial Management Handbook

Second Edition

Financial Management Handbook

Second Edition

Edited by
Jack Broyles, Ian Cooper and **Simon Archer**

Gower

Published by
Gower Publishing Company Limited,
Aldershot, Hants, England
Reprinted 1985

British Library Cataloguing in Publication Data

Financial management handbook.—2nd ed.
  1. Corporations—Finance
  2. Industrial management
  I. Broyles, Jack   II. Cooper, Ian   III. Archer,
  Simon.
  658.1'5   HG4026

ISBN 0 566 02175 7

Printed and bound in Great Britain by
Redwood Burn Limited, Trowbridge, Wiltshire

Contents

Preface   xi

List of illustrations   xiii

Notes on contributors   xvii

PART I   INTRODUCTION

1   **The role and organisation of the finance function**   3
    Peter Ratzer

Historical perspective – Objectives of financial
management – Conceptual framework – Financial
management – Reporting and Control – Organisation –
Conclusion – References

PART II   THE USE OF FUNDS

Overview   17

2   **Capital project planning**   21
    Tessa Ryder Runton, Jack Broyles and Ian Cooper

The goals of project planning – Required rate of return
standards and cost of capital – Traditional techniques for
testing viability – Modern techniques for testing viability –
Cash flow discipline in project analysis – NPV and IRR in
more detail – Computational resources – Data – Sensitivity
analysis – Probability analysis – Risk – The discussion
forum for capital investment problems – Re-appraisal:
ex-post evaluation and capital expenditure reviews –
References

Contents

3 Inflation and financial decisions   **49**
Ian Cooper

Forecasting in real and money units – Inflation and the
cost of funds – Further adjustments when inflation rates
are high – Relative price changes – Forecasting prices –
Long term and short term projects – Lags in cash flows –
Profits and cash flows – Inflation and taxes – Working in
money terms or real terms – The impact of inflation on
profitability – Conclusions – References

4 Managing working capital   **67**
Geoffrey P E Clarkson

Working capital ratios – Decision making – Example of
working capital flows – Timing of flows – Flow of funds –
Product cash cycle – Managing debtors – Managing
stocks – Managing creditors

5 International money management   **91**
Andreas R Prindl

Domestic cash management – International cash
management – International liquidity management

PART III FINANCIAL CONTROL

Overview   **117**

6 Reporting and responsibilities   **121**
Richard M S Wilson

Systems design in managerial accounting – The keys to
control – Organisational and behavioural implications –
Criteria for information usefulness – Internal financial
reporting and management control – Staffing and
operating the management control system – Conclusion

7 Budgets and budgetary control   **147**
Alan R Leaper

What is a budget? – Budget centres – Compiling a budget –
Controlling the plan – Flexible budgets – Use of

computers – Zero-base budgeting – Installing the
system – Conclusions

8   Costing and internal pricing   **169**
   H W Calvert and Simon Archer

Standard costing – Fixing a standard – Cost control
through variance analysis – Marginal costing – Break
even graphs – Make or buy? – The treatment of fixed
production expenses for financial statements preparation –
Internal pricing

9   Internal auditing   **197**
   Harry H Scholefield and P C Elliott

Organisation – Terms of reference – Staffing – Planning –
Audit programmes – The audit review – Reporting – Auditing
of computing systems – Benefits versus costs – Appendix 1 –
Appendix 2 – Appendix 3

PART IV   RAISING FUNDS

Overview   **221**

10   Forecasting financial requirements   **227**
   R L Mansbridge

Timing of cash plans – Monthly cash forecast and control –
Short term cash forecast – Source and application of
funds – Short term cash control – Long term cash
forecasts – Inflation – Dynamic aspect – International
aspects

11   Bank borrowing   **247**
   Michael Clipsham

Identifying the need for bank assistance – Types of finance
offered by the commercial banks – Relations with a bank –
Presenting a case for finance to a bank – Conclusions –
Further reading – Appendix

12   Leasing   **273**
   Colin M Young

Financial benefits of leasing: a simple example – Leasing
and the Inland Revenue – The tax paying lessee – Choice
of a schedule of lease rentals – Residual values – Other
evaluation methods – Conclusions

13 The UK new issue market   **291**
Elroy Dimson

The role of the Stock Exchange – Reasons for obtaining a
listing – Regulations concerning new issues – Methods of
making a new issue – Issue costs – The mechanics of a
flotation – Summary and conclusions – Further reading –
Appendix: New issue glossary

14 Equity rights issues   **325**
Paul Marsh

Issue methods for quoted companies raising money on
the Stock Exchange – The choice between debt and
equity – The rights issue method – The timing of external
funding and rights issues – Rights issue procedures and
timetable – Rights issue costs – Setting the terms and the
underwriting decision – Market reaction to rights issues –
Raising equity at existing market prices – Summary and
conclusions – References

PART V THE EXTERNAL ENVIRONMENT

Overview   **349**

15 Presentation of external financial reports   **353**
George R Thomson

Objectives – Profit and loss account – Balance sheet –
Funds statement – Directors' report – Current cost
accounts – Conclusions – Reference – Appendix

16 Acquisitions and mergers   **375**
J R Franks

Economic benefits of merging – Financial benefits of
merging – Acquisition valuation: four questions – Valuing
a quoted company – Traditional methods of asset valuation –

Conclusions – Further reading

17 Taxation of corporations in the UK   **393**
Raymond K Ashton

The statutory provisions – Corporation tax – How the
system works – Overseas tax – Stock relief – Losses – VAT
– Summary

Bibliography   **419**

Index   **423**

Preface

Financial Management Handbook was first published by Gower in 1972 and for ten years has proved its enduring value as a practical reference for the financial manager, for the chief executive and for accountable heads of departments. While maintaining the comprehensive and practical character of the earlier edition, the editors of this second edition have thoroughly updated the Handbook and extended it in many respects. The objective of the Handbook is to provide an authoritative work on managerial finance, with contributions from acknowledged experts in their respective fields. It provides a comprehensive and accurate summary of financial management techniques that can be used as a basis for action by managers in both large and small companies.

The Handbook is now divided into four main parts, each covering a major facet of financial management: The Use of Funds, Financial Control, Raising Funds, and The External Environment. Although individual chapters in each part are contributed by different authors, a unifying framework and survey of techniques is now provided by the editors in an introduction to each of the four parts of the Handbook, termed an overview; and in those circumstances where concepts can clarify the meaning of practice, the overview provides the necessary links between the two in a straightforward manner.

Part One consists of a new introductory chapter, by Peter Ratzer, on the role and organisation of the finance function. The chapter is a survey of the finance function providing the historical perspective, the objective of financial management, a review of the conceptual framework, the task of financial management, reporting and control and the organisation of the finance function.

Part Two, The Use of Funds, follows with an overview to the part and four chapters dealing respectively with capital investment, coping with inflation, working capital management and international money management. Chapters 2 and 4 have been extensively revised; the chapters on inflation, by Ian Cooper, and on international money management, by Andreas Prindl, are new to this edition and reflect major concerns of contemporary financial management.

Part Three, Financial Control, contains four chapters on reporting and responsibilities, budgetary control, costing and internal pricing and internal auditing. The chapters in this part have been thoroughly revised in collaboration with the editors; and a new author, Harry Scholefield, has revised the chapter on internal auditing. The new and revised chapters provide an up-to-date review of these important activities of the financial control function.

Part Four, Raising Funds, contains chapters dealing with financial planning, bank borrowing, leasing, new issues of securities, and rights issues. Four new authors, Michael Clipsham, Colin Young, Elroy Dimson and Paul Marsh, contribute the latter four chapters, which give greater depth to the Handbook's treatment of long-term financing and round out its coverage of the emerging Treasury function in UK financial management.

Finally, Part Five, The External Environment, contains chapters on external financial reporting, mergers and acquisitions and taxation. Here we deal with three crucial ways in which financial managers relate to the environment and in which external factors influence the financial dimensions of both strategic and tactical decisions. Three new authors, Simon Archer, Julian Franks and Raymond Ashton, have contributed to this part of the Handbook, giving it a new depth and timeliness.

The new material in *Financial Management Handbook* ensures that the second edition is even more comprehensive and up to date. We have selected a combination of authoritatively elucidated topics which should make the Handbook an invaluable, practical companion to the practising manager.

Jack Broyles
Ian Cooper
Simon Archer

Illustrations

Figures

2.1	The use of trial rates to calculate the internal rate of return (IRR)	31
2.2	Example of a decision tree	37
2.3	Graph of the sensitivity of the project's viability to profit variation	40
2.4	Two-variable sensitivity analysis graph	42
2.5	Examples of probability distributions	43
2.6	Example of a profitability/probability graph	43
4.1	Product cash cycle	82
5.1	The collection process in cash management	92
5.2	Components of exchange exposure management	105
6.1	The cycle of control	122
6.2	Statistical control chart	136
6.3	Anatomy of management information	138
6.4	Basic system with feedback loop	142
6.5	Basic cybernetic system	144
8.1	Chart of production cost variance	180
8.2	Example of an orthodox break even graph	185
8.3	Example of a modified break even graph	187
8.4	Example of a profit or contribution chart	189
9.1	Relationship between risk and internal audit	201
11.1	Structure of institutions providing finance for industry	248
12.1	Common methods of obtaining the use of an asset	273
13.1	The structure of the UK new issue market	299
13.2	Conventional costs of issue	306
13.3	The costs of an offer for sale in 1972	307

13.4 Typical offer timetable   313
14.1 Issue methods for quoted companies raising money   328
      on the Stock Exchange
14.2 Timing of rights issues   334
14.3 Timing of rights issues and overall market movements   334
14.4 Rights issue procedures and timetable   335
14.5 Underwriting as a put option   338
14.6 Distribution of excess returns to subunderwriting   340
14.7 Abnormal returns and relative issue size   343
16.1 Growth and the incentive to merge   377

Tables

2.1 Calculating the NPV   30
2.2 Finding the true IRR   32
2.3 The NPV calculation   33
2.4 Example of apparent problem   35
2.5 Variables in the profit estimates   41
3.1 Cash flows in money and real terms   50
3.2 Rates of inflation   53
3.3 Unit prices forecast   53
3.4 Inflation rates and interest rates   54
3.5 Long life projects with varying inflation and real   56
     interest rates
3.6 Net present value effect of payment delay   57
3.7 Monthly income statement on normal accrual basis   58
3.8 Adjusted monthly income statement   58
3.9 Corporation tax on stock gains under FIFO   60
3.10 The impact of stock relief   61
3.11 Investment project with zero inflation   63
3.12 Investment project with 10 per cent inflation and   63
     2 per cent cost escalation
3.13 Example of the impact of inflation on an investment   64
     project
4.1 Balance sheets   74
4.2 Working capital position before and after the   75
     product is manufactured
4.3 Comparison of quarterly balance sheets   77
4.4 Sources and uses of cash for first three quarters   79
4.5 Age classification of die castings   87

7.1	Example of a profit and loss statement	155
7.2	Example of fixed budgeting	160
7.3	Example of flexible budgeting	161
8.1	Example of a cost report	181
8.2	Marginal costing in a time of trade recession	184
8.3	Comparisons of P/V ratios and profit contributions	190
8.4	Cost comparisons between manufactured and bought-in components	191
9.1	Allocation of risk points to each auditable unit	215
9.2	Allocation of risk points to sections within the finance function	215
9.3	Finance	217
9.4	Auditable units summary	218
10.1	Monthly cash forecast and control	230
10.2	Short term cash forecast	233
10.3	Source and application of funds statement	238
12.1	Leased assets broken down by type	275
12.2	Users of lease financing 1981	275
12.3	Lease versus purchase: non-tax-paying lessee	278
12.4	Loan required to support lease payments	279
12.5	Cash flows for the tax-paying lessor	279
12.6	Sinking fund equivalent of the lease	280
12.7	Leasing and the Inland Revenue	281
12.8	Cash flows for the tax-paying lessee	282
12.9	Lessee non-tax-paying for two years	283
12.10	Significance of the duration of non-tax paying	284
12.11	Present values at different levels of interest rates	285
12.12	Effect of length of lease on present value to lessee	286
12.13	Effect of rising rental schedule on present value to lessee	286
12.14	Sinking fund equivalent for IRR	289
12.15	Sinking fund equivalent for actuarial return	290
13.1	The current costs of an offer for sale	301
14.1	Rights issue terms	330
14.2	Summary of rights issue studies	332
14.3	Calculating the value of underwriting	339
15.1	Profit and loss account, following Format 1 of the Companies Act 1981	360
15.2	Balance sheet, following Format 1 of the Companies Act 1981	363

15.3   Sources and application of funds   365
15.4   Example of current cost profit and loss account   369
15.5   Example of current cost balance sheet   370
16.1   Estimate of abnormal gains from share price   386
       movements
16.2   Financial data   387
16.3   Earnings of A and Z before and after the merger   388
17.1   Taxation and miscellaneous receipts   395
17.2   Proforma corporation tax assessment   398
17.3   Example of balancing allowances   400
17.4   Example of corporation tax effects   403
17.5   A corporation tax computation   407
17.6   How a company can benefit from stock relief   412

Notes on contributors

Raymond Ashton *(Taxation of corporations in the UK)* is Lecturer in Finance and Accounting at the London Business School. Formerly he was a Lecturer at the University of Bradford and was Senior Auditor at Armitage and Norton. Dr. Ashton has published extensively on accounting theory and taxation; among his books are *Anti-Avoidance Legislation* (Butterworth, 1981) and *Accounting Standards* (Woodward-Faulkners, forthcoming). Raymond Ashton is a Barrister at Law, a Fellow of the Institute of Chartered Accountants and an Associate of the Institute of Cost and Management Accountants. He obtained the B.Sc, M.Sc and PhD degrees in economics at the University of London.

H. W. Calvert *(Costing and internal pricing)*, now retired, was Principal Lecturer in Management Accountancy at North East London Polytechnic and formerly Senior Lecturer at South West Essex Technical College. He was a cost accountant with British Celanese Limited and cost accountant and budget accountant with Ilford Limited. H. W. Calvert is an Associate Member of the Institute of Cost and Management Accountants and was a member of the Institute's education committee and of its terminology committee.

Geoffrey P. E. Clarkson *(Managing working capital)* is Professor of Business Administration at Northeastern University in Boston, Massachusetts, where he has been Dean of the College of Business Administration. Previously he was National Westminster Bank Professor of Business Finance at the Manchester Business School and has been Visiting Professor at the Sloan School of Management at the Massachusetts Institute of Technology and at the London School of Economics. He was chairman and Chief Executive of Barker and Dobson Ltd., the UK food conglomerate and is Director of Clarkson & Elliott Ltd., financial consultants. He has written numerous articles and six books in finance and economics. He holds three degrees from the Carnegie-Mellon University, and his Ph.D. thesis won the Ford Foundation Dissertation Prize in 1961.

Michael Clipsham *(Bank borrowing)* is assistant general manager responsible for the market planning department at Midland Bank Limited. Formerly he has been manager of the corporate finance division and superintendent of branches at Midland. He was Vice-President of the European-American Bank and Trust Company and also was seconded to the Ministry of Housing and Local Government. He is a graduate of London University, is a Member of the Council of the British Institute of Management and a Fellow and officer of numerous other professional and public service organisations.

Elroy Dimson *(The UK new issue market)* is Prudential Research Fellow in Investment and Lecturer in Finance at the London Business School where he is director of the Investment Management Programme. Previously he was Visiting Associate Professor of Finance at the University of Chicago and at the University of California at Berkeley. Earlier, he was Operational Research Manager at Unilever and Long Range Planning Officer with Tube Investments. He is Associate Editor of the *Chase Financial Quarterly* (New York) and joint editor of the *Risk Measurement Service* (London Business School). Dr. Dimson is the author of many articles concerning corporate finance and portfolio management. He received his B.A. in Economics from the University of Newcastle Upon Tyne, the M.Com. in Business Administration at the University of Birmingham and the Ph.D. from London University.

P. C. Elliot *(Internal auditing)* has been Manager, Corporate Accounts and Central Office Costs, Shell International Petroleum Company Limited, with experience in the Royal Dutch/Shell Group since 1950. He is responsible for the corporate accounts of various subsidiaries of the Group and the administration of budgeting, accounting and cost control for the United Kingdom service companies. Mr Elliott is a Fellow of the Institute of Chartered Accountants in England and

Wales, and a past President of the London Chapter of the Institute of Internal Auditors Incorporated.

Julian R. Franks *(Acquisitions and mergers)* is National Westminster Bank Professor of Finance at the London Business School. Other appointments have included Visiting Professor at the University of Cape Town and Visiting Associate Professor at the University of North Carolina at Chapel Hill. Formerly he was Senior Auditor, Esso Europe Inc., and Auditor, Standard Oil of New Jersey. He is currently Honorary Treasurer of the London Council of Social Services and Chairman of its Finance and General Purposes Committee. Professor Franks is the author of numerous articles on corporate finance and co-author of two textbooks, *Modern Managerial Finance* with J. E. Broyles (Wiley 1979) and *Corporate Financial Management* with Harry Scholefield (Gower, 1977). He is a consultant to major companies and trade unions. Julian Franks obtained his B.A. (econ) at Sheffield University, a B.A. in mathematics at the Open University, the M.B.A. at Columbia University Graduate School of Business Administration and the PhD at London University.

Alan R. Leaper *(Budgets and budgetary control)* was Financial Controller of Hoover Worldwide Eastern Region Headquarters for ten years, in which capacity he was responsible at a regional level for reviewing and controlling the budgets of thirteen overseas subsidiaries. Mr Leaper's experience includes three years in Canada on cost and general accounting assignments and eleven years with the Frigidaire Division of General Motors Limited in various factory accounting positions. Mr. Leaper is now managing his own retail and wholesale business and during his career he has obtained considerable practical experience of budgeting and budgetary control in both manufacturing and commercial environments. Mr. Leaper is a member of the Advisory Committee to the Management Division of Management Centre Europe where he frequently chairs various seminars and Round Table meetings.

R. L. Mansbridge *(Forecasting financial requirements)* is a financial consultant. He was formerly Controller, IMS International Inc. and previously was with Rank Xerox Limited where he spent five years in financial management in the United Kingdom and European operating companies, in various senior headquarters planning and control functions. R. L. Mansbridge is a chartered accountant.

Paul Marsh *(Equity rights issues)* is Bank of England Research Fellow and Lecturer in Finance at the London Business School where he is Director of the London Sloan Fellowship Programme. Previously he was a Systems Analyst with Scicon Limited and with Esso Petroleum Ltd. He is joint editor of the *Risk Measurement Service* (London Business School). Dr. Marsh is the author of many articles concerning corporate finance and portfolio investment management. He is a consultant in both the public and private sectors and in the management of financial institutions. He obtained the Bachelor of Science in economics at the London School of Economics and the Ph.D at the London Business School.

Andreas R. Prindl *(International money management)* has been with Morgan Guaranty Trust Company since 1964 and until recently was on secondment as Chief Executive Officer of Saudi International Bank. Previously, he was General Manager of Morgan Guaranty's Tokyo Office and earlier he managed its International Money Management Group. He is co-author of a book on *International Money Management* and has written books on *Foreign Exchange Risk* and *Japanese Finance* published by Wiley. He gained his B.A. degree at Princeton and the M.A. and Ph.D. degrees at the University of Kentucky.

Peter Ratzer *(The role and organisation of the finance function)* is currently Controller of the Esso Exploration and Production U.K. Division of Esso Petroleum Co. Ltd. Formerly he has been Manager of the Planning and Budgets Division of Exxon Corporation in New York and was Assistant Treasurer of Esso Europe Inc and Treasurer of Esso Petroleum Co. Ltd in London. He was also a Local Councillor for the London Borough of Camden. Peter Ratzer obtained his Bachelors Degree in Economics and Politics from the University of Glasgow and the M.B.A. from the Harvard Business School on a Teagle Scholarship.

Tessa V. Ryder Runton *(Capital investment planning)* is currently a consultant and part-time lecturer on financial and corporate planning. Formerly, she was Administrative Secretary of the Capital Expenditure Committee at the Rio Tinto Zinc Corporation where she had been a Senior Financial Analyst in Group Planning. Her MA at Cambridge University was in Natural Science and Law, and she studied Economics and Accountancy at the London School of Economics.

Harry H. Scholefield *(Internal auditing)* is currently Audit Supervisor, Esso Europe Inc., based in Hamburg and responsible for internal auditing of operations in Germany, Sweden and Finland. Previously he was General Accounting Group Head, Esso Exploration and Production U.K. and has held various senior internal auditing positions within the group. He was a Shell Research Fellow in the Department of Economics, University of Strathclyde, is the author of numerous articles and is co-author with J. R. Franks of the textbook *Corporate Financial Management* (Gower, 1977). Harry Scholefield received his B.A. (Econ) at Sheffield University in Accountancy, Business Studies and Economics.

George R. Thompson *(Presentation of external financial reports)* is a financial consultant engaged in advising companies on financial needs, methods of financing, acquisition opportunities and approaches; he is also concerned with grooming private companies for stock market flotation and advising on private portfolio investment. Mr Thomson's experience includes a period as a stockbrokers' investment manager prior to entering financial journalism, when he became City Editor of the *Sunday Express* and City Editor of the *Sunday Dispatch*; he has been a freelance financial journalist since 1961 and is the author of *The ABC of Investment*.

Richard M. S. Wilson *(Reporting and Responsibilities)* is Senior Lecturer at the University of Sheffield where he is Director of the Post-Graduate Programme in Accounting and Financial Management. He has taught at the Bradford Management Centre and held visiting appointments abroad. Previously, he was Group Chief Accountant of a listed holding company and has experience in the engineering, chemical and construction industries. He has published six books and numerous articles generally in the area of financial and marketing management and is editor of *The Journal of Enterprise Management* (Pergamon). He is a Fellow of the Institute of Cost and Management Accountants and of the Association of Certified Accountants and holds degrees in economics/accounting, management/marketing and technology/sociology.

Colin M. Young *(Leasing)* is Assistant Professor of Finance at Baruch College, City University of New York. Formerly he was Visiting Lecturer at the Cranfield Business School and Systems Analyst with Cavenham Limited. When he was in the Doctoral Programme at the London Business School he was instrumental in setting up the London Business School Leasing Evaluation Service. Colin Young is the author of a doctoral dissertation and several articles on leasing. He obtained the BSc (Econ) degree at University College, London, the MSc (Econ) at the London School of Economics and the Ph.D (Econ) at the London Business School.

PART I
INTRODUCTION

1

The role and organisation of the finance function

Peter Ratzer

'In the broadest sense the function of the financial viewpoint is to serve as the point of contact between the uses of funds within an enterprise and its sources of funds'. This was Ezra Solomon's view of the finance function in his classic work *The Theory of Financial Management* (10). It still stands as a practical definition today.

In this introductory chapter I would like to elaborate on this definition and relate it to four specific concerns of the financial manager: using funds, raising funds, financial control and the external environment.

HISTORICAL PERSPECTIVE

Until the 1950s and early 1960s the primary focus of the finance function was on raising funds. Even today many people still think of the Finance Director or Treasurer as responsible solely for finding money that others in the company need to implement their business plans.

The shift to a concern with the whole financial structure of the company, with both sides of the balance sheet, owes much to Joel Dean's pioneering work in the US on capital budgeting (2). In the UK the work of Merrett and Sykes (6) provided a similar stimulus to broadening the finance function's responsibility. The 1960s saw many firms in the UK change their methods of appraising capital expenditures and shift to approaches such as Discounted Cash Flow

(DCF) or Net Present Value (NPV), that recognised the time value of money and emphasised the expected pattern of cash flows, rather than book profit, of a project. Allied to this development was the work being done on the cost of capital and on the criteria that should be used to judge the acceptability of capital investments.

This work provided the crucial link between the two sides of the balance sheet; between the mix of assets and the mix of finance. It led to the formulation of the key objective of the finance function as maximising the value of the firm and into the challenging and complex fields of risk analysis and modern portfolio theory.

Out of this and related work came three ideas – market efficiency, capital market opportunity cost and the required reward for risk – that provide the conceptual framework for financial management today. The 1980s are likely to see the wider implications of these three concepts having a growing influence on the practice of financial management.

I will describe these key concepts in more detail shortly, but before doing so would like to stress that, while the theoretical underpinnings of finance are important, the main conclusion to be drawn from this brief historical sketch is that the finance function needs to be interpreted broadly if it is to make its full contribution to a company and to meeting corporate goals. As Hunt, Williams and Donaldson (5) put it, the successful financial manager must not only be a 'money man', he must also be a businessman. He is part of the operating team. (4)

OBJECTIVES OF FINANCIAL MANAGEMENT

Profit maximisation has long been recognised as one of the main goals of a company. To some it is the only goal. The problem is to define profit maximisation in a way that makes business sense and that can be used to guide practical decision-making in a company.

How is profit to be defined? Are we talking of maximising operating earnings or net profit attributable to the shareholders? Does it mean an immediate, short term profit? How can a company balance longer term profit potential against shorter term costs? What about risk? These are just some of the questions that come to mind when trying to define profit maximisation.

The solution that has been adopted is to focus on maximising the value of the firm. Valuation is at the heart of the finance function's activity and the key technique is that of discounting. This is described in more detail in Chapter 2. In essence, discounting provides a link between the present and future by the use of a discount or interest rate. It enables all the cash flows of a business at various dates to be valued on a consistent basis at one common time. This is normally the present, hence the term present value, but it can equally well be some time in the future.

Discounting solves the problem of short versus long term profit maximisation. It enables different cash flow profiles to be compared in terms of their present values and it provides a simple tool for determining which profile has the highest present value.

Usually the focus is not on operating earnings or net profit, but on cash flows before any financing charges or depreciation. Financing charges, primarily interest, are omitted since they are a function of a company's financing structure; they determine how the total value of a company is split between shareholders and lenders. Depreciation is omitted since it is a non-cash charge and is only an estimated allocation of earnings to cover the use or decline in value of fixed assets such as plant and machinery. The forecast cash flows are the key to profitability of a company or project. They represent funds that will be available in the future to service debt, pay dividends or make new investment. The forecast cash flow profile is therefore used to determine the viability of companies and of projects.

While the net profit of a company over its life is ultimately the difference between the company's total cash inflows and outflows after allowing for the return of capital to its providers, it is the timing and the pattern of these flows that determine the value of a company and the return that it earns. Two companies could be expected to generate the same net profit over a period but the cash flows, and hence the value of each company, could be very different.

Another factor that affects the value of companies is risk. Two companies could have similar cash flow outlooks, but their values could differ widely if the cash flows of one are subject to considerable risk while the cash flows of the other are dependable. This brings us to the question of the appropriate discount rate to use for valuing future cash flows given their risk, a question dealt with in the next chapter.

Assuming the company has investments that yield more than the rate of interest on additional borrowing, the apparent return to the shareholders could be raised by borrowing more and by increasing its gearing or leverage, or the debt/equity ratio. In the long run this will only increase the riskiness of the shareholders' cash flow since a higher proportion of the total cash flow is allocated to lenders. The shareholders are left to bear potentially greater swings in their cash flow. As the risk increases, so the rate at which these cash flows will be discounted or capitalised by the shareholders will increase. Thus the apparent advantage of additional debt is offset by the greater risk and higher discount rate for the shareholders' equity. Hence the total value of the firm may be unaffected by the way in which claims on assets and cash flow are divided between equity holders and debt holders. The well known Modigliani-Miller theory (8) states that the value of a company is unaffected by how it is financed. An increase in debt will result in a matching decline in the shareholders' interest. Put as baldly as this it might suggest that the financing structure of a company is irrelevant. I hope to show that this is not the case; the financial manager still has a job to do!

In summary, the key objective of financial management is to maximise the value of a company. The value is a function of the expected cash flows and their riskiness.

CONCEPTUAL FRAMEWORK

Three pillars of modern financial management are the efficient markets hypothesis, capital market opportunity costs and the required reward for risk. They relate to the valuation of a company and this explains their central role in financial management.

An efficient market is one in which prices reflect all information available to participants in the market (3). The stock and bond markets are considered efficient and therefore, for example, share prices reflect all the available information about a company. This implies that, in the absence of insider information, there is no way of predicting consistently which way the share price will move next. The next price movement bears no relationship to the last movement – hence the term 'random walk' often associated with share price movements.

Capital market efficiency also implies that the value of a quoted company is the market value of its securities on the stock exchange. This allows the financial manager to draw conclusions about the expectations of shareholders and their attitudes to risk and returns by observing the behaviour of security prices. This information can be fed back into the financial planning of a company.

There is growing evidence that financial markets are efficient. Undoubtedly more research will be done for the benefit of financial management in the coming years on the way the markets work and on the ramifications of this behaviour.

The concept of market efficiency can also be applied to other financial markets such as foreign exchange. This has considerable implications for the way a company manages its foreign exchange activities if it trades or invests abroad. If the market is efficient the expected gain from taking views on future foreign exchange rates is zero. Speculative activity will not pay in the long run.

Financial management has now moved almost full circle from the detailed descriptive work on capital markets and securities that characterised the teaching of finance before the 1950s to a fundamental understanding of how the financial markets work. One of the tasks of the financial manager is to ensure that management takes advantage of the implications of the new insights when running the business.

The concept of capital market opportunity costs is the second pillar of modern finance. It takes as its starting point the valuation of a risk-free cash flow; that is, from a short term government bond. The discount rate used to value the cash flow from such an asset is the government borrowing rate. This is the minimum required return for a risk-free investment.

Capital market opportunity costs imply that a higher return is required for higher risk assets. This accords with common sense since there is no reason why any person or company should accept some risk unless they are offered a return above that available from government bonds. Some inducement is needed to give up a secure, guaranteed income.

The discount rate for valuing the expected cash flow of a company, normally called the cost of capital, will therefore be equal to the risk-free return plus a premium for risk. The amount of the premium can be estimated with reasonable accuracy from long run market data. It is at this point that efficient markets and capital market opportunity costs come together. The required reward for risk, the third pillar of modern finance, therefore provides a link between efficient markets and capital market opportunity costs.

One of the more controversial conclusions of modern financial theory is that, from a strictly financial point of view, a company will not benefit by attempting to spread its risk by diversification. The reason given is that investors can equally well diversify their own portfolios. While such a conclusion omits consideration of the benefits of lower risk to managers and employees, which can also benefit shareholders indirectly through lower wage costs, shareholders do diversify. Thus, the risk for which investors ultimately need compensation is the risk of movement in the general economic situation. That is a risk which investors cannot escape by further diversification of their portfolios.

These concepts clearly have an important contribution to make towards understanding the market valuation of a company. They also imply the need for higher returns on more risky projects.

Again, it is the task of the financial manager to help management understand how the market value of the company is determined and to help management draw the right conclusions on, for example, return criteria for different risk classes of investment, on diversification and on mergers and acquisitions. In this introduction I can only sketch in the foundations of modern financial management. The topics are discussed in more detail in later chapters. Readers are also referred to Franks and Broyles (3).

FINANCIAL MANAGEMENT

The main elements of the conceptual framework – that markets reflect all available information, that a premium is required for risk and that investors diversify their portfolios – may seem self-evident, but I hope I have indicated that even self-evident assumptions about the way markets and investors behave can have controversial implications when it comes to practical financial management. This is one of the factors that makes financial management such a challenging and stimulating activity. It also gives the job a significant educational component.

In this section I would like to summarise some of the key issues on the agenda of the financial manager. I take the basic objective of maximising the value of the company as given. The key long term financing decisions are the target debt/equity ratio, the debt structure and dividend policy.

I explained earlier how increased gearing has a cost in the form of extra risk for the shareholders, which offsets the fact that the interest rate on debt is below the overall cost of funds to the company. This does not mean that the value of a company is unaffected by its financing structure. Since interest is tax deductible, shareholders can benefit from the introduction of some debt into a company and the total market value of shares plus debt securities will be increased by the present value of the tax saving on interest (9). The cost of capital will decline.

At higher levels of debt a company is likely to run up against increasing reluctance on the part of lenders. This can push up the cost of new debt by more than the tax benefit of additional gearing to shareholders. Lenders and shareholders may see increasing risks of bankruptcy and this can lead to a decline in the total market value of a company and to an increase in the cost of capital. The financial manager's job is therefore to recommend a target debt/equity ratio appropriate for the business in question. This is the point at which uses and sources of funds come together since the target debt/equity will be a function of the type of investments and their riskiness, with an added element of market convention reflecting rates applicable to similar companies in the same business.

The United States has rating agencies that grade the quality of corporate debt issues. In such circumstances a company may set a policy of maintaining its rating at a particular level and then design a debt/equity ratio (plus other ratios such as the coverage of all fixed charges) that it is believed will maintain the required rating. I would stress 'believed', since the agencies do not work to mechanical ratio limits. They are also influenced by the quality of company management.

The debt structure or mix of a company is the balance between long, medium and short term debt and, if appropriate, between the currencies of debt. Again, this will be a function of the business, its assets and cash flows, and of the availability of finance. The financial manager needs to be aware of the various sources of finance and their costs and of any opportunities provided by less conventional sources such as leasing companies. He needs to understand the cash flows of the business well since they will determine the basic needs for short term financing to keep interest costs at a minimum and avoid accumulating surplus, idle funds.

Dividend policy is a controversial subject and the literature on this topic alone is immense. One of the most stimulating contributions was made by Miller and Modigliani (7) who argued that dividend policy was irrelevant to the valuation of a company, that shareholders should value dividends and retained earnings equally. As with their argument on the debt/equity ratio this is a simplified proposition that ignores various factors such as taxes and the information value of dividends. Taxes are relevant if the average shareholder pays a different effective marginal rate of taxes than the company on income from investments.

The information value of dividends can be important since changes in dividend levels may reflect more accurately than reported earnings how the directors of a company see the future. It is up to the financial manager to frame recommendations on long run dividend policy that take into account the future needs for retained earnings to support capital investment and, as necessary, additional debt. At this point dividend policy becomes an integral part of the financial planning and business strategy of a company.

The three key financial decisions just discussed – the debt/equity ratio, the debt structure and dividend policy – form the basis of any long term financial plan. They are all related and together make up a company's capital structure plan. The capital structure plan should be one of the financial manager's main planning tools.

REPORTING AND CONTROL

So far I have focused primarily on the basic principles and objectives of financial management, on the conceptual framework and on the major policy elements that make up the capital structure plan of a company.

As the range of chapters of this handbook indicates, the role of the finance function includes many other responsibilities; the main one can be summarised under the heading 'Reporting and Control'. Part Three of this handbook covers Financial Control and Part Five, on the External Environment, includes external financial reporting.

Reporting can be divided into external and internal areas. External reporting covers the reports to shareholders and other interested parties, such as lenders. There has been considerable debate within the accounting profession on the role of published accounts and a useful review of the key issues can be found in *The Corporate Report*, a discussion paper published in 1975 by the Accounting Standards Steering Committee (1).

Of course, there have been changes in accounting standards since 1975, the major innovation being the introduction of a standard on inflation accounting. No doubt this standard will be modified as more experience in reporting the effects of inflation is gained in this country and elsewhere. The important thing is that a start has been made on trying to depict the impact of inflation on companies and this must help to communicate some essential messages on levels of profitability to those outside the business world.

I believe that external financial communications will absorb a greater share of the finance function's time during the 1980s than during the 1960s and 1970s. Part of this emphasis will reflect the growing reporting burden imposed by new accounting standards, but the rest will be dictated by the need to explain in greater detail the contribution a company has made to society.

Internal reporting is an essential part of management control. It is the finance function's responsibility to develop and run the systems for monitoring and reporting all the operations and profitability of a company. Such systems, which are outlined in more detail in later chapters, are an essential control tool. Management needs both current and forecast data to control and steer the business. Internal reporting is another area where the finance function has to contribute its broad business judgement to what is happening in a company. First, it takes a thorough understanding of the business and its key decision variables to design an effective performance monitoring and forecasting system. Second, the finance function can exercise its own judgement in drawing management's attention to issues or trends that may be a cause of concern. Closely related to reporting is control. Control covers the proper and accurate recording of all financial business transactions, the development of appropriate and secure systems for handling all receipts and payments, and internal audit activities. These are all major responsibilities of the finance function and their scope is more likely to increase than to decrease in the 1980s.

ORGANISATION

So far I have discussed the finance function or financial manager in general terms. Obviously the organisation of the finance function in any company will depend upon its size, the nature of its business and its history.

The range of titles that people in the finance function carry is very wide and I can only indicate the general pattern among UK companies.

To a great extent this pattern follows US precedents.

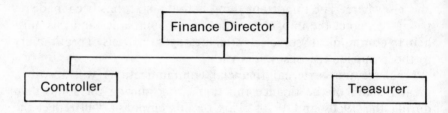

The Finance Director has responsibility as a board member for the whole of the finance function. As a board member he participates in all corporate decisions and can bring the financial viewpoint to bear on the company's business decisions. In view of his wide board responsibilities he has to delegate many of his responsibilities to the Controller and Treasurer. In larger companies the Finance Director may also have a Tax Manager reporting to him and also other departments such as Purchasing.

I will focus on the activities of the Controller and Treasurer since the division of responsibilities between them mirrors the distinction between reporting and control and financial management discussed earlier.

The Controller is the company's accounting and financial control manager. He is responsible for external and internal reporting, for the accounting and information systems, for controlling all receipts and payments and for internal audit and control. The size of a company and its activities will determine how these responsibilities are split into manageable divisions or groups, for example capital budgets, reporting and forecasting, payroll, costs, sales accounting, information systems and so on. I should add that in some companies the computer operations and systems do not form part of the Controller's responsibility, since he is just one of many users. The Controller has the vital task of liaising with the company's statutory auditors. This is a key relationship which is critical in external reporting and in maintaining the financial soundness of a company, since a qualification to the accounts by the auditors can be very damaging.

The Treasurer is the company's finance manager. He is responsible for developing the capital structure plan and basic financial policies outlined earlier. He must ensure that finance is available to meet the needs of the company, both new investments and working capital, and that the flows of cash in and out of the company are managed efficiently. He is the company's main contact with the financial community. He advises on appropriate return criteria for investment decisions. Normally the Treasurer is also responsible for risk management and insurance and for advising on pension fund management. He is also likely to be the point of contact with the company's actuary and must advise on the appropriate valuation assumptions to be used in computing pension liabilities and determining the company's contribution to its pension fund. This is an area of increasing attention owing to the impact of inflation on the real value of pensions and the high costs of providing some degree of protection against the erosion in their value.

If the company is involved in overseas investment or in importing and exporting, then it will be vulnerable to movements in exchange rates. The Treasury, whose department is responsible for all purchases and sales of foreign exchange, must develop appropriate policies for managing foreign exchange exposure. This is another topic that has absorbed an increasing amount of management time and effort in many companies. I mentioned earlier that taking views on exchange rates is an unprofitable activity over the long run. While some would not accept this statement, my own belief is that it is a useful working assumption for managing exposure. It ensures that more effort goes into control and management of foreign exchange risk than into trying to forecast exchange rates.

Although both the Controller and Treasurer are part of the same function, they have a check and balance relationship. While the Treasurer manages the company's cash, the Controller provides the necessary control to ensure that the cash is used as authorised in accordance with company policies.

In summary, every company needs key personnel to shoulder the various responsibilities of the finance function. How these responsibilities are allocated will differ from company to company, but it is clear that an increasing number of companies in the UK have set up separate Treasurer's Departments reporting directly to the Finance Director. In the 1960s this was still a novelty. By 1980 a new professional body, the Association of Corporate Treasurers, had been founded in recognition of this trend.

CONCLUSION

Ezra Solomon posed three inter-related questions for financial management:

1 What specific assets should an enterprise acquire?
2 What total volume of funds should an enterprise commit?
3 How should the funds required be financed?

Although financial theory has developed significantly since he wrote *The Theory of Financial Management*, the questions are still pertinent. I have tried to outline some of the basic considerations that a financial manager should take into account when making recommendations on these topics to management. The following chapters provide more detailed descriptions of some of the concepts I have covered.

REFERENCES

(1) Accounting Standards Steering Committee, 'The Corporate Report', 1975.
(2) J Dean, *Capital Budgeting*, Columbia University Press, 1951.
(3) J R Franks and J E Broyles, *Modern Management Finance*, John Wiley and Sons, 1979.
(4) L V Gerstner, Jr. and M H Anderson, 'The Chief Financial Officer as Activist', *Harvard Business Review*, September-October 1976.
(5) P Hunt, C M Williams and G Donaldson, *Basic Business Finance*, Richard D Irwin, 3rd Edition 1966.
(6) A J Merrett and A Sykes, *The Finance and Analysis of Capital Projects*, Longman, 1963, 2nd Edition, 1973.
(7) M H Miller and F Modigliani, 'Dividend Policy, Growth and the Valuation of Shares', *Journal of Business*, October 1961.
(8) F Modligiani and M H Miller, 'The Cost of Capital, Corporation Finance, and The Theory of Investment', *American Economic Review*, June 1958.
(9) F Modigliani and M H Miller, 'Corporate Income Taxes and the Cost of Capital: A Correction', *American Economic Review*, June 1963.
(10) E Solomon, *The Theory of Financial Management*, Columbia University Press, 1963.

PART II
THE USE OF FUNDS

OVERVIEW

The efficient use of a company's resources is essential to its growth. These resources take many forms: employees, buildings, machinery and stocks, but all involve expenditures of funds for purchase and operation. The ultimate resource that is being employed is the funds of the company. This section deals with four aspects of using funds: capital investment, coping with inflation, working capital management and international money management.

What are the common features of decisions on using funds to purchase resources for the company? Any of these decisions involves an expenditure to create the resource: new buildings or equipment, better trained personnel, new markets through investment in a sales force or marketing organisation. These expenditures anticipate benefits that should arise in the future: the profit contribution from sales from new capacity, the increased productivity of a more skilled workforce, the increased revenues from new markets.

How should such decisions be evaluated from a financial standpoint? The financial resource that is being committed is cash. Cheques are written to purchase the new buildings and machinery and to pay employees. Only when the cash is paid does the company lose the use of its funds. Similarly, the expected benefits should be evaluated in terms of cash flows. If a sale is made, but the cheque is not received for six months, the financial return occurs when the cash flow from the cheque arrives, because the funds are not there for the company to use until that time. Thus the financial costs and benefits should be evaluated in terms of current and expected cash flows.

These cash flows will often differ from accounting profits. The most important difference is the use by accountants of depreciation to spread the costs of capital resources over their lives. If a machine is purchased, the cheque must usually be written for the entire purchase price. This cash flow is a financial cost to the company at the time the machine is purchased, and the company loses the use of funds representing the entire purchase price. In exchange the company receives a machine, which its managers hope will produce sufficient cash flow in the future to compensate for the loss of these funds. The depreciation in the profit statement does not represent a cash flow and is not therefore relevant to the decision being made.

The passage of time means that we should expect to receive interest on our money. Offered £10 one year from now in exchange for £5 now, we would compare this with the interest we could earn by putting our £5 in the bank. The 100 per cent return we are offered compares favourably with the, say, 10 per cent opportunity cost of lending the money to the bank. A good decision in this case involves comparing the rate of return on the 'project' with the rate our money could earn elsewhere.

How much better off does this project make us? To answer this question we must consider the financing arrangements. Suppose we can borrow the £5 at 10 per cent per annum interest to make the investment. In one year we must pay back £5.50, which will leave £4.50 out of the ultimate £10 payment. This is called the net future value of the project, because it represents the net amount by which we will be better off at the final date once we have allowed for the financing costs. This is useful information, but what we really want to know is how much better off we are now. To answer this, suppose we borrow against the entire £10 at 10 per cent. We could borrow £9.09 on this basis, and pay off the loan with the £10 proceeds from our project. Of the £9.09 we must invest £5, but the other £4.09 represents the true gain or profit from the project. This amount is known as the net present value and tells us the value now of making this particular investment.

Uncertainty and inflation affect this decision in several ways. If we are not sure of receiving exactly £10, how should we make the decision? The procedure we followed before was to compute the amount of finance we could raise with the £10 payoff and compare this with the £5 investment to get the net present value. Now the payoff is not certain, so we need to estimate its most likely or expected value. For instance, if the payoff could be £10 or £8 with equal chance, the expected payoff is £9. The rate at which we could raise money to finance the project would also differ. To finance risky ventures investors require higher rates of return. The rate required now might be 20 per cent. In that case, against the £9 expected proceeds, we could raise (9/1.20) = £7.50. The net present value of the project has fallen to £2.50. Uncertainty means that we must use expected payoffs and a higher rate of return.

Inflation also affects payoffs and required rates of return. The interest rate tends to increase when inflation increases, so that we must earn higher returns to beat putting our money into the bank. But the expected cash flows from a project will be affected by inflation. These cash flows may consist of sales proceeds minus labour and material costs. The selling price, wage costs and raw material prices will all be expected to change over time at rates that partly reflect general inflation. As inflation escalates, projected future cash flows from a project should also increase, but so will the rate of return required to finance the project.

Part Two begins with a detailed explanation by Tessa Ryder Runton, Jack Broyles and Ian Cooper of the techniques and organisation required for effective capital investment planning (Chapter 2). They develop the notion of an opportunity cost of funds and explain how this cost of capital can be computed for a company. Testing the viability of capital investments consists of comparing the return from a project with the return required by the company on projects of that sort. Various techniques for doing this are described, including the discounted cash flow method. The chapter then explains how risk can be incorporated into capital investment planning, using techniques such as sensitivity and probability analysis. The authors then place this technical material in an organisational context, discussing the capital investment decision process and the problem of ex-post evaluation of capital investment decisions.

The next chapter, by Ian Cooper (Chapter 3), is concerned with incorporating considerations of inflation into financial decision-making. It begins by showing the impact of inflation on the cash flows from a project and on the cost of capital. The chapter then shows how the principles of effective funds usage can be extended to cope with inflation and changes in relative prices and concludes with the treatment of special tax issues that are heavily affected by inflation, such as stock relief and delays in tax payments.

In the chapter by Geoffrey Clarkson (Chapter 4) the important area of working capital management is addressed. The same notions of profitability apply here, but with additional special techniques for managing the various components of working capital efficiently: stocks, debtors and creditors. These techniques are described by Professor Clarkson. In addition, he shows how the cash flows associated with working capital can be analysed to control profitability in this area. He also provides a useful discussion of conventional ratio analysis as applied to working capital, with the emphasis on the interpretation and use of the ratios, rather than just the mechanics of their computation.

The final chapter of this section (Chapter 5) deals with the important area of international money management. Andreas Prindl demonstrates the basis for effective cash management in a domestic context. He then generalises this approach to international management of the corporate cash resources. Special instruments of international financing are discussed, as well as the effective use of the institutional framework available for effective international money management.

2

Capital project planning

Tessa Ryder Runton, Jack Broyles and Ian Cooper

Capital project planning is the process by which companies allocate funds to various investment projects designed to ensure profitability and growth. Evaluation of such projects involves estimating their future benefits to the company and comparing these with their costs. Such analysis is appropriate not only to the purchase of long lived physical assets, but to any decision which has impacts extending into the future. Thus capital project planning can encompass, for example, long term contracts for goods and services, marketing expenditures, disinvestment by sale, mergers and plant closures.

While capital project planning is a process that takes place in an organisational context over extended periods of time, certain elements of this process are essential to good project planning. These are:

1 Access to the appropriate information.
2 Knowledge of the company's required financial return
3 Realistic evaluation of the prospective cash flow and profit impacts of projects
4 Analysis of the costs and benefits of projects with attention to the timing of their occurrence
5 Evaluation by senior management of the strategic implications of large projects.
6 A well defined approval process.
7 Consistency with strategic planning and budgeting procedures.
8 A review procedure.

THE GOALS OF PROJECT PLANNING

Businesses have responsibilities to various interested groups including employees, customers, suppliers, bankers and shareholders. This goal is met by maximising the total market value of the company's shares. The capital market values shares at the present value of current and future cash flows attributable to shareholders. If the company maximises the net present value of all the operations that make up its business, the sum will be the maximisation of the value of the company. This value net of debt belongs to shareholders. Companies pursuing other objectives, whether social or technological, must primarily be profitable. Should shareholders, corporate members or financiers become dissatisfied with the company's operations, they may withdraw their support, causing such awkward problems as loss of morale and personnel, shortage of funds, a fall in the company's share price if it is publicly quoted, or stormy annual general meetings. Any of these can lead to undesirable vulnerability and result in a takeover, close-down, or governmental interference.

REQUIRED RATE OF RETURN STANDARDS AND COST OF CAPITAL

Cost of capital is a major standard of comparison used in financial analysis and is a vital company statistic needing careful calculation. The return on capital resources must equal or exceed the cost of that capital. Although zero or negative returns are acceptable in special cases, the necessary subsidies may lead to costs in another form.

The realities of commercial life have caused the cost of capital to be a very complex subject. Any comparisons must be made between like numbers. A percentage profit before tax made on a hotel in Bermuda bears no relationship to the same figure made after tax on a farm in Scotland. A profit expressed as a percentage of capital employed should not be compared with a discounted cash flow internal rate of return. Many measures of company performance can be devised but these are valuable only to those who are completely familiar with the definitions involved. The appraisal of projected cash flow discounted at a rate equal to a carefully estimated required rate of return leads to fewer pitfalls. In particular, the time-value of money is taken into account, all the financial effects are assessed and tax and inflation are taken into account in the calculation of the cash flow and the estimation of the cost of capital.

Capital investment analysis aims to discover the financial truth about the plan under investigation. If it does not meet the survival standard of the organisation, that fact should be stated clearly before the discussion as to its desirability begins. In practice, many apparently unprofitable processes go on in any business because they enhance the profitable activities which, of course, should outnumber them. Obvious examples are the provision of catering and other services for the work force, advertising, research and so on. It used to be thought that discounted cash flow analysis led to categorical 'yes' or 'no' judgements on any plan; in fact, all it does is marshal the financial facts for the guidance of the decision takers. In addition, it can point to the least unprofitable way of tackling a loss-making but necessary job.

The cost of capital to the firm

Most companies raise funds from many sources – retained earnings, new equity, grants and many forms of loans. The overall cost of capital to the firm is the return it must earn on its assets to meet the requirements of all those providing it with financing. Lenders require interest payments and shareholders expect to receive dividends and see capital growth.

In the past, UK shareholders have expected to earn a real net return of about 8 per cent after tax on average risk shares. To obtain this required net return in money terms, the expected inflation rate must be added. If this expected inflation rate is 10 per cent, the required return on the company's present equity and retained earnings is 18 per cent. The cost of new equity raised by means of 'rights' is a little more than this to allow for the costs of the issue. Other forms of new equity issues incur further costs of about 2 per cent.

Although the average real expected return on shares is about 8 per cent, companies in risky industries or with high gearing (borrowing relative to equity funds) will have more vulnerable shares than average. The real return required by their shareholders will be commensurately higher. This means, as explained in the overview of Part Four, that borrowing is not necessarily a cheap way of raising funds. Although the interest rate on borrowing may be lower than the return expected by shareholders, increased gearing will raise the risk of shares and not change the overall cost of funds to the company. This is discussed later in this chapter (for a more detailed analysis see Franks and Broyles, 1979).

If a company maintains a proportion of debt capital agreed with its lenders, it can compute a *weighted average cost of capital*. For example, if the interest rate on debt is 10 per cent, and the company has 25 per cent debt and 75 per cent equity, the weighted average cost of capital in money terms including 10 per cent average inflation is (0.25 × 10 per cent) + (0.75 × 18 per cent) = 16 per cent. This cost does not allow for the tax savings from interest payments. This benefit is added separately.

In deciding the appropriate standards for an organisation, the marginal cost of capital is a vital guide. In a growing company, new capital will be needed and, therefore, the return on a project of normal risk should be judged against a standard of the weighted average cost of new capital. Companies making investment decisions continuously should use this marginal cost of capital as the standard for all projects with risks normal to the company's business. If a project cannot pass this test, it will diminish the company's value.

Required rates of return on projects

Obviously projects involve differing risks. Some, such as cost saving investments and lease or buy decisions, are of low risk; others, such as research projects, involve greater than average levels of risk. A company should classify its risk categories for projects and set required returns for each. A large project of risk significantly different from normal can alter the overall character of a company, its cost of capital, its accepted gearing and the returns expected by financiers.

The required rate of return for a project can be significantly different from the weighted average cost of capital for the company. High risk projects are characterised by high fixed operating expenditure and high revenue variability. These should be expected to earn high rates of return. The exact return required will depend upon a judgement about the level of risk in the project compared with the average risk of the company. In the case above, where the weighted average cost of capital in real terms is 6 per cent, the real required return on a project twice as risky as the market should be 12 per cent. With 10 per cent expected inflation the money required return should be 22 per cent.

The use of a separate required rate of return for each individual project is most important when the projects are large relative to the company and/or when the projects being considered have long lives. A typical classification scheme, in increasing order of risk is: cost reduction, replacement, scale expansion, new products. The risks of these different types of investment differ, and so should their required returns.

By evaluating different projects at different required rates of return, the company seeks to protect its shareholders. Shareholders require higher rates of return for higher levels of risk, and receive compensation for high risk in the capital markets. Companies undertaking high risk asset investment decisions must seek to achieve higher returns than their shareholders can earn for that level of risk in the capital markets.

Effect of debt on required returns

Unless there are non-financial incentives, a project is acceptable only if it stands on its own feet; that is, its cash flow should at least meet the company's return criterion for the risks involved. With the possibility of debt financing is the position changed? A typical case arises when new assets simply increase the total assets on a proportion of which debt is available. Some people argue that, even apart from tax advantages, debt is cheap since the interest rate is lower than the cost of equity funds. This argument ignores the hidden cost of debt: the increased vulnerability of the equity as more borrowing is undertaken. The total operating risk of the company remains constant as more debt financing is used, so it is unrealistic to believe that the overall cost of funds can be reduced in this way.

One advantage that borrowing does confer is the reduction in taxes caused by the deductibility of interest payments. The impact on cash flows of this tax saving is simply the future stream of tax payments that are saved by the interest payments on the debt. The value of these tax savings can be added to the value of the operating cash flows from the project to get an overall value including the benefits of debt financing. This is preferable to using a weighted average cost of capital including the cost of debt at an after-tax rate. Use of the latter assumes that the debt available for a project will be very long term and will be the same proportion of the project financing as it is for the company. Both these assumptions can be very erroneous when projects have short maturity debt or very high or low gearing.

Care needs to be taken when a project merits special loans. Usually these are projects of significant size for which government incentives are available, or for which special working capital loans can be raised, or involving mortgageable property. If the result is a new company finance structure, then cost of capital and risk classifications must be reassessed. Some large capital investments, such as in mining, involve parent companies in special financial guarantees and these need special attention. Other capital investments such as in research, do not result in increased total assets which can be partly debt financed.

TRADITIONAL TECHNIQUES FOR TESTING VIABILITY

The natural question: 'When do I get my money back?' has often been answered by the traditional technique of adding up the forecast net cash inflow (sometimes the sum of the profit before depreciation from the forecast profit and loss account) year by year until the amount of the original capital investment is reached, thereby giving the years to payback. Such a calculation is inconclusive because standards vary, definitions of the original capital vary, tax is not always deducted and most of the benefits of tax allowances are obscured. The method ignores the time-value of money, cannot cope with inflation and takes no account of the later profits, if any. Whether, in fact, any profit is made on the investment is not measured at all. Payback calculations give some guidance in matters of liquidity in which case the cash inflow should be carefully defined and be free of any 'accounting numbers' such as 'tax provision' instead of 'tax payable'. A better payback calculation is the discounted payback, which is computed using the present values of the future cash inflows.

Another traditional technique involves the use of balance sheet ratios for current and proposed operations. These include the ratios of profit to capital employed, of profit to sales, and many others concerning stock, current assets and liabilities, and working capital. These ratios are useful for regulating smooth operations but are unhelpful for judging profitability, owing to definition problems and the choice of standards, but mostly because the time-value of money is not included.

One ratio used is the return on capital, known as 'the accountant's return' or the 'book rate of return'. An average profit, before or after tax, is calculated for a number of years of the proposed project and this is expressed as a percentage of the capital employed. The latter is often defined as the initial investment or the average capital employed over the years, thereby allowing for further investment and depreciation. This procedure suffers from the same snags as the techniques mentioned above and, in addition, smooths out the effect of irregular annual profits. Clearly, quick profits are preferable to a slow build up, but advantages or disadvantages are obscured.

MODERN TECHNIQUES FOR TESTING VIABILITY

The traditional techniques take no account of the time value of money. But money received today is much more valuable than the same money received later. Present inflationary conditions magnify the difference. This is the principal fact which modern analysis techniques have incorporated to improve on past procedures. Analysis concentrates on the incremental cash flow of a project. The cash flow is discounted at the project's discount rate to the present time, giving a present value. The work involved has increased, but once an analysis discipline has been set up, decision takers can expect that the realities of the given data for some plan will be clearly identified. They can then concentrate on the non-financial problems involved, judge whether the data is sufficient to work with and act accordingly.

The concept of moving money in time using the relevant discount rate is not new. Today's quoted price for benefits to be received in the future can be judged by netting the price, or capital cost, from the present value of the future cash flow. A positive resultant Net Present Value (NPV), if properly calculated (see page 30), shows that the transaction is financially worthwhile. The value of the transaction can also be assessed by judging its Internal Rate of Return (IRR) (see pages 31–3).

CASH FLOW DISCIPLINE IN PROJECT ANALYSIS

The discounted cash flow techniques use as their raw material the incremental cash flow resulting from some plan. Profit flow study is necessary for proper annual accounting as required by shareholders, but it is the cash flow that should be studied to identify the return forecast and the finance that is required. Provisions for depreciation are excluded, but expenditures on working capital and capital expenditures are included. The cash flow of a project is a forecast of the total monetary effects computed periodically (usually annually or monthly) over the whole life of the project, including scrap values. Such items as tax savings achieved on other profits of the organisation because of allowances due to the new project or any other cash effects which would not occur without the new project, for example, the cost of head office extensions or replacing an executive who would be transferred, should be included. Interest payments are often wrongly deducted from the cash flow, but they are not operating flows, being part of the cost of funds included in the cost of capital. A project can be defined as any procedure which alters the organisation's cash flow. Projects, therefore, include opportunities for cost savings and productivity improvements, where capital cost is not necessarily involved. What, therefore, is analysed is the total cash flow effect of an opportunity, that is, the net incremental cash flow, which is the difference between the cash flow in the company if the project is undertaken and the cash flow if it is not.

This analysis must be in real terms or in money terms with respect to inflation and, if necessary, alterations must be made so that real terms cash flows are judged by a real terms required return standard and money cash flows are judged by a money terms required return standard. Tax allowances and loan servicing schedules are always in money terms but sales and cost figures are usually forecast in real terms. It is usual for the marketing and production departments to project schedules showing changes in sales percentages or production costs without allowing for external price changes. However, the estimation of taxable profits and taxes requires that these data be converted to money terms. In cases of high inflation forecasts, or different effects on prices and costs, and for lengthy projects, some estimate must be made of the inflation pattern over the life of the project. This estimate could differ for use on prices, on costs and on the overall situation including the cost of capital. All figures must then be converted to money terms so that expected tax payments can be estimated.

It should go without saying that cash flows are forecast after the effects of company taxes when paid. Because tax allowances are normally in money terms, consistent cash flows almost certainly have to be forecast in money terms, unless real terms tax allowances can be calculated. Sometimes it is necessary to consider any likely future changes in tax structure. In this, as in treating inflation and in all problems of data uncertainties, it is important not to be over meticulous, particularly at the outset. Analysis of the most roughly prepared cash flow will show whether it is worth spending any further time attending to the details. The first question to answer is: 'What is the profitability of the given set of data, warts included?' If the answer looks promising it is then sensible to take the time to examine the given data, prepare a detailed net incremental cash flow in money terms and look at possible outcomes of the project as opposed to one set of data. The analysis should then examine sensitivities, risks and probabilities and the effect of the project on the organisation as a whole. Decision takers prefer consistent analysis disciplines so that they can use consistent standards of judgement and comparison.

For a fuller discussion of inflation and its effects on required rates of return and cash flows, see Chapter 3.

NPV AND IRR IN MORE DETAIL

The use of the concept of present value (NPV)

The net present value, NPV, of a project is the net present value of the net incremental cash flow discounted at the project's required rate of return. A zero NPV shows that the project repays the capital invested plus the minimum acceptable return on the invested capital throughout the project's life. The minimum acceptable return is equal to the opportunity cost of that capital including a return required for the risk taken by investing in that operation for that period. NPVs show that the minimum return is achieved plus extra value. Given a discount rate of 11 per cent for a project, the NPV is found as shown in Table 2.1.

Other things being equal, this project looks financially acceptable. One could pay up to £199 more for the opportunity and still not lose. NPV represents the analyst's estimate of the net increase in the value of the company which would accrue from the project. If the discount rate used is the capital market's capitalisation rate for the risk of the project, the NPV represents an estimate of the incremental market value of the firm due to the project. The NPV technique thus gives a simple assessment tool, but is inaccurate if there is doubt or dispute as to the correct discount rate.

Table 2.1
Calculating the NPV

Time in years from today	Cash flow (£)	11% Discount factor	Present value (£)
0	(1500)	1.000	(1500)
1	100	0.901	90
2	1000	0.812	812
3	1000	0.731	731
4	100	0.659	66

The NPV, the sum of the present values of the cash flow = +£199

The use of the concept of internal rate of return (IRR)

The internal rates of return, IRR, is also known as the discounted cash flow yield, DCF, the DCF return or the actuarial return. IRR is defined as the break-even financing rate for the project. This is not to say that the capital released by the project earns such a return. Reinvestments, whether wise or not, should be kept separate from the analysis of a project on its own merits. The IRR of a project is judged against the cost of capital standard or the minimum required return.

The mathematical definition of the IRR is that it is the discount rate which, when used to discount the net incremental cash flow, gives a zero net present value for the project. The NPV (which is calculated at the project's required rate of return discount rate) should not be confused with the many net present values which can be calculated using other rates.

The calculation of the NPV consists in setting out the cash flow, discounting it to the present time and adding up the net total. DCF or IRR calculations necessitate trial and error. If, however, the graph shown in Figure 2.1 is borne in mind, the process need not be lengthy.

Most practitioners find it convenient to calculate the NPV first. If this shows, for example by being positive, that it is worth doing more sums, a guess must be made of the next trial rate. A positive NPV indicates that the DCF/IRR will be greater than the cost of capital rate; how much greater can sometimes be guessed by the size of the

NPV. Trial rate A per cent is used and will give a net present value VA. Consideration of this result might lead to trial rate B per cent and VB. Having thus both over and underestimated the answer, the true IRR can be found by mathematical interpolation, or by drawing a similar graph (always provided the trial rates are not more than one or two percentage points apart – if they are, the curve that represents the relationship will give too inaccurate a result, which should be checked by the another trial and interpolation or extrapolation).

The following example shows how this procedure applies. Suppose the cost of capital is 11 per cent and an investment is being considered which costs £1500, lasts four years and has no terminal value:

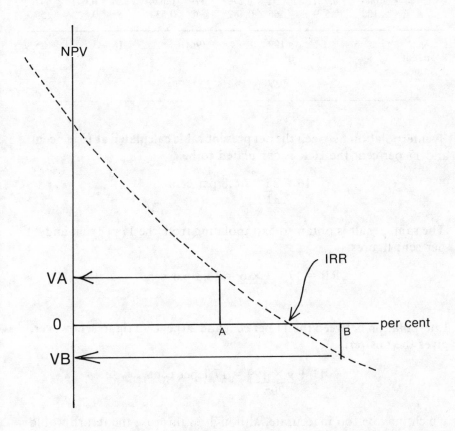

Fig. 2.1   The use of trial rates to calculate the internal rate of return

Table 2.2
Finding the true IRR

Time in years from today	Cash flow £	11 per cent Discount factor	value	20 per cent factor	value	17 per cent factor	value	16 per cent factor	value
0	(1500)	1.000	(1500)	1.000	(1500)	1.000	(1500)	1.000	(1500)
1	100	0.901	90	0.833	83	0.855	86	0.862	86
2	1000	0.812	812	0.694	694	0.731	731	0.743	743
3	1000	0.731	731	0.579	579	0.624	624	0.641	641
4	100	0.659	66	0.482	48	0.534	53	0.522	55
Net present values			199 this is the NPV		(96)		(6)		25

Cash flow discounted at:

By interpolation between the net present value calculated at 16 per cent and 17 per cent the IRR is calculated to be:

$$16 + \frac{25}{31} = 16.8 \text{ per cent}$$

The same result is obtained extrapolating from the 17 per cent and 20 per cent figures:

$$IRR = 17 - \frac{3 \times 6}{90} = 16.8 \text{ per cent}$$

Interpolation between the 11 per cent and 20 per cent figures, however, gives the answer:

$$11 + \frac{9 \times 199}{295} = 17.1 \text{ per cent}$$

which may be too inaccurate, although in this case the return would probably be quoted at 17 per cent. These figures could also be found graphically.

The use of present value: mid-year discounting

Discount tables are available for all periods – weeks, quarters, years – and to various numbers of places of decimals. It is not normally helpful to calculate the cash flow in too small periods or to discount it using more than four-figure tables. it is more important to notice that the tables usually refer to points of time and the cash flows represent a total for a period. A fitting assumption is needed. It is easy if the majority of receipts and payments occur at the beginning or at the end of the periods. For flows which are continuous and irregular over the periods, the total cash flow is often assumed to arise mid-year. The calculation should therefore be refined. If only annual discount tables are available, the half-year discount factor at r per cent can be calculated from the equation:

$$\text{Discount factor} = \frac{1}{\text{Square root of } (1+r \text{ expressed as a decimal})}$$

Examples

(*A*)   In the example suppose the investment is bought today and the operation is immediate and continuous. The NPV calculation becomes:

Table 2.3
The NPV calculation

Time from today	Cash flow £	Present value at 11 per cent Discount factor	Present value
0	(1500)	1.000	(1500)
$\frac{1}{2}$	100	0.949	95
$1\frac{1}{2}$	1000	0.901 × 0.949	855
$2\frac{1}{2}$	1000	0.812 × 0.949	770
$3\frac{1}{2}$	100	0.731 × 0.949	69
		NPV = 289	

The IRR now needs to be recalculated to take account of the refined timing. The IRR is now $21\frac{1}{2}$ per cent because of the earlier cash flow.

(*B*)   Suppose again that the operation were to be built up and paid for over one construction year. In this case the £1 500 cash flow is similarly assumed to be mid-year and the other cash flows occur six months later than before. The NPV can then be obtained from the first calculation, which has so far given a present value six months from today, by discounting the result by six months. NPV today =

$$199 \times 0.949 = £189$$

The IRR is 17 per cent in this case, as at first, because it is mathematically true that the same yield is given wherever period zero is assumed to occur if the succeeding time periods bear the same relationship to period zero.

In some cases, such as natural resource projects, which involve large negative cash flows at the end of the project, a special problem arises in using IRR. Projects of this sort can have more than one IRR, some of which may be above the required return and some below. Complex techniques have been developed to salvage the IRR method in these circumstances. These adjustments usually involve procedures similar to the present value approach, and fewer problems will be encountered by the use of the NPV rule in these circumstances.

The use of present value – optimisation of mutually exclusive alternatives

Financial analysts are constantly being asked to advise as to which of two viable alternatives is financially preferable. Such choices include large long life machinery versus cheaper short life machinery, labour versus automation, the choice of site, speed of construction, shaft versus open pit mining, air versus sea transport, and so on; in each case choice of one excludes the possibility of choosing the other alternative. Use of the net present value calculation is the easiest approach. Suppose that in a company with a cost of capital of eleven per cent the choice is between:

> method A (which is capital intensive) showing a NPV of + £1 500
> *and* method B (with a lower capital cost) showing a NPV of + £1 300

If the analyst calculates the NPVs using the minimum acceptable return discount rate for the risk of the project, different discount rates might be appropriate to A and B. For example, one method might involve installing a possibly risky unproven technological improvement, whereas the other method would re-equip as before.

The actual question to be answered, since both methods are financially desirable, is whether the expenditure of the extra capital involved on Method A is worth while. The incremental investment, which is represented by the difference between the cash flows of the two alternatives (cash flow A and cash flow B, for each period), shows an NPV of + £200 (NPV A – NPV B). It is therefore worth spending the extra money. Where the patterns of the alternative cash flows are very different, the incremental approach avoids problems in comparing projects with different levels of capital expenditure. Indeed, different cash flows can arise from the same total capital invested but the incremental cash flow analysis still gives the financially preferable operational plan.

Use of the DCF/IRR approach is also straightforward but contains a snare for the unwary. The question of whether the incremental investment would be desirable is answered by finding the DCF/IRR on the incremental cash flow (cash flow A minus cash flow B, for each period). If the incremental IRR is greater than the company's minimum acceptable return, then alternative A is financially preferable. When setting out the results, however, an apparent problem frequently arises.

Table 2.4
Example of apparent problem

Method		11 per cent NPV	IRR
A	Expensive	+ £1 500	14 per cent
B	Cheaper	+ £1 300	16 per cent
A–B	Incremental investment	+ £200	13 per cent

It looks as though one should choose method B because the IRR is better than that in A. This is an illusion because the capital on which the yield is earned is different in each case. The analysis of the incremental investment points to the same answer whichever method is used. It is often argued that, perhaps, the incremental capital should be spent on some other investment which might show a better return than the 13 per cent here. This could be the case in conditions of severe capital rationing when investments yielding 13 per cent cannot be financed. In other conditions there is no conflict and both investments are desirable. Of course, more than two projects might be available, in which case, several incremental investment choices would be necessary. It is easier simply to compare the NPVs; the most preferable choice has the highest NPV.

Some practitioners approve the calculation of the NPV but find the answer, which is of necessity expressed in currency, difficult to use. The profitability index is therefore sometimes used, particularly when projects need to be ranked because budgets are limited. The index is calculated by dividing the present value of the net cash returns by the present value of the net cash investments. In the example on page 32 the profitability index is 1 699/1 500 = 1.13 which means that every unit of investment earns 1.13 units of present value in the project. Care must be taken not to confuse this with the IRR, which is 17 per cent. In practice analysts report the profitability of a project both in terms of NPV in currency and of IRR as a percentage, to assist understanding.

When mutually exclusive opportunities are being analysed, equal project lives should be compared. This is often difficult, but a three-year life machine can be compared with a five-year machine by assuming that the longer life machine will be sold at the end of the third year. Alternatively a fifteen-year period can be taken with five three-year machines compared with three five-year machines. The most sensible assumption will be obvious.

Present value and expected value: decision trees

Much of capital investment planning involves arranging a continuous series of actions which may be altered in the light of future events or future actual patterns of marketing. It is possible to set out likely outcomes in a map known as a decision tree – it grows as it is extended further into the future. NPVs of each likely chain of events can be prepared and this could help the decision that must be taken later. Very often decision tree calculations are of the expected value of the outcome. To calculate expected values, the probabilities of likely intermediate events of outcomes are incorporated. Decision trees have been described extensively. A decision tree is shown in Figure 2.2.

Faced with the need to decide whether to install a computer, the possibilities or likely events might appear as shown. The decision taken would depend, financially, on the relative NPVs or expected values of the three good possibilities. Expected values are weighted by the relevant probability; for example, if there is a 60 per cent chance of an NPV of £100 and a 40 per cent chance of an NPV of zero, the expected value is £60.

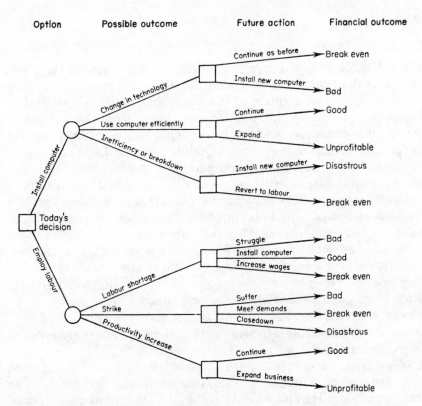

Fig. 2.2 Example of a decision tree

COMPUTATIONAL RESOURCES

Although computers, big and small, are invaluable as calculating aids for complex problems they should not be used indiscriminately because the cost, and the time taken to eliminate errors, can become disproportionate to the problem being analysed. Time sharing on computer terminals using borrowed working programs can be invaluable. Modern analytical methods can generally be employed for simple problems, using everyday hand calculators.

Calculation shortcuts and standard procedures for all problems are often sought in this field. If, however, they are used without understanding or without necessary adaption to the different circumstances of each case, much more time can easily be wasted than if the problem were initially approached from first principles.

DATA

The collection and sifting of project data normally leads to far more problems than the analysis. This is no reason for allowing less than rigorous analytical techniques. If a quick look at the first set of data indicates a promising idea, it is sensible to re-examine the data before extending the analysis. Data is given, begged, borrowed or stolen, but in spite of, or because of, the uncertainties involved, the best way to obtain good understanding leading to better decisions is to establish good communications with the project initiators as a top priority.

Discussions should be held 'on site' as early as possible so that there is no suggestion of ivory tower thinking. Diplomatic approaches to the hard-worked estimators who have to grapple with difficult forecasting problems can lead to a good understanding, not only of the best realistic guess at some figure, but also of the possible range in which it may lie and of the probabilities involved. Conversation with outsiders often helps clarification. Much the best hunches are those agreed by two or more experts. Special and outside experts can be called in to advise on variables found by sensitivity analysis to be critical enough to merit the cost of the advice.

A special problem to be tackled is that of inflation, particularly when costs are subject to special pressures leading to price rises greater than the general rate. The analyst will have to take a view as to when it is safe to assume that, on balance, costs and revenue will be similarly inflated. (See also Chapter 3.)

Missing data – reverse economics

Very often, data is simply not available for such vital factors as the achievable price for a new product, the size of the reserves in a new oil field, the time required to obtain safety clearance or planning permission or the market or technological life period. Reverse economics is the formal technique whereby it is possible to define the achievable or viable range for the missing data. If a graph is drawn of the profitability (NPV or IRR/DCF) of the project against invented values of the missing data, it is possible to find the value that gives the minimum acceptable result. If that value is very unrealistic, it may be possible to conclude that the new product will not be profitable, or that the oilfield cannot be exploited economically under present circumstances. A decision might then be taken to stop any further expenditure on the promotion of the idea. If a project must be killed off or frozen it is far better halted early, before reputations become involved.

This technique is also useful when considering the merger, takeover or sale of a company, or its flotation on the public market. An attempt is made to forecast the foreseeable cash flow of the company, possibly including benefits caused by savings in the new managerial context. The difference between the present value of the forecast cash flow and the debt divided by the number of issued shares will give a measure of the acceptability of a quoted or offered price, or will indicate what price to set at the beginning of negotiations. In a takeover situation the buyer should use the incremental required return for the project, that is the required rate of return for the risk of the company being taken over. If the company is quoted, the value of its equity share capital is given in the market place, unless there are undisclosed facts such as technological advance, or unless the market has anticipated a possible merger. The premium paid should be less than the NPV of the merger benefits (see also Chapter 16).

Uncertain and erroneous data

A good approach to uncertain data is to attempt to identify the range in which the answer may lie. This is sometimes done by adding to the best guess two more guesses, one of which is the most pessimistic and the other the most optimistic. In this way it may be possible to exclude too much subjectivity on the part of the estimator, who might previously have thought that his future depended on the success of his estimates and who therefore, understandably, introduced too much conservatism. In large organisations a chain of conservatism may be introduced. In such cases the analyst must try to assess the realities, and it is helpful if the motivations of the personnel are adjusted so as not to interfere. Overestimating can be as wrong as underestimating and can easily lead to raising too much finance, or to premature expansion.

Often, data is manipulated, either innocently or deliberately, to achieve the desired result – perhaps acceptance of a scheme by head office or of a contract in a tendering competition. The results can lead to public embarrassment, if not disaster. A good review discipline can help to avoid or to sort out such problems.

Once the range in which critical data lies is found, sensitivity analysis can be carried out. Alternatively, a calculation of the likely profit or loss, should everything turn out for the worst, can help in a discussion. If the organisation simply cannot survive such a loss and the chances of it are significant, then the project may well have to be forgone.

SENSITIVITY ANALYSIS

This technique can highlight the facts and problems caused by the risks and uncertainties of the plan under discussion. It has limitations but can be carried out with a minimum of calculating aids if necessary. The aim of this analysis is to discover the value of an uncertain variable at which the project is just profitable. Two or three calculations will give the necessary sensitivity curve.

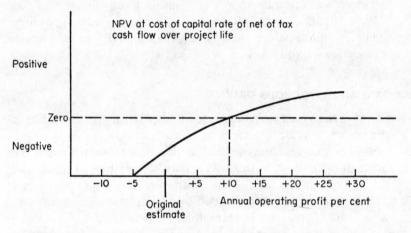

Fig. 2.3 Graph of the sensitivity of the project's viability to profit variation

Example

A project is showing a negative net present value at the company's cost of capital rate. What would need to be done to make it profitable? The sensitivity graph is drawn (Figure 2.3) and shows that the operating profit would need to be raised by ten per cent to give a zero NPV of the net incremental cash flow for the project. All other things are assumed at first to remain constant (capital cost, speed of coming into operation, life of the project, tax, inflation, etc.). Table 2.5 shows data which give the desired result.

Table 2.5
Variables in the profit estimates

	Original estimate	Acceptable estimates				
Price per unit £	20	21	20	20	20	20	20.3
Volume/Number sold	10	10	10.5	10	10	10	10.15
Labour cost £	40	40	40	30	40	40	38
Materials cost £	50	50	50	50	40	50	47.5
Overhead cost £	10	10	10	10	10	0	9.5
Operating profit	100	110	110	110	110	110	111.045

It is thus possible to say that the project would be acceptable if either the price could be raised by 5 per cent, or the volume sold is increased by 5 per cent, or if the labour cost could be lowered by 25 per cent, or the material cost by 20 per cent or the overhead cost by 100 per cent. Another possibility to explore would be if (as shown in the final column) both the price and volume sold could be raised by $1\frac{1}{2}$ per cent at the same time as all costs are reduced by 5 per cent. However, one should try to ensure that joint changes in variables are not contradictory and fit a plausible and consistent scenario.

The graph could have been plotted using IRR and the company's required rate of return as the cut-off line but this involves more sums.

One more uncertainty can be explored to extend the analysis. Suppose, for example, that the market for the product is thought to last ten years but could be hit by competition in eight to twelve years' time; further calculations give the graph shown in Figure 2.4. Annual operating profit is thought likely to lie between 95 and 120. Assuming the variables examined to be the most critical, the profitability 'envelope' is shown by the two outer curves and the dotted connecting lines. This envelope is divided into two parts by the cut-off line of zero net present value. By inspection of the two areas it is possible to conclude that the project has roughly only a forty per cent chance of being viable. The worst likely outcome is also shown. The decision may then be taken more easily.

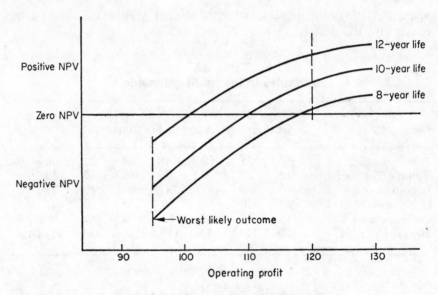

Fig. 2.4 Two-variable sensitivity analysis graph

Should the whole envelope be above the cut-off line it would be possible to conclude that the project is profitable in spite of the uncertainty in the variables considered, which are then defined as uncritical. Further effort could then be concentrated on other variables. This technique is limited to two dimensions. It is, however, of great value, even without calculating aids, because of its simplicity in demonstrating the effect of apparently daunting uncertainties.

PROBABILITY ANALYSIS

This is the ideal towards which sensitivity analysis is the first step, but the calculation usually requires the help of a computer. Great efforts are being made by large organisations and consultants to prepare flexible computer programs to conduct probability analyses on a wide variety of projects.

Sensitivity analysis tells one the impact of each variable on the profitability of the project. If probabilities can be assigned to each variable in different parts of its range, the probability of various outcomes for the profitability of the project can be examined.

Subjectivity is not avoided by this, but the further discussion can sometimes help clarify the situation. The results could be shown for each variable in a histogram, which is a practical approach to the underlying mathematical curve. An example is shown in Figure 2.5.

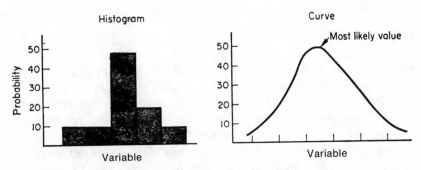

Fig. 2.5 Examples of probability distributions

Mathematical sampling using such data for each significant variable results in the type of profitability/probability graph shown in Figure 2.6.

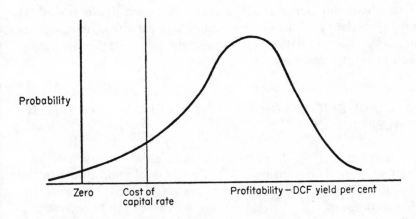

Fig. 2.6 Example of a profitability/probability graph

The peak of the curve shows the most likely outcome, but there is a significant chance that the yield might be negative or that the original investment would not be recovered. The area under the curve being taken as unity, the area to the left of the cost of capital or required rate of return cut-off line, if measured, gives the probability of unprofitability. The use of sensitivity and probability analyses does not remove uncertainty and subjectivity of data; it helps decision takers to judge the likelihood of profit or loss in projects.

RISK

Uncertainty of data is not the only unknown bedevilling projects. Many possible events could have a highly significant effect. Such events include acts of God (earthquake, flood) of governments (tariffs, nationalisation), of competitors, of technological improvement. Some risks can be insured against. In every case it is helpful to define the risk and assess its possible effect (what happens if . . . ?), and in particular when such an effect might occur. If the likely loss caused by the risky circumstances were to be disastrous to the company, then perhaps the venture is too risky. There are several ways in which organisations of different kinds can proceed to minimise the effect of risk. Obvious examples are diversification, both geographically and in the nature of the business, the tying of customers or suppliers to long term contracts, and the cautious introduction of new or different scale business. Other risks can be eliminated through markets in which risk is traded. A surprising variety of risks can be insured against and others, such as commodity price variation and exchange rate variations, can be hedged in futures markets.

THE DISCUSSION FORUM FOR CAPITAL INVESTMENT PROBLEMS

Good decision taking depends more than anything else on good communication. The decision takers (at the level appropriate to the size of the proposal) do well to arrange a free debate between the project sponsors, the experts, the analysts and themselves. Documentation of the proposal, the analysis, the decision and any argument or discussion are of great value to all concerned in future planning, as well as the relevance to interrelated projects in the context of the organisation's future as a whole. The techniques described in this chapter contribute only by assembling such facts as can be established and highlighting the likely probabilities. This, however, is of great value in releasing management effort for the interpretation of the problems.

Most private organisations are to some extent limited as to the amount of capital available, particularly for unspectacular investments. It would be convenient if all projects turned up simultaneously and could be ranked in order of profitability and then accepted in turn until available funds were used up. (Such a procedure is to a certain extent available to the public sector at budget time). In most companies, however, capital investment or operational optimisation opportunities turn up irregularly. It is therefore highly desirable to establish and monitor a clearly understood set of criteria and discount rates, reflecting the company's required rates of return for different risks, against which each scheme can be measured as it arises and progresses. With the aid of the right criteria there is some chance that a good source of investments will have been chosen so that, at the minimum, returns can exceed costs and the company's value can be increased, leading to a healthy financial context for future development.

Tactics

When analysis precedes or accompanies negotiations with governments, financiers, associates or opponents, it is usually helpful to make calculations in order that one can understand the opposite point of view, which might be based on different methods or criteria.

Few organisations can avoid differences of opinion which lead to apparent or very real conflicts. The experienced decision taker and his advisers can normally recognise the behavioural signs. Discussion is not always avoided for good reasons, such as a real emergency. Emergencies can be contrived by skilful delays and, perhaps, decisions can be precipitated by prompted outside pressures. Decisions taken in real emergencies should be appraised and documented as soon as possible. If a decision taker is known to be susceptible to private discussions, then project sponsors will be quick to arrange suitable lobbying. Such a situation has obvious dangers.

A very real problem can arise in planning investments which can or should be phased. The purchase of options or expenditure on pilot plants, which lead either to subsequent large investment or to embarrassment if the second stage is deemed unacceptable, should not be appraised in isolation. Appraisal of the first stage should be accompanied by a best guess of the likely subsequent history, and the project should be discussed at the level relevant to the whole operation, in which case the decision will be taken after consideration of the future commitments. The decision tree technique examined earlier can help.

When a superficially attractive proposal is financially marginal, special care must be taken. At this time criticism may be made of the company's criteria which were otherwise accepted when the proposals were better than marginal. Such criticism at this time may not always be valid. In this situation excessive subjectivity may be introduced into uncertain data; in fact, some estimators claim to be able to produce estimates which pass company tests. Wide discussions of parameters, perhaps calling in outside advice, as well as the discipline contained in carrying out sensitivity and probability analysis, go some way to reduce the risk. Afterwards, a well established routine of project monitoring reappraisal, review or *ex-post* evaluation, or whatever the subsequent comparison of forecast with actual results is called, may be especially appropriate.

RE-APPRAISAL: EX-POST EVALUATION AND CAPITAL EXPENDITURE REVIEWS

It has been said that, without subsequent re-examination, formal planning appraisal techniques are largely counter-productive. *Ex ante* evaluation – the prior preparation of forecast results – is very necessary when raising finance for a project, either internally or externally, and obtaining the desired go-ahead. There is, however, no certainty that the combined estimates and skills which resulted in the forecasts have been optimised unless a subsequent view is taken.

There are well established commercial routines whereby periodic (weekly, monthly, quarterly, annual) accounts are compiled of both financial and physical resources used and benefits achieved, and reports are made to relevant technical and financial monitors. Usually the results are compared with annual and three or five-year plans for the project or the organisation as a whole. Variations are studied and adjustments are made.

Projects which were initially appraised using cash flow disciplines should be reviewed using the same diciplines. If the conclusions drawn differ, speedy action may be desirable or, if it is not, it would be nice to know that it is not.

Unfortunately, it is necessary to take a cynical look at projects built for less than the forecast cost, sales that noticeably exceed budget, and other successes. If the planners' faults were not in their stars but in themselves they should remain as underlings. People have gone as far as saying that it is useless to plan at all unless one also reviews the results. But, as always, too much is as bad as too little.

It is not always clear who should conduct re-appraisal reviews. Conflicts may be avoided if the project operators undertake the review in the normal course of their duties. It is highly desirable also to include some sort of outside view to ensure a balanced opinion as to why the resulting return differs from the first forecast. The review should, of course, cover all the unquantifiable as well as the measurable aspects. If the organisation sets up a separate reviewing team, its members may need great powers of diplomacy as well as of detection and endurance.

Reviews are discussed preferably at the same forum as are capital expenditure proposals, or, at least, the decision takers should check that re-evaluation has taken place. Very often the lessons do not need to be driven home but have been learnt in the course of the operation.

The introduction of this routine is often problematical. As usual, opposition may be a cover. Other avoidance tactics can include radical changes of scope of a project leading, among other things, to a delay in the review date. Significant changes of scope should be appraised as rigorously as new projects.

FURTHER READING

J. R. Franks and J. E. Broyles, *Modern Managerial Finance*, John Wiley & Sons, 1979.

A. J. Merrett and Allen Sykes, *The Finance and Analysis of Capital Projects*, Second Edition, Longmans, 1973.

A. J. Merrett and Allen Sykes, *Capital Budgeting & Company Finance*, Second Edition, Longmans, 1973.

Howard Thomas, *Decision Theory and the Manager*, Pitman, 1972.

3

Inflation and financial decisions

Ian Cooper

Inflation affects profitability in four ways. It changes the cost of funds used to finance an enterprise; it increases costs of labour, materials and the price of the product; it affects the tax bill to be paid; it causes shifts in demand patterns. In this chapter we will consider how to analyse these problems and make good decisions when faced with inflation.

FORECASTING IN REAL AND MONEY UNITS

Most companies make forecasts of the number of units of output they will produce and sell, the man-hours and machine-hours that production will require and the volume of material purchases. These forecasts in terms of physical units can be converted to cash flows by multiplying by the appropriate prices. If the prices used are those expected to hold at future dates, the resulting forecasts of cash flows are in money terms. If, however, today's prices are applied, the resulting forecasts of cash flows are in real (constant price) terms.

Table 3.1 illustrates this. Unit forecasts and price forecasts are given. These are used to calculate cash flow forecasts in money terms or real (current price) terms. Since in this case the same inflation rate is forecast for the three components of cash flows: sales, materials and labour, the real cash flows and the money cash flows are related simply by the general inflation rate forecast, which is assumed to be 10 per cent.

If the various costs and revenues were forecast to inflate at different rates, this simple relationship would not hold. In that case, relative price changes would have to be included, as discussed later in this chapter.

Table 3.1
Cash flows in money and real terms

Year	1	2	3	4
Units:				
Sales units	100	110	130	90
Material lbs	100	110	130	90
Labour hrs	50	55	65	45
Unit prices forecast:				
Sales £/unit	10	11	12	13
Materials £/lb	3.0	3.3	3.6	3.9
Labour £/hr	4.0	4.4	4.8	5.2
Cash flows: money terms				
Sales	1000	1210	1560	1170
Materials	300	363	468	351
Labour	200	242	312	234
Net cash flow	500	605	780	585
Cash flows: real terms				
Sales	1000	1100	1300	900
Materials	300	330	390	270
Labour	200	220	260	180
Net cash flow	500	550	650	450

Just as the cash flows can be forecast in real or money terms, so the cost of funds used to finance the business can be stated as a real or money rate. The money rate is just the overall or weighted average cost of funds computed using the actual interest rate charged and the actual money return required by the equity investors. The real rate is the overall money rate adjusted for inflation:

Real rate = Money rate – Expected inflation

In the case above, where inflation was forecast at 10 per cent, a money rate of 16 per cent would correspond to a real cost of funds of 6 per cent (the 16 per cent cost of funds less the 10 per cent expected inflation).

When making decisions by discounting forecast cash flows at the cost of funds, it is important to be consistent. Money flows should be discounted at a money rate or real cash flows at a real rate. Used correctly, both methods give the same answer, but it is easier in general, to work in money terms. This is discussed further later on.

INFLATION AND THE COST OF FUNDS

The cost of funds to a company is related to the level of interest rates. Because business enterprise is risky, the overall cost of funds is higher than the interest rate, but will rise and fall as the interest rate changes.

$$\text{Overall cost of funds} = \text{Interest rate} + \text{Risk premium}$$

As discussed in Chapter 2 the weighted averaged risk premium for UK companies is about 6 per cent.

The interest rate reflects expectations of inflation. The proposition that the interest rate completely reflects the expected inflation rate is known as the Fisher effect. This is equivalent to saying that the expected real rate of interest is zero. In fact, for the UK and US the real interest rate seems to have averaged about zero during the post-war period. In normal times:

$$\text{Interest rate} = \text{Expected inflation rate}$$

In periods of low economic activity, such as 1974, the real interest rate often becomes negative, and in periods of high economic activity it changes to positive. It seldom, however, seems to depart by more than a few per cent from zero. Recently the real rate of interest in OECD countries has been positive for an extended period even though economic activity has been depressed. This has been caused by a heavy demand for borrowing from both the public and private sectors to fund operating deficits.

This relationship between expected inflation and the cost of funds is useful in two ways If we wish to forecast inflation, one of the best places to start is by looking at interest rates. For instance, a one-year interest rate of 14 per cent suggests in normal times a general expectation of inflation around 14 per cent over the next year.

Second, if you choose to make financial decisions by forecasting real cash flows and discounting at a real rate, the Fisher effect tells you roughly what real rate you should be using. It should be the real interest rate of approximately zero plus a risk premium of approximately 6 per cent for the average risk company.

FURTHER ADJUSTMENTS WHEN INFLATION RATES ARE HIGH

The simple relationship between interest rates and the cost of funds where the cost of funds is computed by simply adding the 6 per cent risk premium to the interest rate is only an approximation. In fact, the exact relationship is:

$$1 + \text{Cost of funds} = (1 + \text{Interest rate})(1 + \text{Risk premium})$$

where all rates are expressed as decimals. When interest rates are low, this gives an answer very similar to just adding the premium to the interest rate. When rates are high, the multiplicative relationship must be used.

Similarly, the real interest rate, when inflation is high, is correctly computed as:

$$(1 + \text{Real interest rate} = \frac{(1 + \text{Money interest rate})}{(1 + \text{Expected inflation rate})}$$

Making these adjustments in the correct way is especially important when considering projects in high inflation countries. When inflation rates are low (less than 10 per cent) the errors involved in the approximations are small.

RELATIVE PRICE CHANGES

As we saw earlier, if we were so fortunate that costs and revenues all experienced the same rate of inflation, working with real or nominal forecasts would be a simple matter of adjusting all cash flows and the discount rate by the forecast overall inflation rate. Unfortunately, life is not so simple. Table 3.2 shows the inflation experience of different goods and services over the period 1974–80.

It is clear from Table 3.2 that different costs and revenues can experience very different rates of inflation. Although inflation rates for various products will tend to move with the general rate of inflation, a significant volume of price movement is not related to general inflation. For instance, in 1979 the cost of the inputs to the chemical industry increased by more than double the general rate of retail price inflation.

Table 3.2
Rates of inflation (%)

		Retail prices		Materials purchased by	
	All items	Housing	Fuel and light	Chemicals	Motor vehicles
1976	17	14	18	24	25
1977	10	7	11	2	9
1978	9	16	6	15	9
1979	18	25	19	50	15
1980	13	20	28	-8	7
1981	12	23	13	13	8

Sources: Annual Abstract of Statistics, HMSO Monthly Digest of Statistics, Central Statistical Office

How do we incorporate this into the cash flow forecasts we use to make financial decisions? If we are working in money terms, the answer is straightforward. If, for instance the labour price in Table 3.1 were forecast to increase at a higher rate than materials cost and sales cost, we would just factor in the increased forecasts when converting from physical units to cash flows (as shown in Table 3.3).

Table 3.3
Unit prices forecast

Year	1	2	3	4
Labour £/hr.	4.0	4.7	5.3	5.8
Cash flows: Money terms				
Sales	1000	1210	1560	1170
Materials	300	363	468	351
Labour	200	259	345	261
Net cash flow	500	588	747	558

These cash flows should then be discounted at the money cost of funds given by the money interest rate plus a risk premium. To make this adjustment if we were working in real terms we would have to adjust by the forecast relative movement of labour costs against the overall inflation rate.

FORECASTING PRICES

As the interest rate normally approximately equals the expected inflation rate, it forms a good starting point when forecasting inflation. The three-month interest rates at the beginning of each year from 1960 to 1980 are given in Table 3.4. The actual retail price inflation that occurred is also given. Although the outcome for inflation differed from the forecast implicit in the interest rates, other forecasts of inflation produced by economic forecasters did not do much better. Whatever forecast is used, unforeseen factors will almost inevitably cause the actual outcome to differ from the forecast.

Forecasts can, of course, be purchased from various economic experts. These often include forecasts for various components of the general price index. In making such forecasts of relative price movements, a number of factors should be considered. In general, wage inflation will exceed retail price inflation by the rate of productivity growth. This will not always be the case, though, since temporary or local imbalances in the demand and supply for labour can disturb the relationship. The relative rates of inflation of different goods and services will be determined by demand and supply conditions in those markets. Demand components that should be considered include the stage of the business cycle, the level of export

Table 3.4
Inflation rates and interest rates

Year	Interest rate at beginning of year (%)	Inflation during the year (%)	Year	Interest rate at beginning of year (%)	Inflation during the year (%)
1960	4.2	1.8	1971	6.9	9.0
1961	4.4	4.4	1972	4.5	7.7
1962	5.5	2.3	1973	8.5	10.6
1963	3.5	1.9	1974	12.8	19.1
1964	3.8	4.8	1975	11.3	24.9
1965	6.7	4.5	1976	10.9	15.1
1966	5.6	3.4	1977	14.0	12.1
1967	6.6	2.5	1978	6.4	8.4
1968	7.6	5.9	1979	11.9	17.2
1969	6.9	4.7	1980	16.5	15.1
1970	7.8	7.9	1981	13.6	12.0

demand, the re-distributional effects of general inflation and the strength of the consuming industry, if an intermediate product is being considered. On the supply side, the degree of competition within the industry, the level of capacity usage, the rate of technological innovation, and the speed of learning and cost reduction with new technology should be included as factors when assessing the likely rate of inflation.

All these elements help to produce forecasts of the price movements for the individual components of the cash flow stream. Even so, the expected outcome will seldom be the one that actually occurs, but that is no reason not to try to make forecasts. In some cases free forecasts are available. For those commodities which are traded in futures markets, the futures price represents the market forecast of the price movement for that commodity. Such markets also provide a vehicle for hedging risk as discussed in Chapter 2.

When making inflation forecasts for individual components of the expected cash flow, it is important to retain an overall perspective. The ultimate purpose is to make good financial decisions, so more detail should only be added if it is likely to influence the decision. For instance, if a separate inflation estimate is included for labour costs, it would only make sense to break this down further into different types of labour if the costs of each type were substantial and likely to increase at very different rates.

LONG TERM AND SHORT TERM PROJECTS

In making a forecast of general inflation or of specific price changes, it is important to define precisely the period to which the inflation forecast refers. For instance, forecasts based on the current level of short term interest rates refer only to the next year or so. Longer term projects require forecasts of inflation over their whole lives, and this should include separate forecasts for each year if the inflation rate is expected to vary.

Similarly, if the real interest rate is currently high, this situation may not be expected to persist. For long life projects, a forecast must be made of the way that the real interest rate will change over the life of the project. Table 3.5 gives an example of the way that the cost of funds and present value of a project can be computed including inflation rates and real interest rates which are expected to vary over the life of the project.

Table 3.5
Long life project with varying inflation and real interest rates

Year	1	2	3	4	5	6	7	8
Inflation forecast (%)	15	14	13	12	11	10	10	10
Real interest rate (%)	3	2	1	0	0	0	0	0
Total money cost of funds including 6% risk premium* (%)	26	23	21	19	18	17	17	17
Total money cash flows including general inflation, and relative price changes	100	140	170	170	160	150	140	80
Present value factor**	0.79	0.65	0.53	0.45	0.38	0.32	0.28	0.24
Present value	79	91	90	76	61	48	39	19

*(1 + Total cost of funds) = (1 + Inflation forecast) (1 + Real interest rate) (1 + .06).
**The present value factor for year five, for instance is computed as: $1/[(1.26)(1.23)(1.21)(1.19)(1.18)]$.

If a project has cash flows originating in foreign countries, these cash flow forecasts should take account of local inflation rates. This will give a forecast of the money cash flow in the local currency. These money cash flows should then be discounted at a local cost of funds. Alternatively, the money cash flows can be converted to real cash flows by deflating by the local inflation rate. These real cash flows can then be discounted at the local real rate of interest plus a risk premium.

LAGS IN CASH FLOWS

The example given in Table 3.1 incorporates estimates of future prices in calculating the cash flows resulting from the project. In many cases the cash may not be received at the time a sale is made. The lag in receipt of payment of accounts receivable or of payment of tax bills is often large, and the effects of inflation on their values are correspondingly significant.

Suppose that the £1 000 sales revenue at time zero in Table 3.4 will not be received until the second year. How much will this delay in payment cost? The money value of the cash flow will not have changed, but, because of the one-year delay in receipt, one year's interest will have been lost on it. In terms of net present value this is set out in Table 3.6. The year's delay when interest rates are 10 per cent costs £91. When rates are 20 per cent due to higher inflation, the cost of the delay almost doubles in net present value terms. Of course, were this a delay in making a payment, the higher interest rate would be beneficial.

Table 3.6
Net present value effect of payment delay

Year	0	1	NPV 10%	NPV 20%
Cash flow	1000		1000	1000
With delay		1000	909	833
NPV cost of delay			91	167

Since, as we have seen, high interest rates are usually caused by high inflation rates, the costs of delayed receipts rise and the benefits of delayed payments are also increased when inflation is high. The most important impact of this effect is on the cost of carrying accounts receivable. Receivables (trade debtors) are loans given to customers. Since they usually carry no explicit interest charge, the cost of financing the receivables should be reflected in the price of the goods supplied. For instance, the cost of granting six months' credit when the interest rate is 20 per cent is 10 per cent, and the price charged should reflect this.

PROFITS AND CASH FLOWS

Apart from their impact on profitability, lagged cash flows cause differences between the accounting earnings used by most companies for forecasting and the cash flows of the companies. Periods of high inflation are often those when companies face the most severe cash crises, but also those when the difference between cash flow and accounting profit is the greatest. While forecasts of accounting profits are useful, short term forecasts need to include the impact of the timing of cash flows.

Table 3.7 gives an example of a simple monthly income statement prepared on the normal accrual basis. An annual inflation rate of 12 per cent is assumed. What are the differences between this and a cash flow statement of the same business? First, as we have seen above, billed sales do not correspond to cash flow received from payments of accounts receivable.

Table 3.7
Monthly income statement on normal accrual basis

	Month			
	1	2	3	4
Sales	222.0	224.0	226.0	228.0
Expenses (FIFO)	(54.5)	(55.0)	(55.5)	(56.0)
Depreciation	(100.0)	(100.0)	(100.0)	(100.0)
Sales & administration	22.2	22.4	22.6	22.8
Net operating profit	45.3	46.6	47.9	49.2
Taxes accrued at 50%	(22.7)	(23.3)	(23.9)	(24.6)

In the initial stages, the lag of payments shows up as a large increase in receivables. After two months, the receivables increase at the rate of inflation as long as the physical volume of sales remains constant. This is shown in Table 3.8.

Another difference between cash flows and accounting profit arises from the accrual accounting treatment of costs. Costs enter the profit and loss account as cost of goods sold when the associated sale is made. The cash flow associated with these costs occurs when the payment is made on purchases. Just as accounting sales can be adjusted to a cash flow figure by subtracting a forecast of the investment in accounts receivable (debtors), so cost of goods sold can be adjusted to a cash

Table 3.8
Adjusted monthly income statement

	Month			
	1	2	3	4
Sales	222.0	224.0	226.0	228.0
Cash payments			222.0	224.0
Difference (Build-up of receivables)	222.0	224.0	4.0	4.0

flow cost figure by subtracting inventory investment and adding the build-up of accounts payable (creditors).

These working capital flows are extremely important in evaluating projects. In inflationary times, the investment in working capital is not just the initial investment required to bring working capital up to its normal level. This balance must be continually topped up to maintain the real value of the working capital. These topping up flows appear as additional investments in working capital over the life of the project. At the end of the project the working capital may be released, as inventories, receivables and payables are run down.

One final adjustment that should be made is for the depreciation, included as an accounting cost, which is not a cash flow. The cash flow effect of purchasing capital goods is the payment made. Depreciation amortizes this payment over the life of the asset. To convert reported earnings to cash flows, depreciation must be added back and capital expenditures deducted.

To summarise the general relationship between accounting profit and cash flow:

Cash flow equals:
Accounting profit
plus non-cash charges (such as depreciation)
minus capital expenditure
minus investments in working capital (other than cash)
plus adjustments for timing of tax payments etc.

As we have seen, these adjustments correct for the way in which accrual accounting imputes costs and benefits to times other than those at which the associated cash flow occurs. The effects of this difference are greater when inflation and interest rates are high, so the use of accounting profit rather than cash flow as a guide to financial decisions is likely to be most misleading at such times.

Working capital flows adjust profit forecasts to give forecasts of cash flows. In some circumstances, it is easier to forecast cash flows directly. For instance, if a project has a series of stage payments, the resulting cash flows can be forecast directly. This is more appropriate than forecasting sales on an accrual basis and then including a forecast of accounts receivable to get back to a cash flow figure. If the amount of such payments is large, their timing may be important, and it will be necessary to forecast cash flows on a quarterly or monthly basis rather than annually.

INFLATION AND TAXES

Taxes paid by UK companies are based on taxable income net of capital allowances and stock relief. Taxable income is based on FIFO stock accounting. Stock relief can be viewed as an allowance against taxable income for changes in inventory investment. The adjustment differs from an allowance, however, since it is based on changes in values of stocks held.

Table 3.9 shows the tax paid on stockholding gains without tax relief. The company holds £100 000 of stock and inflation is 10 per cent. Tax is paid, under FIFO, on gains in the money value of stock, even though the physical amount of stock held is constant. It is clear that the tax paid on stock gains increases with higher rates of inflation and that the tax on stock gains adds substantially to the cost of holding stocks when inflation is rapid.

Table 3.9
Corporation tax on stock gains under FIFO

	0	1	2	3	(£'000)
Value of stocks at end of period	1 000	1 100	1 210	1 331	. . .
Value at beginning of period		1 000	1 100	1 210	. . .
Stock gain		100	110	121	
Corporation tax* at 52 per cent on stock gain			–52	–57	–63

A constant physical volume of stock is assumed
*A one-year lag in payment of corporation tax is assumed

Stock relief reduces the tax liability on stock gains which result from inflation. Since 1981, stock relief has been given as an allowance on stocks in excess of £2 000. The allowance is defined as the increase in the value of such stocks held at the beginning of the accounting period. This increase in value is computed using a general price index published by the government statistical service. Table 3.10 gives an example of the impact of stock relief. (The details of stock relief are described in more detail in Chapter 17.)

Table 3.10
The impact of stock relief

Profits	£400 000 (including £100 000 stock gain)
Opening stocks	£1 000 000
Opening index	179.2
Closing index	194.5
Stock relief	$(1\ 000\ 000 - 2\ 000) \times \dfrac{194.5 - 179.2}{179.2} = £85\ 209.$

Note that in this case, the stock relief does not completely offset the £100 000 holding gain on stocks. This is because £2 000 of the stock is excluded from the computation of relief and because the stock relief index has gone up by only 8.5 per cent whereas the price of the stocks concerned has gone up by 10 per cent. Another feature of the stock relief system introduced in the 1981 Finance Act is that relief is not given on increases in the value of stocks resulting from a physical increase in the volume of stocks held. Conversely, reductions in the physical volume of stocks held do not now result in a clawback of stock relief.

The main impact of the present stock relief system is that companies whose material costs are rising more rapidly than the general rate of inflation will receive incomplete relief for the tax on their inventory holding gains resulting from FIFO tax accounting. Companies with input costs increasing at less than the general rate of inflation will benefit. There is no incentive, however, to manipulate the physical volume of stocks, since this does not affect the amount of stock relief.

In Table 3.9 a one-year delay in tax payment is assumed. This approximates to the actual situation for most UK companies. The delay in tax payment is beneficial, since taxes are levied in money rather than real terms. As with other lags in payments, the effect of the delay becomes greater as inflation and interest rates rise. So at high rates of inflation, the postponement of tax payments has significant value. For deductions such as capital allowances, the effect works the other way. Since the benefits are received after a delay, by way of a lower tax bill, the value of such allowances falls as inflation increases. This delay in receipt of the tax benefits may be very large for companies which are not currently paying taxes, so providing a motivation for leasing rather than buying assets, as discussed in Chapter 12.

WORKING IN MONEY TERMS OR REAL TERMS

Apart from increasing all cash flows associated with business decisions, we have identified other impacts of inflation. Relative price changes, lags in payments and receipts, and the impact of stock relief on taxes all mean that the real cash flows that occur with inflation are different from those with no inflation. If money cash flows and a money discount rate are used for decision making these factors can be incorporated directly. If real cash flows and a real discount rate are used, relative price changes, lags and tax effects must still be included.

To adjust for relative price changes when working with real cash flows, the price of each cash flow stream must be forecast as if it would inflate or deflate at the difference between its own predicted inflation rate and the general forecast inflation rate. For instance, if labour costs are expected to increase at 3 per cent more than the general inflation rate, the real hourly labour cost would be calculated as increasing by 3 per cent per year. Adjustments can also be made for lags in tax payments, by deflating the tax by the amount of inflation expected to occur between the dates the tax is incurred and paid. For instance, if a real net income of 200 is forecast in year 2, and tax will be paid in year 3, the real value of tax payment in year 3 will be 104 divided by 1.1, assuming that the tax rate is 52 per cent and the expected inflation rate is 10 per cent.

Because these adjustments are quite complicated, it is usually preferable to work in money terms. Furthermore, the results actually achieved will be in terms of money, not real values, so comparison of actual with forecast outcome is simplified if planning and forecasting are expressed in money terms.

THE IMPACT OF INFLATION ON PROFITABILITY

Table 3.11 gives an example of the cash flows expected from an investment project assuming zero inflation. For simplicity, the net impact of stock appreciation and stock relief have been omitted. This is a profitable project, with a net present value of £109 000. Table 3.12 shows the after-tax cash flows from the project when inflation increases from zero, as in Table 3.11, to 10 per cent. Along with this general rise in the inflation rate, Table 3.12 includes a 3 per cent rise in the real interest rate. The total cost of funds rises from 8 per cent to 22

Table 3.11
Investment project with zero inflation

Year	0	1	2	3	4
Investment in plant	−1 000				
Working capital	−600				
Revenues		+1 900	+1 900	+1 900	
Costs		−1 000	−1 000	−1 000	
Tax on net income			−450	−450	−450
Tax affect on capital allowance		+500			
Net cash flow	−1 600	+1 400	+450	+450	−450

NPV at 8% = 109

per cent*. Also, costs are expected to increase at 2 per cent above the general rate of inflation. The net effect is to reduce the net present value of the project by £51 000.

Table 3.12
Investment project with 10% inflation and 2% cost escalation

Year	0	1	2	3	4
Investment in plant	−1 000				
Working capital	−600				
Revenue		+2 090	+2 299	+2 529	
Costs		−1 120	−1 254	−1 405	
Tax on net income			−485	−525	−562
Tax effect of capital allowance		+500			
Net cash flow	−1 500	+1 470	+560	+601	−562

NPV at 22% = 58

Table 3.13 shows how the net change in profitability of the project results from several different causes. The rise in the real interest rate and the cost escalation both reduce the NPV by about £50 000. A

*The computation is: $(1.08 + .03) \times (1.10) = 1.22$

similar effect results from the delay of one year in receipt of the tax benefit from the capital allowance. As inflation and interest rates rise, the present value of this tax saving falls. The benefit which partially offsets these costs of inflation is the delay in tax payments on net income. The real value of these payments decreases as inflation rises.

Table 3.13
Example of the impact of inflation on an investment project

		NPV effect
1	Rise in real interest rate (0% to 3%)	−50
2	Cost escalation of 2%	−59
3	Delay in tax saving on capital allowance	−52
4	Delay in tax payments on net revenue	+110
Total		−51

CONCLUSIONS

Interest rates, and therefore discount rates, tend to increase with the rate of inflation. Inflation also affects project cash flow forecasts. This does not mean that net present values remain unchanged, however. Since prices negotiated on credit transactions at one point in time are not paid for until, perhaps, months later, the leads and lags in working capital payments and receipts affect net present value when an expected increase in the rate of inflation increases the discount rate.

Because the cost of goods sold is based upon FIFO in the UK, inventory appreciation due to inflation increases accounting profits. The resulting increase in taxes reduces net present value. In other countries LIFO valuation helps to preserve net present value under inflation by delaying taxes payable on inventory profits. Since fiscal depreciation (capital allowances) is usually based upon initial cost and remains unaffected by inflation during the life of an asset, the present value of the tax savings from depreciation is reduced when inflation increases the discount rate.

Inflation increases the burden of taxes on both individuals and companies. The resulting redistribution of wealth affects demand for different products and may materially affect revenue forecasts of specific projects. If inflation reduces real macro economic growth, then the profitability of capital investment in the private sector must be affected adversely.

We have shown how to reflect the effect of these factors in the discounted cash flow of capital projects, and we have suggested ways of avoiding common pitfalls in the analysis of capital investment under inflation.

4

Managing working capital

Geoffrey P E Clarkson

Working capital is that proportion of a company's total capital which
is employed in short term operations. It is customary to divide working
capital into two categories: gross and net. Gross working capital is the
sum total of all current assets, while net working capital is the amount
by which the value of current assets exceeds the value of current
liabilities. The former presents the financial manager with the problem
of how to manage the individual components which comprise the list of
current assets. The latter has financial significance for two reasons.
The amount of net working capital represents the net volume of
current assets which are being financed by long term sources. Though
current assets and liabilities customarily are turned over within
relatively short periods of time, the net balance of current assets is that
proportion which requires permanent financing by the company. The
second point is that creditors have a particular interest in the net
working capital position and regard these assets as the ultimate source
of funds for the repayment of their loans.

Current assets consist of all stocks (inventories), including finished
goods, work in process and raw materials; debtors; short term
investments (near cash) and cash.

Current liabilities are the sum total of a company's debts which must
be settled within the following twelve months. They include creditors,
overdrafts (short term bank loans), current portions of long term debt
due, as well as the remaining credit obligations of the firm. They may
require early settlement, or involve an interest charge which can vary
from zero in the case of net monthly accounts due, to bank charge rates
on overdrafts. Current liabilities represent the total amount of short
term debt. They are the cheaper forms of debt but involve the highest

insolvency risks. Current liabilities have relatively short term due dates for payment and cash or further credits must be found to settle these accounts.

It is the function of financial management to fund the company debt at the lowest cost consistent with acceptable risk. This is readily evident when the net working capital position is examined. Since net working capital is the net value of current assets this balance must be totally financed from long term sources. Since long term funds are usually more costly than short term funds, the management of current assets and current liabilities is an important part of financial management.

WORKING CAPITAL RATIOS

The liquidity and solvency of a firm are closely related to its working capital position. Solvency represents the time state of liquidity. To be solvent entails an ability to meet debt payments on due dates by having money available in the form of cash, near cash or unused credit. To be and remain solvent, it is not necessary to be liquid. It is only necessary to be able to become sufficiently liquid should the need arise.

The ability to become liquid is a function of time and the state of assets in relation to cash. If too high a proportion of assets exist in a state far removed from cash, a problem of solvency can arise. To be unable to generate cash or credit when required creates the risk of insolvency. This condition is known as overtrading. Firms which overtrade cause concern in the minds of their creditors. This can lead creditors to shorten credit lines, and in some cases, to demand immediate settlement of their debts. If sufficient cash cannot be obtained, the company may be declared technically insolvent.

Technical insolvency, as distinct from legal insolvency, occurs when a firm has sufficient assets to meet all financial obligations but not enough time to convert those assets into cash. Legal insolvency is a condition of permanent cash shortage no matter how much time is provided.

A customary way to measure a company's liquidity is to divide its current assets, the gross working capital, by its current liabilities to get what is called the current ratio:

$$\text{current ratio} = \frac{\text{current assets}}{\text{current liabilities}}$$

This ratio, sometimes called the working capital ratio, provides a rough measure of the safety afforded the firm's short term creditors. For, in the event of a technical liquidation, current assets are more likely to yield a high percentage of their book value than are many of the fixed assets. Moreover, short term lenders look to the current assets as the prime source for the repayment of their loans. Clearly, the higher the value of the current ratio, the greater is their feeling of security.

Despite the feelings of security it may generate, the working capital ratio is frequently misleading. Often it has little value as a tool for financial management. To calculate the ratio, figures are taken from a balance sheet. These numbers reflect the past activities of the firm. Though it may comfort a manager to know that his current ratio was in a satisfactory state last month, this data point may not relate to present activities. Not only do balance sheets usually represent the past, but they are also summary statements of the accounts. They do not provide information on timing, particularly with reference to the periods within which the current liabilities are falling due. A company could have a current ratio of four to one at the time of its audit, but if its current assets were primarily made up of work in process and most of its current liabilities were due at the end of the month it might face a severe shortage of cash. On the other hand a company which acted as an agent buying and selling finished goods for clients could have a low current ratio and a sound liquidity position.

One way of coping with the inadequacies of the current ratio is to recognise the inherent illiquidity of most companies' stocks (inventories), particularly if the majority of their value is tied up in work in process. A first solution to this problem is to exclude all stocks from consideration and focus attention instead on the current assets that stand nearer to cash. Under this approach, a quick ratio is created which takes as the numerator the value of cash, near cash, and debtors (accounts receivable), and as the denominator the value of the current liabilities:

$$\text{quick ratio} = \frac{\text{cash} + \text{near cash} + \text{debtors}}{\text{current liabilities}}$$

The quick ratio unquestionably provides a stricter test of a firm's liquidity. But it still does not represent or measure the underlying short term credit strength of a company. Nor does it reflect or measure the timing of the flow of funds.

One way to overcome the inadequacies of the current and quick ratios is to calculate the borrowing power of a company's current assets. This borrowing power or potential is then compared to the actual borrowings or current liabilities to determine the proportion of its short term borrowing power the company has already consumed. Since existing borrowings, namely the current liabilities, are known with accuracy, the only difficulty in calculating this ratio lies in assessing the borrowing power of a company's current assets.

Borrowing power depends upon holdings of cash, near cash, debtors and stocks. In order to calculate the total borrowing power, it is necessary to look at each item separately since each has a different liquidity value and hence a different borrowing power.

Cash and near cash have the highest liquidity. While near cash may well represent 90 or 120-day deposits or securities, their borrowing power is quite high. Clearly, instead of borrowing against such assets they could be sold for cash. Frequently, however, there are severe interest penalties for early encashment. Hence, genuine savings can be effected by borrowing against the market value of such time deposits and securities. Though conditions can vary, particularly in periods of rapid inflation, it is realistic to assume the borrowing power of cash and near cash combined to be 95 per cent of face value.

Debtors can readily be used as security for short term loans. The borrowing power of a company's debtors is calculated as a percentage of their book or face value. This percentage is directly related to their quality which in turn reflects the credit worthiness of the customers as well as their payment record. Banks and finance houses that specialise in granting loans on debtors make it their business to assess accurately the quality of such assets. Though percentages will vary between companies, it is realistic to assume that the borrowing power of their debtors is 80 per cent of face value.

Stocks are by far the hardest to assess. In order to calculate their borrowing power, it is necessary to break stocks down into the three main categories of raw materials, work in process, and finished goods. Companies that use raw materials listed on commodity exchanges can borrow a high proportion of their market value. Such items as steel, copper, silver, crude or refined petroleum products, hides for leather, chemicals, grains, and so on, may vary in price from day to day, but their liquidity remains high. When used as security for a loan, the bank or lender will lend a proportion of their market value, usually specifying a minimum level which must be maintained. Percentages vary with the liquidity of the item, but in general, it is realistic to assume that the borrowing power of these raw materials is 80 per cent of their market value.

Some companies use as the raw materials for their manufacturing process sub-components or assemblies built by other firms. Though listed on their books as raw materials, the borrowing power of such items is in the same category as that of work in process. Work in process can have a high scrap value, particularly if the scrapping process is neither lengthy nor complicated. But scrap value is not a good indicator of borrowing power as bankers and other financial institutions are not in business to behave as scrap merchants. Hence, unless a company's products have some unusual or special features, the borrowing power of work in process is effectively zero.

Finished goods can have a high level of borrowing power. Once again, the exact percentage will depend on the time and effort it customarily takes to sell these items. For example, a specially designed machine tool will have less value as security for a loan than a like value of standard sized ball and roller bearings. On average, however, a company should be able to borrow up to 70 per cent of the book value of its finished goods stock.

The liquid asset ratio is thus given by dividing the value of liquid assets by the value of the current liabilities:

$$\text{liquid asset ratio} = \frac{\text{liquid assets}}{\text{current liabilities}}$$

The liquid asset ratio has several important features. The first is that it provides the financial manager with an accurate assessment of the company's short term liquidity and solvency. If the ratio has a value greater than one, the firm still has additional credit available to it should the need arise. A ratio of less than one says that the borrowing power of the current assets is no longer sufficient to cover the current liabilities already on the books. From a financial point of view, the most efficient use of short term borrowing power is being made when the liquid asset ratio is approximately equal to one. At that point, the minimum amount of current assets is being kept in a needlessly liquid condition.

Despite the refinements provided by the liquid asset ratio, none of the above ratios deal with the flow of cash through the company's accounts. This flow is of prime importance to the company's operating liquidity and solvency.

DECISION MAKING

The management of working capital is concerned with two distinct but interwoven sets of activities: short term and long term financial operations. The former poses the problem of managing the individual current asset balances which make up the gross working capital position. Long term working capital management is concerned with providing and funding the volume of net working capital required by the company's current and future activities.

An obvious problem concerning the management of a company's net working capital is the impact of inflation on the value of these assets. In times of high rates of inflation the money values of stocks and debtors can rise very rapidly. The value of trade creditors will also rise, but if the company is engaged in manufacturing, the impact of inflation is greater on the asset side of the balance sheet. As a result, incremental long term funds have to be found to finance this inflationary addition to the value of net working capital. To the extent that the company's long term funds are partly represented by long term debt, the exposure of these net assets to erosion by inflation is lessened. Incremental debt brings incremental financial risk. And to achieve an acceptable balance this risk has to be weighed against the certain erosion of value caused by inflation.

It would be very convenient if it were possible to prescribe the precise amount of gross and net working capital each company needs. Unfortunately, such is not the case. Manufacturing and merchandising enterprises, to mention but two examples, will invest different proportions of their total available monetary resources in working capital. Furthermore, some businesses will buy their fixed assets such as land, buildings and machinery, while others will lease these items. Each situation creates its own working capital problems that must be decided within the constraints and plans of the individual company. The object of this chapter, therefore, is not to tell managers what working capital they require. Rather it is to present a number of analytic techniques which will identify the decisions to be made when applied to the data of any company. It is management's job to make and take decisions. All that technical analysis can do is to identify the decisions that have to be made and the paths to their resolution.

The fundamental problem posed in the management of net and gross working capital can best be illustrated by examining the effects on a company of an increase in sales. To fill new orders extra units must be produced. Extra production requires additional raw materials, labour and overhead expenses. Even after the sale is effected an interval of time will elapse before payment is received. Throughout the manufacturing, selling and delivery period the company's activities have to be financed. Though the effects of this financing will eventually be reflected in the current and quick ratios, it is the pattern and timing of the expenditures and receipts that generates the company's current liquidity and solvency.

EXAMPLE OF WORKING CAPITAL FLOWS

Consider the consequences of the following sequence of events on the much simplified balance sheets of two companies, Liquidity Company Limited and Efficiency Company Limited, whose starting balances are given in Table 4.1. Both companies now receive an order for £500 000 of their products. The order itself has no effect on their working capital, it merely becomes an entry in the order book. Suppose each firm has sufficient productive capacity available to handle the order. To manufacture the products each company has to buy £100 000 of raw materials. These materials are purchased on terms of net cash monthly. Gross working capital grows immediately by £100 000. So do current liabilities, since the increase in gross working capital is being financed by the supplier who is not paid until the end of the month.

The raw material begins its passage through the manufacturing process and a direct wages bill of £100 000 is incurred. By the time the products are manufactured, labour, overhead, and other costs have risen to a total of £200 000. Thus, to produce these orders the companies have had to find £300 000 to pay for wages, overheads, and supplies.

Suppose both firms borrowed the required funds from their respective banks by extending their overdrafts (short term loan facilities). Current assets rise by £300 000 and current liabilities register a similar increase. As can be seen in Table 4.2, both companies are now noticeably less liquid. Though the Efficiency Company was and is in the weaker financial position, the Liquidity Company has incurred a proportionately greater reduction in its current liquidity.

Consider now the effects of completing the sale transaction. The orders are delivered and invoices are sent out for £500 000 with terms of net cash monthly. By sending out the goods, as well as the invoice, the

Table 4.1
Balance sheets   (all figures £'000s)

Liquidity Company

	£			£
Net worth	4 000	Fixed assets		2 500
		current assets		
Current liabilities	500	Stock	500	
		Debtors	1 000	
		Cash & deposits	500	2 000
	4 500			4 500

Efficiency Company

	£			£
Net worth	3 000	Fixed assets		1 700
		current assets		
Current liabilities	1 500	Stock	1 000	
		Debtors	1 300	
		Cash & deposits	500	2 800
	4 500			4 500

stock of finished goods is turned into a debtor valued at the selling price, presuming no loss due to bad debts. The value of liquid assets for both firms rises immediately, as do their quick and liquid assets ratios. Current liquidity has improved when judged by these ratio tests, but a cash shortage will remain until the buyer pays for the goods he has purchased.

TIMING OF FLOWS

The pattern of payments and receipts which are a part of all business operations, depicts the occasions when financing is required. The purchase of materials generates trade creditors, and the manufacturing process creates labour and overhead expenses, all of which have to be paid for. Stocks of work in process and finished goods have to be handled, stored, and shipped. Each operation incurs additional expense that has to be paid for as it comes due. Finished goods which have been sold are then delivered, usually on credit terms. Credit sales generate trade debtors. It is at this point that cash shortages reach their

Table 4.2
Working capital position before and after the product is manufactured

Liquidity Company

	Before	After
Cash & deposits	500	500
Debtors	1000	1000
Stock	500	800
Liquid assets* (95:80:50)	1525	1675
Current assets	2000	2300
Current liabilities	500	800
Net working capital	1500	1500
Current ratio	4 to 1	2.88 to 1
Quick ratio	3 to 1	2.25 to 1
Liquid asset ratio	3.05 to 1	2.09 to 1

Efficiency Company

	Before	After
Cash & deposits	500	500
Debtors	1300	1300
Stock	1000	1300
Liquid assets* (95:80:50)	1540	1690
Current assets	2800	3100
Current liabilities	1500	1800
Net working capital	1300	1300
Current ratio	1.87 to 1	1.72 to 1
Quick ratio	1.20 to 1	1 to 1
Liquid asset ratio	1.03 to 1	0.94 to 1

*Borrowing power is taken as cash 95%; debtors 80%; stock 50%

peak. Companies face a variety of cash demands, including tax payments, all with individual timing. As a rule, there is only one major source of cash revenue: credit sales which have yet another timing.

The management of the cash flows is crucial to the financial life of an enterprise. It may be necessary, as well as desirable, to finance cash shortages with short term borrowing. Such borrowing must be planned. It is as foolish to borrow money and not use it as it is to discover a sudden need for cash that can only be satisfied by an immediate increase in short term loans. Banks, like other lenders, dislike lending at short notice. They also have their cash flow problems. Further, when a company needs cash urgently the risk of insolvency is at its highest, and willing lenders become scarce as the risk increases. Many profitable firms have gone bankrupt because they ran out of cash. Solvency can always be maintained by holding large amounts of cash or deposits, but excessive cash implies a high level of net working capital. Net working capital is financed for long term sources. An efficient financial manager will determine the minimum cash required, will study the pattern of receipts and payments, and will plan both his short term borrowings and investments so that the company is neither wasting its funds nor running unnecessary risks. He will manage the company's cash so that it is neither idle nor over traded.

FLOW OF FUNDS

The pattern of payments and receipts described above gives a simple example of the flow of funds through a company's activities. These flows are usually audited on specific dates such as the end of each month, quarter, or year. Over such intervals of time, the total net flows represent a balance of all cash transactions. Receipts from sales, for example, are balanced against the funds used in the generation of those sales. Similarly, cash borrowed during the period is offset by payments made on the debt.

Total net cash flows are calculated by comparing balance sheet entries for consecutive time periods. Table 4.3 represents a simplified statement of a company's balances at the end of each of three consecutive quarters. In addition, two columns note the increases or decreases in assets and liabilities that took place during each period. The changes in assets and liabilities are important, for they identify the fund transfers that have been made. A decrease in an asset's value implies that a corresponding increase in cash has been generated from this asset. Alternatively, an increase in an asset's value means that additional funds have been invested, which implies a decrease in cash. A decrease in cash can also be achieved by reducing liabilities, while any increases in liabilities or net worth, or shareholders' equity, mean an increase in funds. These sources and uses of funds can be summarised as follows:

Table 4.3
Comparison of quarterly balance sheets

	Fourth Quarter	First Quarter	Increase (Decrease)	Second Quarter	Increase (Decrease)	Third Quarter	Increase (Decrease)
	£	£	£	£	£	£	£
Net worth							
Ordinary shares	220 000	220 000		220 000		250 000	30 000
Retained earnings	275 000	293 000	18 000	316 000	23 000	341 000	25 000
Total	495 000	513 000		536 000		591 000	
Long-term liabilities							
Mortgages	180 000	180 000		180 000		200 000	20 000
Machinery loans	90 000	100 000	10 000	103 000	3 000	121 000	18 000
Total	270 000	280 000		283 000		321 000	
Fixed assets							
Building & property	230 000	227 000	(3 000)	224 000	(3 000)	250 000	26 000
Machinery	320 000	340 000	20 000	345 000	5 000	360 000	25 000
Total	550 000	567 000		569 000		610 000	
Net increase (decrease) in long-term funds			11 000		24 000		52 000
Current liabilities							
Bank overdraft	33 000	85 000	52 000	29 000	(56 000)	41 000	12 000
Creditors	95 000	145 000	50 000	112 000	(33 000)	153 000	41 000
Other payables	17 000	8 000	(9 000)	15 000	7 000	10 000	(3 000)
Total	145 000	238 000		156 000		204 000	
Current assets							
Stock	230 000	268 000	38 000	245 000	(23 000)	298 000	53 000
Debtors	105 000	150 000	45 000	130 000	(20 000)	165 000	35 000
Cash and deposits	25 000	46 000	21 000	31 000	(15 000)	46 000	15 000
Total	360 000	464 000		406 000		508 000	
Net increase (decrease) in short-term funds			(11 000)		(24 000)		(52 000)

Sources of Funds	Uses of Funds
Decrease in assets	Increase in assets
Increase in liabilities	Decrease in liabilities
Increase in net worth	Decrease in net worth

In order to illustrate how to identify these flows of funds in detail, the flows of three quarters' worth of balance sheets are set out in Table 4.4. As can now be readily seen, during the first quarter cash was generated by negotiating an increase in bank borrowings, by taking an increase in trade credit, by financing new machinery purchases partly with term loans, and by earning enough profit to increase retained earnings after taking care of taxes and dividends. Most of these funds were used to build up current assets in the form of stocks and debtors. During the second quarter, this pattern of sources and uses is reversed. Funds are still raised from the reinvestment of retained earnings and by raising of more machinery loans, but the largest sums are generated by reducing the value of current assets. These funds are applied to the reduction of current liabilities. The funds flow in the third quarter is very similar to that of the first, the one main exception being the sale of additional equity.

From the flow of cash depicted in Table 4.4, it is possible to make a number of inferences about the company's financial behaviour thorughout the three quarters. The company began the year by increasing both stocks and sales. Either sales are subject to seasonal swings or the firm has launched a new sales campaign. The effect of increasing sales on current assets and cash flows has already been partially described in the analysis of the activities of the Liquidity and Efficiency Companies (see Table 4.2). There it was noted that a growth in sales needs to be supported by a corresponding growth in raw materials, work in process, and finished goods and debtors. All these activities require cash, and it can be seen from Table 4.4 that this company chose to finance its first quarter growth by borrowing short term from its bankers and suppliers, and long term by financing new machinery purchases, and by making an adequate and retainable profit.

By the end of the second quarter either the sales drive has come to an end or the company does produce seasonal items. In either event, the growth rate of sales fell during this quarter. Typically, a lower rate of sales generates cash if there is a corresponding reduction in creditors and stock. During the second quarter most of the cash generated by the

Table 4.4
Sources and uses of cash for first three quarters

	First Quarter	Second Quarter	Third Quarter
	£	£	£
Sources: long-term			
Ordinary shares			30 000
Retained earnings	18 000	23 000	25 000
Mortgages			20 000
Machinery loans	10 000	3 000	18 000
Buildings & property	3 000	3 000	
Total	31 000	29 000	93 000
Uses: long-term			
Buildings & property			26 000
Machinery	20 000	5 000	15 000
Total	20 000	5 000	41 000
Net sources (uses): long-term	11 000	24 000	52 000
Sources: short-term			
Bank overdraft	52 000		12 000
Creditors	50 000		41 000
Other payables		7 000	
Stock		23 000	
Debtors		20 000	
Cash & deposits		15 000	
Total	102 000	65 000	53 000
Uses: short-term			
Bank overdraft		56 000	
Creditors		33 000	
Other payables	9 000		3 000
Stock	38 000		53 000
Debtors	45 000		35 000
Cash & deposits	21 000		14 000
Total	113 000	89 000	105 000
Net sources (uses): short-term	(11 000)	(24 000)	(52 000)

reduction in current assets was used to reduce current liabilities. One could therefore infer that the company was working itself back to a level of sales and production based on its experience of demand in the previous fourth quarter.

The third quarter, however, was another period of rapid growth in sales. Once again the surge in current assets was financed by borrowing short term from bankers and suppliers. This time, management must have judged the rate of growth in sales to be reasonably secure because additions were made to buildings as well as machinery. These additions were financed by increasing both the amount of the mortgage, and the machinery loan. Another indicator of management's belief that the sales had indeed grown at least to a new plateau, is the fact that they chose to raise further funds by selling additional equity during this quarter.

Another interesting feature of these cash flows is that in each quarter the company was taking cash raised from long term sources and investing these funds in short term assets. As can be seen in Table 4.4, the amount of cash invested in short term assets increased each quarter. As a result, one can conclude that over these three quarters the company was becoming progressively more liquid. In effect, the company has been a net borrower of long term funds which it has chosen to invest in current assets.

PRODUCT CASH CYCLE

An equally important aspect of working capital behaviour is the way cash flows are related to the life cycle of individual products. The life cycle begins when a company decides to develop a new product. Development costs may be large or small but inevitably they require cash payments. In addition to design and development costs, the firm may have to incur the costs of extensive market testing. Also, some reorganisation of the manufacturing process may be required if the tests indicate that the new product should go into production. In addition, various engineering and other costs will be incurred if a new production line has to be set up. Raw materials must then be purchased and labour and overhead expenses be applied in order to create the required stocks of partially and completely finished products. During this last stage, some form of sales campaign must be launched. Finally, if orders are generated, deliveries can begin.

The design, development, marketing and production stages may represent years of time and effort. However long the time period, the cash flows during this part of a product's life cycle are wholly negative. It is not until some weeks after the first delivery has been made that the first sales revenue is received. For many products, particularly those requiring advanced technology, the research and development phase alone occupies a number of years. Testing and refining prototypes can add many more months, as faults are discovered and improvements are made. Manufacturing and marketing also take time. Throughout this period the firm has to finance the new product's development from revenue and money sources to which the new product is not yet contributing. In order to manage and control these expenses, companies frequently set up a research and development department with its own budget. This department or division then becomes responsible for initiating studies and helping to make marketing and production decisions which identify and create profitable additions to the product line. Research and development is expensive. It is successful only when a new product sells sufficiently well to earn a suitable share of the company's profit. No product, however, earns cash returns while it is being developed. All such development must be financed, perhaps by an advanced sale of a franchise or royalty rights, perhaps by government grants or from internal funds. Whatever the cost, the required volume of funds as well as the timing of the outlays must be estimated, and the necessary funds obtained, or the new product cannot be developed, let alone brought to the market to earn profits.

Example of the cash flows of a new product

Figure 4.1 provides a graphic illustration of the behaviour of the cash flows for a product that is launched successfully. At the first, the cash revenue is small. As sales and deliveries build up, cash receipts rise. It is frequently the case, however, that the cash costs of generating sales and effecting the deliveries rise faster than the cash inflows from those sales. The net result is an extended period of cash shortages, shortages that are not relieved until the rate of growth tapers off. A rapid growth in the sales of a product can eventually be very profitable, but it always causes a heavy drain on cash.

Taking a closer look at Figure 4.1, one can see that if the intervals on the horizontal axis represent quarters, the first net cash receipts are not received until two and a half years after the first expenses are incurred.

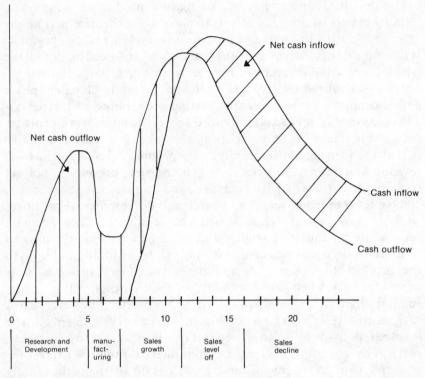

Fig. 4.1 Product cash cycle

This schedule of cash flows is typical of many products. There are some products, notably fashion items, which can be created, developed and brought to the market in a matter of months. Equally, there are high technology products for which the intervals of time in the cash cycle are measured in years. Whatever the duration of the cash outflows, it is important to notice that large net cash receipts only begin when the rate of growth in sales slows down. The greatest net inflow of cash occurs when manufacturing expenses decline and the product can be sold without extensive advertising and marketing costs. This is a period where the growth in sales is declining. It may well signify that the useful life of the product is coming to an end.

The net cash inflows that are generated during the later, or mature, stages of a product's life can be, and frequently are, used to finance the development of other new products. When companies state that 80 per cent of their current sales comes from products that didn't exist five years ago and that this pattern is expected to continue, it is clear that these firms have learned to balance and manage the many streams of cash flows.

MANAGING DEBTORS

Trade debtors are a product of credit sales. If a company were to make all sales for cash it would have no debtors and no need to finance its sales by the use of current debt. Most companies, particularly in manufacturing, sell on credit and it is these companies with debtor balances that this section concerns.

Net cash value

The average collection period (or age) is an important indicator of the liquidity of receivables. The longer an invoice goes unpaid the less likely it is ever to be paid. Doubtful accounts turn into bad debts when they are left uncollected. Hence, to assess the liquidity of a given balance of receivables it is necessary to investigate the relation between the age of an account and the likelihood of its being collected. An inspection of past accounts will reveal the proportions to use. For illustrative purposes suppose the collectable percentages are as follows:

Age of Accounts	Collectable percentages
1–30	99
31–60	98
61–90	95
90–120	70
121+	50

Applying these percentages to the receivables balance recorded at a particular time period will produce the net cash value of those receivables. Thus a £100 000 credit sale in the age category 1–30 would have a net cash value of £99 000. The same sized sale in the 121 days plus category would have a net cash value of only £50 000. It follows that an increase in the average age of receivables means a deterioration both in liquidity and real value.

Suppose that management has decided to do something about its deteriorating receivables position. What are the possible actions it can take and what credit policy should be adopted? Solutions vary from leaving things as they are to the opposite extreme of withdrawing credit facilities and insisting that all future sales be contracted for cash. Every solution will generate its own pattern of cash receipts and, depending upon its stringency, will entail certain costs. Thus, an increase in cash flow can be measured against the cost of generation. The net value to the company, given by a variety of alternatives, will help management to decide which credit policy to adopt.

It is most unlikely that a new, more stringent credit policy can be effected without cost. Management will wish to determine the probable cost of persuading customers to pay their bills within a new time limit. Obviously, such cost must not exceed the benefits to be derived from the new policy. The limit to the cost is determined by calculating the discount which the company could afford to offer as an incentive leaving itself no worse off than under the old credit policy. In other words, the interest rate or discount that will equalise the present value of these two streams of income must be calculated.

Financing debtors

Encashing receivables, like obtaining an overdraft or trade credit, is an important part of short term working capital management. The basic objective in financing accounts receivable is to generate the maximum cash inflow at the lowest possible cost. One possible strategy was noted above: to offer a discount for prompt payment and a maximum credit period of 30 days. Although there is a large range of alternative financing policies, three important types of approach exist. The first is to sell, each month, all receivables to a commercial factor for cash. The second is to borrow against the receivables balance. The third is to develop a credit and collection department of such capability that other companies' receivables can be purchased and processed with the company's own assets to yield additional earnings.

Factoring debtors

The factoring of debtors is accomplished by offering the entire collection of receivables to a commercial factor. If a satisfactory price is negotiated and the sale is made, the factor takes on the responsibility for collecting all accounts due. As a consequence he also accepts the risk that some accounts will prove to be uncollectable. The purchase price is determined on the basis of the net cash value of the receivables balance. Though practices can differ, the purchase price is usually stated in terms of an advance payment of, say, 90 per cent of the net cash value. The balance, less service and financing charges, which may amount to 4 or 5 per cent, is paid to the company on the average due date of the accounts.

For example, suppose a company has a debtor balance with a net cash value of £100 000. The average age of these receivables is 30 days. The factor offers £90 000 cash now, and the balance less service and finance charges in thirty days. The amount of this balance depends upon the quality of the receivables. If the credit worthiness of these accounts is high, the factor's charge is low. It increases in line with the risk of bad debts.

The total cost of factoring can be quite heavy, particularly in times of high interest rates. However, if a company uses a factor for all its credit sales then the company has no direct collection charges of its own. The factoring cost has to be compared with this saving. The evaluation criterion is the company's cost of its own credit and collection department for the year. Moreover, cash today is worth more than cash at some future period. In any assessment of the cost of factoring the fact that the company's own credit department will not produce 90 per cent of the cash value of all receivables on the first day of every month must be costed and allowed. Hence the factoring cost may well look quite attractive compared to the alternative costs.

Borrowing on debtors

An alternative method of raising money on debtors is to pledge them as collateral for a loan. Many companies do not like the thought of having a factor collect from their customers. None the less, they cannot afford to tie up cash in receivables. A loan based on these receivables can be readily negotiated with commercial or merchant banks and may well provide a more acceptable financing vehicle.

With a loan of this type, the company retains the obligation to collect the debtors as well as the risk of doubtful accounts becoming bad debts. The usual practice is for the finance house to lend the company a proportion, say 70 or 80 per cent, of the net value of the receivables. Interest can be charged either on a daily basis or on the actual cash advanced. A service charge may also be included. Usually, the company will pay off the loan as debtors are collected and, as a result, the net cost to the company will be less than that charged by the factor on an outright sale. It must be noted, however, that the factor carries out credit accounting, ledger keeping and collecting as part of his services. The company is responsible for all these activities if it merely borrows money on its receivables.

Buying debtors

Many companies are in a position where they manage and finance their own credit sales. Such companies have credit departments and managers whose task is to service their customers' accounts and collect the receipts when due. One alternative to selling or borrowing on debtors is to go into the business of collecting receivables in a serious way. If the company already has a credit department, why not put it to work in a more efficient and effective manner? A satisfactory credit department will find little difficulty in providing a collection service for receivables from other companies with similar customers. The question to answer has two parts and can be stated as follows: is it cheaper to sell receivables outright to a factor or to process them? Whatever set of reasons persuade a company not to sell its receivables, economies of scale suggest it will be cheaper, per account collected, to behave as a factor and buy other companies' receivables. For debtors can be purchased just as they can be sold.

MANAGING STOCKS

Stocks of raw materials, goods in progress and finished goods pose a number of management problems. On the one hand there are the questions of warehousing and storage. Decisions on what levels of stock to keep are determined by economic order and production batch size considerations. These, in turn, help to specify the minimum and maximum stock levels required. On the other hand there is the question of how to finance these stocks and how to control the investment of funds in this type of asset. Finally, there is the impact of stocks and taxation, as discussed in Chapter 3.

The average age of stocks on hand can be computed. The stock balances at the beginning of the period are divided by the purchases expected during the period and multiplied by the number of days in the accounting period. This calculation can be made for each category of stock as well as for the total balance. For example, within the raw material stocks used in a particular company's manufacturing process there is a variety of items such as sheet steel, copper bars and metal rods, which are purchased in substantial quantities. Raw materials, as far as this company is concerned, also include items which are the finished products of other companies, such as die castings, gear assemblies and many types of fittings. The manufacturing process takes some time to complete and in so doing produces a number of stages of goods in progress. Raw materials have been partially assembled into finished goods and stocks of goods in progress are normally held at a fairly high level, representing a substantial amount of invested funds. Finished goods stocks are not large and every effort is made to keep them within reasonable bounds.

Suppose the age classification of the die casting stocks are as given in Table 4.5. It can be readily seen that over 60 per cent of these die castings have been on hand for more than 45 days. Suppose a check on the composition of these aged stocks shows that some castings are used early in the productive process while others are not employed until much later. Moreover, some of the castings are speciality items which may remain in stock for many months at a time. In short, the company really uses two classes of die castings: those which are processed within 30 days and those which may take many months to clear.

Efficient management of raw materials requires that these stocks are turned over rapidly. The longer a given item remains in stock the more difficult it becomes to collect the full cost through the sale price. In many instances, however, there are some items, such as special die castings, sub-assemblies, and so on, which cannot be moved through

Table 4.5
Age classification of die castings

Classification (Days)	Amount	Percentage each is of total
	£	
0–15	17 000	16.0
16–30	13 000	12.2
31–45	9 000	8.5
46–60	29 000	27.4
61+	38 000	35.9
	106 000	100.0

the productive process with the desired speed. The financing of stocks can be readily geared to the ageing process, and it is this criterion which is featured in Table 4.5 and discussed in the next paragraph.

Types of stock finance

Stocks can be used to raise funds in a number of ways. The simplest procedure is to use these assets as collateral for a secured loan from a commercial or merchant bank. To do so the value of each item or class of items must be noted and approved. As in the case of debtors, the loan will be based upon an agreed percentage of the net cash value of the stocks. As stocks are consumed in the productive process, the net cash value declines and unless the balance is maintained by new purchases the size of the loan has to be reduced by a proportionate amount. As a result, taking a secured loan on rapidly moving raw materials is a complicated process and may not be worth the effort. An analysis of the age classifications reveals those stocks which remain unused for the greatest periods of time. These are the items to use as collateral if loan financing is desired. If the average age of certain materials, say die castings or other speciality items, is 80 days, this length of time is sufficient to make a collateral loan worthy of investigation.

Raw materials which are purchased in bulk and which take some time to be delivered to the company can be financed *en route* by means of a trade bill and/or warehouse receipt. In either case, the financing instrument is, in effect, a secured loan on the value of the itemised goods. Warehouse receipts are issued by the warehousing company and can be used by the company: to reclaim the goods when required; to borrow funds by pledging the receipt as collateral; or to sell the goods in question by presenting the receipt for sale on the commodity market. The trade bill is based upon the bills of lading, which represent the goods in transit from the supplier. These bills become negotiable if endorsed by a commercial or merchant bank and can be sold outright or used as collateral for a loan. In both of these cases the company is delaying the investment of its own funds until such time as the goods are actually delivered to its factory for processing.

MANAGING CREDITORS

The management of trade creditors is essentially a simple operation.

As indicated earlier, it is both informative and useful to maintain control over the average age of the outstanding trade credit. The decision whether to settle these accounts at once or later depends upon the discounts, if any, that are offered for prompt and early cash payment. If discounts are available from suppliers, then advantage should be taken of the offer. Such reductions in cost can always be compared to the value of keeping the same amount of credit unpaid. In most cases it is a sound financial rule to accept cash discounts whenever possible.

Some suppliers do not offer cash discounts. In this event, they should be approached with a view to striking a bargain. The promise of prompt settlement will often reduce an agreed discount even if this is not part of the company's normal sales policies. If all efforts to achieve discounts for immediate cash payment fail, there is no incentive to settle the account and every reason to delay payment until the last possible moment.

The management of trade creditors can be broken down into two parts:

1 For all accounts on which attractive cash discounts are available, ensure that settlements occur before the cash due date.
2 For all accounts with no discount, ensure that payment is not made until the maximum due date, but no later.

Financial management is responsible for maintaining the credit standing of the company as well as generating the necessary credit financing. To be known as a late payer does not enhance the company's reputation. To be known as a company that is aware of the value of money and insists on bargaining for its most effective use engenders respect and, in all likelihood, will lead to even higher credit rating.

The remaining current liabilities offer little scope for active financial management. PAYE withholdings are taken out of wages and salaries every time employees are paid. These withholdings do not have to be paid to the appropriate authority until certain calendar dates have been reached. Companies have free use of these funds for an average 30 to 40 days. If total wage and salary payments are rising, so will the amount of credit that this free source of funds represents. Since the size of the withholdings is outside the company's control, management only has responsibility to use these funds while it can and to make sure they are paid to the tax authorities when due.

Similar comments pertain to payment of the company's tax

obligations. Though tax assessments must be paid, there is no justification for paying them in advance. Tax reserve certificates are offered for sale to tempt companies, by a small discount, to settle their obligations in advance. But a tax reserve certificate can only be used in dealings with the Inland Revenue. All other short term or long term investments have a degree of liquidity and many exist which also provide higher rates of return. Thus, before purchasing tax reserve certificates their rate of return should be compared with other available short term investments. The money market can always supply an investment with a high degree of liquidity and a due date coincident with tax outlays.

5

International money management

Andreas R Prindl

International Money Management (IMM) deals with the problem of collecting, utilising and protecting the financial assets of internationally involved companies. The term 'IMM' is used to designate both the operating responsibility of the treasury of a multi-national corporation and the array of techniques and tools available to co-ordinate that task. This problem is difficult enough in domestic firms; greater structural and environmental impediments for the multi-national company place its treasury's responsibilities on a different level of complexity.

Despite the size and power of many multinational companies, they can be characterised as fragmented, rather than monolithic. Multi-national companies are divided into a number of local units, separated by distance, exchange control, and tax and legal systems. Such technical barriers to treating a company's finance as a whole are structural ones. They include the obvious problems of being far away from parent or subsidiaries, speaking in different languages, relying on inefficient communications systems, accounting for worldwide operations under various principles, following diverse legal practices, paying differing rates of tax and being restricted by exchange control systems.

These elements have always been found in international companies which have set up operations abroad. A quantum change in financial management problems, however, has come from the chaotic environment since exchange rates began to float in the late 1960s. Thus, added to structural impediments are today's unpredictable and fast moving exchange rates, as well as large interest and inflation differentials, all of which are environmental factors. Not only must assets be correctly collected and maintained, they must be protected against depreciation caused by outside economic changes which have taken on a magnitude not seen since Depression years.

The field of IMM attempts to give an ordered approach to these various problems. Much of it is based on correct reporting systems and optimal use of banks, while the remainder is anticipatory, attempting to forecast the liquidity and foreign exchange risks of the firm, in order to position the company's assets and liabilities properly. The field is separated into two major parts: International Cash Management, which deals with the more mechanical areas of cash collection, holding and disbursement, and International Financial Management, which involves utilisation of liquidity and foreign exchange risk management.

DOMESTIC CASH MANAGEMENT

The collection process

Domestic cash management has three distinct stages: collection, treasury management and disbursement. While the outer stages are mechanical and semi-automatic, they are used to maximise the amounts of funds for treasury management, which should then concentrate on optimal deployment of available resources and reducing external borrowing to a minimum.

It is instructive to analyse these activities in more detail. Collections, for example, are broken down into distinct stages, as shown in Figure 5.1.

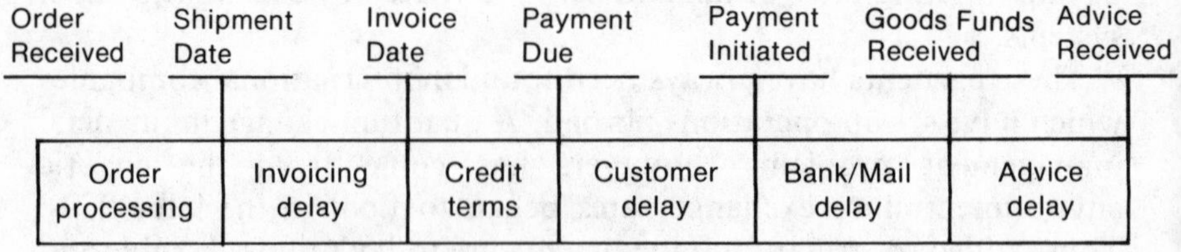

Order Received	Shipment Date	Invoice Date	Payment Due	Payment Initiated	Goods Funds Received	Advice Received
Order processing	Invoicing delay	Credit terms	Customer delay	Bank/Mail delay	Advice delay	

Fig. 5.1 The collection process in cash management

Besides credit terms extended to customers, other possible delays before sales proceeds can be utilised include invoicing delays within the company, customer non-adherence to credit terms, and delays within the banking/mail system. The last are designated as 'float', and each type deserves careful study.

Order and invoice systems

The first step of cash management is internal: to check whether the billing procedure involves unnecessary delays or inadvertent credit extension. For example, if credit terms are stated to be X days from date of invoice, and invoice creation is delayed after shipment, extra credit is given to customers; this can be particularly costly if a weekend is involved. Even if month-end terms are used, late invoicing can dip over a month-end, and allow greater credit to buyers. It is a simple matter, particularly with computers, to ensure that statements are created simultaneously with shipment, or back-dated to coincide with shipment dates.

Customer payment methods

More important is the way in which local customers are asked to pay, as many methods are generally available, for example: paying cash, using bank transfers, sending cheques, accepting direct debiting by the supplier.

The treasury should analyse customer payment habits to determine what delay, if any, derives from non-adherence to maturity dates. The competitive situation will determine which pressures can be put on customers to pay promptly, or whether different credit instruments can be used to ensure payment at maturity. Discount practices need to be studied as well; discounts offered to customers may have become inconsistent with market rates of interest.

Bank delays can benefit either the payer, if he sends his own cheques, or the banks making the transfers. Proper utilisation of bank systems forms a major portion of account receivable management: it requires analysis of customers' locations, how they pay or instruct their banks, which banks are used, and to which accounts funds are paid.

An excellent collection instrument, now available in a number of European countries, is direct debiting. This can reduce customer delay to zero (the payment is tapped by the supplier at maturity) and cut bank delay to minimal levels, as the payment request can be put into the system in advance. In effect, the supplier takes cash from its customers with good value at maturity – an optimal system from both delay and forecasting standpoints.

Guidelines for accounts receivable management

If arranged correctly, a company's collections can be set up in a virtually automatic way and float reduced to a minimum. The following questions should be studied:

1 Is inadvertent credit given to customers by slow billing?
2 Do discounts offered reflect the true value of funds invested or costs saved from reduced overdrafts?
3 Are clear instructions given to customers as to payment method?
4 Can a single nationwide bank's network be used to collect, and then concentrate, inflows?
5 Are salesmen or messengers, who pick up cheques, depositing them in the most efficient manner?
6 Is the best use being made of computerised bank transfer possibilities?
7 Are inflows being directed to banks where overdraft lines are maintained, so that net borrowing is reduced?
8 Is direct debiting possible?

Local treasury management

In a one-country setting, the treasury management function is that of identifying cash surpluses and cash needs at the various domestic locations during the production/sales cycle. The chief task is to do so in advance, so that appropriate funding or borrowing procedures can be undertaken, eliminating the chances that funds will lie idle somewhere in the system. Given a single tax, legal and currency system, this relies primarily on good cash forecasting, portfolio management and banking relationships. Banking ties must be examined; commonly there are too many accounts and too many banks. A subsidiary in one part of the country may have surplus cash while another has to borrow. Pooling of local subsidiaries' funds can be achieved in a number of ways, through negotiation with a nationwide bank or daily adjustment of positions. Where possible, payments should be made into accounts where overdrafts are held, to reduce them on a daily basis.

Disbursements

Disbursement control is the converse of account receivable management: to accrue float and thus longer use of funds to the paying company. Although the firm tries to reduce its customers' payment delays, its suppliers will act accordingly regarding its own payments. Disbursement analysis ascertains that discounts offered are properly evaluated, that all but small local payments are centralised and reported and that payments are not made before maturity.

INTERNATIONAL CASH MANAGEMENT

The international transfer of funds

International cash management involves longer distances, exchange controls, different currency units and unrelated banks. The sequence of the international collection process, however, is the same as that of local account management, and delays are analysed in the same fashion.

A variety of instruments exist for the international transfer of funds. Lodged in and flowing between banks, they can be simple payment instructions in written form or evolve from documentary sales incorporating some form of credit. The standard method of transferring funds internationally is by mail payment order. In it, the remitter of funds asks its bank to make a transfer to the recipient in its own or another currency. The remitter's local currency account will be debited on the day the remitter presents the payment order to its bank (in some countries with back value).

Mail transfer is a lengthy process, despite the routine use of airmail. The remitter's local bank may not maintain foreign currency accounts abroad as they are chiefly held by the head offices of the large indigenous banks. It must then send the payment instructions through its main office, central savings bank organisation or domestic bank correspondent. Allowing for mailing time and processing at each bank, a mail transfer which involves several banks in two countries can take eight to ten business days or more.

Cable transfers reduce remittance time appreciably. By instructing its local bank to inaugurate payments by cable, the remitter ensures that the recipient of funds is paid as soon as the foreign bank receives the cable order from its correspondent. A cable transfer results in a debit to the paying bank's foreign account more quickly than mail transfer does, and involves a higher cost or less favourable rate of exchange when a conversion is involved. In addition, a nominal charge is made, usually $5 to $10 equivalent per cable, depending upon the length of the text.

Other international payment instruments include bank drafts, cheques and trade bills. A subsidiary may purchase a bank draft from its house bank to send directly to the payee. Bank drafts are payable to order upon presentation and are drawn by a bank upon itself or another branch of the same bank.

Sight and time drafts, acceptances and letters of credit fall into the area of documentary credit. A sight draft is an international financial instrument in which the importer's (drawee's) obligation to pay a certain amount at sight to the drawer is formally confirmed in writing. Time drafts add a credit element as the payment is designated as due at a certain future date and the obligation is accepted by the drawee. Acceptances (time drafts drawn on a foreign buyer whose obligation is accepted by its bank) and letters of credit are extensions of payment orders that take into account the credit risk of dealing with distant customers. These instruments are well known and are generally processed by international banks in a structured manner that has long proven to be efficient. Thus cash management concentrates on payments arising from open account sales.

The underlying principle of international payments is that currencies are ultimately transferred on the books of banks in the country whose currency is involved. Dollars sent from Tokyo to Zurich become entries in the books of a US bank in which the working accounts of international banks are held in dollars. Acceleration or interception of international dollar payments thus lies in the US banking system. Deutschemark transactions are made over the books of German banks, pounds over those of British banks, and similarly with other currencies. This structure determines the way in which export proceeds can be intercepted and accelerated.

Acceleration of export proceeds

A foreign customer has no reason to accelerate payments abroad after its own account is debited, and banks have no incentive to expedite the transfer of funds to a foreign entity. Many banks traditionally depend more on float and commissions than on compensating balances, which accounts for part of the slowness of mail transfers. By using cable transfers increased yields can accrue to the recipient even if it absorbs the cable charges of its customers. A minimum break even amount (where interest gained on funds available earlier exceeds the cable cost) should be set and instructions given to customers to make all payments above that minimum by cable net of its cost.

Smaller export payments can often be intercepted in the country whose currency is involved. For US dollars, this involves directing payments to a US bank, rather than using the lengthy procedure that characterises international transfers. When export receipts are in large numbers but in amounts that do not warrant cable transfers, the standard procedure is to use a dollar lockbox system, incorporating a post office box in a major US money centre.

A US bank has the authority to open and empty daily a postal box held in the name of the exporter, which instructs its customers to have dollar-denominated cheques or drafts sent directly to the specific postal box rather than to the exporter or its bank for the account of the exporter. The cheque, drawn on a US bank, is airmailed to the postal box, whereupon the responsible bank will process and present it immediately to the Federal Reserve clearing system. Delays are reduced to the mailing time plus one day for clearance and credit to the exporter's US dollar account. Usually, the standard delay in receiving export mail payments is reduced by three to five days or more.

Dollar interception of non-US exporters

Since the underlying principle is that US dollars are transferred by banks in the United States, an identical procedure can be followed even if the exporter is not a US company. An exporting company located in France and invoicing in dollars, can also use a dollar lockbox in New York to accelerate dollar collections. Ideally, it will maintain one account in America and another with the Paris branch of the US bank that processes the lockbox items. The US head office will collate payments made and advise its Paris branch by cable of the amounts received; it will give details of each remittance to comply with French exchange control regulations. Larger amounts can be received by cable and credited in the same manner. Similarly, dollar amounts received in favour of a British exporter can be intercepted and credited to a retained dollar account in the United Kingdom.

Interception in other currencies

In most European countries, IMM systems can be set up to allow interception of a currency in its home country. The principle remains to intercept the funds from abroad at a point close to the account to which the funds are directed. Belgian franc payments, for example, can be requested from an importer or foreign dealer in the form of a Belgian franc cheque sent directly to the bank holding export documents. The Belgian bank will present the cheque directly to the clearing system after matching payments and documents and immediately credit the proceeds to the exporter's account. Both acceleration of receipts and compliance with exchange control regulations are assimilated in such a system. Similar mechanisms can be inaugurated for British exporters invoicing in pounds sterling, Dutch exporters invoicing in guilders and so forth.

Retained foreign currency accounts

The use of retained foreign currency or 'hold' accounts complements control over international cash flows. Exchange control commonly recognises that a trading or exporting company, which receives foreign currencies for its exports, may have foreign currency obligations against which such proceeds can be applied. In most countries, domestic exporting companies are permitted to hold foreign currency receipts in local accounts set up for that purpose. Upon presentation of the proper documents, foreign currency export proceeds can be credited to such accounts held at local banks or abroad and held in suspense until they are needed for authorised payments in that currency. There should be a reciprocal, although not necessarily identical, flow; in general, funds may not be held in such accounts for a indefinite period.

Foreign currency accounts give an exporter a twofold advantage. They avoid exchange conversion costs, which would normally be borne twice if proceeds were converted and reconverted, and they maintain a neutral exposure position in the currency for those transactions. In fact, such foreign currency holdings may constitute a short term hedge against the exporter's local currency. Conversion costs of transferring dividends in foreign currency to a parent company can also be avoided.

Accumulation accounts

In certain countries, currency accounts can earn interest at Euro-currency rates, which transforms them into an accumulation account, maintained over longer periods. Exchange control authorities may require that they be converted into local currency, because investment in foreign currency is not their underlying justiciation. The same advantages of and rationale for foreign currency accounts exist for exporters in countries where there are no restrictions on international transfers or foreign exchange holdings.

Intercompany transfers

Intercompany transfers arise from sales between affiliates and from such financial transactions as royalties and dividends. Since the time lost in transferring funds from one affiliate to another represents a loss of availability of funds to the group, it is important to rationalise intercompany transactions.

Intercompany transfers of sizeable amounts should be made by cable as of routine. A simple comparison of cable cost and interest saved by reduction of overdrafts or gained by short term investment of accelerated payments shows the advantage of making even relatively small payments by cable. If overseas subsidiaries are reluctant to absorb recurring cable costs, they should be instructed to make payments net of cable charge.

Value compensations

To reduce the transit time of intercompany transfers further when foreign exchange conversion is necessary, value compensations should be negotiated. Under standard foreign exchange procedures, the remitter's account is often debited two days before the foreign currency counterpart is actually provided. Assuming two-day notice is given, the remitting bank should agree to debit the local currency account on the actual day of transfer and thus save two interest days for the remitter.

International bank branches that make payments between two subsidiaries, both of which are customers, offer value-compensated cable transfers, as a routine matter. They look at their relationship with a multinational company globally and make concessions at one paying branch in the light of activity or relationships at another. They may even waive cable charges for intercompany, intrabank payments.

Netting

The systems discussed so far are rather mechanical and can be designed to operate virtually automatically by using careful instructions and agreement with banks. The area of intercompany transfers leads to more managerial decisions, such as the use of payment dates to keep liquidity in a subsidiary, or to accelerate it to another – moves which have both liquidity and exchange exposure implications. Manipulation of intercompany transfers ties together the field of cash management and that of international financial management (IFM).

A first step towards IFM is to institute netting systems where applicable. Even though value compensation and cables may reduce most intercompany float, there are still conversion and payment costs to bear; these are often estimated around one eighth per cent flat on average. One should analyse whether intercompany payments can be offset bilaterally or multilaterally on the books of subsidiaries, thus saving the potential costs of converting and moving gross payable amounts by paying only the net balance. A group of subsidiaries selling to each other multilaterally will report their gross intercompany payable/receivable position to a central point, which then works out mathematically the net payments to be made at precise dates and so informs the participants. Exchange controls in most countries permit this system. Export and import documentation continues as before and needs to be centralised in the banks making the net payment. Such systems nearly always go through the branch network of a single multinational bank to ensure efficiency. Once the reporting and central control systems are set up, changing the matrix of the payments can give rise to more sophisticated use of group funds.

INTERNATIONAL LIQUIDITY MANAGEMENT

The management of liquidity held in the international firm is limited by exchange control and other barriers, which usually prohibit the flow of funds in desired directions. Funds held by individual subsidiaries in different countries cannot be considered fungible and there is little or no chance of international pooling of funds. Even intracountry liquidity management can be impeded by weak capital markets which offer few investment media or banking systems which delay transfers. Expropriation or funds blockage are continual possibilities in certain parts of the world.

The area is also affected by mechanical impediments in banking and mail systems. As shown above, an appreciable portion of a company's apparent liquidity may be delayed or in transit due to the slowness of customers in paying and the tardiness of banks in transferring funds in settlement of international transactions. These inefficiencies and delays diminish liquidity, impair credit control and add to the general difficulties of financial management. Good IFM is thus based on good cash management systems at both the local and the international level.

International liquidity management cannot be divorced from exchange factors. Almost every borrowing/investment decision made is implicitly exchange related. To leave funds in one country, to convert and deposit them covered or uncovered, or to lend them internationally, involves an acceptance or a transmittal of exchange risks. Uncertainty about future rates shapes the policy of the international treasurer's liquidity decisions as it does his attempt to optimise exchange risk management.

Thus, liquidity management directly embodies the fragmentation which characterises the multinational firm. Government monetary or financial policies, specifically those designed to influence balance of payments flows, can limit the deployment of the firm's working capital. Most government measures constructed on macro-economic grounds can be seen as hampering the international company's micro-economic liquidity policies.

Need for centralisation

Given these parameters, liquidity management must be centrally co-ordinated and directed by a control point which has full knowledge of resources and needs. Normally, this function will be based at the parent level, although it may be partially delegated to regional centres. Local implementation of policy may be carried out with appropriate guidelines.

Liquidity management needs to be based on a detailed, treasury orientated reporting system which goes beyond that necessary for accounting purposes. It must be anticipatory, fostering proper determination of liquidity implications of all financial transactions in advance. It should allow proper response by forecasting liquidity shortages or uninvested surpluses.

Such centralisation has implications for profit centre accounting. Interest income/costs beyond purely local levels, where directed from above, may be eliminated from the internal operating reports of subsidiaries. This correction eliminates group considerations from local operating statements without eliminating subsidiaries' responsibility to keep asset levels down.

Centralisation assists in reducing the total amount of liquidity needed by the corporation. Total assets held abroad and their related financing costs will be minimised. The specialised knowledge needed to place and optimise the use of liquidity can more easily be built up in one central location, which has ready access to tax and accounting assistance which the local locations may not enjoy. As in multilateral netting, only a central point is in a position to see liquidity shortfalls and surpluses, to appraise different markets and evaluate interest arbitrage opportunities.

Utilisation of funds internationally

There are a number of ways in which liquidity can be utilised internationally:

1 Leading/lagging, i.e., extending longer, or shorter, credit terms to importing affiliates, or paying before maturity.
2 Pre-paying import payables to third parties.
3 Intercompany lending.
4 Covered arbitrage abroad (i.e., investing in a foreign currency asset while covering the exchange risk by forward sale of that currency).
5 Uncovered arbitrage abroad.
6 Parallel loans with companies in a second country, in which each side makes its local currency available to a subsidiary of the other for a fixed period of time.
7 Repayment of international borrowings.

Liquidity decisions have an effect on exposure by definition, unless totally covered, and it is a moot point whether the corporate treasurer, grappling with an array of assets and risks should turn first to the liquidity problem or the exchange risk aspects. Since the risk of parity change is the common denominator, prior assessment of that risk should form the initiative to analysing opportunities.

Vehicle companies

The use of vehicle companies can optimise liquidity management. Such intermediary companies are usually located in a country with nominal exchange control and low rates of taxation, such as Switzerland or Bermuda. They are incorporated resident companies with a local board and set of accounts. Typically, their major role is to buy the export products of the group, and to reinvoice these for sale to the ultimate customers. The credit terms, currency of invoicing and price to third party borrowers remain unchanged.

Reinvoicing takes place either manually or by computer and the actual goods are shipped as before; thus the tariff/customs framework is unaffected. This is particularly important in multinational groupings with advantageous internal tariff regulations such as the EEC.

The intermediary company may also buy from each exporting affiliate in its local currency, and purchase their imports for them, reinvoicing back in local currency. If carried out rigorously, this puts all the trading exposure of the group into a central entity and creates a linkage of intercompany receivables.

Such centralisation of funds is as close to international pooling as is now possible; by using intercompany trade and other transactions, adjustment of credit terms can change, augment or reduce liquidity as desired. A vehicle company creates more ties between the subsidiaries, even where there is no direct trade between them, and materially increases the flexibility and range of liquidity management. The network of intercompany linkages thereby created is among the more powerful tools open to the large, sophisticated company which has the initiative to create such an enterprise, and the understanding to operate it successfully.

Foreign exchange exposure

Definition of exposure. The term 'exchange exposure' has several meanings. *Accounting exposure* relates to the necessity to value (translate) disparate financial items in terms of a single currency. The publicly stated value in local currency of the company's assets, equity and income may be affected adversely by the movement of currencies in which it has dealings. Translation losses in terms of the base currency can reduce its reported profits and nominal net worth. A corporation's image may be endangered, its stock market appeal diminished, or its ability to raise loans or equity put into question after reporting such losses.

Transaction exposure is a second commonly used term. It refers to the actual receipt or payment in foreign currency of funds which result from trade or financial transactions. Payments larger, or receipts smaller, than originally booked, (because rates have changed) have an actual operating effect on the company.

Some companies regard the risk of adverse accounting changes as ephemeral, depending on their own stockholder makeup and perception of risk. Translation losses are seen more as an embarrassment, or as an unavoidable cost of doing business abroad. The firm may be regarded as a permanent ongoing concern where realised profits and remitted dividends are more material factors. Long range implications of rate movements on investments or profit streams will be of more concern than short term bookkeeping effects. This approach to foreign exchange risk concentrates on *economic exposure*: the long term operating effects of parity changes.

Foreign exchange risk management is an integral part of the overall financial management of the firm. The international monetary system remains highly volatile and relationships among currencies are impossible to predict in the short run. Multinational companies must weigh the foreign exchange risk element in each major decision area: management of liquidity and borrowing, reporting financial results, declaration or payment of dividends, and long term investment decisions.

Financing decisions are affected directly by the appreciation or depreciation of the borrower's currency or that which is borrowed; nominal interest rates alone are only part of the decision making analysis. The timing of dividends requires an exchange rate judgement and falls into the overall strategy of dealing with exchange risk. Foreign investment decisions, normally based on productivity, competition, market and economic factors, must include a perception of long term exchange risk. Equivalent investments in different countries, otherwise offering the same apparent advantages, can be differentiated, and thus graded, by the long term outlook for currencies involved.

Main components of exchange risk management

After defining the nature of the risks borne by the company, a series of reporting and analytical stages follows: identification of exposed positions, analysis of the potential impact of future rate changes on present and forecast positions, strategy setting to deal with these risks, and carrying out appropriate tactics, all within a larger framework integrating with liquidity and tax management.

I Definition of exposure	II Identification of present and projected exposed positions	III Analysis of potential impact
(a) That based on accounting rules (b) Risks of actual transactions (c) Economic exposure	(a) Reporting systems: – internal positions – external data (b) Forecasting systems	Effect of forecast exchange rate movements on corporate positions
IV Strategy setting	V Tactics for implementing strategy	VI Integration
(a) Cost/risk analysis (b) Use of mathematical tools	(a) Selection of hedging techniques – internal – external (b) Regulatory limitations	(a) Co-ordination with liquidity management (b) Tax considerations (c) Personnel implications

Fig. 5.2 Components of exchange exposure management

Identification of exposed positions

Actual transactions in foreign currency on a realised basis present different operating effects at all levels of the company. These may or may not be anticipated in traditional accounting statements. Additional definition and reporting elements are necessary to quantify changes in the company's positions over time and to identify the exchange risks engendered.

Reporting systems are at the heart of the identification and analysis systems, which also identify the external constraints on company response. Only after the projection of all types of exposure is achieved can the potential impact on a firm and its constituent parts be quantified. Only then can a company develop a strategy to eliminate, reduce or accept its perceived risks. The company will review its position individually by currency and by location.

Projection of possible losses

Assessing the potential impact of exchange exposure on any company is the next stage. Once adequate reporting and forecasting are achieved, the determination of impact on the firm becomes a process of comparing future expected rate changes to the positions maintained – and expected to be maintained – by the group on a currency-by-currency basis. Determining that impact involves an assessment of market trends which can be graded in terms of probability.

Setting strategy

The previous stages are analytical, a strategy of accepting or covering individual risks. Creating a strategy is again a function of the individual firm's attitude to risk, the degree to which any bad results must be reported publicly and the actual after-tax effects if the worst possible set of events happens. A policy of maximising earnings might foster a different strategy from one directed towards preservation of assets or maintenance of sales volumes. If a firm's policy is simply to protect reported income, it might consider covering all risks; this would be appropriate for a simple exporting or importing firm. A more sophisticated firm might decide which potential risks are unacceptable from the point of view of potential realised losses or reduced liquidity.

The firm should perform cost/risk analysis based on the above criteria, its own particular risk structure and flexibility in hedging risks. The logic in covering only certain exchange hazards derives from the calculation of individual risks in each currency, deciding which are acceptable and which are not, and selecting one, or an array of, methods to cover the latter at the lowest cost.

Decision responsibility

The way in which a firm goes about this task is also important. The centralisation necessary for ascertaining all types of risks and alternatives can be achieved in more than one way, if strict guidelines for co-ordination are developed. The corporation must designate clear responsibility for exposure management. One way to do so is to make the finance department a profit centre, with direct attribution of foreign exchange gains, losses and hedging costs, as well as certain interest costs and yields. It is also necessary to decide how hedging or risk-acceptance decisions are made: whether they are the responsibility of a single designated individual or a committee. The role of regional headquarters can form an effective complement to the whole process, if a structure is created in which the experience of more than one source can be used. Any independent action by subsidiaries should not be undertaken without central approval.

Computer application

Due to the complexity of the area, the amount of data to be assimilated and the element of uncertainty, mathematical/computer application is of major interest. For compilation and permutation of statistical data, computers are increasingly useful, as they are also in simple simulation models. Owing to the unpredictability of short term rates in the exchange markets and the unknown co-variances between spot rates and interest rates, more ambitious optimisation programs have not been very successful to date.

Hedging

The international company has a variety of techniques at its disposal to neutralise, minimise or avoid exchange risks. The application and selection of hedging techniques vary directly and proportionately with the complexity and international penetration of the firm. Thus the exporting/importing company has only certain hedging methods available, while a much fuller range is open to the true multinationals. Both types of company must consider in advance the appropriateness of internal as well as external hedging possibilities, regulatory limitations, tax effects and cost factors. Techniques used to change or reduce risk have a basic cost, although this may fall in marketing areas. All are based on the firm's accounting conventions used to translate foreign currency items, which shape the way in which the corporation will select and apply hedging techniques. All need to be reviewed on an after-tax basis.

Internal techniques affecting outstanding positions

Pre-payment of existing third-party commitments

Exchange risks arising from third-party transactions fall into export, import or financial categories. Outstanding third-party export receivables cannot be changed by internal adjustments. Import commitments, however, normally can be pre-paid if the currency in which they are invoiced is expected to appreciate *vis-à-vis* that of the importer. Foreign currency loans, where there is a pre-payment option, may be paid down. The cost of such transactions is the domestic financing expense (or the interest foregone) from the time of early payment to the original maturity. The principal restrictions are found in the exchange control regulations of the importer's country, which may rule out pre-payments, or of the exporting/lending country, which may prohibit the premature receipt of funds by explicit decree or financial charges.

Intercompany term adjustment

Greater scope is offered in intercompany positions where original payment dates can be accelerated or delayed to change the basic position of the group in a specific currency. Commonly called leading and lagging, this is a widely used and legitimate technique to shift risk or liquidity.

Exposure netting involves creating or acceptance of open positions in two (or more) currencies, which are considered to balance each other and, therefore, to require no further internal or external hedging.

A short position in such a currency can be considered offset to some degree by a long position in a closely related currency. An exporter with Belgian franc payables and Dutch guilder receivables might decide that these two positions covered each other and that forward contracts were not necessary. A long position in a traditionally hard currency, such as the Deutschemark, might be used to offset eventual depreciation of assets in a softer currency.

Internal techniques affecting future positions

The above techniques – chiefly lagging or leading payments – form a limited and short term range of hedging techniques related to existing positions. Anticipatory exposure management offers a greater variety of useful risk adjustment possibilities. These fall into two types: changes in pricing/currency billing policy, and changes in balance sheet positions.

Anticipatory local subsidiary price increases are often the only way to protect against the negative effect of depreciation of a local currency. For example, if the local sales price can be raised before devaluation, the reported income stream and ultimate dividends are protected, which will prove doubly valuable if a local price freeze follows currency devaluation. Treasury input can be an important factor in a decision which has more than one justification.

Export price increases depend on marketing factors, since there are often both international and local competitive products. When exports are denominated in a currency likely to depreciate, selective price increases protect revenues just as local price adjustments do. A discount option for more prompt payment has somewhat the same effect.

A more subtle price adjustment strategy is through *changing the currency of billing* to that of a parent or to a stronger currency. Billing in weaker currencies, when the home currency is inherently strong, can be considered if sales increases are fostered, with sufficient margins to allow external protection methods. Exchange risk enters even if one switches from a supposedly weak currency of billing to a stronger one. No currency trends are so predictable, or so long lived, that one can assume with certainty that a billing switch will remain as attractive in the future. Currencies of billing cannot easily be reversed and cannot be changed often.

The second major area of internal anticipatory changes in exposure management comes in *asset or liability adjustment*. The goal is to wind up with reduced assets/increased liabilities in currencies likely to depreciate, and increased assets/reduced liabilities in harder currencies.

Either the parent itself, or a subsidiary concerned can build up cash, short term investments, receivables and/or inventories denominated in currencies expected to revalue. Subsidiaries will be instructed to pay bills as slowly as possible, to convert foreign currency holdings or investments into local ones and to delay intercompany settlements or dividends. They may also delay purchase of, or settlement for, raw materials. All these moves will build up short term local currency assets, those items both translated/consolidated at spot rates and likely to be realised in the near future. A net increase in short term asset positions could also be achieved by reducing group members' short term debt denominated in hard currencies, by pre-payment of hard currency payables, and analogous techniques.

When a devaluation-prone currency is involved, the techniques apply in reverse. Cash and short term security holdings will be run down, local debt increased, certain payables accelerated, and intercompany payments rescheduled. The goal is to reduce long positions or increase debt and other commitments in a soft currency so as to benefit from, or be protected against, its expected depreciation.

Export financing vehicles

Hedging of foreign commitments is constrained by the restrictions imposed by each exchange control and by exchange market structure. The typical situation is that each local affiliate must cover its own transaction exposures locally under specific external regulations.

A way to rationalise this situation is to create a finance company vehicle which buys the export receivables of the group and assumes the credit risk and covering responsibility. The vehicle company purchases the export receivables of each group member as created or buys outstanding receivables under previous agreement. The finance vehicle's assets consist of export receivables with varying dates and currencies; its liabilities of short term borrowings. It can cover those risks and maturities exactly, or can leave them uncovered as to timing and amount as part of an overall risk strategy. Centralisation in a vehicle operating essentially 'off-shore' in the Euro-markets gives a great deal more flexibility and the ability to put a trained group in charge of all such risks. Such a vehicle can usually be established with moderate capital input and legal costs (the former since its borrowings will be guaranteed by the parent).

Reinvoicing vehicles

A finance house, however, can only react in the receivable portion of risks. Since it holds title solely to the underlying paper involved, legal recourse in the case of customer default is also more problematic. A more useful approach is to use a reinvoicing intermediary company, as already discussed. Advantages for exposure management are:

1 Local personnel are left to concentrate on production, marketing or local financing.
2 Identification of exposure and any requisite hedging are facilitated.
3 Exposures may be mutually offsetting.

External hedges

External hedgings are more clearly delineated and usually their cost can be precisely determined in advance. They fall into the following categories:

1   Forward exchange contracts.
2   Foreign currency loans.
3   Discount/sale of foreign receivables.
4   Retained currency accounts.
5   Borrowing/deposit arrangements in two currencies.
6   Factoring.
7   Leasing.
8   Export risk guarantees.

With *forward exchange contracts*, future receipts or payments are sold, or bought, for the same date forward as the payment maturity, at a fixed price. In the final analysis, forward rates are a function of the interest rate differentials of the two countries involved. In the major currencies and larger markets, forward exchange contracts can be negotiated not only for periods beginning with the present to some fixed maturity, but also from one future date to another. Similarly, it is possible to have two simultaneous forward sale/purchase contracts, in essence a swap, which cover the company for any time period up to one year (or whatever limits the markets permit). This cover is achieved for instance by buying a currency forward for three months and selling it forward for six months. These contracts give cover for exchange risk exposure between the two dates permitting both a more flexible and directed hedging policy and a reduction of hedging costs, since the cost factors involved will comprise the discount (or premium) only in the exact period covered. A forward contract is not irrevocable, and in normal markets can be closed out during its existence. This would be done if the underlying reason for the hedge had changed or if other exogenous factors had intervened to make the hedge superfluous.

   Where an exporter is invoicing in a currency other than its own, and which is expected to weaken, it can consider borrowing the same foreign currency for the tenor of the outstanding receivable and selling the loan proceeds spot at the outset for its own currency and placing them on time deposit. The ensuing interest yield will reduce the gross borrowing expense.

Export bills denominated in foreign currency can usually be discounted in local markets, exchange controls allowing this as an aid to exporters. The bank discounting such currency bills will itself apply a mixture of the domestic rate and the net cost/yield of the swap transaction. This technique is not possible in many exchange control-based countries, where foreign currency borrowings are permitted only under strict limitation, or not at all.

An analogous risk-avoiding possibility for importers owing foreign currency is to borrow their own currency, use the proceeds to buy the foreign currency spot and place the funds on deposit.

Where an exporter is selling on open account and therefore receives no discountable bills, it is sometimes possible to assign the actual receivables as collateral for related bank financing. Both commercial banks and specialised factoring institutions in certain countries offer factoring facilities for this purpose. It is possible to factor receivables denominated in foreign currency, as well as those in local units. The equivalent local value of the receivables is then advanced to the exporter until maturity.

A less used hedging method for the export of capital goods is *leasing*. For marketing reasons, an exporter of capital goods may not be able to bill in his own currency nor wish to receive an importer's weak currency. It may be possible to sell the goods outright to a leasing company in the country of the importer, which leases them on to the ultimate user. Neither side then has an exchange risk, and the exporter is paid immediately. While attractive in certain cases, it is not always easy to negotiate a tripartite arrangment covering all the legal and fiscal considerations between seller, leasing company and buyer/lessee.

Even the above wide range of external risk hedging techniques does not cover every eventuality, since exchange and banking markets are neither perfect nor long term in orientation. For this reason, several governments have established *exchange risk guarantee* (ERG) programmes to add to the flexibility of exporters. These programmes are usually found in hard currency countries where exporters of industrial equipment sell under long term contracts and where traditional short term cover is neither available nor appropriate.

Banking policy, market limitations and/or exchange control regulations will constrain or prohibit the use of these techniques in many instances. All methods will seldom be available to any company, nor will all be equally advantageous. The relevance and cost of each method should form part of the normal managerial analysis when setting hedging strategy.

Summary

To summarise, the international corporations dealing with exchange risk should:

1 Review the definitions used internally to determine exchange risk.
2 Make its exposure management anticipatory, based on perception of future risk as well as present positions.
3 Centralise control over exposure risk as far as possible.
4 Review reporting systems as regards their adequacy and timeliness.
5 Cover economic and transactional exposures generally and translation risk when the maximum potential translation losses are considered to be unacceptable by definitive corporate criteria. This implies a selective coverage policy, not one of complete cover at all times in all currencies. All hedging possibilities – internal and external – should be studied and their cost effectiveness determined.
6 Analyse and make exposure decisions on a post-tax basis.
7 Co-ordinate exchange management closely with liquidity management, as both have common goals and are equally affected by environmental and structural constraints.
8 Be aware of the non-financial implications of exposure strategy, particularly the personnel effects of centralisation and the necessity to deal with an array of governmental and institutional contacts.

PART III
FINANCIAL CONTROL

OVERVIEW

Financial measurement is an essential ingredient in all commercial activities in a market economy. Thus the challenge of financial management lies in the interdependence of finance and all other activities in the firm. Financial management encompasses not only the treasury function, that is, raising capital and the management of working capital and of capital investment, but also the controllership function involving the operation of a financial control system which aims to depict the financial aspect of all the firm's planned and actual activities. This means that as well as being a financial specialist, a financial manager may need to be a management systems generalist. Financial information systems must be articulated with operational information systems in sales and marketing, production, physical distribution, personnel, and so on. Hence, when discussing control, one should consider companies and their various parts as systems and sub-systems (systems within systems.)

Part Three of this handbook deals with these control aspects of financial management. Broadly speaking, control requires that objectives be established, that actual outcomes be measured and compared to objectives, and that actions be taken to avoid any major divergences between expected outcomes and objectives. For the financial manager, the relevant aspects of objectives and outcomes are the financial ones, that is, in the last analysis, cash flows. Certain financial objectives and outcomes can be, and often are, also expressed in terms of profits, which are perhaps best considered as cash flows which have been smoothed by removing two kinds of fluctuations:

1 Fluctuations due to the operation of the working capital cycle;

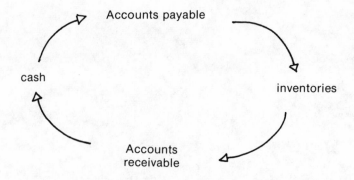

2   Fluctuations due to the lumpy nature of expenditure on fixed assets.

How far this kind of smoothing contributes to the usefulness of the information will depend on the circumstances in which it is being used. It should be recognised that because the financial control system works by abstracting the financial aspects of the firm's activities, a degree of abstraction is essential to the system. An excessive degree of abstraction is, however, a common failing in accounting systems.

To achieve control, a management system has two interrelated kinds of systemic requirements: an information system or systems, and a system of responsibilities or management organisation. These requirements are the subject of Richard Wilson's chapter 'Reporting and Responsibilities' (Chapter 6). Within this overall system, the budget control sub-system is concerned particularly with the expression of operational objectives in financial terms, and the comparison of financial outcomes (profits and cash flows) with these objectives. This forms the subject of Alan Leaper's chapter 'Budgets and Budgetary Control' (Chapter 7).

Both the establishment of objectives and the measurement of financial outcomes require information subsystems which provide knowledge of the costs of the organisation's final outputs (products) and of intermediate outputs (goods and services produced and used within the organisation in the production of those final outputs). These subsystems for Costing and Internal (or Transfer) Pricing are the subject of Chapter 8 by H. W. Calvert and Simon Archer.

Finally, the Internal Audit subsystem is intended to provide a check on the operation of the management system as a whole. As described in the chapter on Internal Auditing by Harry Scholefield and P. C. Elliott, it constitutes an off-line or second-level appraisal activity designed to evaluate the adequacy, efficiency and effectiveness of the company's on-line or first-level control subsystems (Chapter 9). Internal Audit, then, is not part of financial control as exercised by the Financial Manager; rather, it is complementary to it.

Thus, the four chapters deal with the principles which govern the design and operation of financial control systems in business organisations. Certain important system requirements tend, however, to be specific to particular kinds of business (retailing, for example, as compared with manufacturing or transport); others may be specific to certain areas of the business (marketing, production, etc.).

Such situation-specific requirements are potentially vast in number. Part Three does not aim to cover the control requirements of particular types of business or, in detail, of particular areas in a business; rather, the aim is to deal with those principles and approaches which apply to a wide range of business situations.

6

Reporting and responsibilities

Richard M S Wilson

The aim of this chapter is to indicate how the accountant might design
and develop reporting procedures under the total systems concept by
adopting a control perspective.

SYSTEMS DESIGN IN MANAGERIAL ACCOUNTING

The objects of managerial accounting systems design are: to assist
managers to take planning and control decisions in the light of their
financial impact on the whole organisation; to motivate employees
towards a high level of performance; and to evaluate actual
performance. Internal financial reporting is the 'output' subsystem of
managerial accounting, designed to supply managers with relevant and
usable information. Other subsystems of managerial accounting are
concerned with collecting and processing raw data to provide these
outputs.

Planning and control systems: the cycle of control

The necessary company-wide perspective for establishing reporting
systems is given by the cycle of control. Diagramatically, this can be
shown as in Figure 6.1. Reporting systems should be designed to
include procedures for carrying out each of the steps within the cycle.
This requires:

1   Means of determining and communicating the objectives that the
    system is to serve (step 1).
2   Means of adding the additional detail to complete and gain

approval of the planning phases (steps 2, 3, 4 and 5).

3 Means of communicating with the performance groups (step 7).

4 Methods of comparing performance with the plan and identifying significant variations (steps 7 and 8).

5 Methods of reporting accomplishments (step 8).

6 Identification of the various corrective actions which may be taken and the means of taking them (steps 8 and 9).

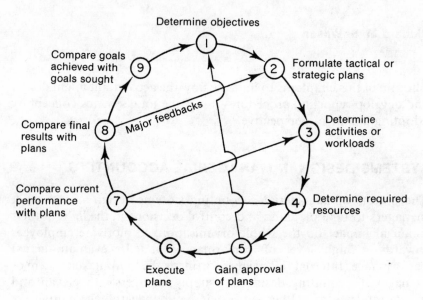

Fig. 6.1 The cycle of control

In these terms, the managerial accounting system forms a significant part of a web of management information systems designed to facilitate the articulation and achievement of the company's objectives. These information systems, in turn, form part of the overall set of operational activities making up the business enterprise as a total system.

Operating principles of systems design

Decision needs and associated information flows are the primary centres of attention for accounting systems designers and the actual design of accounting systems must concentrate on the desired arrangement of resources and activities within the organisation, and on the desired outputs from those resources and activities.

Initially, then, the systems designer must know:
1 What the organisation and its sub-units are required to achieve.
2 To what standards they are required to do this.
3 How their performance is to be evaluated against these standards.

The requirements of the system can then be expressed in terms of information outputs that its reporting subsystem must produce; data that its data input subsystem must accept; processing operations that its data processing subsystem must perform; and resources that it is constrained to use.

Its performance may then be measured in terms of whichever criteria are appropriate. For example, relevant criteria of system operating performance will usually include some of the following:

1 Cost.
2 Timeliness.
3 Accuracy.
4 Reliability
5 Security.
6 Quality.
7 Flexibility.
8 Capacity.
9 Efficiency.
10 Acceptability.

The successful operation of a managerial accounting system depends upon both the accounting techniques employed and the behavioural response of the result. Given this, the basic steps in designing a new system are to:

1 Study the enterprise and the information needs of its decision makers.
2 Develop a basic system design: overall system and major subsystems.
3 Identify the activities to be performed within each subsystem and the interfaces between the various subsystems.
4 Specify the resources needed to perform these activities and assure the interfaces.

5 Prepare a preliminary plan for system implementation.
6 Determine the impact of the design on profitability (or other objectives or constraints).
7 Document the new system design.

These steps are often best accomplished by a project team comprising representatives from the main decision making units and account and data processing specialists, directed by a project leader. The responsible individual must ensure that he has the authority of management to implement the system once it has been designed.

The installation of a new accounting system involves recruiting new staff, re-training existing staff, re-allocating duties, etc. As a result, job classifications, job specifications and the proper division of labour must be considered carefully. If the system is large, phased implementation is preferable to a single complete change, due to the latter's sheer complexity.

Every system should possess sufficient flexibility to allow for a constantly changing environment. (For example, sufficient free classifications should be built in to an account coding system to allow subsequent expansion to be accommodated.) Furthermore, a system producing too much information can obscure that which is relevant, while a system producing too little information does not favour good decision making. Balance and flexibility are prerequisites for success.

If an existing system is to be improved, four basic steps should be followed; it is necessary to:

1 Identify the critical aspects that need to be planned and controlled (i.e., ascertain the types of decisions to be made).
2 Determine what specific information is required, and amend the system by adding omitted data-flows and deleting unnecessary data-flows.
3 Motivate and train line-management to use the revised system, involving them in its design to an appropriate extent.
4 Determine the best method of improving the required information within prescribed time limits.

This highlights the need for a systematic, rather than an *ad hoc*, approach.

Control as the perspective for accounting systems

If progress towards goals is to be supervised, it must be observed and measured; there must be some assessment of where the organisation is, compared to where it ought to be. This is achieved through control. Control involves the use of a reliable, readily understood and sensitive system of information and standards as a basis for the management decisions that have to be taken.

All control is not necessarily financial or accounting-based. The company consists of the subsystems of production, marketing, R and D, personnel, administration, etc., all of which have their specific control aspects. However, the accountant or financial manager, by the very nature of his duties, is in a better position than most to see the total spectrum of corporate activities in an integrated manner, even though this overall view is biased in favour of emphasising the aspects most readily expressed in terms of money at the expense of those not so readily expressed. Yet, money is certainly the most convenient, if not the only, common yardstick for planning and gauging performance; and this is the accountant's or financial manager's domain. The accountant can discharge his responsibility adequately however, only if he appreciates the type of decisions made and the nature of the activities to be controlled. (The masculine pronoun is used for convenience; no disrespect to women accountants is intended). Indeed, there are good reasons to believe that improvements can be made on the stereotyped accountant's approach to reporting.

Additionally, the accountant is in a good position to consider the economics of control. The aim should be to provide an information system that facilitates control in such a way that the value is maximised for a given cost, (or alternatively, cost is minimised for a given level of control information).

In the capacity of controller, the accountant will be responsible for:

1 Selecting the key factors and control points.
2 Segregating the non-controllable factors so that the picture of the controllable aspects is not confused.
3 Relating the plans and controls to individual accountability at the various organisational levels.
4 Ensuring that the setting of standards meets the needs of the control system and can be built into departmental plans.
5 Co-ordinating the building up of the overall plan from subsidiary plans.

6 Designing the reporting system for effective display of required feed-back data.

Distinctions in accounting systems for planning and control

In the context of designing financial reporting systems for control purposes, it is helpful to distinguish the various types of accounting, namely: financial (or external) accounting and management accounting in its cost, decision and control aspects.

Financial accounting systems report to the outside world on management, rather than to management. The traditionally aggregated figures must meet the criterion of objectivity, but this often conflicts with the more important control criterion of usefulness. While financial accounting reports focus on the whole business, they must be compiled in accordance with statutory requirements and are historical in perspective. It will be evident, therefore, that financial accounting is of little value to management in exercising control.

In contrast, the term *management accounting* is used to designate a subset of information systems which fall into three main categories: cost accounting, decision accounting and control accounting. Such systems are intended as tools for management, and their outputs are not subject to the objectivity criteria and formal requirements characteristic of financial accounting.

Cost accounting is concerned with specific segments of the company, relating costs and revenues (and, hence, profits) to products, processes and divisions. Operational control is made effective through the analysis of variances from standard, but, essentially, cost accounting is concerned with planning and controlling costs in great detail, often at the unit cost level.

Decision accounting is perhaps more aptly referred to as economic decision analysis. It aims to provide information that is useful to management for specific decisions or planning purposes. Thus, its activities consist of a series of one-off studies of particular problems which routine cost or control accounting activities are designed to illuminate only partly, such as whether to produce internally or to subcontract certain manufactured items or service activities.

The purpose of *control accounting* is to indicate how successful the company is in achieving its goals. It permits the inclusion of goals other than profit (or cost reduction), and pays special attention (through the planning phase) to securing consistency among the objectives of the company as a whole and the objectives of its constituent parts.

Inevitably, these four broad types of accounting overlap considerably, but the demands of a variety of primary and secondary goals within the control process require that the control aspect of management accounting, supplemented by the other forms as appropriate, be the focus of attention for designers of reporting systems.

Accounting control systems considered

Given the purpose of accounting for control, several accounting subsystems can successfully supplement the budgetary control system (which is discussed in the next chapter).

Internal control is the process and means of safeguarding assets, checking the reliability of accounting data, monitoring operational efficiency and encouraging adherence to managerial policies with which the accountant is normally associated. However, in its broadest sense, internal control embraces every type of accounting technique and even extends beyond internal audit to the rigorous management audit. Since any system of controls requires human application, internal control exists, essentially, to ensure that the human factor acts in accordance with instructions, plans and policies.

Conventional product cost accounting can be usefully supplemented by *distribution cost analysis*, thereby bringing marketing and distribution activities under the same micro-control as production activities.

It is worth bearing in mind that cost itself is not a homogeneous concept, although the notion of sacrifice is common to all cost concepts. The costs of tangible phenomena can be defined and measured in many ways depending on how money values are assigned to the resources involved and precisely which resources are considered as being involved. Opportunity cost, direct cost, indirect cost, overhead cost, fixed cost, variable cost, marginal cost, incremental (or differential) cost, semi-fixed cost, semi-variable cost, average cost, full (or absorption) cost, joint cost, separable cost, sunk cost, avoidable cost, unavoidable cost, imputed cost, controllable cost, uncontrollable cost, replacement cost, standard cost – this list indicates the multiplicity of cost concepts which a systems designer may have to consider.

Clearly, the accountant must consider carefully (in conjunction with those who will use his reports) the types of costs to include in any financial reporting system. His role will be both provider of information and educator on how to use it.

It must be borne in mind, then, that any accounting technique has limitations. For example, allocations of indirect costs between products and of direct fixed costs to units of product, are arbitrary; ratios may hide compensating factors or trends and cost-volume-profit (or break-even) analysis is essentially a static technique, being largely based on static assumptions of linear, that is, straight-line, relationships between volumes, on the one hand, and revenues and costs on the other.

Nevertheless, the distinction between fixed and variable costs and the related *flexible budgeting* approach, help to depict the financial implications of alternative scenarios and in the analysis of past performance. *Ratio analysis* can also be used to assist in the same process.

THE KEYS TO CONTROL

The first, and, perhaps, the most obvious requirement, is that measurement must be relevant to management's needs, and measures themselves must be designed to aid interpretation.

What to measure

Many companies tend to measure only material factors that are readily expressed in production or financial terms, such as time, quantity and quality. However, it is important that certain non-material factors should be measured, especially those indicating the performance of responsible individuals throughout the company.

Interpretation

Interpretation is the essential link between measurement (information) and decision making (action). The demands on top management are such that it is important that reports emphasise departures from plan or standard (exception reporting) and interpret the exceptions, in order both to conserve the manager's time and aid him in decision making. A policy decision must be therefore made in designing control systems to determine the extent to which the interpretation of exceptions and the resultant decisions can be delegated as routine procedures to subordinate staff.

Where practicable, trends should be displayed graphically, as, for instance, the behaviour of overhead costs in relation to the level of productive activity.

Selectivity

When considering the scope of exception reporting, one must bear in mind that control can break down because management attempts to control too much, and really important issues become submerged in a mass of irrelevancies. In any control series, a small proportion of elements will always tend to account for a large proportion of effects. Examples of the frequently-met 80/20 rule, illustrate this, when 80 per cent of a company's sales are accounted for by 20 per cent of its customers, or 20 per cent of items in stock account for 80 per cent of the value of inventory. Accordingly, the key factors for control must be selected carefully and reporting systems should be designed to highlight significant items.

In practice, most managements attempt to control many factors which, in a control sense, are unimportant because their behaviour pattern will follow that of other more essential factors such as the level of sales.

Accountability and controllability

It is essential to the success of any financial control system that an individual (the budgetee) is only held responsible for results when the following conditions prevail:

1   That he knows what he is expected to achieve.
2   That he knows what he is actually achieving.
3   That it is substantially within his power to regulate what is happening.

When all these conditions do not exist simultaneously, it may be unjust and ineffective to hold the budgetee responsible, and the desired control will become impossible to achieve. Nevertheless, the fact that a system fairly reflects commercial reality is just as important as ensuring fair treatment for the budgetee. These considerations lead us to the principles of responsibility accounting.

ORGANISATIONAL AND BEHAVIOURAL IMPLICATIONS

A financial reporting system is a means of bringing information to each level of management in order that responsibilities to the organisation may be fulfilled. It follows that accounting figures should be compiled so that the results may be considered attributable to one person's performance. This requirement causes accounting to cross the threshold into behavioural science (especially the areas of motivation and human relations), which forms the basis for management control.

Responsibility accounting

Each responsible individual should prepare his budget on the basis of controllable costs (and revenues, where appropriate) at his level of authority. Essentially, the responsibility centre is a personalised concept, whereas the notion of cost centre may well be impersonal. For example, a machine shop in an engineering company will be composed of several cost centres – milling machines, turret lathes, auto-robots, and so on – but the whole shop is under the authority of the foreman. This is his responsibility centre for which he is the responsible individual.

Responsibility accounting changes the emphasis of cost and management accounting from products, which are passive inanimate objects, to people who are led to participate in vigorous planning and cost control through the budgetary process.

Cost classification is a vital area of responsibility accounting, the aim being to assign costs to the individuals who are responsible for their incurrence. However, charging individuals with only those costs subject to their control has many attendant practical problems when joint costs are involved. The general rule is to charge the person who can bring the greatest influence to bear on cost incurrence with responsibility for any joint cost, rather than making some meaningless apportionment.

Responsibility centres as a basis for reporting

Accounting control reports should be fitted to the various areas of individual responsibility, and as one moves further up the managerial hierarchy, more cost items will be reported at each level, since more costs are controllable as the scope of managerial responsibility enlarges. Top management will therefore receive a summary of all costs, made up of summaries of controllable costs at each subordinate level, plus details of those relevant to the top level.

Such reports can do little to rectify previous mistakes, but by indicating exceptions to plan they ensure that causes are investigated and appropriate corrective action taken to prevent similar mistakes in the future. The orientation must clearly be towards the future rather than to the past.

A common weakness in many companies is an over emphasis on current profit performance. For example, return on capital by division, plant, or product line helps to explain changes in the rate of return for the company as a whole, as well as assisting in appraising the performance of individual managers. But two principal dangers exist in this approach. First, both profits and the capital base must be clearly defined to avoid misunderstanding; for example, whether profit is measured before tax, or the investment base is net of depreciation and other specific items. Secondly, sub-optimisation through departmental orientation rather than corporate orientation on the part of individual managers can result from emphasising the department to the exclusion of the company as a whole. In addition, there are more general problems of arbitrary cost allocations and holding individuals responsible for costs over which they have no control.

Adopting a systems approach should ensure the highest degree of consistency between departmental and corporate goals. However, divisional responsibilities must be specific, since control must be specific. An individual manager's budget should only be modified after negotiation between the manager and his superior together with the budget officer. The manager should accept the modification as reasonable and feel committed to the new target. If this practice is not followed, the manager may lose confidence in the attainability of the budget, no matter how specific it may be, and may fail to see how his budget fits into the overall corporate pattern. The guiding principle is that those charged with responsibility should be consulted on all matters relevant to it.

In summary, anyone fixing responsibility and implementing the control related to it should:

1　Define clearly the organisational structure, and delegate responsibility so that each person knows his role.
2　Determine the extent and limits of functional control.
3　Ensure that responsible individuals are fully involved in preparing budget estimates, since they will be held liable for deviations.
4　Provide those responsible with means of exercising control, in the form of regular, relevant statements of cost and, where appropriate, of revenues.
5　Organise ways and means by which subordinates may report to superiors on significant variances and corrective action taken (or to be taken).
6　By the above procedure, confirm that every item of expense is the responsibility of some person within the organisation and also that every responsible individual knows for what expenditures he must account, and to whom.

The ability to delegate is one sign of a good manager, and the budgeting process enables the control of expenditure, segmental revenue-generation and profit responsibility to be delegated. Specifically charging managers with responsibilities forms an important way of ensuring that tasks are performed satisfactorily, since few people will reduce costs or otherwise seek to improve profitability unless responsibility has been specifically delegated to them.

The impact of control on individuals

As already noted, the design of planning and control systems takes us into the territory of the behavioural sciences. The question of motivation is particularly relevant. For control (as distinct from planning) purposes, the use of accurate calculations and their transmission (in the form of results) to others may be beneficial, harmful, or neutral, depending upon:

1　The kind of persons and tasks involved.
2　The setting in which operations are conducted.
3　The vehicle, time sequence, etc., used for information transmittal.

Clearly, therefore, the effect of control on individuals can play a large part in the effective control of the company.

Budgets have been known to unite employees against management where reports show results rather than reasons, or are excessively historical in relation to future goals, or are prepared by inflexible and narrow-minded accountants.

One vital study in this area (C. Argyris, *Personality and Organisation*, New York: Harper Brothers 1957) quotes the following statements about budget reports from supervisory management:

> *"I'm violently against the figures. I keep away from showing them to the workers. I know the boys are doing a good job. They're trying to to their best. If I give them the heat with this stuff they'll blow their top."*

> *"You can't use budgets on people. Just can't do anything like that. People have to be handled carefully and in our plant carefully doesn't mean with budgets. Besides I don't think my people are lazy."*

As a result of the pressure, tension and general mistrust of management controls, the above mentioned tendency of employees to unite against management may result. Such controls as budgets tend to make employees feel dependent and passive, which emphasises their subordination to management – not only are they told what to do, but also how to do it. Consequently, a great care must be taken in administering management controls to ensure that employees do not experience excessive exposure to such factors as pressure, inter-departmental strife, barriers to communication, or inclinations to be department centred rather than organisation centred. Such care will involve:

1 Reporting both results and (insofar as possible) reasons for those results.
2 Emphasising both past and present performance.
3 Maintaining flexibility.
4 Stressing the established goals (and future expectations).

The problem of directing activities towards goals is one of motivation, which is often overlooked by conventional budgeting methods. The budget is not the goal, it is the plan that should aim to motivate goal attainment. As such, it should be based on realistic expectations, and this demands effective communications between the different operating levels of the company.

Good attitudes must provide the key to successful budgeting. This is facilitated by satisfactory relationships between subordinates and superiors, which rest on the existence of clear cut organisational lines and the disposition to delegate authority along with responsibility. Budgets should not be used as pressure devices, since this will prohibit the development of team spirit in striving to achieve planned goals. A budget should be seen as a yardstick – not an instrument of pressure.

By helping to clarify targets and by demonstrating the inter-dependence of the different sections of the business, budgets form a powerful means of motivation. If the budgetary process does not aid in motivating people in the right direction, then serious thought should be given to discounting or thoroughly revising the procedures practised. The ideal situation is that in which a control system is so designed that it leads people to take actions that are not only in their own best interests but are also in the best interests of the company.

It becomes necessary, therefore, to consider the aspiration levels of different individuals. This requires incorporating sufficient flexibility within the budgetary system to improve motivation by the upwards or downwards movement of targets in order to achieve continuous improvements in goal-attainment. For example, an individual's aspiration level will tend to decrease following a failure in his goal striving behaviour. Similarly, his aspiration level will tend to increase following success. In addition, aspirations are affected by external events other than task performance (such as his relationship with his superior, his personal financial condition, his domestic situation, etc.), but these effects tend to decrease as experience with the task increases. Since each individual's aspiration level will be unique to him (and to his pattern of success/failure and non-task circumstances) it is necessary to reflect recent past performance levels with revised future target levels if positive motivation is to be ensured.

Weaknesses of budgetary control

From the standpoint of internal financial reporting, the budget is an all-pervading consideration. We conclude this section by re-emphasising the problems encountered in using budgets and describing an approach which will minimise these difficulties.

Four major problem areas are frequently encountered in the use of budget systems:

1 They can grow to be so complex, detailed, cumbersome,

meaningless and expensive that they become dangerous.

2 Budgetary goals may come to supersede organisational goals, requiring care in using budgets as a means and not an end.

3 Budgets may tend to hide inefficiencies by continuing initial expenditures in succeeding periods without proper evaluation. The budgetary system must contain provisions for re-examination of standards and other bases of planning, by which policies are translated into numerical terms.

4 The use of budgets as pressure devices defeats their basic purpose.

To allow for different levels of activity, and the inherent inaccuracies of forecasting in an uncertain world, budgets must be flexible.

The inability to forecast with total accuracy does not nullify the value of the budget as a managerial tool. It does mean, however, that the budget should not be a static device that is insensitive to changing conditions. Flexibility is an obvious necessity in providing meaningful current standards for guiding operations and judging performance.

Although cost-volume-profit analysis can be a useful adjunct to effective budgeting, it must be accepted as a relatively inflexible tool that hinders the comparison of alternatives on account of its static nature. In more detail, it fails to take account of:

1 The dynamic nature of industrial activity.
2 The efficiency of management.
3 The efficiency of labour.
4 Technological progress.
5 The size of plant and resource limitations.
6 Price changes.
7 Varying product/sales mix.
8 Objectives other than profit (derived from specified cost and sales levels) such as the degree of consumer satisfaction to be achieved.

Even when budgets have been prepared, based on accurate, currently attainable and internally derived standards, the financial reporting system should have tolerance levels built into it. It cannot be expected that standards will be met perfectly, thereby requiring some measure of the significance of results *vis-à-vis* plans to be developed – results beyond this tolerance limit being the subject of control action,

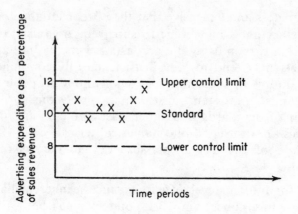

Fig. 6.2   Statistical control chart

and results within this limit being accepted as random variations.

The tolerance range should not be so broad as to excuse all levels of performance, nor so narrow as to cause control action and investigation to be applied too frequently.

The statistical control chart in Figure 6.2 allows successive levels of performance for a particular factor to be observed in relation to standards, and tolerance limits set accordingly.

CRITERIA FOR INFORMATION USEFULNESS

How effective a manager is in his job will tend to depend upon his general ability; his knowledge of what he is seeking to achieve; and how much, how relevant and how good his information is, along with how well he interprets and acts upon it.

Management information needs

Nevertheless, one hears frequent complaints from managers that information is too late, of the wrong type, unverified or even suppressed. It is evident, therefore, that if information is to be of value, it must be clear, detailed, timely, accurate and complete – not merely some vague figures thrown out by an unplanned system. Management information and its presentation must observe the important concepts of control, namely: accountability, controllability and selectivity. In addition, data should be checked for the important qualities of impartiality, reliability and internal consistency.

Basically, the manager needs information to:

1 Help him in making plans and setting standards (to indicate what is expected of him).
2 Indicate his performance and achievement in executing those plans.
3 Assist him in decision making (to bring 1 and 2 closer together).

As frequently happens, the manager may not know the precise information he needs (or, alternatively, what information is available). The systems designer can help by observing the types of decisions made, testing the adequacy of existing information, suggesting alternate data-flows, determining what information is available and indicating the means and costs of providing it.

The process of specifying, collecting, analysing, reporting and using information is essentially the same in any size of business, whether for routine purposes or for special projects. What do vary however, are the methods of collection and analysis. The differences lie in the relative employment of manual as opposed to mechanical or electronic methods. The increasing adoption of electronic data-processing should ensure that fewer managers will have cause to complain about insufficient, inaccurate or delayed information – provided that systems designers ensure that relevance, reliability, and timeliness are taken into account. The danger, rather, is that they may be inundated with data which is too voluminous and poorly formulated for them to use.

In aiming to provide the right information to the right people at the right time and at low cost, the financial reporting systems should, ideally, be designed as part of a total systems framework such as that portrayed in Figure 6.3, which is derived from D. R. Daniel, 'Management Information Crisis', *Harvard Business Review*, Sept.-Oct., 1961.

Uses of financial information

A great deal of information, while useful for planning and control, is primarily generated for some other purpose that is only tangentially related to planning and control purposes.

In most companies the accounting routine provides the bulk of data which are derived from:

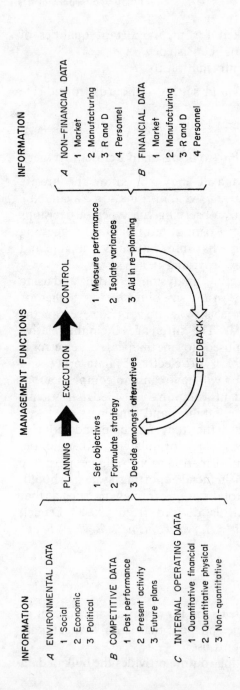

INFORMATION

A ENVIRONMENTAL DATA
1 Social
2 Economic
3 Political

B COMPETITIVE DATA
1 Past performance
2 Present activity
3 Future plans

C INTERNAL OPERATING DATA
1 Quantitative financial
2 Quantitative physical
3 Non-quantitative

MANAGEMENT FUNCTIONS

PLANNING
1 Set objectives
2 Formulate strategy
3 Decide amongst alternatives

EXECUTION

CONTROL
1 Measure performance
2 Isolate variances
3 Aid in re-planning

FEEDBACK

INFORMATION

A NON-FINANCIAL DATA
1 Market
2 Manufacturing
3 R and D
4 Personnel

B FINANCIAL DATA
1 Market
2 Manufacturing
3 R and D
4 Personnel

INFORMATION SYSTEM CHARACTERISTICS

PLANNING INFORMATION
1 Transcends organisational lines
2 Covers long time periods
3 Shows trends
4 Non-financial data important
5 Future-oriented

CONTROL INFORMATION
1 Follows organisational lines
2 Covers short time periods
3 Non-financial data important
4 Very detailed
5 Past-oriented

Fig. 6.3 Anatomy of management information

1 Payroll procedures.
2 The order processing cycle, beginning with the receipt of an order and ending with the issue of invoices and the collection of accounts receivable.
3 The procurement and accounts payable cycle.

Since so much information is within the accounting sphere, the accountant will play a most important role in reporting on accomplishments.

Financial reports are essentially statistical tables, the brevity, arrangement and content of which should all be subject to the prime test of usefulness. However, accounting statements generally describe what has already happened within the company, and omit such items as:

1 Information about the future.
2 Data expressed in non-financial terms, such as that concerning market share, productivity, quality levels and adequacy of customer service, etc.
3 Information dealing with external conditions as they might bear on a particular company's operations.

Given that all these elements are essential to the intelligent management of a business, the key to the development of a dynamic and usable system of management information is to move beyond the limits of conventional accounting reports and to conceive of information as it relates to the vital areas of planning and control.

The organisational structure of a company and its managers' information requirements are inextricably linked. In order to translate a statement of his duties into action a manager must use, as well as receive, relevant information. This involves considering all the data and intelligence – financial and non-financial – that are available, rather than relying wholly on the accounting system and the reports it produces, to satisfy a particular manager's information requirements.

A structured approach to reporting

To achieve the aim of successfully communicating the essential facts about the business to its managers, the accountant, as systems designer and operator, must have a clear conception of the purposes, possibilities and limitations of the many different types of statements and reports. Also, he must understand the problems and viewpoints of their users in order to ensure that they, in turn, appreciate the true meaning, and limitations, of the reports that he prepares for them.

At each level of management, and especially at the lower levels of the hierarchy, the accountant should pose two questions:

1 What are the necessary and controllable factors pertinent to the level of authority in question?
2 In what form are they best presented to aid in decision making at this level?

At this stage, the two complementary forms of controlling corporate activities must also be considered. They are:

1 Control against long range objectives or plans.
2 Control against standards, representing short term goals or targets.

Both forms are essential to effective overall control, but top management is more interested in the former, and supervisory management in the latter, for obvious reasons.

A structured approach to reporting by areas of responsibility will enable top management to view the results and efficiencies of individual departments in the light of their contributions to overall objectives. If corrective action is required from the top, this may well indicate a failure to achieve control at a lower level.

Similarly, the existence of a time lag between actual events and the reporting of these events, through the top management control system, may create the need for corrective action that is more drastic than if such action had been instituted at a lower level of control which could be associated more closely with the actual events.

This requires that the interface of top management with subordinate management control systems should provide a rapid feedback of financial data to the former. Without this rapid feedback, when top management is obliged to instigate corrective action it is often found that this action is delayed, that it becomes more complex and that more people become involved. This is not the most favourable setting for effective control.

Within the control framework, the characteristics of good reports are that they should:

1 Be oriented towards the user, considering both his level and function.

2 Give as much information as possible in quantitative terms and flow both ways in the organisation.

3 Be based on a flexible system that allows quick changes to meet new conditions.

On a tangible plane, succinctness is a great virtue in reporting, while on an intangible plane, one major advantage of an adequate reporting system is that the mere act of reporting requires a manager to pause and think.

INTERNAL FINANCIAL REPORTING AND MANAGEMENT CONTROL

Definition and distinctions

Management control can be defined as the use of a reliable, readily understood and sensitive system of information and standards which ensures that resources are obtained and used effectively and efficiently in the accomplishment of the company's objectives.

Clear distinctions should be drawn between:

1 Strategic planning, which is concerned with overall policies and objectives.

2 Management control (as defined above, which has a month by month focus).

3 Operational control (relating to day to day tasks).

To illustrate these different activities we can consider the setting of financial policies as a strategic planning activity, whereas planning and reporting on working capital requirements is a management control matter. At a more detailed level, the control of credit extensions falls within the sphere of operational control.

Financial reporting subsystems within managerial accounting are therefore an important element of management control, which should be their primary focus. Management control has the following characteristics:

1 It is complex because it is concerned with the total organisation.

2 The information within it tends to be precise, integrated, and developed within a prescribed set of procedures.

3 Although communication is difficult, it aims to lead to desired results by catering for the needs of many personnel, especially

line and top management.

4 It has its roots in social psychology and the mental activities involved are those of persuasion and motivation over a relatively short time span.

Accounting systems themselves cannot be the starting point in constructing an overall system, since it is management control rather than pure accounting that deals with the on-going operation of the whole enterprise. Internal financial reporting systems are subsystems of both the management control system and the financial accounting system, but in the case of conflict, the needs of the former should predominate. In turn, however, since management control is the system around which others should be constructed, this system must itself be predominantly financial. Only in this way can it encompass all the parts of the company in common terms so as to assist management in determining that the parts are in balance.

Management control systems

In terms of management control, a suitable system may be defined as a set of policies, procedures, and associated information processing designed to give direction to corporate activities. This direction results from a knowledge of the objectives sought, the progress made towards them and the need for corrective action (if any).

While a control sytem is able to exercise a positive influence on events, the system alone cannot control; it can only help the manager to achieve control.

This he will seek to do by, first, using information and knowledge to *explain* the behaviour of phenomena making up the processes that are of interest to him. Such an understanding will enable him to *predict* future outcomes from those behaviour patterns. As a consequence of explanation and predictive ability, the manager will be able to *adapt* his decision making in order to achieve the outcomes he desires, or, to put it another way, he will be able *to exercise control*.

Feedback and effective systems

The information link between output and input (or, strictly, revised input) is the feedback channel. (See Figure 6.4). For control to be effective, information must pass along this channel rapidly. In a dynamic environment, the time interval between deviation and

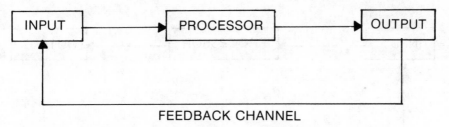

Fig. 6.4   Basic system with feedback loop

correction must be kept to a minimum.

In the psychology field, and especially in learning theory, it has been shown that motivation is maintained at a high level when the time lag between action and knowledge of results is minimised. This emphasises the need for a system to supply feedback information as rapidly as possible. Furthermore, it must be designed to report to those responsible for taking corrective action and not to intermediaries in the information networks of the company.

The danger exists that feedback carrying messages of failure may tempt the recipient to attack the control system rather than take corrective action. The concept of individual aspiration levels is especially relevant in this context. Furthermore, feedback may show that objectives are unattainable in terms of corporate, as distinct from individual, aspiration levels, in which case corrective action should take the form of a search for alternative objectives that are attainable.

It should always be recognised that systems and feedback seldom operate perfectly. In addition, people and equipment (as facilitating agents) are usually far from perfect and, even when constrained by a system, frequently produce peculiar problems and situations.

Characteristics of cybernetic systems

When the input-output model of a system is fully developed with feedback loops, one enters the domain of self-regulating or cybernetic models. (This type of system is illustrated in Figure 6.5.)

Such systems are closed rather than open; they operate independently of the human factor once established. The best example is, perhaps, a simple thermostat. The computer (suitably programmed with decision rules) is the analogous business example.

Complexity characterises cybernetic systems, with the proliferation

143

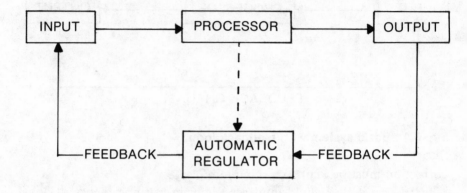

Fig. 6.5 Basic cybernetic system

of variety characterising the control problem. ('Variety' in this context relates to the number of distinguishable elements or variables in the business situation.)

Cybernetics, described as the science of control and communication in the animal and the machine by the man who coined the term, specifically sets out to recognise, describe and handle (through feedback principles) the complexities of the real world. By considering 'variable' systems (that is, those that exist beyond a certain complexity barrier), it never errs by treating systems in an over simplified way.

STAFFING AND OPERATING THE MANAGEMENT CONTROL SYSTEM

The organisational implications of the systems approach are not such as to require wholesale changes in the organisational structure, or in administrative behaviour. While some would suggest significant (and commendable) changes, from the financial point of view it is mainly necessary to ensure that accountants take a company-wide view in discharging their duties.

The accounting department

The size of the company will determine the degree of specialisation and exact staffing requirements. However, the starting point will be the statement of objectives, from which the organisational plan for the accounting department can be derived by:

1 Preparing an organisational chart with job specifications for all accounting posts.
2 Appointing suitably qualified people to these posts.
3 Instituting effective methods of controlling these persons once in post.

In a company of any size, the dichotomy between reporting on stewardship (to shareholders, bankers, etc.) and to management will be recognised by the appointment of a financial accountant with responsibility for the former, and a management accountant with responsibility for the latter.

Together with the duties of the internal auditor, these functions will typically be co-ordinated by the chief accountant (or financial controller). In a similar manner, the management accountant will co-ordinate the duties of the budget officer and the cost accountant along with their staff, whilst the financial accountant will co-ordinate the payroll, bought ledger, sales ledger, cashiers and general sections of his department.

The budget committee

The budget committee is responsible, on a consultative basis, for overseeing the preparation of budgets. It usually consists of several members of the top management group, together with the budget officer who will act as convenor and secretary to the committee.

This committee establishes the general guidelines to be followed in budget preparation, and subsequently exists to:

1 Resolve inter-departmental differences in preparing budgets.
2 Offer general advice on the preparation of budgets.
3 Co-ordinate the preparation of budgets.
4 Scrutinise budget reports, comparing results with the plan and submitting appropriate recommendations upwards or down-wards as the situation demands.

It is emphasised that budget proposals should be made by the line organisation (subject to modification and approval from above), with the budget committee forming an advisory group responsible for the consolidation of the budget and the speed and accuracy of the budgetary process, rather than for the detailed content of the budget.

Management control/systems committee

The establishment of a management control committee, composed of senior executives from all functions, should increase the probability of success in adopting systematic control procedures.

As with the budget committee, it should not be responsible for designing or imposing systems upon the organisation, but should play a role of guidance, leadership and co-ordination. Its particular aims may be:

1 Welding the whole company into a team, working continually towards systems improvement.
2 Aiding this team by providing technical assistance.
3 Both controlling and evaluating the results of system development from a managerial point of view.

CONCLUSION

An effective reporting and control system must be based on personalised organisational centres of responsibility, and be sufficiently flexible to maintain a high level of motivation. Within this framework, usefulness must always be the overriding consideration.

7

Budgets and budgetary control

Alan R Leaper

All businesses have some form of budgetary control in existence whether or not they recognise it or call it by that name. Someone in the organisation co-ordinates the resources of the business in some degree to achieve some sort of plan, but whether they examine alternative plans, ideal criteria and harmony of objectives is possibly another question.

There are many benefits to be derived from the introduction of a formalised budgetary control system, among which are:

1 It defines the objectives of an organisation as a whole and in financial terms.
2 It provides yardsticks by which to measure efficiency for various parts of the organisation.
3 It reveals the extent by which actual results have varied from the defined objective.
4 It provides a guide for corrective action.
5 It facilitates centralised control with delegated responsibility.

The disadvantages of a formalised procedure are by no means so readily identifiable; in general terms they usually concern the following:

1 The additional costs/personnel necessary to perform the function.
2 The suspicions aroused by its introduction, that it is merely another vehicle to implement cost reduction programmes.
3 The complacency of paper work becoming routine with the eventual possibility that little notice or action is taken.

Immediate benefits should not be expected from the introduction of a budget procedure; it may take a year or two to educate those concerned in the proper compilation of the data required and in the proper application of the data subsequently made available.

WHAT IS A BUDGET?

A budget in business planning is the expression in financial (and rather summarised) terms of a comprehensive short term operational plan for a business entity. The financial numbers relate to specific action programmes which give rise to asset acquisitions and disposals, earning of revenues and incurring expenses. A budget in which the financial numbers have been 'pulled out of the air' is worse than useless.

Many alternative plans may be considered before the final one showing the most practical profit is chosen. Executives and other responsible officials from all functions of the company must contribute towards the plan. Data in the unit terms of each of the functions concerned must be collected and translated into monetary terms. For example, the sale manager is primarily concerned with units of the finished article or service and would therefore contribute the volume and models to be included in the plan. The production manager talks in standard hours and efficiencies. The personnel manager will be responsible for the levels of wage rates, absenteeism factors, welfare schemes, etc. The chief executive must be fully convinced of the benefits to be derived from the plan and really believe in it.

Budgetary control is the process of managing these facets – planning and co-ordinating all functions so that they work in harmony and control performances and costs. It establishes the responsibility, throughout the corporate structure, of all managers for achieving the company's budgeted objectives. It entails measuring at suitable intervals how the plan is actually progressing and, if divergencies are occurring, taking the necessary corrective action to ensure that the company gets back on course again.

By having a budget built up in this manner it is possible to fix responsibility at every level of the organisation – and this is important.

Most managements have found that it is not sufficient to face the problems of a business on a day to day basis or even on a year to year basis; medium term operational (or programme) planning is therefore carried out over a time horizon of three to five years ahead. Generally, such planning involves a projection of the total market for the company's products and an assessment of what the company's share of that market should be, based on historical performance and management objectives. Obviously the degree of accuracy of the projections and plans varies with the period covered. In practice, in view of the many uncertainties involved in projecting activities over, say, a three-year period, the usual procedure is to prepare plans for the first year in considerable detail, and then to resort to summary projections for the remaining two years. As each year's plan is done, refinements are made on the basis of recent experience and a new third year is added.

BUDGET CENTRES

Efficient control requires acceptance that costs are best controlled at the point where they are incurred. The transport manager should therefore control the transport department's costs. The span of control of any one person should not be unduly large, however.

The area controlled by an individual is known as a budget centre. The Institute of Cost and Management Accountants has defined a budget centre as:

> *A section of the organisation of the undertaking defined for the purposes of budgetary control.*

The budgets prepared at a given level of budget centre are then consolidated at the next level up (profit centre, division or company, as the case may be).

A substantial business organisation will generally comprise a number of operating units, each of which has primary responsibility for its own profits and cash flow, (profit centres) as well, perhaps, as its capital investment (investment centres).

Thus, a business may comprise several profit centres, and in a larger organisation these may be grouped into investment centres or divisions. Each division will normally have its own financial controller who will prepare the divisional master budget (see the following sections); larger profit centres may also have their own management accountants who prepare the draft profit and loss and cash budgets.

Within the budget centre there may be other smaller areas to which costs are attributable and for which it is deemed desirable to control a particular group of assets. For example, in the transport department fleet vehicles may be grouped by type or area. Each such smaller group may be defined as a cost centre.

The Institute of Cost and Management Accountants has defined a cost centre as being:

> *A location, person or item of equipment, or a group of these, in or connected with an undertaking in relation to which costs may be ascertained and used for purposes of cost control.*

One person only should be responsible for incurring costs within the defined budget centre and the ultimate responsibility for budgetary control lies with the chief executive.

COMPILING A BUDGET

There is really no established order in which budgets should be prepared provided all parts are geared into a common factor. This is generally the principal limiting or bottleneck factor which varies for each individual company.

Most companies tend to establish a sales target determined on market potential and their share of the market as the basis of their budgets. Many others prefer to establish their production capacity and plan a budget to ensure the full utilisation of available equipment. The ideal, of course, is to achieve a harmony of both of these important items. However, many other factors may determine the level of activity to be budgeted, among which are insufficient cash to finance expansion, a scarce raw material, and a possible shortage of skilled labour.

Having established the basis for compiling the budget all known external factors which could have a bearing on its fulfilment must be examined – national wage awards, sales taxes, credit squeezes, the movement of purchase prices and so on.

In larger organisations a budget committee is usually formed to review these items and determine, as best it can, the likely effect they will have on business during the period to be used in the budget. Having determined these external factors, the budget accountant/committee will advise functional and departmental managers of their effects and provide guidelines for the compilation of the subsidiary departmental budgets, the main examples of which are considered below.

Sales budget

The sales budget should show total sales in quantity and value. It may be analysed further by product, by area, by customer and, of course, by seasonal pattern of expected sales.

The main problems arise in the determination of quantities and the calculation of standard prices.

Constraints such as competitive activity (new products and aggressive pricing polices) have to be borne in mind.

The budget should be compiled by the sales manager, who will seek the opinions of his salesmen and use any statistical forecasting techniques arising from market research. Other considerations include general business and economic conditions, company policies regarding advertising, new products, supplies, product demand and plant capacity.

A special pricing study is usually helpful at this stage. It should show the complete product range, the sector of the market involved, competitive models or products (both pricing and features available), introduction dates, discount structures and advertising strategy.

In some cases, when jobbing production is involved, budgets must be made in terms of the expected sales value only.

Production budget

The production budget is a statement of the output by product and is generally expressed in standard hours. It should take into consideration the sales budget, plant capacity, whether stocks are to be increased or decreased and outside purchases.

The form the budget will take depends upon circumstances. Usually the quantities are shown for each department (known as budget centres) and information is taken from machine loading charts, material specifications, time schedules and other production or time-study records.

When computing labour cost, the average labour rate to be used depends on the wage plan in effect. For hourly rated employees not on incentive bonuses, an overall plant rate may be sufficient. In other cases, departmental or labour grade rates may be used. When a straight piece rate plan is in effect, the labour cost is the amount paid per unit produced. When other types of incentive plans are used, average labour rates that include an estimated amount of bonus payments must be computed. In companies where standard costs are used, cost accounting records can be very useful in determining budget requirements for non-productive direct labour. Many cost accounting systems are sophisticated enough to indicate the extent to which direct labour is non-productive and involves down time, waiting time, changeover or set-up time and so on.

The production budget will be prepared by the plant manager in close co-operation and collaboration with accountants, production engineers, work study engineers and other key personnel. Adequate lead times for delivery of new equipment and/or development of new processes will be considered.

At this stage, the sales and production budgets should be compared to ensure the maximum utilisation of capacity aligned to satisfactory sales growth. If the sales budget exceeds the production capacity, decisions on capital expenditure and new plant may be required before proceeding further. If significant under-utilisation of existing capacity is denoted, examination of how best to use this spare capacity must be undertaken to determine, for instance, if sub-contract work is profitable, if a revised pricing structure could increase volume or if plant should be declared redundant and scrapped.

Production costs budget

This supplementary budget should determine the 'cost of sales' allied to the required production.

Generally, by far the largest element in cost terms is direct material. This part should be compiled by the chief buyer in conjunction with the production manager. Using the sales and production budgets, it will determine the requirements of raw material and piece-parts, period by period, to meet the output, and will be evaluated in cash cost terms. Considerations should take into account bulk buying, delivery periods, stock holding, suppliers' credit terms and trade discounts, as well as recognising any changes in material specifications, new model introductions, etc. In timing such purchases as raw materials and piece-parts, consideration must be given to the necessity to keep inventory levels to the very minimum and thereby not tie up valuable capital. Competitive pricing exercises should be undertaken with potential suppliers to ensure that costs are strictly controlled and keen.

Direct labour is another most important element of production costs. The work study department should be called upon to establish standard times for individual units. These may then be evaluated by the required volumes and converted into direct labour needs. The degree of labour efficiency must be determined, as must the type of employee necessary, that is, male/female; skilled/semi-skilled/unskilled.

Direct expense budgets covering warehousing, transport, warranty and special tools should be determined by the appropriate managers responsible for incurring or approving the respective expenses.

Factory overhead costs (burden) should be established by departmental foremen and consolidated by the production manager. Expenses of all types should be considered and some assistance may be necessary from the finance department in determining depreciation, insurance and other expenses possibly beyond the control of the local foremen.

Chapter Eight provides further guidance on establishing production cost standards.

Personnel budgets

This is a headcount schedule of the total labour requirements necessary to carry out the sales and production budgets and, in fact, run the whole business from managing director to office boy and production worker to office cleaner. It should be prepared by the personnel department in conjunction with all other functional departmental heads.

The schedule will show the number of personnel required, the hours to be worked, wage rates, salaries, etc., and should be built up by departments. The respective costs should, of course, be included in the applicable departmental budgets. The recruitment and training policies of the company will be incorporated in the budget and cognisance should be taken of all labour related costs, for example, national insurance and pension schemes.

Operating and service department budgets

The type of department falling into this category may be administration, finance, selling, advertising and service, and may also include warehousing and shipping.

The departmental head of each of these functions will be responsible for compiling his individual budgets. The data included will cover personnel requirements by number and grade and be cost-determined in conjunction with the personnel manager; it will cover departmental running costs detailed by account, namely, utilities, operating expenses, depreciation, insurance, rates, and so on.

Special note should be taken of competitors' activity in determining the size and use of the advertising budget.

If raw material or bulk purchases are necessary, the usage and cost of these will be planned with the purchasing agent or chief buyer.

The basis of determining costs included in these budgets invariably depends on the established trend in previous years, adjusted for known changes. It should also be remembered that historical costs will include inefficiencies and these must be identified and determined if likely to continue. The considered effects of volume and activity should also be borne in mind.

Capital expenditure budget

This supplementary budget is usually compiled by senior management in conjunction with engineering and technical services.

The budget will show details of the capital expenditure proposals in the period of the master budget and will probably be prepared for a number of years ahead because of its longer term implications. Items included will be distinguished by the various types of assets – land, buildings, equipment, furniture, etc., and should also state the reasons for proposals – for example, replacement, new methods, capacity.

Back-up data should also accompany the proposals to justify the expenditures. This will take the usual forms of capital evaluations, such as return on investment and discounted cash flow analysis. The strain on cash resources should also be considered when compiling this budget.

Profit and loss account

The first component of the master budget is the budgeted profit and loss account. This budget will summarise the effects of all the relevant data contained in the supplementary operating and service department budgets, sales, purchasing, personnel and capital expenditure (depreciation, salvage receipts) budgets. It will be prepared in months or other chosen periods and be compiled by the financial controller. A sample profit and loss statement incorporating provisions for budget and standards is shown in Table 7.1.

Table 7.1

Example of a profit and loss statement

	BUDGET	%	STANDARD	%	ACTUAL	%	VARIANCE
CURRENT MONTH							
Gross Sales							
Less: Deductions from sales							
Total Net Sales							
Manufacturing Standard Costs							
Material							
Labour							
Burden							
Direct expense							
Total Standard Costs							
Standard Manufacturing Gross Profit							
Budget and Volume Variances							
Actual Manufacturing Gross Profit							
Expenses							
Selling							
Advertising							
Administrative							
Engineering							
Total Expenses							
Operating Profit							
Other Income and Deductions							
Net Profit Before Taxes							
Income Tax Provision							
Net Profit							

Cash budget

The second component of the master budget is the cash budget, which is critical in view of the possible constraints that an unsatisfactory cash position may have on the required expansion of a business and hence on the acceptability of the master budget as a whole.

The financial controller, with the assistance of all other management, should determine the timing by period, usually monthly, of production, sales, fixed asset purchases etc., and then calculate the effects on the cash balance. The reason for this budget is to determine by period where additional cash may be required or where surplus cash may be available for short term investment.

The income side is built up from the sales and debtors budget plus any other miscellaneous receipts, such as loans, new capital, sale of assets, grants, interest. The expenditure side will show the incurred expenses of the production and service department budgets, purchasing and capital expenditure budgets plus other payments relating to the distribution of profits, such as dividends and income taxes.

Balance sheet

The third component of the master budget is the projected balance sheet which will show the net effect of the budgets on the financial position of the company. Again, being compiled by the financial controller, it will consider information contained in the budgeted profit and loss account, capital expenditures and cash and the related movement of the working capital and financing.

Management must examine these results of the profit and loss, cash and balance sheet master budgets that result from consolidating the subsidiary budgets and determine if they are acceptable. Do they show the most practicable overall profit to be accepted as a plan for the ensuing year or period to be budgeted? If the answer is negative then the problem areas should be determined and the departments concerned advised specifically of their shortcomings. As all the budgets are mainly inter-related, such a change generally entails resubmission of all the subsidiary budgets. This exercise may appear to be rather long-winded and even time wasting, but one of the real values of preparing budgets in this manner is that the consideration, discussion and communication of the short term profit objective of the company involves all levels of management in its achievement, and by this process is most likely to reveal the maximum practicable profit objective for the company.

In practice, a lot of companies tend to take either sales or production in isolation and agree independently what the level of activity should be in these fields; once decided on, they proceed to build all the other budgets around them. If the resultant profit is in excess of the outlook for the current year, they are happy to leave it as such. However, assuming that the job is to be tackled properly, it is at this stage of review that any attempts at over budgeting or, worse still, conservative budgeting, should be weeded out. The level of responsibility for performance of the plan from each manager should be agreed upon, so that he fully commits himself to its attainment.

When the master budgets have been finally agreed and accepted, they should be adopted formally by management as its policy and plan for the forthcoming year or period and thereby provide a budget against which performance or achievement will be measured.

CONTROLLING THE PLAN

As indicated, the budgets are built up by progressive areas of responsibility. It follows, therefore, that operating statements will be prepared for each of the budget centres involved. These should form part of the management information system used to control actual performance against the budget plan.

Good budgetary control follows the management theory of 'management by exception.' While management is given full details of expenditure, sales, production, etc., under its functional control, reports and information should be focused on matters that are adverse, or that show an unusual favourable variance, so that its energy is concentrated in the right direction and its effort is not diluted by a lot of information which merely indicates that things are going as planned.

There are differing schools of thought on the amount of detail that should be provided to management. Some management accountants prefer to provide only data over which managers have some degree of control. For instance, if depreciation policy is decided by the board, there is no point in giving an operational manager a depreciation charge for, say, the machine shop. He has no control over what that charge will be; according to this theory, this information is unnecessary and does not help him to perform his part of the plan under normal conditions. This theory does not give management the full picture and lacks the important benefit of enabling management to see the overall effect and contribution of its department to the business as a whole. The statement may be broken down into two sections labelled 'controllable' and 'uncontrollable.' Just what is controllable or uncontrollable can be surprising. For example, if a shop foreman is shown a list of fixed assets in his area on which there is a depreciation charge he may well indicate items of equipment which are surplus to his requirements but for which he has not bothered to raise a disposal request. These items can then be removed from the department and sold at good salvage prices, releasing valuable floor space, eliminating routine maintenance checks and saving administration time and effort searching for and identifying equipment at physical inventory time.

Timing of feedback

When considering the subject of control the question of timing is of great importance. When should the measurement of control be effected and over what period? Having decided the period the budget is to cover, which is usually annual (see the next section), the budget itself will be set out in terms of sub-periods: months and/or quarters, or perhaps a thirteen four-weekly basis for the subject year, depending on the type of business. In addition to the detailed annual budget, most companies have some form of long range plans for a number of years ahead, covering, for instance, the profit and loss account, balance sheet, cash flow and probably capital expenditures.

This longer term planning concerns itself primarily with determining whether or not the internal fund flow of the business will cover its commitments and capital expenditure programme, etc., but of course the longer term plans will not be prepared in anything like the same detail as the yearly short term operating budget. It is a matter of individual company requirements to determine which data is best controlled on a quarterly, monthly, weekly or even daily basis.

An organisation needs a fairly sophisticated accounting system to generate and disseminate information on a daily basis and this type of data is generally confined to production data. Standard hours produced, finished units, efficiences, absenteeism, etc., all lend themselves to daily control. Billings in terms of unit sales and value would best be reviewed on a weekly basis, although for local consumption this, again, may be preferred on a rough daily basis. All other profit and loss and cash flow data would be embodied in monthly financial statements and a balance sheet could be prepared on a quarterly basis.

The best system for a business must be determined by the constraints within which it works and what is needed to control the situation. Normally, data of a daily and weekly nature is restricted to middle management to facilitate operational control and is not fed through the pyramid of top management unless a special situation demands such close control. As a general rule, the lower down the management line one goes, the sooner information should be in management's hands. The foreman should have his output in standard hours measured against budget and his material usage for his batch of machines during the following morning so that he can take the necessary action to correct any deviation from his target.

Thus it has been said that this first-line information is the life blood of the business, and the accounting results which follow at the end of the month confirm and quantify an already known situation.

FLEXIBLE BUDGETS

One criticism of budgetary control which is sometimes raised is its rigidity, where actual results may be the outcome of circumstances which have changed since the budget was originally prepared.

Budgets, when set and agreed upon, can only take into consideration one set of circumstances. As actual conditions seldom equate with budgeted conditions, the difference between actual costs and budgeted costs must be demonstrated. Information should, therefore, be available to suggest the appropriate level of expenses, generally known as budget standards, which fluctuate at varying levels of production activity or sales volume.

In order to achieve control of this situation, flexible budgetary control was introduced – as opposed to fixed budgets. Flexible budgeting is applied in businesses where it is impossible to make a firm forecast of the future conditions. Fixed budgeting should be satisfactory for the more stable industries; however, these are very few and far between and flexible budgeting is more widely applicable.

Flexible budgeting is designed to provide a more realistic picture of the variance between actual expenses and budgeted expenses. One expects to be able to distinguish that part of the variance which is due to volume and for which a manager will not have control, and that part of the variance over which the manager should have control. To achieve this, one must be in a position to calculate budget standards at varying levels of activity.

The application of this calculation is demonstrated below by considering first a report on the basis of fixed budgeting and then showing a similar report calculated on a flexible budgeting basis. Before looking at these reports, it must be clear that costs are classified for flexible budgeting purposes. This in itself is a most difficult task and one that may be tackled in many ways which cannot be amplified in this chapter. However, for the purpose of this exercise, the following broad categories are used:

1   Fixed costs. Costs which do not vary in the short term with volume.
2   Variable costs. Costs which do so vary.
3   Semi-variable costs. Costs which will vary with volume but not in direct relationship.

The chapter on costing provides detailed examples of these types of expenses; of course, if standard costing is already applied in the company, the setting of a flexible budget is rendered considerably easier. If standard costs are not available, the technique of marginal costing will need to be applied in dealing with individual costs to determine the degree of variability. Scatter graphs or the regression theory may be used. Table 7.2 is based on fixed budgeting and demonstrates how much the actual is off target. This type of measurement is an improvement on, say, measuring against last year's performance when

Table 7.2
Example of fixed budgeting

Expense type	Budget £	Actual £	Variance £
Material	10 000	12 500	+ 2500
Labour	5000	5900	+ 900
Rent	3000	3000	—
Salaries	1000	1100	+ 100
	19 000	22 500	+ 3500

circumstances may have been different. The report provides some conception of the amount by which actual experience varies from budgeted plans.

However, if one is to adhere to one of the basic principles of budgetary control, that people should only be responsible for costs over which they have control, this report may not provide the solution.

Table 7.3 applies similar information but is calculated on the basis of flexible budgeting. Thus, clearly, the advantages of flexible budgeting are demonstrated by the second report. It shows in reality that instead of the manager being responsible for an adverse variance of £3 500 as he was in the first report, he is, in fact, only responsible for the adverse variance of £500, the remaining £3 000 being due to increased volume in production which may be the result of conservative sales forecasting, or some other factor which must be taken up with a different department in the organisation.

Flexible budgeting is thus extremely useful for getting behind the causes of variances, particularly if quantities, as well as costs, have

Table 7.3
Example of flexible budgeting

		BUDGET		ACTUAL	VARIANCE ANALYSIS	
	Standard per unit	Fixed budget	Flexed budget		Control-lable	Volume
Output in units		10 000	12 000	12 000	—	+2000
% of original budget		100%	120%	120%	—	+20%
		£	£	£	£	£
Variable costs						
Material	£1.00	10 000	12 000	12 500	+500	+2000
Labour	£0.50	5000	6000	5900	−100	+1000
Fixed costs						
Rent		3000	3000	3000	—	—
Salaries		1000	1000	1100	+100	—
Total		19 000	22 000	22 500	+500	+3000

been budgeted. For example, with sales variances one can determine whether the variance is due to prices, volume, outlet mixture, product mixture or a combination of all these elements.

USE OF COMPUTERS

Generally, manual methods of making the planning computations are time consuming, with the result that only a few alternative plans of operation can be fully evaluated when setting a budget and analysis of variances may be limited by time constraints. Computerised financial models have been developed to assist in simulating the results under many different assumptions as to volume, products and plans of operation. Most steps in budgeting involve some alternative assumptions or decisions, and the final outcome of the budget process can vary greatly in terms of the profits and resources which will result from each assumption or decision. As a practical matter, the burden of making the planning and budgeting computations under even one set of assumptions is generally considered to be all that a company can expect its people to carry in addition to their other operating responsibilities. Very often the work is such that deadlines are missed and budgets for the new year are not available on time. The computerised financial model takes the drudgery out of the calculations, once the computer programs are prepared, by applying the given relationships to different sets of assumptions and conditions. This process of simulating different methods of operations is a big help in exploring the alternatives available in the planning process.

ZERO-BASE BUDGETING

Zero-base budgeting is a technique for short term operational planning, whereby existing levels of expenditure on ongoing activities are systematically questioned. This is in contrast to the more common 'incremental' approach. In incremental budgeting, the benchmark tends to be the level of activity and expenditure in the immediate past, budget proposals being related to this in terms of 'more' or 'less'. In Zero-base budgeting, the benchmark is the 'minimum survival' level of activity and expenditure as seen by the manager of the activity in question. If the budget proposal is only to maintain the existing level of activity, assuming this to be above the 'minimum survival' level, the proposal must explain why the additional expenditure involved over and above the 'minimum survival' level is justified. A manager in charge of several activities will be required to state which level of expenditure on each of these activities he would choose if he could only spend, say, 80 per cent of his budget. The point of this approach is to squeeze out 'budget slack' at the lower levels of decision making and to allow the senior levels to decide how, if at all, the balance of the budget will be spent.

INSTALLING THE SYSTEM

The organisational chart should be examined with a view to determining where the responsibility for sales, costs and profits really lies. Revisions, where appropriate, may be considered at this time. The organisation structure should be so developed as to fix responsibility right down the line. There must be an organisation chart which clearly defines the levels of responsibility and the chain of command, setting out who is responsible for what and to whom. It is desirable to support each functional position with a job description defining the function, duty and responsibility. Tradition must be ignored, responsibility and control being given to those who are responsible for taking the decisions, but care must be taken to preserve the 'business flair' of an organisation, and those given the responsibility should be placed where their individual resources can be used best.

The key factors should then be determined before designing the system most suitable to the company's needs. The system design should cover flow diagrams of the information generated, collection data necessary for budget preparation and control reports to be subsequently prepared. During this period consideration should be given to the level of sophistication of the existing information system, whether the proposed system will provide an improvement and also the level of human resources with which one has to work the new system.

Having obtained a positive reaction to these considerations, the next step is to test the initial design with various personnel at all levels in order to determine its suitability to meet their requirements for management information.

Once initial design is finalised, the next step is to prepare a series of seminars and teach-ins to explain the thinking behind the purpose and operation of the system. Questions, constructive criticisms and improvements should be invited so that all are involved and communicate at all levels.

A timetable for installation of the programme should be established. A critical path analysis is the ideal basis for identifying the order in which the budget data should be collected and which information is to be cross-referred to two or more departments.

Now is the time for the collection of information for the 'first budget.' Considerable time, assistance and guidance should be made available to staff at this stage, and perseverance on behalf of those taking responsibility for the installation of the system will be required. It is vital that all levels of management go through the discipline of thinking through and preparing their portion of the budgets. Miracles should not be expected from the first results. It is not unusual for a company to take two or three years to get a control system of this nature fully operational. However, at each stage one should expect to produce some results which are usable even in the first year. What these results will be may differ from company to company but initially they usually provide a good insight to sales and cash flow data. An important by-product is management education and awareness of what the business is all about.

Budget period

There is no general rule governing the selection of a period of time for a budget. This will be decided by the particular circumstances of the business. For instance the fashion industry must, of necessity, have a very short budget period, sometimes of three or four months duration, whereas in the shipbuilding industry a budget may range over three or four years. For most businesses, however, the calendar year is normally the accepted period: it is broken down into twelve monthly periods and the information is complementary to the published accounts.

However, if there is a strong seasonal influence affecting sales, it is sometimes prudent to have a 'model year' upon which to base the budget and this usually starts just ahead of the main selling period. Businesses which rely mainly on the summer or Christmas trade may well justify a model year. Model years, as the name implies, usually commence with the introduction of new models. A car manufacturer, for example, may run its model year from September to the following

August in order to have a good start to the year following the autumn motor shows and new year car registrations. The motive behind this is that if business has not gone as well as expected there is still sufficient time before the end of the model year to curtail activity, restrict costs and reconsider expansion programmes or introduce special promotions in order to keep profits in line with, or better than, budget.

Budget manual

It is helpful to have such a document available within the company so that there is no ambiguity about what is required of each individual in relation to budgets. The type of information one might expect the budget manual to contain is a brief explanation of the purposes of budgetary control as practised within the company and organisation charts and job descriptions showing the specific budget responsibilities for each function; routing of budgetary control forms for collection and control documentation; timetables or programmes for completion of budgets and control data feedback; budget periods; samples of reports and statements to be employed and accounts classification and coding data.

Budget committees

The question of who should control the preparation of the budgets and who should review these controls is one that each organisation arrives at during some stage of the budget preparation.

It is desirable that top and middle management contribute to and agree levels of activity to be budgeted, although it must be recognised that the human factor involved makes this difficult to achieve. A keen manager, anxious to please at a budget review meeting, will possibly incorporate a stretch element to his plan. Another manager setting his own targets against which his performance will be measured may be inclined to be over cautious (particularly if an achievement bonus is paid). Investigations have been made in this area and the results carry important lessons for the businessman interested in making the most of his budget system. One conclusion is that the budgets studied were used as pressure devices for constantly increasing efficiency, but because of the effects on people, the budgets tended to generate a long run result of decreased efficiency. Naturally enough, this is attributed to the lack of participation in the budget preparation phase by those being budgeted and to the lack of sales ability on the part of accounting personnel. Another study concludes that successful budgeting is more concerned with human relationships than with accounting techniques and that if good principles of human relationships are applied, successful budget practices will be inevitable. Yet another appraisal of current business budgeting indicates that important weaknesses in practice are the result of superficial appreciation of budget concepts by management, inadequate techniques, and the absence of a disciplined environment in many organisations. Upon reflection, it becomes apparent that the requirements for a successful budget operation are not restricted to accounting or finance planning techniques but that successful managers are those who keep wider considerations in mind while executing the more mechanical aspects of the budget process.

Various views are held on this point of responsibility. If operating managements are made responsible for profits, then one of the objectives of budgetary control, that is, the proper co-ordination of the organisation, is achieved.

The same processes should be involved as with the control aspect. What an organisation should attempt to achieve is the total commitment of all levels of management to the plan. Each level of management should review its plans and performances through the usual management committees, be they formal or informal groupings, right up to the chief executive, and the overall objective should be clear and unambiguous at each stage.

However, one person will be responsible for pulling together the various parts of the master budget. This job usually falls on the chief accountant or financial controller or his department. Larger companies employ a budget manager and, of course, this co-ordinating exercise naturally falls into his lap. He may be called upon to undertake a number of exercises to determine what the various results thrown up mean within the overall company objectives, but it must be emphasised that his role is one of support. The responsibility is fixed upon the persons committing and accepting stewardship over resources.

The budget organisation can be regarded as analogous to a telephone company operating an important communications system; it is responsible for the speed, accuracy and clarity with which the messages flow through the system, but not for the content of the messages themselves.

Information codes

Budgetary control has extended control information beyond the more traditional accounting information to broader aspects of control, setting out data in terms of hours worked, output of production in standard hours, information on market share, quality of product, etc. This is all necessary for the achievement of the plan. However, looking at the pure accounting contribution to budgetary control, a suitable system of accounts coding should be designed so that the information is collected and analysed within the budget and cost centres.

The accounting code should be what is commonly called a subjective/objective system. The subjective part of the code should qualify information into its primary or traditional classification, that is, the nature of the expense, for example wages, fuel, rent, etc. The objective part of the code will be used to analyse the expenditure to the cost and burden centres, that is, machine X in the machine shop.

It is important to give considerable thought to the design of the coding system, as it should not only allow for coping with existing needs for information, but also have the flexibility to be expanded to meet future demands. A system of this sort should enable a company, using the subjective code, to produce information necessary for the preparation of the traditional statutory accounts. And by going through the objective section of the code, the information required for budgetary control and management accounting can be produced which should be made available to those drawing up the budgets as appropriate.

CONCLUSIONS

Budgetary control often strikes apprehension or fear into non-financial people. People tend to be sceptical or mistrust having their performances measured against a standard. This is a human and understandable response. Most people, at some time during their careers, have had budgetary control used against them as a cost reduction tool.

It is up to finance managers, to clarify and emphasise that budget flexing and control is an essential and deliberate need of modern day management. It is a management tool designed as a *fair* basis upon which to measure performance against a predetermined plan, and conduct business in the most efficient manner possible, thereby improving profitability.

8

Costing and internal pricing

H W Calvert and Simon Archer

The purpose of costing is generally to find out the cost of an organisation's outputs. These can be either its final outputs (products or services made available to the outside world) or intermediate outputs used within the organisation in the production of its final outputs. Costing therefore involves two phases of fact finding activities:

1 Finding out the quantities of inputs required or used in the production of outputs.
2 Finding out the cost of those quantities of inputs.

Internal pricing refers to the situation where one organisational sub-unit produces an output which is used as an input by another sub-unit of the same organisation, and it is desired to charge the second sub-unit with a transferred-in cost.

Apart from its purely fact finding aspects, a major problem in costing arises when a number of outputs are joint products of some input. Typically this is the case with those inputs of an organisation we generally call 'overheads'. The problem here is that the determination of exactly how much of these inputs has gone into any given quantity of outputs is arbitrary. This problem occurs in a severe form in many transport businesses: how to deal with overheads or 'system costs' in working out, say, the cost per passenger mile or tonne mile. A similar difficulty arises in businesses such as petrochemicals, where a given quantity of a particular raw material is turned into a number of joint products within a sequence of processes. The problem here is how to allocate the cost of the raw material to the various joint products derived from it. Again, any such allocation is arbitrary. These kinds of *ad hoc* allocations can be misleading if they are used as data for a decision (such as product pricing) without their arbitrariness being recognised. This problem poses a particular challenge to management accountants working within the kinds of industries mentioned, but they are liable to arise to some extent in almost any kind of organisation.

The information provided by costing is clearly among the most vital to any organisation. The production and marketing activities cannot proceed in a rational manner without it. Good costing pre-supposes an accurate and detailed knowledge of how outputs are produced, and typically requires co-operation between accountants on the one hand and engineers or others having the required knowledge of the product on the other. Depending on the complexity of the product, good costing may also require the application of well developed data processing capabilities, for example computerised bill of materials systems. Often, therefore, it is best to regard costing as a co-operative effort between accountants and other colleagues having the necessary knowledge and skills.

The need for co-operation with engineers or production people is particularly evident where a standard costing approach is adopted. In standard costing, a cost is developed for each output, intermediate or final, so as to act as a norm or guideline for the purpose of cost control. Costs actually incurred can then be compared against the standards, and the *differences or variances* can be analysed in a number of ways so that requirements or opportunities for cost improvements can be identified. Standard costs may also be useful for internal pricing and as a check on prices charged for final outputs.

STANDARD COSTING

Standard costing has much in common with budgetary control, which was considered in Chapter 7. On the one hand, standard cost data can be extremely useful in compiling budgets, particularly for such items as raw material costs; on the other hand, budget data may be required to establish the standard cost allowances for overhead items. We return to these matters later in this chapter. Since costs are built up on the basis of the determination of input quantities followed by the determination of the costs of those quantities, a full standard costing approach involves standards both for the input quantities and for the unit costs applicable to those quantities. In certain cases, however, it may be possible to establish standard data for quantities but not for unit costs, or vise versa. For example, an important raw material may be subject to extreme price volatility so that the usefulness of a standard cost may be questionable; nevertheless it may be perfectly feasible and useful to establish standard quantities. Alternatively, the products may be essentially of a non-standard nature, made to customer order, so that the establishment of standard quantities may be possible only for a limited number of inputs, while the establishment of standard unit prices for those inputs may not be difficult at all.

Apart from their use in cost control, standard cost data are often more convenient to use than 'actual' cost data. For example, if a stock of raw materials is accounted for using standard costs, variances from standard purchase prices (material purchase price variances) are isolated when the materials are purchased. Thus, the raw materials may be held in stock at standard cost, and any subsequent movements of the materials out of stores and through work in progress into furnished goods stock will be likewise accounted for at standard costs. This avoids the need to establish 'actual' costs for materials subsequent to purchase, whether on a first-in-first-out, weighted-average or other conventional basis.

In costing, the original or prime inputs are conventionally divided into three categories of cost elements:

1 Materials – these are the materials which go physically into the final output in some shape or form, and this is emphasised by the frequently used term direct materials.
2 Labour – again, this category normally includes only the labour which is a direct physical input to the product, and excludes the work of supervisors etc. It is likewise frequently referred to as direct labour.
3 Overheads – which are any cost elements not falling into either of the two previously mentioned categories.

FIXING A STANDARD

Standard costing being a technique of comparisons – the actual with the standard – the first problem is to fix the standard. Three types of standard are generally considered.

Historical

This is based on costs previously achieved and may easily be ascertained, but it has two principal defects. Standard costing will be of major value when applied to an industrial unit where control has been inadequate. In such an organisation the past performance may provide a weak standard which could be easily attained and so give little incentive to management and factory supervision. Also, if standard costs based on such a foundation are used as a guide to price fixing, then either prices may be fixed at an uncompetitive level or the sales department may consider that many lines cannot be remunerative.

Ideal

This is based on the assumptions that plant will always work at full available capacity; there will be no unavoidable loss of material; the highest grade of labour will be available and there will be no lost time. Such a standard would present a target which the most energetic supervisor would not attempt to attain and a cost which could never be achieved in practice. The result might be that the sales department would be tempted to offer products at unremunerative prices.

Normal or expected

This is based, probably after work study, on agreement between the management functions concerned – production, personnel, purchasing and costing – on the levels which could be attained under normal working conditions. For most purposes this type of standard is to be preferred.

Revision of standards

In conditions of inflation, and generally when prices are unstable, it is most important that standards be kept up to date. How frequently it may be possible to revise the standards at an acceptable cost depends both on the complexity of the product involved and on the extent to which the required product information is available in an appropriate form for computerised updating of standard costs. It is not uncommon for standards to be updated more than once a year, say, six-monthly or even quarterly. On the other hand, in some industries the complexity of the product is such that a high degree of data processing sophistication is necessary for thorough updating to be feasible at all. In the absence of such a capability, reliance has to be placed upon approximate methods such as the application of indices on an across the board basis rather than on updating the costs of individual cost elements. The problem with this latter approach is that the revised standards progressively lose their character as cost norms which can be used for control purposes. Variances are as much a function of the indices being used as of cost abnormality which requires follow-up action.

In addition to updating prices or unit costs, standards must be revised whenever there is a change in the technical specification of a product. This requires co-operation between the engineering section where specification changes are worked out, the purchasing and production sections whose actions govern the introduction of the revised items, and the costing section. Lack of co-ordination after leads to a situation where inputs are being accounted for on the basis of one set of standards (typically, the new standards), while the outputs are being accounted for on the basis of another set of standards (typically, the old or unrevised standards). This discrepancy leads to an accumulation of erroneous charges or credits in the accounts for stock or work in progress.

Direct materials

The standard cost of direct materials will depend on the standard quantity of material to be used per unit produced and the standard price of that material. The quantity will be based on the specification of the product and the process losses and rejects which are agreed as the standard between production management and the cost department. The standard price will be based on the average price which should be paid over the period under consideration, taking into account that a material may have to be purchased from several suppliers.

Direct labour

Where possible the standard cost of direct labour should be based on a work study of the operations involved. This will fix the standard times for each process and, where an incentive scheme is in operation, the standard hourly rate will be that which would be payable at the standard efficiency.

Conventionally, the standard cost of direct labour tends to be considered in a manner analogous to the standard cost of direct materials, that is, as a straight forward multiple of the units of output.

In many circumstances, however, the cost of direct labour may be relatively invariable with respect to the level of output in the short term. In other words, the cost of direct labour may behave in a manner much closer to that of overheads than to that of direct materials. In such circumstances, it may be advisable to abandon or modify the conventional treatment of direct labour; for example, by treating it similarly to a semi-variable overhead as described below.

Overheads

For the purpose of standard costing, three elements of overhead costs need to be distinguished:

1 Fixed costs – costs which do not vary in the short term with volume.
2 Variable costs – costs which do so vary.
3 Semi-variable costs – costs which will vary with volume but not in direct relationship.

In determining standard unit costs of outputs, it might appear obvious that only the variable overheads can properly be taken into account. It is not possible to establish the amount of fixed or semi-variable costs at the unit level, since the amounts of such costs do not vary proportionately with the number of units. The most logical approach is to integrate the standard costs per unit with a system of flexible budgets as described in Chapter 7. With such an approach, variances with respect to unit standard costs can be identified separately from variances with respect to the budget allowances for fixed and semi-variable costs. The standard or allowed cost per unit will vary according to the level of output achieved: it is equal to the standard variable cost per unit as shown in Table 7.3 in Chapter 7 plus the total budget allowance for fixed and semi-variable costs at the relevent level of output divided by the number of units produced.

An alternative, but less satisfactory, approach is to assume a normal level of production or output, and to calculate the standard overhead cost per unit by taking the total overhead budget allowance at that level of output and dividing it by the number of units to be produced at that level. This approach gives rise to 'volume variances' whenever the level of output is different from the pre-established normal level. Given the inherent uncertainties of most business activities, however, it is questionable how informative such 'volume variances' are for control purposes. Certainly, the flexible budget approach is far more powerful for cost control purposes. Moreover, it is probably misleading to speak of a 'normal level' of output rather than a 'normal range' which will correspond to, or fall within, the range of outputs allowed for in the flexible budget. Where the 'normal level' approach is adopted, however, one of the three bases mentioned above (historical, ideal or expected) will be used for fixing the standard unit overhead cost. The appropriate procedures for dealing with overhead costs on this basis are described in the relevant sections below.

One significant advantage of the flexible budget approach is that it can be used to give guidance on what is often a very important piece of information: the additional cost, at a given level of output, of producing one or more additional units (or the costs avoided if one or more fewer units are produced). This is known as the differential or marginal cost of the units in question. The topic of marginal costing is explored later in this chapter.

COST CONTROL THROUGH VARIANCE ANALYSIS

The most important service which standard costing can give to management is information for the control of costs through variance analysis. The difference between the variation of the production for a period at standard cost and the actual cost for that period is of great use to management, but even greater is the consideration of changes in this variance from one period to another. This shows how efficiency is moving.

The standard cost of the production of each section for the period under consideration will be calculated first. This will be the quantity of each item actually produced, multiplied by its standard cost in that process. It will represent the cost which should have been incurred under standard conditions. The actual cost incurred will be available from the records kept in the financial and cost accounting departments. As already noted, it is common to account for raw materials held in stock and their subsequent movements at standard cost, the material purchase price variance being isolated upon purchase. Variances in the quantities of raw materials used will, however, be identified in production; these materials usage variances will be expressed in money using the standard prices of the materials concerned. They will be identified for particular production cost centres and perhaps, in job order type businesses, by customer order as well. Moreover, in a job order kind of business, it may be important to identify also the material purchase price variances associated with particular customer orders, and in that case actual material costs will be made available from the stores issues and invoices for materials charged direct to individual orders.

The direct and indirect labour costs of production will be available from the wages analysis. Again, the labour cost variance typically comprises a price (or rate) variance and a quantity (or efficiency) variance. These variances will be calculated for each production cost centre, and in addition, as in the case of materials, it may be necessary to identify the variances at the level of particular customer orders. Other items of overheads can be obtained from suppliers' invoices and from the apportionment of whole items of expense to the various production cost centres. The latter will apply to service charges, electricity, insurance, rates, and similar items which are not allocated in the original charge.

Direct materials

The analysis of direct material costs can be obtained in the following manner. If the standard for producing one unit of product Z is, say, 10lb of material XY at a standard price of 20p per lb, that is £2.00 per unit, and if the production in week eight is 2 000 units, the standard cost of material for the week will be

$$£2.00 \times 2\,000 = £4\,000$$

If the actual consumption of material has been 20 500 lb which has cost £4 260, there will have been an adverse direct material cost variance of £260(A), where (A) stands for 'adverse'. This information is useful to management as £260 is a significant amount which must be investigated. The variance may be due to a number of factors which must be isolated. The most important are the price and usage variances into which the direct material cost variance is usually analysed.

The direct material price variance is the difference between what the material used should have cost and what it actually cost. In this case the material used should have cost

$$£0.20 \times 20\,500 = £4\,100$$

As the actual cost was £4 260, the direct material price variance is £160(A). The quantity of material which should have been used was

$$2000 \times 10\text{lb} = 20\,000 \text{ lb}$$

so there is an excess usage of 500 lb which at the standard price of 20p, costs £100. This is the direct material usage variance which, again, is adverse. Note that the price and usage variances together make up the total direct material cost variance, that is,

$$£160(A) + £100(A) = £260(A)$$

Where more than one material is used in making a product the price variance is generally shown in respect of each material. The usage variance can be calculated for each material, but in cases where the proportions of certain materials may vary, if there is a difference in the price of the materials, a cost variance will arise from any variation in the composition of the mixture.

If an alloy is made of 70 per cent of 'X' and 30 per cent of 'B' which cost, at standard prices, £200 per ton and £300 per ton respectively, and a batch of metal is made up from 600 tons of 'X' and 400 tons of 'Y', there will be a materials mixture variance. At standard prices the 1000 tons should have cost

$$£(700 \times 200) + £(300 \times 300) = £230\,000$$

whereas it cost

$$£(600 \times 200) + £(400 \times 300) = £240\,000$$

giving a material mixture variance of £100(A).

The material mixture variance is always calculated on the standard prices after the price variance has been taken on the actual material used. The fact that the proportions of the materials in a mixture are not as standard is no guarantee that a mixture variance presents reliable information. The use of an excess of one or more of the materials may be due to process technicalities.

The direct material usage variance is defined as that portion of the direct materials cost variance which is due to the difference between the standard quantity specified and the actual quantity used. Where there is a mixture variance, the difference from standard due to the total quantity of materials used is referred to as the direct materials yield variance. The mixture and yield variances will together equal the usage variance so that where there is no mixture variance shown, the usage variance and the yield variance will be the same.

Labour

The analysis of cost variances for labour is similar to that of materials, except that the major sub-variances are referred to as rate and efficiency instead of price and usage. Each production manager will require a further analysis of the efficiency variance according to the techniques of the operations and the relative significance of the individual variances.

If, in the above mentioned case, the labour cost had been set at a standard of a production of 5 units per labour hour with an hourly wage rate at this level of productivity of 60p per hour, that is, 12p per unit, and the wages cost of production in week eight had been 420 hours, which cost £246, there would be a direct wages variance of £6(A) because the standard wages cost was

$$2\,000 \times £0.12 = £240$$

The analysis of this variance would be direct wages rate variance

$$420 \times £0.60 - £246 = £6(F)$$

The variance is favourable, (F), because the actual cost was less than the hours worked at the standard rate.

The direct labour efficiency variance will be

$$(420-400) \times £0.60 = £12(A)$$

– adverse because the actual hours worked exceeded the standard hours for the actual production.

Where a financial incentive scheme is in operation, it is generally found that an adverse efficiency variance will result in a favourable rate variance owing to the average rate earned being less than the standard. Conversely, if there is a favourable efficiency variance, the bonus will be high and there will be an adverse rate variance.

Overheads

For the purpose of variance analysis it is advisable to have the overheads divided into variable and fixed costs. A standard having been agreed for the variable overhead, the variable overhead variance can be calculated by multiplying the production for the period by this unit standard cost and comparing the result with the actual expenditure on account of the relative indirect costs. These items can be obtained from the stores requisitions, wages analysis, etc. A more detailed analysis of variable overhead variance may not be justified on account of the expense, but, if required, that part which is due to prices can be calculated, as can variances in the quantities of the items utilised.

As mentioned earlier, fixed overheads are a 'period' cost so that the unit cost must be compiled from the expenditure, production and working hours budgeted for the same period. In the case of product XYZ, assuming that the budget for the year is a production of 110 000 units to be produced in 50 working weeks of 440 hours each at a fixed overhead cost of £5 500, the unit cost of fixed overheads will thus be 5p, and the rate per hour worked 25p. If the actual fixed overhead is recorded as £122 for week eight, the standard cost of the production is

$$2\,000 \times £0.05 = £100$$

so the fixed overhead cost variance is £22(A). This variance arises from two factors: the difference between the actual expenditure (£122) and the budget amount allowed for the period (£110) which gives a fixed overhead expenditure variance of £12(A), and the difference between the actual production for the week (2 000 units) and the budgeted production (2 200 units) which gives the overhead volume variance

$$(2\,200–2\,000) \times £0.05 = £10(A)$$

Again, the expenditure variance and the volume variance add up to the fixed overhead cost variance.

$$£12(A) + £10(A) = £22(A)$$

The expenditure variance arises from the prices of the items included in the fixed overhead and the utilisation of the factors employed – higher wattage lamps being used in corridors, extra security staff being required. The volume variance is due to the production being above or below the budgeted figure, the result of the number of hours worked being above or below the budget, and the labour efficiency being favourable or adverse.

The capacity usage variance is favourable if more hours than the budgeted number have been worked. This can cause some difficulty unless it is remembered that the more hours worked, the more should be produced, other things being equal. In week eight, 420 hours were worked against a budget of 440, so there was a loss of twenty working hours which, at the fixed overhead cost of 25p per hour, is a variance of £5(A).

The volume efficiency variance is related to the labour efficiency variance if the former has been based on labour hours. In some cases it may be based on machine hours. As the production is equal to 400 standard hours there is again a loss;

$$(420-400) \times £0.25 = £5(A)$$

The capacity usage variance and the volume efficiency variance are together equal to the volume variance.

Where the fixed overhead is budgeted on a monthly basis and the number of working days in the month varies, the volume variance may include a calendar variance. This will be favourable when the number of working days in a month exceeds the average, and adverse when it is less. The greater the number of days in the month, the higher the production should be, thus tending to improve the volume variances.

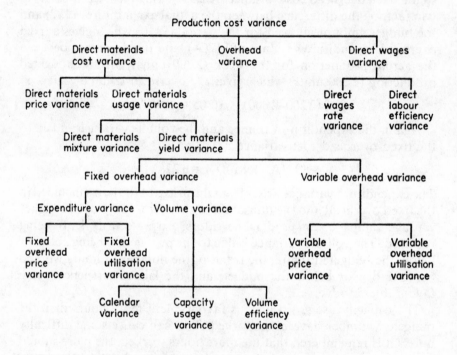

Fig. 8.1   Chart of production cost variance

Table 8.1
Example of a cost report

DEPARTMENT X   OPERATION X12A   PRODUCT XYZ

Report for week no. 8, ending 2 May 19.. Standard cost per unit: £2.22

	Budget	Standard	Actual	Variance	Analysis
Production units	2200		2000	200 (A)	
Materials lb.	22 000	20 000	20 500	500 (A)	
Labour hours	440	400	420	20 (A)	
Costs					
Direct materials £	4400	4000	4260	260 (A)	
Price					160 (A)
Usage					100 (A)
Direct labour	264	240	246	6 (A)	
Rate					6 (F)
Efficiency					12 (A)
Overhead variable	110	100	106	6 (A)	
Price					8 (A)
Utilisation					2 (F)
Overhead fixed	110	100	122	22 (A)	
Price					10 (A)
Utilisation					2 (A)
= Expenditure					12 (A)
Calendar					—
Capacity usage					5 (A)
Volume efficiency					5 (A)
= Volume					10 (A)
Totals £	4884	4440	4734	294 (A)	

Note: The standard cost for the period will bear the same ratio to the budgeted cost as the *actual* production bears to the budgeted production.

The sum of the calendar variance for the year will always be nil.

It has been shown how the total production cost variance can be analysed so as to give more accurate information regarding the cause of cost excesses and savings. A chart of this analysis, such as that shown in Figure 8.1 may be useful. It is not exhaustive and further analysis can be made to suit individual requirements.

Presentation

The presentation of the analysis of the cost variances is very important; it should be prepared so as to show the maximum information in the minimum space and with economy of figures. A cost report on week eight from the figures previously quoted might appear as shown in Table 8.1.

MARGINAL COSTING

As already mentioned earlier, the differential or marginal cost of one or more units of output is equal to the change in the total cost of output dependent on whether or not a company produces that unit or those units. In the case of one marginal unit, marginal cost is equal to the standard unit cost plus the change in the total semi-variable costs. The latter may be zero or may be relatively large depending on whether the change in output level encounters a capacity constraint and, if so, the financial implications of that constraint.

One possible capacity constraint relates to direct labour. The decision to produce the marginal unit or marginal lot of units may or may not saturate the capacity of normal shift working and give rise to overtime payments or shift premium payments which exceed the basic standard direct labour cost per unit. Such overtime or additional shift work may also call for an increase in supervisory labour expense, and so forth. In this connection, the warning given earlier about the treatment of direct labour as an element of standard variable cost per unit needs to be recalled. Direct labour used to be considered a variable cost because, if trade was slack, workers were discharged or stood off without pay. More recently, the cost of training labour, periodic difficulty in obtaining even untrained labour and the economic consequences of the guaranteed working week and redundancy provisions have tended to make labour costs a fixed expense which only changes with large and prolonged variations in the volume of production.

Marginal production cost should not, however, be taken to be identical to standard variable unit production cost. To equate these is to ignore the kinds of production capacity constraints referred to earlier. The technique of direct costing (sometimes erroneously called marginal costing or, more correctly, variable costing) involves the use of the standard variable unit cost as the basis for keeping the accounts for finished stock and work in progress. In addition, production cost variances are related either to the standard variable cost per unit on the one hand, or to the flexible budget for semi-variable and fixed expenses on the other.

Moreover, the use of flexible budgets does not concern production costs alone. It also relates to the costs of selling and distributing output. Here too, some costs may vary directly with the level of sales, others may be fixed in regard to that level and others may be semi-variable. Thus, a profit and loss statement based on a marginal costing approach will generally show a 'contribution margin' which is equal to sales less total directly variable costs. This contribution margin can also be calculated at the unit level for individual products.

The term 'contribution margin' is perhaps, somewhat misleading insofar as the amount calculated as just described is not identical with the true marginal contribution to profit of the unit or units in question. This is because no account has been taken of possible changes in the level of the semi-variable expenses. Nevertheless, the standard contribution margin and variances from it have proved to be useful control tools, especially in high volume consumer product businesses where marketing activities are organised on a product management basis. For this reason, and for the sake of simplicity, the behaviour of semi-variable expenses is ignored in the following example.

The first applications of marginal costing were as a technique for use in times of trade recession when plant was under utilised and business could not be obtained at prices which would cover the total unit costs, i.e. the variable unit cost plus the total fixed expenses divided by the number of units produced. The simple example contained in Table 8.2 illustrates such a situation.

At a sales price of £8 per unit a profit of £100 000 will be made, and this may be a fair return on the capital employed in the business. However, if the plant is working at only 80 per cent of capacity the variable cost will be 80 per cent of £420 000 or £336 000. The fixed expenses will remain at £280 000, a total cost of £616 000. The sales at £8 per unit will be £640 000 giving a net profit of only £24 000. The sales department is unable to obtain any further business at £8 to fill the vacant capacity, but a customer can be found for 10 000 units at £6.50. This business appears to be unremunerative as the total cost is £7.00 per unit. However on a marginal cost basis the unit cost is £4.20, so that the price of £6.50 will show a contribution of £2.30 per unit and this will increase

Table 8.2
Marginal costing in a time of trade recession

Plant capacity	100 000 units
Cost of 100 000 units	£
Direct materials	300 000
Direct labour	100 000
Variable production overhead	10 000
Fixed production overhead	150 000
Administration expenses	80 000
Variable selling expenses	10 000
Fixed selling expenses	50 000
	£700 000 = £7 per unit

the net profit by £23 000, nearly doubling that important figure.

Useful as the marginal costing technique is, certain precautions must be observed when using it and there are certain restrictions on its use. The most significant of these are:

1 Business at such cut prices must not be taken on long term contracts where there is a chance that before the contract is completed trade may improve and orders at more remunerative prices could be booked.

2 Business must not be taken on a marginal cost basis in the same market where more normal prices are being obtained. This policy might offend established customers and, in the case of overseas business, care must be taken that the low price exports do not come back into this country in competition with the company's own sales in the home market.

BREAK EVEN GRAPHS

On the assumption that no significant distortion will occur if costs are divided into directly variable and fixed, so that variable cost is a good approximation of marginal cost, it is possible to draw simple break even graphs or profit charts. Assuming that all expenses other than directly variable costs are stable throughout the probable range of sales, the marginal cost aspect can be presented in the following manner.

A graph is drawn taking the horizontal axis as the amount of the sales, either in quantity or in value; if a number of items are sold the total figure must be expressed in value. The sales figure will start at zero and cover the maximum range of the sales. The vertical axis will represent the receipts from sales and the expenses incurred, both fixed and variable.

Having estimated the fixed expenses for the period under review, this point is located on the vertical axis and from it a line is drawn parallel to the horizontal axis. From the production cost budget and the selling cost budget the marginal cost of the budgeted sales can be ascertained. A line can now be drawn from the point on the vertical axis from which the fixed cost line started so as to show at the budgeted sales the total expenses of the organisation for that level of sales. In the graph in Figure 8.2 the fixed expenses have been taken as £280 000 per annum, and the variable costs of £100 000 units as £420 000.

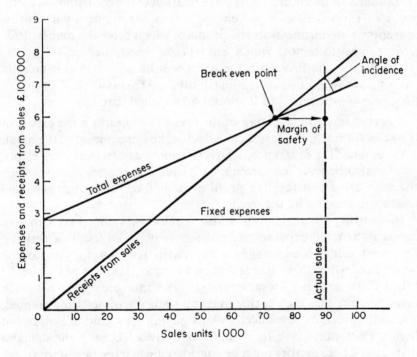

Fig. 8.2 **Example of an orthodox break even graph**

The 'receipts from sales' line can now be drawn, commencing from the origin where the vertical and horizontal axes meet to show sales of £800 000 for £100 000 units. Assuming that there is a contribution, that is, that the sales price exceeds the variable cost, this line will cut the line of total cost at a point where the receipt from sales equals the total cost. This junction is called the break even point, the level of activity at which there is neither profit nor loss. The distance of the receipt from sales line above or below the total cost line will show the net profit at the relative level of sales.

The profit/volume (P/V) ratio

The break even graph will show at a glance the sales which must be achieved to obtain any required net profit, and also the effect on the profit potential of variations in the fixed expenses and the profit volume ratio. The P/V ratio is an important factor in planning the profitability of an enterprise; it is the relation of the contribution to the net sales expressed as a percentage. A trading concern will aim to concentrate its business on the products which offer the highest P/V ratio, subject to factors which will be considered later.

The greater the P/V ratio the wider will be the angle at which the receipt from sales line cuts the line of total cost. This angle is known as the *angle of incidence* and it should be watched carefully.

Another important feature of the break even graph is the excess of the sales for any period over the sales for the same period at the break even point. This difference, which is known as the *margin of safety*, should also be watched carefully as it indicates the amount by which the sales can fall before the profit made will be reduced to zero and losses will start to be incurred.

In drawing a break even graph it must be remembered that in practice the fixed expenses are not constant for all levels of activity; they tend to increase in stages as the activity rises, but they do not fall so quickly when there is a recession in trade. Account must also be taken of the tendency for sales prices to fall if sales are pushed beyond a certain point. This may be due to larger trade discounts being granted. Variable costs may be reduced by bulk buying when trade expands, but higher rates may have to be paid for skilled labour if the demand increases. These factors must be considered when the line of total cost is drawn; in practice it will not be straight but may curve upwards or downwards.

The break even graph may be used for other purposes as well as showing the effect of varying levels of sales on the net profit. Other applications include the evaluation of different methods of distribution. Should the company run its own van or send its goods by carrier? Here the comparison is that of a fixed cost per article or per ton mile (the total cost depending on the quantity carried) with the fixed cost of a van (tax, insurance, depreciation, garage and driver's costs) plus a running cost per mile or ton mile. The break even graph may be used to show the amount of traffic which must be handled to make the introduction of the van an economic project.

The graph in Figure 8.2 shows a break even chart based on the figures given earlier. The graph in Figure 8.3 gives an indication of the effect of allowing for the behaviour of the semi-variable expenses which have been included with the fixed expenses. The effect of the capacity constraints which determine the behaviour of the semi-variable expenses is shown in the characteristic step function of the latter.

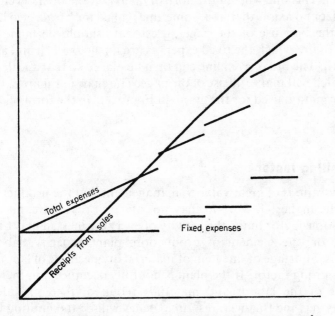

Fig. 8.3 Example of a modified break even graph

The 'profit' or 'contribution' chart

The break even graph is fairly well known in industry, but for most purposes the profit chart will present the same information in a simpler manner, with less probability of errors in drafting, and in a way which often displays the effect of a policy more clearly. In the profit chart the horizontal axis can be drawn as for the break even graph, but to obtain the best effect, the way this is positioned on the page is most important. The vertical axis will be drawn below, as well as above, the horizontal axis. It will be graded in values but, instead of showing costs and receipts from sales, it will show profits above the horizontal axis and losses below the horizontal axis.

Taking the case previously quoted, if there were no sales there would be a loss equal to the fixed expenses of £280 000. This fixes one point on the profit line; zero on the sales line and minus £280 on the profit axis. As there is a contribution of £3.80 per unit sold the profit line will start from this point and rise £3.80 per unit until, at sales of 100 000 units, the loss of £280 000 is converted into a profit of £100 000.

The graph thus drawn is that not of cost and sales but of the contribution. This line will cut the horizontal axis at the break even point; the horizontal axis is therefore sometimes called the break even line. To obtain the best use of the page an estimate should be made of the highest figure which the fixed expenses are likely to reach and also the net profit. The break even line can then be placed so that a scale can be used which will make full use of the page. The chart in Figure 8.4 shows the information used for the graph in Figure 8.2 in the form of a profit chart.

The limiting factor

The P/V ratio is of great value to management, but the product which shows the highest P/V ratio may not always provide the maximum profit. Some factor limits the activity of every business; it may be sales, finance, or one element of production, plant capacity, labour or materials. Shortage of one item of material or one grade of labour may be the limiting factor. If the plant is not fully occupied and there is no shortage of the labour and materials required, then provided the company has the financial resources, sales will be the limiting factor. The sales department will push the sales of the items with the highest P/V ratios.

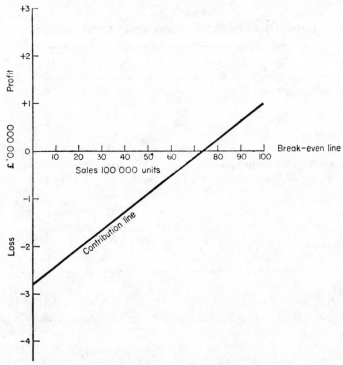

Fig. 8.4   Example of a profit or contribution chart

Where, however, the plant can be fully employed, the use of restricted facilities must be taken into consideration. In the following illustration (see Table 8.3, overleaf) it is assumed that the sales department has ample orders to employ the factory at the prices quoted.

Although the P/V ratio of A is much higher than B, the contribution per unit of B is greater than for A, and the contribution per hour will be £29 for B against £11.60 for product A, because twice as many units of B can be produced as units of A. Where products have to pass through several processes, the planning of production and sales to obtain the optimum product mixture is most important. It is not always best to concentrate on the products which show the highest P/V ratio or even the highest contribution per unit. Sometimes a product mixture which leaves certain units of the plant under employed will yield the highest contribution and *profit*.

This example shows the danger of a sales department fixing selling

Table 8.3
Comparisons of P/V ratios and profit contrubutions

Product	A	B
Units produced per hour	10	20
	£	£
Direct materials	4.00	8.00
Direct labour	0.08	0.04
Variable production overhead	0.16	0.08
Variable selling overhead	0.40	0.60
Total marginal cost	4.64	8.72
Selling price	5.80	10.17
Contribution	£1.16	1.45
P/V ratio per cent	20	14

prices on the basis of costs, total or marginal, without understanding the implication of limiting factors which may operate with regard to certain processes.

MAKE OR BUY?

An important decision may often face the management when the plant is fully occupied and components are required which could be made in the factory or purchased from outside sources. Apart from considerations of quality, reliability of delivery and credit terms, the profit position can be assessed by the application of marginal costing. The following simple example will demonstrate the basis for a management decision.

If there is not sufficient plant capacity to produce the requirements of both components, it will pay to make Z and buy X, for although the saving on Z is only £0.80 per unit as compared with £1.00 per unit for X, the saving per machine hour is £24 for Z against £20 for X. Assuming fixed overhead on the machine will be the same in each case, an apportionment of this cost to the two components is unnecessary and has therefore been ignored.

The application of marginal costing may highlight important factors

Table 8.4
Cost comparisons between manufactured and bought-in components

Component units produced per hour	X 20	Z 30
Direct labour	£0.05	0.033
Direct materials	4.00	3.00
Other variable costs	0.45	0.167
Total marginal cost	4.50	3.20
Purchase price outside	5.50	4.00
Saving per unit if made in the factory	1.00	0.80
Saving per hour if made in the factory	20.00	24.00

when a decision has to be made as to which of two or more factories should be closed because capacity exceeds needs.

Opportunity costs

The example just given is also helpful in illustrating the concept of opportunity cost which is often highly relevant to management decisions. The saving per hour if component Z is made in the factory can also be described as the opportunity cost of transferring one hour's worth of production of Z to outside purchase. The corresponding opportunity cost of relieving in-house production of one hour's production of X is £20. An opportunity cost of £20 is clearly more acceptable than an opportunity cost of £24, so that it is preferable to transfer the production of X to outside purchase.

THE TREATMENT OF FIXED PRODUCTION EXPENSES FOR FINANCIAL STATEMENTS PREPARATION

Generally accepted accounting principles for external financial reporting purposes, as well as the Inland Revenue, require stock and profit figures to be calculated on the basis that the value of stock includes an allowance for fixed costs per unit. Thus, where marginal or variable costing is used for management accounting purposes, it will be necessary to make a calculation at the end of each major financial reporting period (i.e., yearly, quarterly or even monthly) of the amount of fixed overhead to be included in the closing stock and work in progress figure for that period. Since any such allocation of fixed expenses to individual units is arbitrary, there would seem to be no point in seeking an elaborate and cumbersome solution to this problem. For example, a relationship can be established between standard variable cost and the total of fixed and semi-variable costs per period so that for the purpose of calculating stock and cost of goods sold a percentage is added to the standard directly variable costs in respect of the fixed and semi-variable cost elements.

Suppose that for the period in question the total fixed and semi-variable costs of production amounted to three times the total standard directly variable costs of production. Then it would be reasonable to add a three hundred per cent overhead burden to the standard variable cost of stock to arrive at the balance sheet figure. This figure would therefore be entered in the stock account and a corresponding credit would be made to the account for cost of goods sold. At the beginning of the ensuing period, these entries would be reversed, thus reducing stock to standard variable cost and charging the same amount back to the account for cost of goods sold. The same procedure would be followed at the end of this ensuing period, using the appropriate corresponding data. Thus, the figure of cost of goods sold for this period will be reduced by the additional overheads applied to stock at the end of the period but also increased by the amount of additional overheads which had been applied to stock at the end of the previous period.

In certain cases, it may be thought desirable to sub-divide stock in the various categories so as to establish more detailed figures for the fixed overhead applied. However, it is difficult to see the point of this unless the business in question is faced with a situation where the concept of 'full cost per unit' has a particularly important significance. Businesses which work extensively on contracts established on the basis of 'full cost plus' are a case in point; however, such businesses do not generally find it so useful to employ variable or marginal costing in the first place.

INTERNAL PRICING

When considering the issues of internal pricing, it is necessary to recall what was said in chapter 6 about responsibility centres. The issue here is somewhat different, depending on whether the goods or services transferred internally pass between two cost centres or two profit centres.

Transfers between cost centres

The obvious basis for making transfers between two cost centres is to use the standard cost of the goods or services transferred. This would be a standard 'full' cost or a standard variable cost depending on the type of costing system in use. However, this approach can be used only when a standard cost for the goods or services transferred has been established. In addition, there are circumstances when the inclusion of an element of fixed cost may have a counter-productive effect on the decisions made by the people involved.

To deal with the first point, it will generally be possible to arrive at a standard, or at least at a budgeted, cost per unit of the transferred goods or service (provided, in the case of services, a convenient measuring unit is available). But whether this standard or budget allowance per unit should be so calaculated as to include a unit fixed cost element is a more delicate issue. Under the internal pricing mechanism, the standard cost per unit is used to charge the transferee cost centre for each unit it uses, and to credit the transferor cost centre for each unit it transfers. Where the use of the transferred good or service represents a discretionary cost to the transferee cost centre, the situation is similar to a transfer between two profit centres.

A fairly familiar example is the use of the services of a duplicating department by other departments in an organisation. The duplicating department establishes a standard cost per page for various types of duplicating work, and these costs are used as transfer prices to charge the various user departments for the work done on their behalf. The calculation of unit fixed costs and the inclusion of these in the standard costs used as transfer prices mean that costs which are fixed to the duplicating department appear as variable costs in the accounts of the user departments, since, of course, they vary according to the amount of duplicating work done for them. Increased use of the duplicating facility, therefore, will cause an apparent cost increase in the accounts of the user department or departments concerned in excess of the increased cost to the organisation as a whole. (The latter, of course, is equal to the marginal cost of the additional work, not the so called 'full' cost). This may lead to wrong decisions, as discussed in the next section.

Transfers between profit centres

The appropriate way to account for transfers between profit centres depends on two factors:

1 Whether or not the goods or services transferred are of a kind for which an external market exists, so that arms length market prices can be determined.
2 Whether or not it is the organisation's policy to allow the goods or services in question to be sold and/or bought in such an external market, if it exists.

Where an external market exists and the organisation's policy allows the profit centres to buy and sell in that market, arms length market price is clearly the logical basis on which to account for transfers between them. Even where the level of an arms length market price can vary, there is nothing to prevent profit centres negotiating with each other to establish transfer prices which are mutually satisfactory.

The problem is not so simple if, for one reason or another, the organisation wishes to restrict the right of profit centres to buy the goods or service in question from the external market. This might be the case because the profit centre producing the goods or service within the organisation has excess capacity. The converse situation arises when the organisation wishes to restrict the right of the transferor (or up-stream) profit centre to sell the goods or service on the open market. This might be the case when one or more of the transferee (or down-stream) profit centres are particularly dependent on supplies of the product in question, and the latter is scarce. In such cases, while it is still appropriate to use market-based transfer prices, friction may arise because either the transferee or the transferor may find a more advantageous price externally, or may claim to have done so as a bargaining tactic. Where the bulk of a profit centre's output, or its input, is sold or procured within the organisation as a matter of policy, the existence of such a policy is, in fact, a denial of the true profit centre status of the 'profit centre' involved. In such circumstances the existence of external market prices for the goods or services transferred is somewhat irrelevant, and the situation is analogous to that described in the next paragraph.

Where the bulk of the profit centre's outputs or inputs is sold or procured within the organisation and is such that arms length external market prices do not exist, then it is more appropriate to speak of a 'pseudo profit centre'. Opinions differ as to whether it is worthwhile having pseudo profit centres rather than designating the responsibility centres in question as straightforward cost centres. On the other hand, a situation may exist where the bulk of the responsibility centre's outputs or inputs relates to products for which the arms length external market price can be ascertained, but it is also involved with a certain quantity of transfers for which no arms length market prices exist. In these circumstances, the responsibility centre is not a 'pseudo profit centre', and it is desirable to find a method of accounting for the latter category of transfers in a way which is consistent with its profit centre status.

Two part and three part transfer price systems

Where market based transfer prices are either unavailable or inappropriate for the reasons mentioned above, the most effective approach is to use a multi-part transfer price system. In such a system, transfers are accounted for on a unit basis at standard variable cost plus a lump sum per period in respect of fixed costs. Where the transferor is a profit centre, but not when it is a cost centre, a further lump sum is added which is calculated as an allowed rate of return on the assets employed in producing the transferred outputs.

The advantage of treating the fixed overhead and profit elements as lump sums rather than as an amount per unit transferred is that decisions regarding the quantities to be transferred can be taken on the basis of what is most profitable for the organisation as a whole. The lump sum allowances for fixed costs and return on assets employed are agreed as part of the budget; they represent the cost of committed capacity and do not alter as a function of the number of units actually transferred during the budget period. Thus, the down-stream responsibility centre perceives the economics of the situation as it affects the organisation as a whole. This is not the case when the fixed costs of the up-stream responsibility centre are made to look like variable costs to the down-stream responsibility centre by being included as an element in the unit transfer price.

Where the semi-variable costs are an important element of the cost of the transferred items, it may be preferable not to treat them in the same way as the fixed costs. Rather, the transfer price may be obtained by consulting a previously agreed flexible budget schedule, so that the changes in the level of the semi-variable costs are reflected, the fixed cost and return on asset elements being dealt with as previously described.

To sum up, in situations where it is not feasible or inappropriate to use arms length market transfer prices, it is important that the responsibility centres involved are presented with the accounting information regarding the transfers in a manner which reflects their impact on the economics of the business as a whole. This is not achieved when the transfer pricing system ignores the differences between variable costs and fixed costs, and between these two categories and semi-variable costs where the latter are a significant element.

Where the transferred items cross an international or other fiscal border, the multi-part transfer pricing approach described above will not generally be satisfactory for customs duty purposes. It may therefore be necessary to use unit transfer prices incorporating a fixed cost element for invoicing purposes in order to satisfy the requirements of the customs or other fiscal authorities. However, there is no obligation to use these invoice transfer prices for management accounting purposes and, for the reasons described above, it will generally be better not to do so.

9

Internal auditing*

Harry H Scholefield and P C Elliott

In a small business consisting of an owner/manager and a small number of employees the owner will be able to keep in close touch with all activities. However, as the size of the business increases this becomes more and more difficult. The statutory auditors will assist management to ensure that financial records, accounts and other statements are kept correctly and drawn up to reflect the progress of the business; but in addition, management needs to know that controls are operating·satisfactorily in all activities. Typically, management establishes its control systems using two basic approaches corresponding to two different levels of control:

On-line controls (first level)

The on-line control function consists of on going measures and procedures designed to provide reasonable assurance that all significant actions of the company are taken in accordance with company policies and with appropriate regard for efficiency and the protection of corporate assets.

Off-line controls (second level)

The off-line control function is an appraisal activity designed to evaluate the adequacy, efficiency and effectiveness of the company's on-line controls and to promote more efficient and effective controls through constructive recommendations.

*The authors wish to thank B J B Driver, P J Henry and A J Somers for their valuable comments on an earlier draft of this chapter.

The off-line control function is performed by internal auditors. The modern internal auditor appraises controls rather than acting as the control and his activity is not confined to data records. The efforts of the Institute of Internal Auditors have done much to ensure that the responsibilities of an internal auditor are more fully understood and practised.

ORGANISATION

If the chief internal auditor reports directly to top management, he will be independent and will carry, without question, the appropriate status to review controls over all activities. In a smaller company he will probably report to the chief executive. However, in larger organisations, partly for historical reasons, he may report to the financial director or comptroller.

The financial function also provides a service to other functions and there is no reason why a chief internal auditor reporting within finance should be hampered in reviewing activities of other functions provided that he is given the full support of top management. It is therefore important that the internal auditor reports to a strong corporate officer who can guarantee his independence, his access to all company records, and also shield him from internal pressure to alter or suppress his findings. Moreover, the executive to whom the internal auditor reports must be in a position to assure that the internal auditor's reports are read by every level of management concerned.

If the internal auditor reports to the financial director or comptroller there is, however, a danger that he may not be free, then, to express himself fully on financial activities. A necessary safeguard against such an impediment is for it to be agreed, and included in his terms of reference, that the internal auditor has the right of direct access to top management should he feel that this is warranted. In the US, and to a lesser extent in the UK, this safeguard is extended further in some companies where he has access as a final resort to the Board Audit Committee, which is typically composed of non-executive directors.

TERMS OF REFERENCE

The internal audit function helps senior management to attain corporate objectives and seeks to protect shareholders' interests. In the final analysis it is this latter role which predominates; even senior management can be corrupt. Recommended responsibilities of the internal auditor were set out in a statement approved by the Institute of Internal Auditors' Board of Directors in 1947 and revised in 1957, 1971 and 1976. The revised statement is included in Appendix 1 to this chapter.

Every management must decide on the particular terms of reference which it proposes to give its internal audit department. After agreement, terms of reference should be produced in writing giving a firm base for planning, staffing and carrying out internal audit work without objection and resentment from those responsible for activities to be audited. Senior management should make clear throughout the organisation the importance they attach to the internal audit function.

The work of internal audit is not easy. It is, after all, an inspection, and people normally resent being inspected. A very careful path has to be trodden, to ensure that controls are reviewed and that the organisation's policies are being carried out without giving the impression that the internal audit department is either criticising policy or that it will be making adverse criticisms on decisions taken, when those decisions could have been proved wrong only after the event.

STAFFING

It will be clear from the preceding sections that internal auditing is a responsible job, involving contact with senior staff and requiring skill and tact in personal relationships. Having decided to establish such a department, it would be folly to staff it with people incapable of the performance required.

Opinions differ as to whether internal auditing is a profession in itself or whether it is a useful step in the career development of those with management potential. Whether the more senior positions of the internal audit department are filled with those having a career in internal auditing or not, it is generally agreed that this department affords an excellent early training ground for those with management potential. Because of the department's interest in all activities, shorter term recruitment for the lower levels should encompass not only those employees with financial backgrounds but also those from other disciplines. The perfect internal auditor will, perhaps, possess both financial and applied science qualifications, but such staff are not plentiful. A balance can be achieved by a mixture of staff from different functions in appropriate proportions.

Criteria for selection of staff should encompass education, experience, performance and potential. A points system can be developed for each area of selection so that only in exceptional circumstances would audit candidates be accepted who did not meet an overall minimum points requirement. In addition to 'control mindedness' and the usual virtues, the internal auditor needs perseverance, empathy and a logical approach with analytical ability. Given staff who have satisfied the above requirements, internal auditing has the best opportunity to meet and maintain its objectives.

Those employed on internal auditing early in their career should not serve too long; say, up to 4 years. This time is sufficient for them to gain an insight into many aspects of the organisation, to learn and carry with them throughout their careers the value and basic requirements of good control, and to contribute significantly to the work of the department. A longer term may lessen their enthusiasm, with the exception of those internal auditors envisaged as career audit specialists. The movement of good staff into internal auditing together with promotion of many on leaving it, will be an excellent advertisement and will banish any earlier images of internal auditing as a department where finance staff finish their working years.

PLANNING

All business activities require a plan, a budget and a stewardship review, and internal auditing is no exception.

The audit plan

The list of activities to be covered should be separated into auditable units. These units should be of such a size that the chief executive does not receive too many reports and that the time spent on auditing each unit is not excessive. A broad guideline would be 100–150 man-days per audit.

The review of all activities every year, regardless of the stability of organisation, adequacy of controls or chance of loss or profit improvement, is wasteful and a decision should be made regarding the time cycle over which activities are to be reviewed.

It may be considered appropriate to audit every 2–3 years those activities with major financial or other potentially harmful exposure. The period will depend on relative exposure, on-line controls and strength of management. Where audit evaluation indicates weak or inadequate controls, or where for other reasons financial exposure or risks due to non-compliance with company policies are particularly high, the interval should be reduced to less than 2 years. Intervals between audits for activities which do not have major financial exposure may be greater than 3 years and will vary according to the relative exposure as judged by management and the internal audit manager involved.

The above approach to planning is appropriate in an organisation where internal auditing has been conducted for some time and experience gained in the activity. How can an audit plan be developed, based on a systematic approach to risk measurement, for an internal audit group in its infancy or for one which is extending its activities?

Let us consider the relationship between risk and internal audit as depicted in Figure 9.1.

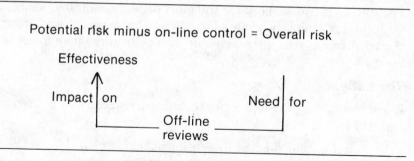

Potential risk minus on-line control = Overall risk

Fig. 9.1   Relationship between risk and internal audit

The greater the overall risk, the greater the need for off-line reviews; these in turn should contribute to the effectiveness of on-line control and hence reduce the overall risk. Thus the extent of off-line reviews needed should, other things being equal, diminish over time. An assessment of potential risk is derived from a good knowledge of an area and could be provided by internal audit management in those areas where they possess considerable experience. However, in those areas where they lack experience, discussions would have to take place with line management. Similarly, in the case of on-line control effectiveness in a previously unaudited area, line management's input will have to be sought, since the audit function will be able to make an evaluation only after the audit. A possible approach to allocating risk to auditable units by line management is outlined in Appendix 2.

Calculation of staff numbers

An assessment of the plan must be made in terms of audit man-days, including travelling time, in order to determine staff requirements. Initially, timing is rather difficult to assess but, as experience is gained on actual audit timing, estimates will improve. After adding the man-days audit effort for each year in the time cycle, some adjustments to allocation of audits within the year may be necessary to give a more even distribution of effort. Staff requirements can then be estimated: an allowance for leave, sickness, training courses, *ad hoc* requirements and public holidays is needed. In a later section it is recommended that internal audit staff keep time-sheets; time-sheets summarised for previous years will help when estimating both audit time and the additional allowance, as well as providing input for allocation of costs. An example of a 5-year internal audit plan is shown in Appendix 3. There will, of course, be some trade-off between audit frequency and manpower, despite the evaluation of risk. An overall 2-year interval extended to a 3-year interval would reduce required manpower by a third.

The budget

Based on the plan, the budget for the coming year can now be prepared and will include:

1 Salaries (plus on-cost to pension schemes, etc.).
2 Travelling and accommodation expenses.
3 Training courses.
4 Computer time.
5 General share of overheads.

Management agreement and stewardship

The next requirement is management's approval of the budgeted cost of the department and of the broad plan within the agreed terms of reference. The budget may be the particular responsibility of one member of management, but the plan needs to be discussed with management as a whole if controls on all activities are subject to review.

It is recommended that the chief internal auditor should meet periodically with senior management to review audit effort and progress against the plan. Such a meeting can be used to review each year's new plan. Copies of the plan should be circulated before the meeting, giving management the opportunity to review the list of activities to be covered and the proposed timing, possibly leading to adjustments in timing, staffing and costs. It also allows the chief internal auditor to obtain input from senior management and to discover their concerns.

After approval of both the plan and the budget, the chief internal auditor is in a position to adjust staffing ready for the coming year. He is also in a position to calculate the estimated average cost of an audit man-day, by dividing the budgeted cost of the department by the planned audit man-days. This figure is very significant. It can be used to assess the limit of time that can reasonably be spent on audits, having regard to the possibility of benefits that may arise, either from preventing loss or improving profit in other ways.

AUDIT PROGRAMMES

It is a sound approach for the senior auditor and audit manager to meet before the review to prepare an audit programme. The programme will set down the audit objectives, followed by the detailed steps designed to achieve them, leaving room for adjustments as the audit progresses.

Auditing of financial controls

This type of auditing verifies the existence of both a strong system of internal control, and of the corporation's assets. It involves review of the general accounting function, debtors and creditors, receipts and payments of cash, payrolls, banking transactions, and materials and equipment purchasing. In addition, it involves the verification of fixed assets and stocks. The financial audit also includes an assessment of adherence to management policies, procedures and guidelines which includes such matters as contracting, the adequacy and accuracy of cost reporting systems, budget systems and compliance with laws.

Operational auditing

Operational auditing involves the extension of internal auditing to all operations of the business. The principal objects of such audits are to assist the management in the effective discharge of their responsibilities by furnishing them with objective analyses, appraisals and recommendations designed to improve profits, and to protect the corporation from losses of all kinds.

The operational audit is a comprehensive examination of an organisational strucutre (or one of its components), of policies and objectives, mode of operations, and stewardship of human and physical resources. It can be said that operational auditing is characterised by the approach and the state of mind of the auditor – not by distinctive methods. Operational audits are seldom undertaken as special and distinct audits; instead they complement and augment the scope of appraisal systems by applying the talents, background and techniques of the internal auditor to the operating controls which exist in the business. The operational audit provides an independent appraisal of all activities within the company performed in such a manner as to serve all levels of management and to obtain the most profitable results.

Examples of internal audit extensions into operational areas during the course of the audit are:

1 An appraisal of a company's inventory levels (including, for example, a review of order quantities), the adequacy of warehousing facilities and staffing at the same time as the accuracy of inventory is verified.

2 An appraisal of alternative methods of transport and possible savings at the same time that rates and services received are verified against payments made.

3 A review of policies relating to the maintenance of plant and equipment at the same time that contract payments for repair services are verified.

4 A determination of the quality of materials and services received as well as the quantity when payments for them are being verified.

Audits, however, do not fall neatly into one of the two categories, financial and operational. Rather, they involve a difference in approach and no internal auditor should proceed with any type of audit without an operational approach.

It is emphasised that the internal audit is an appraisal of controls and not the control itself. For example, stock checking should not be carried out by staff from the internal audit department. The internal auditor will, however, appraise the controls by reviewing the work of the checkers and by carrying out spot tests.

THE AUDIT REVIEW

Normally, prior notification is given of an audit. However, when fraud is suspected, an investigation must be carried out without warning. The overall plan is agreed with management but the actual date of the audit will not be known until close to the time. Notice of the date should be given to management and there should be sufficient tolerance in the plan to avoid descending on an activity at peak periods or at a time of emergency. The auditor, or audit team, will outline the nature of the work to be conducted with the senior management of the area to be reviewed as well as inquiring whether there are any management, financial, operational, or other controls with which senior management is not entirely satisfied. Such concerns should be incorporated into the programme. In addition, the most recent reports of the statutory accountants, the last internal audit report and working papers should be obtained for review; follow-up items should be noted.

The auditor, or audit team, will then start discussions with the appropriate level of management supervising the activity, having obtained the necessary introductions via senior levels of management. The auditor will ask for the relevant organisation charts and main job descriptions of the personnel in the area covered by the audit and request a quick review of the department, thus becoming aware of organisational and other changes since the last audit and gaining some knowledge of proposed changes. He or she should ask for introductions to those people he expects to contact during the investigation.

Controls cannot be appraised without knowledge of the activity. The auditor will, therefore, gather the facts and ask questions of the appropriate personnel in the area being audited to obtain a good understanding of the activities. A complex operation is better understood if it is flow charted. Flow charts should be kept as simple as possible, using symbols with the minimum of narration, produced as useful working papers rather than works of art involving the cost of several man-days or weeks.

The activity may involve the use of land, buildings, plant, equipment or people to move or change physical things or data. When the movements or changes are understood, the established controls can be reviewed to see that they are working as intended. In clerical operations it was once the fashion to select a week's or month's transactions which were checked in detail. Recently the fashion has changed to the use of statistical sampling techniques, on the theory that a random sample of calculated size taken over a whole period gives a sample more truly representative of the whole and, therefore, gives a better test than one of a block period selected at random.

Audit in depth

Before discussing the comparative merits of these methods, mention should be made of another internal audit technique known as audit in depth. In this technique a record or voucher is selected, not merely to test the authorisation and accuracy of the supporting documentation, but to carry out an investigation of one item right through the organisation.

The vouching technique compares with an audit in depth as follows, where there is an item of cash expenditure of £750 (for example, the cost of photographing a piece of equipment).

1 Vouching technique. Find the original invoice supporting this payment, check that it is made out in the name of the organisation, is properly authorised, currently dated, cancelled and that appropriate discounts have been taken.
2 Audit in depth technique. Carry out vouching technique; check expense account to which it is carried; ascertain the budget unit (or cost centre) bearing the charge; visit the budget unit to discover the purpose of the expense (for example, advertising), whether it is within the approved budget (for example, was this within the province of the budget unit?), how the photographer was selected (possibly the charge includes unnecessary travel and accommodation), how the photograph was used; review the controls operating along the route.

Such audit in depth may open up areas for future investigation of considerably more importance than the item of £750, for example, clarification of departmental responsibilities, the existence of an advertising policy, procedures and the general cost consciousness of the departments concerned. These are the type of questions that the owner of the business would want answered if he had time, and a report on these aspects is of much more interest to management than trivial errors arising in recording the item of expense.

The internal auditor cannot carry out such an investigation while sitting at his desk or within the accounting department. He should use the calculations and supporting documents as a record of something real that has happened and should go to the point of activity to further his investigations. Worthwhile investigations often start from trivial items of expenditure or income and to review only items exceeding a certain figure can be shortsighted. It will be appreciated that auditing in depth is a time consuming activity.

Sampling methods

Let us now consider the comparative merits of block period, statistical or other random sampling methods for testing established controls. All three methods have their uses.

Selecting a block period has the advantage of covering all items for a period; it is simple and vouchers are normally easier to find.

The statistical sample gives a random and representative review of the whole period but the method is not so simple and vouchers are harder to find.

Neither of these methods lends itself to audit in depth because transactions are too numerous. The best method for this technique is a truly random sample but restricted to a much smaller number than the statistical sample.

The small random sample is also of value in testing non-clerical controls. For example, an employee may be checking weights of filled packages; the random selection of a few items by the internal auditor for re-checking will indicate the value of this control.

The internal auditor should be aware of all these techniques and select the one, or combination, appropriate to the job in hand.

REPORTING

Some managements prefer verbal reports. It is recommended, however, that written reports are always produced following an internal audit review. These lead to better disciplines in the audit department; no opportunity arises for argument about the recommendations made, and there is a greater likelihood of success in follow-up. In addition, in the event of litigation against the company, written reports may assist the company's defence.

A sound overall reporting procedure would provide:

1 Draft audit memos for discussion with the first-line management of operations being audited, followed by formal audit memos.
2 A draft report to the next superior in line for discussion, and incorporation of replies.
3 A final report to the chief executive, with a covering letter highlighting major findings.

The main purpose of producing the draft audit memos for discussion with the first-line management of the department being audited, is to ascertain their actual validity. The audit memos and draft report allow management to provide input to the final report from all levels in the area being audited. They are an added check that the facts have been gathered properly, that the emphasis is right and recommendations are sensible. Statements dealing with each area of concern in the final report should outline the problem, its magnitude, its cause and the audit recommendations, and should incorporate management's comments. In addition, an overall comment on control adequacy should be made in the covering letter and in this regard it is helpful if a standard terminology is laid down so that management understand clearly what the control assessment means.

The report should be completed as rapidly as possible so that it is still fresh and relevant when presented. It is usually accepted that the report should be distributed to the department or section head audited and the next superior in-line and the chief executive. The internal auditor should appraise controls on behalf of top management and his independence of all executive functions should be apparent. This independence can be reinforced by the chief internal auditor making a presentation to management at least annually. He can then offer a brief review of his investigations, prompt action where follow-up of the recommendations has been unnecessarily delayed, report on his performance compared with the plan and review future plans as necessary.

An important part of any internal audit is the preparation and filing of working papers. 'Working papers' is the term applied to all schedules, memoranda, check lists, questionnaires and other papers assembled during an audit. The purposes of working papers are to provide a record of work performed, to substantiate the auditor's findings, to record his discussions with management, to serve as a base for review of the auditor's work and as a guide for subsequent audits.

The essentials of good working papers are completeness, neatness, legibility and indexation. Completeness should not be attained at the expense of preparing voluminous papers with information which could be included in the working papers by mere reference to company records. However, working papers should be prepared so that a comprehensive review can be made of them in a minimum of time and with a minimum of recourse to the auditor who prepared them.

Working papers should be indexed as they are prepared to facilitate cross referencing. On completion of the audit an index summary of the working papers should be prepared which would typically include:

1 Final report and follow-up correspondence to report.
2 Audit memoranda and replies and cross reference to working papers.
3 Administration and general correspondence, time budget, job critique.
4 Background – organisation charts, authority levels, flow charts etc.
5 Audit programme.
6 Detailed working papers by subject.

As mentioned, working papers are an important part of any internal audit and minimum standards need to be agreed and laid down by audit management. Clearly, preparing and indexing working papers is time consuming and it would be reasonable to spend 5 per cent of total audit time on this activity.

AUDITING OF COMPUTING SYSTEMS

Internal audit is responsible for all activities and reviews controls on both efficiency and data. The internal auditor, therefore, is interested in the controls on all systems. He will pay greater regard to data processing systems than to mathematical systems because, apart from the smaller chance of his making an effective contribution, mathematical systems are, generally speaking, conceived by employees already organisationally independent of the executive function.

Auditing computing systems includes auditing the general controls operating in the computing department as well as in the systems themselves. The lack of elementary precautions to safeguard equipment and information can jeopardise the best of systems and, in any case, the computing department, as a budget unit, needs to be reviewed as much as any other activity.

Systems are created, *inter alia*, to control assets outside the computing department. Thus, the issues to be examined will be, first, the effectiveness of the controls created by the system to operate on those assets and, secondly, the effectiveness of the controls built into the system, whether manual, mechanical or electronic, to ensure proper processing of data within the system.

Systems are expensive to create and expensive to alter. It is therefore good common sense for the internal auditor to involve himself in, and comment on, systems during development as well as systems that are operational. This is sometimes referred to as 'pre-audit'. Important though pre-audit is, however, it is vital that the auditor maintains his off-line role.

In summary, the internal audit review of computing systems falls into three parts:

1 Review of the computing department as a budget unit, and of the general controls operating in relation to staff, equipment and information.
2 Review of systems under development, examining the effectiveness of the proposals and the controls envisaged within them.
3 Review of operational systems for accuracy and effectiveness.

Significantly, external auditors are coming much nearer to an efficiency audit in their reviews of the first part than they have thought appropriate for any other activity. Some external auditors, however, have so far restricted their investigations to the third part, and have then carried out these reviews only on financial projects. Internal auditors should complement rather than duplicate the work of external auditing and a considerable contribution from the internal audit department can come from the review of the controls in the computing department and in new systems. It is, therefore, important to have a combination of data processing and audit specialists to conduct the internal auditing of computer systems. Good controls and disciplines in the computing department not only lead to efficient safeguards on, and usage of, staff, equipment and information, but also to effective systems development and subsequent operation.

Audit of computing department

Controls to be reviewed will include those on:

1 Division of responsibilities.
2 Purchase and hire of equipment.
3 Fire precautions and general security.
4 Stand-by equipment.
5 Fall-back procedures.
6 Usage of equipment and information.
7 Acceptance of systems for development (for example, feasibility studies and justification statements).
8 Standards of documentation.
9 Testing of new systems and subsequent amendments.
10 Training.
11 Normal administrative responsibilities.

Audit of systems under development (pre-audit)

After the new system has been thought out, but before detailed programming and testing begin, the project leader in charge of the systems development should prepare documentation in accordance with laid down standards and send copies to the user department and internal auditing function. A meeting should be held soon afterwards to review the system and its proposed controls and the internal auditor should include consideration of the impact of the system on the business environment and the surrounding control needs.

The internal auditing department will examine the system, consider its effectiveness and, after breaking it down into its different sections of activity, review the controls helping to ensure that only accurate, properly authorised input is accepted for processing, that no information can be added or lost after acceptance, that master files and amendments are authorised, that the processing is correct and that the output, whether visible or invisible, is correctly distributed.

With knowledge of other facets of the organisation, the internal auditor may be able to suggest further integration to satisfy other requirements. The internal auditor will also review the statement of justification for the development.

Audit of operational systems

Errors in programs are either accidental or made with intent to defraud. If accidental, the application of proper testing routines or the controls built into the operational system will discover them. If made with intent (which will be more difficult if there is proper segregation of duties and good supervision) errors will not be documented and will remain undetected if the normal controls are not sound. The job of the internal auditor, as for other activities, is to appraise controls, not to act as the control. He will appraise controls by reviewing the organisation and the system, selecting items for following through the system, using, perhaps, test-decks to compare results with those expected, and using the computer itself for random selection of items from master files and so on.

As with manual systems, he will choose the technique most suitable to the requirements. Various audit packages now exist to help select random items from master files, to sort and compare information and to prepare reports. Nearly all commentaries of so-called computer frauds indicate the absence of basic controls, so that, had the systems been manual, similar frauds could have been perpetrated even more easily.

Wherever possible, for efficiency reasons audits of operational systems should be incorporated with the audit of the function concerned.

BENEFITS VERSUS COSTS

Internal auditors should keep time sheets to the nearest day or half-day. Time sheets provide audit job times and records of training leave, sickness and other absences. As such they are also control documents.

The audit job-time in man-days can be multiplied by the average cost per audit man-day to arrive at a job cost. The cost side is thus relatively easy to determine. The benefits side is impossible to quantify in total: it consists of losses discovered and recovered that would not otherwise have been found, of reductions in costs or improvements in income as a direct result of recommendations made, of losses that would have occurred if it were known that there would not be an internal audit appraisal, and finally, of the value in training staff for a future career in the organisation. Even if it were possible to quantify all the benefits, the audit department should not be judged on the surplus or deficit of benefits versus costs. If on-line controls were operating perfectly, most managements would have an off-line function, and it is on this basis that internal auditing should be justified.

APPENDIX 1

The Statement of Responsibilities of Internal Auditors issued by the Institute of Internal Auditors is as follows:

Nature

Internal auditing is an independent appraisal activity within an organisation for the review of operations as a service to management. It is managerial control which functions by measuring and evaluating the effectiveness of other controls.

Objectives and scope

The objective of internal auditing is to assist all members of management in the effective discharge of their responsibilities, by furnishing them with analyses, appraisals, recommendations and pertinent comments concerning the activities reviewed. Internal auditors are concerned with any phase of business activity in which they may be of service to management. This involves going beyond the accounting and financial records to obtain a full understanding of the operations under review. The attainment of this overall objective involves such activities as:

1 Reviewing and appraising the soundness, adequacy and application of accounting, financial and other operating controls, and promoting effective control at reasonable cost.
2 Ascertaining the extent of compliance with established policies, plans and procedures.
3 Ascertaining the extent to which company assets are accounted for and safeguarded from losses of all kinds.
4 Ascertaining the reliability of management data developed within the organisation.
5 Appraising the quality of performance in carrying out assigned responsibilities.
6 Recommending operating improvements.

Responsibility and authority

The responsibilities of internal auditing in the organisation should be clearly established by management policy. The related authority should provide the internal auditor full access to all of the organisation's records, properties and personnel relevant to the subject under review. The internal auditor should be free to review and appraise policies, plans, procedures and records.

The internal auditor's responsibilities should be:

1 To inform and advise management, and to discharge this responsibility in a manner that is consistent with the *Code of Ethics of The Institute of Internal Auditors.*

2 To co-ordinate internal audit activities with others so as best to achieve the audit objectives and the objectives of the organisation.

In performing their functions, internal auditors have no direct responsibilities for, nor authority over, any of the activities reviewed. Therefore, the internal audit review and appraisal does not in any way relieve other persons in the organisation of the responsibilities assigned to them.

Independence

Independence is essential to the effectiveness of internal auditing. This independence is obtained primarily through organisational status and objectivity:

1 The organisational status of the internal auditing function and the support accorded to it by management are major determinants of its range and value. The head of the internal auditing function, therefore, should be responsible to an officer whose authority is sufficient to assure both a broad range of audit coverage and the adequate consideration of and effective action on the audit findings and recommendations.

2 Objectivity is essential to the audit function. Therefore, internal auditors should not develop and install procedures, prepare records or engage in any other activity which they would normally review and appraise and which could reasonably be construed to compromise the independence of the internal auditor. The internal auditor's objectivity need not be adversely affected, however, by determining and recommending standards of control to be applied in the development of systems and procedures being reviewed.

APPENDIX 2

Allocation of risk to auditable units

If an internal audit function is being set up or the existing function being extended the question to be answered is 'Who can identify the risk areas in the company and weight them between functions?' The rational reply would appear to be that line managers are in the best position to do this. Line managers at each level are asked to allocate 100 points on a risk basis to the activities for which the personnel reporting to them are responsible. This exercise is conducted for all levels of management from the Chief Executive to first-line management.

The next stage is to calculate the risk points applicable to each auditable unit dependent on the decisions made by line management starting with the Chief Executive. The result will look like:

Table 9.1
Allocation of risk points to each auditable unit

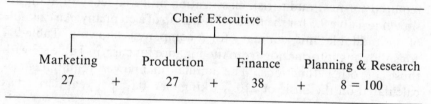

	Chief Executive		
Marketing	Production	Finance	Planning & Research
27 +	27 +	38 +	8 = 100

If we then continue with the finance function, for example:

Table 9.2
Allocation of risk points to sections within the finance function

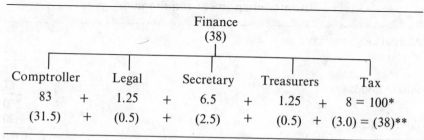

		Finance (38)		
Comptroller	Legal	Secretary	Treasurers	Tax
83 +	1.25 +	6.5 +	1.25 +	8 = 100*
(31.5) +	(0.5) +	(2.5) +	(0.5) +	(3.0) = (38)**

*Allocation of 100 risk points by Finance Director.
**Application of Finance Director's allocation to the 38 points allocated to the finance function by the Chief Executive.

This procedure for allocating risk is continued to first-line management level so that each auditable unit has risk points associated with it. Risk point bands can then be decided for high, medium and low risk and each auditable unit can be classified by risk category. The next stage is to decide on the frequency of audit for each risk category.

APPENDIX 3

Example of a 5-year internal audit plan

The year of last audit, man-days of last audit, estimated man-days required for next audit, risk classiciation and frequency of audit are shown in Table 9.3 for the Finance function of a company. An example of an auditable unit summary for a company is shown in Table 9.4 consolidating information from the Finance function in Table 9.3 with those of other functions. The annual manpower requirement is calculated on the basis of 210 working man-days per year derived as follows:

Annual manpower requirement

Annual calendar days	365
Weekends	104
	261
Public holidays	11
	250
Annual leave	20
	230
Training, sickness, other	20
	210

Table 9.3
Finance

	Last audit 1975–1979	Man-days	Estimated total man-days required	Risk*	Interval of coverage years	Annual equivalent audit man-days	Quarter	Audit plan man-days 1980	1981	1982	1983	1984
Computer systems & operations												
Computer operations	1975	130	150	H	3	50	1	150			150	
System development	1979	80	100	H	1	100	1–4	100	100	100	100	100
Other	1977	130	150	M	4	38			150			
Comptrollers – marketing												
Management accounting	1979	120	110	M	4	28				110		
Stocks	1976	60	90	H	3	30	2	90			90	
Sales accounting	1979	160	150	H	3	50				150		
Comptrollers – corporate												
Financial accounting	1975	60	80	M	5	16	3	80				
Purchases accounting	1977	138	140	H	3	47	3	140			140	
Capital budget & reporting	1979	80	90	M	4	22						90
Payroll	1979	90	80	H	3	27				80		
Treasurers	1978	170	150	H	3	50			150			
Secretaries, legal. tax	1978	105	120	L	5	24				120		
			1410			482		560	400	560	480	190

*H = High, M = Medium, L = Low

Table 9.4

Auditable units summary

	Total man-days required	Annual equivalent audit	Audit plan 1980	1981	1982	1983	1984
Production	1885	599	615	630	680	455	750
Marketing	3350	981	890	1180	860	740	1410
Finance	1410	482	560	400	560	480	190
Other	820	287	350	240	220	360	450
	7465	2349	2415	2450	2320	2035	2800
Manpower	35.5	11.2	11.5	11.7	11.0	9.7	13.3

PART IV
RAISING FUNDS

OVERVIEW

In Part Four we discuss both the conceptual problems and the practical issues associated with raising finance for companies. Financing can be classified broadly under the headings of debt and equity, and in this introduction we shall summarise the relative advantages of debt and equity in the capital structure, the importance of financial planning and the methods of raising finance for quoted and unquoted companies.

When making a choice between debt and equity financing one should be aware that there is no theoretical case for the notion that the cost of debt is different from the cost of a company's equity. That the cost of debt and equity could be the same is not obvious since these costs take different forms. To the dividend costs of equity one must add capital gains. To the interest payments on debt one must add the implicit cost of debt. The implicit cost of debt is reflected in the impact of additional debt on the cost of equity. Financial gearing increases risk per pound of equity, as equity is replaced by debt in the capital structure. The increased equity risk increases the cost of equity, which takes the form of dividends and capital gains required by shareholders as a reward for risk taking.

Modigliani and Miller (1958), (1), in a number of famous propositions showed that the true pre-tax cost of debt and equity is the same in a competitive capital market because the operational risks of the underlying assets are not changed by the method of financing. They showed why arbitrage would ensure that investors would not pay more for an operating cash flow partially financed by equity. Miller (1977), (2), later claimed that the same result holds after tax. Thus financial management should not imagine that there are any strong theoretical grounds for expecting an economic advantage to be gained from the choice between equity and debt financing. The theory, however, is incomplete, as pointed out by Paul Marsh in Chapter 14. Other factors such as convenience, flotations costs and the risk of liquidation arising from the possibility of default must govern the balance between equity and debt in the capital structure of the company.

What is the implication of the equality of cost between debt and equity after tax for the weighted average cost of capital (WACC)? For the purpose of illustration suppose we begin with a company which has no debt. The cost of equity capital for such a company simply reflects the risk and required rate of return for the assets of the company (including its growth opportunities or goodwill). Now let us introduce some debt into the capital structure. The after-tax interest cost of the debt may appear low, but it does not alter the weighted average cost of capital according to the Miller argument. The increased gearing increases the cost of equity (expected dividends and capital gains per pound of equity) just sufficiently to keep the weighted average cost of capital the same as it would have been if there had been no debt financing. In other words the cost of capital reflects only the required rate of return on the company's underlying operations and does not reflect the particular way those operations may have been financed. The financial community is not giving anything away and does not bless companies with extra debt any more than companies with less debt.

Unless one knows how to alter the cost of equity to reflect the extra cost per pound of equity due to gearing, one cannot calculate the weighted average cost of equity correctly. The purpose of obtaining the WACC is to try to determine a discount rate for an asset that is independent of the particular way the asset might be financed. A more useful way of determining this discount rate was discussed by Tessa Ryder Runton in Chapter 2. The required rate of return is merely the shareholder's personal rate of interest after tax plus a premium for the systematic risk of the individual asset.

While the existing theory of finance provides little guidance as to the optimum capital structure of a company, many practical guidelines are available to help management maintain a sensible and prudent balance between equity and debt finance. Since borrowing entails legal obligations to pay interest and to repay principal, borrowing incurs a risk of reorganisation or liquidation in the event of default. In an industry characterised by highly variable and uncertain cash flows, borrowing can entail greater financial risk than in less volatile industries. Thus a study of industry debt ratios can provide useful rules of thumb for the capital structure of a company in the same industry. A more sophisticated approach involves the projection of future sources and uses of funds for the company including funds required for dividends, interest and repayment of debt. A sensitivity analysis of sales revenues, costs, working capital and capital investment requirements under alternative scenarios of business conditions can indicate whether conditions are likely to occur which might cause the company to default given a planned level of debt financing. Prudent financial managers keep the burden of interest payments and repayment of loan capital within the bounds of the company's expected ability to pay under a variety of possible business conditions.

Arrangements for sufficient finance must be provided to ensure not only the continued financial viability of the firm under the most adverse circumstances but also to ensure that all likely options to invest in worthwhile growth can be exercised as profitable opportunities emerge in the course of time.

In Chapter 10 R. L. Mansbridge discusses the methods and importance of financial planning to determine the implications of operational plans, capital investments, acquisitions and divestments on the future financing requirements of the firm. Financial plans based on alternative scenarios of possible future economic conditions and investment opportunities provide the framework within which appropriate financing requirements can be determined. If there are sufficiently likely scenarios of future economic events and opportunities for which the sources of internally generated funds fall short of projected uses, then arrangements are required for external financing to meet the additional cash requirements.

When internal funds from retained earnings, liquidations, and other sources temporarily fall short of requirements, the company's bankers represent a natural source of short term funds. Overdraft facilities to cover foreseeable short term requirements can readily be agreed in advance if the company has cultivated a continuing close relationship with its bankers. For longer term requirements banks now offer term loan financing up to about ten years, usually at variable rates of interest if the company's total borrowing does not exceed prudent levels for the industry.

In Chapter 11 Michael Clipsham discusses how to identify the need for bank assistance, methods of presenting a case for finance to a bank, and the nature of security usually required for bank loans. The chapter also provides a useful rundown of eleven types of finance offered by the commercial banks including, for example, leasing and export financing. The close relationship which a bank can maintain with its corporate customers through a variety of banking services means that banks can provide flexible and easily accessible financing facilities without the high flotations costs which would be associated with the sale of small issues of the company's securities.

An increasingly important form of term debt financing is equipment leasing. Lease financing now accounts for approximately 12 per cent of capital investment in the United Kingdom or about one quarter of new external financing. Since the title to the leased asset remains with the lessor, lease financing makes it possible for tax paying lessors to pass on some of the financial benefits of capital allowances to non-tax-paying lessees in the form of lower rental payments. For companies which have insufficient expected taxable profits to take full advantage of capital allowances, properly structured leases can provide one of the cheapest sources of finance. Colin Young defines in Chapter 12 the precise tax benefits available to certain companies through lease financing and describes methods of structuring leases to maximise these benefits.

If a combination of bank borrowing and lease financing cannot be expected to meet the company's future requirements for funds fully, then a public issue of either debt or equity may be required. Occasionally, a company may wish to make a public issue of debt securities. These may take the form of unsecured Loan stock or of Debentures which are secured on specific assets and therefore rank before unsecured loan stock in terms of entitlement to interest and repayment in liquidation. Interest on most corporate borrowing is allowable for tax, but the market for corporate debt is relatively inactive in the UK. The relative lack of corporate debt issues in the UK is often ascribed to vigorous competition from public sector borrowing, which makes the cost of debt issues relatively high compared to other forms of debt.

Elroy Dimson in Chapter 13 describes the various methods of making a new issue of securities including public issues by prospectus, offer for sale, placings, offer for sale by tender, public issue by tender and a Stock Exchange introduction. Securities other than debt which might be issued are preference shares (often considered as a class of debt with fixed dividend payments but without the benefit of tax deductibility for the dividends), or various classes of equity or ordinary share capital. Finally, warrants can be issued (usually in conjunction with other securities) giving the holder the right to purchase a specified number of ordinary shares from the company at stated prices during specified periods of years.

Next to undistributed income and bank borrowing the largest single source of funds to quoted companies results from the issue to existing shareholders of 'rights' to subscribe to a specified number of additional ordinary shares at a stated price within a limited period of weeks. To help ensure that the issue will be fully subscribed the rights price is fixed below the current market price of the shares. Furthermore underwriters are usually employed, who effectively insure the success of the issue by agreeing to purchase any shares remaining unsold. Since the rights are issued to existing shareholders proportionally to the number of shares already held, existing shareholders can maintain the proportion of ownership that they have in the company simply by exercising their rights. Alternatively they may sell the rights. Paul Marsh in Chapter 14 explains why rights issues do not dilute the value of existing shareholdings, why rights issues rarely fail and how to quantify the insurance benefits that underwriters provide.

Chapter 14 also indicates the likely flotations costs of rights issues including administrative, legal and underwriting costs. These costs undoubtedly explain why companies prefer to use internal sources of funds and bank borrowing when possible, and issue securities almost exclusively to raise large tranches of long term finance.

To summarise, the choice of financing is determined in practice by industry norms, limitations prescribed in a company's Articles of Association, convenience, term of requirement, taxes and flotations costs. The choice, amount and timing of funds raised from various sources must be planned within the context of projected sources and uses, indicating both the needs for funds and the ability to pay the cash costs of funds under various possible future business conditions. The chapters in Part Four provide a comprehensive review of the main external sources of funds available to companies in the UK.

REFERENCES

(1) Franco Modigliani and Merton H Miller, 'The Cost of Capital, Corporation Finance and the Theory of Investment', *American Economic Review*, 48, pp.261–277, June 1958.

(2) Merton H Miller, 'Debt and Taxes', Presidential Address at the Annual Meeting of the American Finance Association, *Journal of Finance*, 32, pp.261–275, May 1977.

10

Forecasting financial requirements

R L Mansbridge

This chapter concentrates on how to plan and control that very necessary resource in every company – money. Effective financial planning is essential to company survival. It is not only important to managers and employees whose jobs are at stake in the event of financial distress, but also to shareholders, banks and others who finance the company. Financial managers must understand the cash implications of various future possible contingencies, in order to know the types and amounts of funding which may be required, well in advance of actual needs. Financial planning provides the framework guiding the company's relationships to providers of funds. Therefore, systematic financial planning and forecasting should play a central role in the managerial process.

TIMING OF CASH PLANS

There are essentially three time spans which a financial manager should cover in his cash planning. The planning is mentioned first at this stage as it comes first in time, but the control is equally important.

Plans are of no use unless there is a good control mechanism to highlight when, where and how events are off plan. This probably applies more in cash planning than in profit planning. If a company makes an unplanned loss one month or one year, the effect is less devastating than not being able to pay the wages on a Friday.

The three time spans are:

1 Monthly cash forecasts for, say, the next three months.
2 Short term cash forecasts of, say, one or two years, probably by month.

3   Long term cash forecasts for five to ten years, usually by year.

The day to day planning and control of cash is omitted here as this is purely the arithmetic and checking of bank statements.

The timings of the cash plans are dictated mainly by the budgeting or planning cycle of the operation. It is essential that the cash plans lock into profit and balance sheet planning.

MONTHLY CASH FORECAST AND CONTROL

Assuming that the company's planning and reporting system runs by calendar month, this forecast should be produced as near the beginning of the month as possible. It shows:

1   Actuals for the last month, over/under plan and over/under last month's forecast.
2   Forecast for next month, over/under plan.
3   Forecast for month two, etc., over/under plan.

A schedule of this is shown in Table 10.1. This is a simple statement of money received and paid, showing how last month compared to the plan and prior forecast. Similarly, it shows forecasts for months one, two, three etc., against the plan. The length of the forecast is determined by the urgency of the cash position. Thus, if the overdraft is right up to the limit in a tight money situation and there are large seasonal payments, the forecast will go further than three months to cover this.

The plan column mentioned will be the short term forecast showing the month by month movement of cash which links in with the budget of profits.

The forecast for next month will be those figures which the financial manager is planning to pay and receive next month. To do this he will use the following sources of information:

1   Calendarised profit and cash plan.
2   Short term profit outlook for next month (if this is done month by month).
3   Debtors' and creditors' ledger.
4   Information on taxes, loans, etc.
5   Capital expenditure authorisations.

6   Last month's actuals.

Thus, the short term forecast should accurately give the money movements picture for the next two or three months. It will also be closely locked in with the activities of the company, that is, production, sales costs, and so forth.

The variance from plan will be analysed in conjunction with the profit and cost variance statement. Variances will highlight some of the questions itemised below:

1   *Trade debtors*

Is this due to lower turnover or late payment by debtors?
Is the number of days outstanding on the debtors' ledger increasing?
Is this seasonal or is a trend developing which may need more financing in future?

2   *Investment income*

Does the company still own the investments as planned?
Should future income be adjusted?

3   *Receipts/payments – overseas subsidiaries*

Is this lower business activity or are international money transactions being blocked or restricted?

4   *Loans or financing received*

Is this due to a change in capital spending?
Are planned loans not forthcoming?

5   *Purchases, salaries and overheads*

Is this due to operating volume, price variations or late payment of creditors?

6   *Capital expenditure*

Is planned spending cancelled or delayed?
Are costs different from plan due to price only or has there been any change in specification?

7   *Interest*

Is the rate of interest different from the plan or is the overdraft size different?

Table 10.1
Monthly cash forecast and control

	LAST MONTH			MONTH 1		MONTH 2		MONTH 3, ETC.	
	Actual	o/u Plan	o/u Fore-cast	Fore-cast	o/u Plan	Fore-cast	o/u Plan	Fore-cast	o/u Plan
Receipts									
Trade debtors									
Investment income									
Receipts from Overseas sub-sidiaries									
Loans or financing received									
Other									
Total Receipts									
Payments									
Stock purchases									
Salaries and costs of employment									
Other overheads									
Capital expenditure									
Interest									
Tax									
Payment to Overseas sub-sidiaries									
Repayments of loans									
Other									
Total payments									
Surplus (deficit)									
Opening cash/ (overdraft)									
Closing cash/ (overdraft)									
Overdraft facility									

8   *Tax*

Is this due to a change in rates or in taxable profits?

The purpose of showing over/under forecast is to see:

1   How good a forecast was done one month prior to events.
2   What changes have happened in one month which could not have been forecast.

The immediate object of point one above is not to see whether the financial manager is a good forecaster, although over a series of forecasts an opinion can be formed, but to judge how accurate the next few months' forecasts are likely to be.

Total receipts less total payments equal surplus or (deficit) each month. Hence the running balance for the next three months is forecast.

Specific decisions which should be made are:

1   If there is a cash balance, should this be invested? For what period can this be done (30 days, 90 days, etc.)?
2   If there is an overdraft, what items of payment can be delayed? Can the overdraft facility be increased?

SHORT TERM CASH FORECAST

This forecast links in with the budget or operating plan for the next financial year. Its timing should be on the same basis; thus, if the plan is by month, then the cash forecast will be monthly. Many companies now plan two years ahead in their short term planning cycle, the second year in less detail and without such a commitment as the first. This avoids the cliff-hanging situation in which, at the close of the company's fiscal year, the world stops on one day and starts again on the next.

Cash is simply one of the resources which go to make the budget work. Within the budget all resources must be planned – manning, facilities and money.

The main objective of the short term cash forecast is to see how the cash balances move, if the company does what it is planning to do. This forecast must highlight, on a phased basis, the need for any short term borrowing. This is particularly relevant in a seasonal business, even if high profits are being made. Long term borrowing should be decided from the figures in the long term forecast (see later in this chapter).

It is obviously better to plan in advance for any overdraft requirements than to borrow on an emergency basis. When a request to borrow is made, a profit budget and cash forecast is often required by a potential lender.

Cash forecasts can be produced either by converting the profit budget into receipts and payments or from the budgeted balance sheets. The latter method is probably more appropriate for longer term forecasts. Basically the end result is the same in that the movement of the cash balance from one balance sheet to the next is shown.

As already indicated, the cash forecast must lock into the company's profit plan. The first cycle is to agree a marketing/sales plan and production plan. This is merged with the overhead plan to produce a profit plan. This and the capital expenditure plan are the necessary tools for the cash forecast.

Because all the work in producing a budget must be done before the financial year commences, an up-to-date forecast for the current year must also be calculated. The cash forecast must obviously start from a factual balance, progress to the year end and then be calculated for the next year. This means that not only does the cash balance have to be known at the last month end or quarter date, but a balance sheet must be prepared also so that the oustandings are correctly brought into account.

Assuming that there is a profit forecast for the current year and that the profit and capital budgets for the next two years are agreed, the cash forecast using the receipts and payments method would show similar headings to Table 10.2.

If the balance sheet forecast method is used, a source and application of funds statement would be produced as shown later in the chapter. This statement traces the items in the profit statement and any extraneous items which cause a cash movement for both receipts and payments. This facilitates a quick check of the numbers against the profit budget. It is particularly valuable on the payments side where items such as salary costs and overheads are specifically identifiable.

The opening balance each month (or quarter) plus the surplus (or minus the deficit) gives the closing balance before any borrowings or loans which have not yet been agreed. This immediately shows whether loans are required. By studying the phasing it can be seen whether this is a seasonal dip or whether it looks like a permanent borrowing requirement. The correct overdraft facility is the amount up to which the bank has agreed to pass cheques.

Headings on the cash forecast shown in Table 10.2 could be calculated on the basis set out below.

Table 10.2
Short term cash forecast

Quarter/Month	1	2	3	4, etc.	Total
Receipts					
Trade debtors					
Investment income					
Loans/financing arranged					
Other					
Total Receipts					
Payments					
Stock purchases					
Salaries and costs of employment					
Other overheads					
Capital expenditure					
Interest					
Tax					
Repayment of loans					
Dividends					
Other					
Total payments					
Surplus/(deficit)					
Opening cash/(deficit)					
Closing cash/(deficit)					
Current overdraft facility					

Receipts from debtors

By reference to the debt collection department, the forecast of number of days outstanding for the average debtor will be made for the next year. Receipts from debtors will be calculated on the basis of the current situation and the budgeted turnover. The financial manager should question precisely how debt collection will be speeded up. This is a good objective, but as the cash forecast is always very sensitive to changes in this number, it must not be over-optimistic. With most companies this is the only receipt of any size, so there is no compensation if an error in forecasting is made.

Investment income

The investment income credited to the phased profit statement will be used after allowing for the receipt of cash.

Loans/financing arranged

This heading will only include financing which has been arranged prior to the budget. It does not include overdraft facilities as these will be shown at the bottom of the forecast. The object of the forecast is to see how the cash deficit measures against the current overdraft facility. The types of financing entered on this line will be mortgage money which will be received against capital expenditure, or a fixed loan or debenture of which the proceeds have not yet been received.

Other receipts

These receipts are essentially non-trading cash receipts and would include items such as the sale of fixed assets. These are sometimes accounted for by reducing the capital expenditure but unless a simultaneous purchase and trade-in (as with motor vehicles) is involved it is better to separate the receipt from the payment.

Stock purchases

The payments side of the forecast follows the logic of splitting expenditure as it appears in the profit budget. Thus, in a trading company, stock purchases equals the charge in the profit budget plus opening creditors less closing creditors.

To determine the closing creditors, an assumption will be made as to whether the company wishes to, or has to, pay creditors more quickly or slowly than at present. Stock purchases in many companies represent a large portion of total payments and can be a useful form of financing. The ethics of this must be carefully weighed, especially for large companies which have a monopolistic buying power over small suppliers. The problem for a small company trying to finance itself out of creditors is (short of being sued) whether it obtains a name for being a bad payer and whether this affects business.

Salaries and costs of employment

Net salaries and wages in the profit budget are usually phased in line with the cash payments. The only items to be allowed for would be commissions or bonuses which are paid at a later date. Deducted tax and costs of employment as charged to the profit statement should be adjusted for creditors at the beginning and end of the period, as for stock purchases.

Other overheads

These consist of all items of cost (other than purchases and salary costs) between turnover and profit before depreciation. On the working papers it is easiest to run through the calculation from the charge by item to the profit budget, adding beginning creditors and deducting beginning prepayments. With expenses which are the normal invoice and payment type, the same logic applies as for stock purchases. With cash items such as travelling, etc., the profit charge needs no adjustment for the cash budget. Items such as rent and rates are usually paid in advance on specific days and this determines the phasing of the cash budget.

Capital expenditure

The capital plan must be produced alongside the profit plan, which in turn incorporates the production and sales plans. Plant to produce the end product is as much a plannable item as the purchase of raw material. Usually, it is more important to plan capital, especially facilities which have a long lead-time. For each item of capital expenditure in the plan the phases of management approval, commitment and cash spending should be specified, with dates and amounts. In the smaller business, management approval is basically when the owner says that a certain asset must be purchased. In many companies commitment is synonymous with approval. This date is important, however, as once a commitment is made it will cost the company money if it reverses its decision.

At the time of a capital budget the dates of the cash spending should be forecast. This forecast would be based on experience. With capital items having long lead-times from order to delivery (for instance a factory or specially designed machine tools), the capital requisition and management approval have probably taken place before the budget. In this case the cash budget is dictated by the pre-calculated figures. For short lead-time items, the capital budget should operate from the date the asset is required. It must be determined whether payment will be made on the delivery invoice or by stage payments.

Interest

The interest charge in the profit budget is calculated from the result of the cash forecast. The apparent problem of putting the cart before the horse can be resolved in one of two ways: either by calculating all items in the cash forecast (except interest), completing this before finishing the profit budget; or by using the last cash forecast with a rough adjustment for known large changes to produce the interest charge (the same logic applies to interest receivable) in the profit budget. The latter would appear easier in most cases.

Payment of interest on fixed loans and mortgages would be determined by the agreements.

Tax

Many companies end their formal planning at the profit before tax level, on the premise that as tax is unavoidable and uncontrollable it is not worth planning. This thinking is erroneous because the payment of tax is a significant item for a profitable company.

Tax planning is essential for a company based in the United Kingdom. It is even more vital if the company has overseas investments.

The payment of tax in the cash forecast is based on the rates and rules current at the time of the budget. The only deviation from this would be when a government has made a firm commitment to change the rates of corporation tax or capital allowances.

Repayment of loans

This item will include those repayments to which the company is committed. It is an item easily overlooked and could lead the company into serious legal problems if it is unable to repay loans or mortgages on time. Before completing the cash forecast the finance manager should check the last balance sheet published and any loans received since with the loan agreements to ensure that he is planning repayment at the correct time.

Dividends

These payments will consist of the final dividend on the current year's trading and probably an interim based on the first half of the budget year's trading. The amount of the dividend on preference shares is pre-determined. The ordinary dividend forecast would be based on the company's dividend policy.

Dates of payment would be similar to the prior year unless circumstances have changed.

Other payments

This covers any payments not itemised above. These would include non-trading or extraneous loss items and would be shown in the cash forecast as circumstances might dictate.

SOURCE AND APPLICATION OF FUNDS

This statement requires the prior production of the profit budget and forecast balance sheets. There must be a balance sheet at the end of each period for which the cash forecast is required.

Many companies budget profit on a monthly basis but balance sheets are only budgeted quarterly or annually. This makes a monthly source and application of funds statement more difficult to produce.

Table 10.3 gives a possible layout for the source and application of funds statement.

This statement links into the profit figure then adds back all the items in the profit budget which are non-cash. This is mainly depreciation, but 'other' would include provisions for bad debts, stock, and writing off patents, etc. The total of these line items represents the cash inflow due to trading.

Table 10.3
Source and application of funds statement

Quarter/Month	1	2	3	4, etc.	Total
Profit before tax					
Depreciation					
Other non-cash items in profit statement					
Increase/decrease in:					
Fixed assets					
Stocks					
Debtors					
Creditors					
Tax payment					
Dividends paid					
Loans received					
Loans repaid					
Net movement in cash					
Opening cash surplus/ (deficit)					
Closing cash surplus/ (deficit)					
Current overdraft facility					

The outflow of cash is shown by balance sheet heading. The gross increase in fixed and current assets is deducted. This is calculated by reference to the balance sheets at the beginning and end of the forecast period.

The cash movement section will show tax and dividend payments. These figures will be opening creditor plus profit charge less closing creditor.

Loans received will be only those loans which have been arranged prior to the budget being prepared. Loan repayments will be repayments of existing loans.

The net movement in cash will, accordingly, be the change between opening and closing cash balances.

SHORT TERM CASH CONTROL

Most companies segregate their cash control away from the profit performance control. Concentration is nearly always on the latter until cash problems arise. The statement that a company has 'got to make money' is heard frequently, but money in this sense is profit and not specifically cash. Many businessmen equate profit with cash, but unless the two are linked it does not always happen that one follows the other.

The reporting of cash to central management should be at least as often as the profit reporting and could be on formats similar to Tables 10.2 or 10.3. The line narrative would be the same as the plans and the headings could be:

This month
Actual | Plan | Over/under plan

Year to date
Actual | Plan | Over/under plan

A facing page would explain variances which would correlate with the profit variance statement.

In this way there would be two types of variance – those related to profit performance, that is, volume or cost variances on production, sales or overheads, and those related to cash management. These would include such items as:

1 Improvement in debtor collection.
2 Delay in payment of creditors.
3 Early repayment of loans.
4 Changes in tax or dividend payments.

Control of the accuracy of forecasts is exercised by the comparison of actuals to budget. But the effect of any variance is as important as knowing what the variances are. If a variance is caused by a large payment being made one day late, and therefore included in the next month's figures, this must be highlighted so that the short term forecast, which gives a picture of the cash for the next two or three months, can pick it up.

LONG TERM CASH FORECASTS

The basic principles of forecasting over a period longer than two years are essentially the same as for the short term but the process and style of approach are different. The figures tend to be less accurate, of course, and the interest lies more in long term trends than short term fluctuations.

Objective

The objective of a long term cash forecast is to see the cash flows which will be generated by the company's long term profit plan and to assess the capital expenditure needed to attain that plan. The borrowing requirements of the company will be seen from the cash flows and decision be made as to how the finance can be raised. Alternatively, if cash surpluses build up, decisions can be made whether to increase dividends, or invest the cash outside the company, or invest within the company in the form of more revenue earning assets.

If the forecast shows up a short term requirement for finance, this could be covered by borrowing from the bank. A decision could alternatively be made to slow down or delay expansion.

A long term requirement for cash would initiate a study into how that cash should be raised – by share capital increase, debenture issue or mortgage of property. This would depend on a lot of factors but quite a number of these could be decided by figures in the long term forecast. The balance sheets would show the fixed asset movements, the unmortgaged fixed assets, the debt/equity ratio, and the current asset situation. Outside factors, such as the general business climate and likely movement of interest rates, would be part of the basic assumptions behind the long range plan.

Format

The format of the long term cash forecast could be almost identical to the short term source and application of funds. As a balance sheet would be produced (probably yearly) for the long range forecast, this document would be used to produce the cash forecast; the cash forecast really becomes an integral part of the creation of the long range plan, and is produced at the same time as the balance sheets.

The cash forecast in the short term is a fairly self-contained exercise, but the long range cash forecast covers a lot of corporate activities.

The profit before tax will be calculated from the profit forecast. This is determined by the forecast of new products, the costs and volumes, the marketing policy and the trend of overheads.

Depreciation will be based on the current policy with respect to the assets as forecast in the capital plan. This creates a problem as the capital plan is based on the facilities required to manufacture and sell the forecast products. One way to get round this is to assume a certain depreciation content in the unit manufacturing cost and the overheads.

The fixed assets increase is calculated from a facilities plan. This plan, basically, starts from the production and marketing plan to determine what facilities in terms of factories, offices and training centres are required, and from this the space requirement is calculated. This is then costed and plant, vehicles and furniture are added to produce the forecast of capital expenditure. As this is one of the major long term decisions made in any company it is a vital part of the long term plan.

The stock levels would be based on historical trends of the ratio to cost of sales, updated by the marketing strategy which could specify a stock build-up just prior to launch of a new product.

Debtors and creditors would also be based on trends. Debtors bear a direct relationship to turnover and creditors to purchases and overheads.

The tax payment will be based on the profits after calculating capital allowances. Normally, the current rates and timings of tax would be used, unless there is firm evidence that these would change.

The dividend payment requires a corporate decision as to the company's dividend policy. Failing a policy, the current rate as a percentage of distributable profit would be used.

It is unlikely that any loans arranged at the present time would be received more than two years ahead, that is, after the period covered by the short term cash forecast. But the repayment of existing loans must be covered.

From this it will be seen that overlapping decisions and calculations are required for the balance sheets and cash forecasts.

In the same way as the long range profit forecast locks into each yearly balance sheet and shows the performance of the business as planned in terms of turnover and costs, so also does the long range forecast in terms of where the money comes from and where it goes.

By definition, all forecasts are inaccurate as they are calculated from what the company planners think at one point in time. Tomorrow the strategy could be completely different. The cash forecaster has two problems here: first, how uncertain is the profit statement, and second, how uncertain are the other assumptions concerning cash?

Many companies now use a computer to produce the profit effect of various strategies, and having thus homed in on a politically accept-able profit figure, proceed to calculate the cash forecast in a deterministic way with just one set of rules. It is just as important to see a best and worst case for cash as it is on the profit side – in fact, more so if the company is in a capital-restricted situation. The calculations dis-cussed earlier should therefore each be examined to see what chances there are of the situation being better or worse. Areas of specific flexibility would be:

1　The length of credit affecting debtors and creditors.
2　Any significant change in interest rates.
3　Changes in the tax laws affecting the rate of tax, calculations of capital allowances, tax on interest and dividends or the time of payment.
4　Changes in national dividend policies.
5　Changes in the international situation affecting remittances, blocked currencies, overseas borrowings and exchange rates.

Without a computer program it would be impossible to flex the above without vast manual calculations. Obviously, it would be impossible ever to finish a forecast if every contingency were to be thought of and evaluated. But it is important to look at the risks and opportunities as far as they can be foreseen at the present time. This determines the areas of the company's operation which should be analysed more closely. Very often the original policies which were used at the start of the long range cash forecast have to be changed.

INFLATION

There is much argument as to whether inflation should be brought into long range plans and, therefore, long range cash forecasts.

The arguments for leaving inflation out of long range plans are:

1　The long term marketing strategy of the company can be evaluated more correctly.
2　Sales prices can be inflated as costs inflate so that profit margins are not eroded.

3   The rate of inflation cannot easily be forecast and decisions
    could be erroneous if based on an incorrect rate.
4   If every figure is inflated by a fixed percentage each year, why
    bother?
5   Trends are more easily identified if based on the current year's
    value of money.

Against this are the arguments for inflating long term forecasts:

1   Costs do inflate automatically, there is nothing management can
    do about this, but sales prices only go up on the basis of a man-
    agement decision.
2   Future requirements of cash will be in that year's value of money
    and not today's.
3   Taxes are paid in that year's money.
4   As inflation is here to stay it should be taken into account.

The net result of this is that the inclusion of inflation will depend on
what the forecast is to be used for.

The problem can be solved by running two or three cases of each
long-range strategy:

1   Without inflation, to look at the profitability of the marketing
    strategy and trends of sales, costs and profits.
2   With costs inflated to determine how much prices will have to be
    increased to maintain margins.
3   With costs inflated and sales prices increased to determine future
    cash requirements.

The long term cash forecast must show each year, in that year's money,
what cash will be generated and on what it will be spent.

This effect of inflation on after-tax cash flow is dealt with in more
detail in Chapter 3.

DYNAMIC ASPECT

The actual cash movements change from plan in the same way as the
actual profits. It is therefore essential to update forecasts continuously.

In the long term the frequency with which forecasts are updated
should be the same as for profit. This would be determined by the
frequency of changed strategies and markets, and the effect of these on

the resources of the company.

In the short term the cash situation of the company and the significance of changes from the year's plan should dictate the frequency of reviews of the cash forecast. It is useless to update a no-change cash forecast where there is plenty of cash available. However, where cash is the restraining item in the company's policies, more frequent review than monthly may be required. It is most important to differentiate between trends and random daily variations.

INTERNATIONAL ASPECTS

An international company's objective for cash does not necessarily correlate exactly with the policy for profits. Whereas the profit objective could be to maximise after tax profit so that on consolidation the group shows the best earnings per share situation, cash does not necessarily show this.

The cash policy should be determined by what the cash is to be used for. This is usually a mixture of paying the dividend of the holding company and ploughing back for internally financed expansion.

The methods of getting cash into the holding company from overseas subsidiaries are:

1 Dividends.
2 Repayment of loans or share capital.
3 Payment for goods exported by the holding company to a subsidiary.
4 Payment by a subsidiary of management fees, fees for techno-logical know how or royalites.

All these cash transactions are subject to the roles of each country's national bank. They change frequently and are designed to guard the balance of payments positions. This often runs contrary to a company's policy of trying to reduce its exposure to parity changes. That is, money is borrowed in a country likely to devalue and held in a country likely to revalue. Against this, of course, interest rates tend to be high in the former countries and low in the latter. This produces a compensating effect.

It is the financial manager's responsibility to safeguard company assets and take reasonable precautions against currency risks – not to play the money market.

International cash management is dealt with in more detail in Chapter 5.

11

Bank borrowing

Michael Clipsham

In this chapter we explain how the commercial banks, and the clearing banks in particular, either directly or through their interests in related financial institutions, provide corporate borrowers with a comprehensive package of short, medium and long term finance which can be tailored to suit individual requirements. The commercial banks now offer facilities in such diverse fields as instalment credit, leasing, factoring and merchant banking, which they regard as an integral part of lending in the broadest sense.

The position of the commercial banks in the general structure of institutions providing finance for industry is shown in Figure 11.1, which illustrates that the commercial banks are far from the only major institutions involved in providing finance for industry: the Stock Exchange and the National Enterprise Board, for example, are prominent in this respect. Other institutions provide special finance which includes longer term lending through organisations such as Finance for Industry and Equity Capital for Industry, and export finance by way of the accepting, confirming and export houses. The diversification of the commercial banks has meant that they sometimes have an interest in such organisations.

The major sources of finance for industrial and commercial companies in the UK are undistributed profits, bank borrowing, external sources other than bank borrowing and capital issues, in that order of magnitude. Over the past decade bank borrowing has, on occasions, provided almost a third of corporate requirements and has come second only to undistributed profits as a major source of finance.

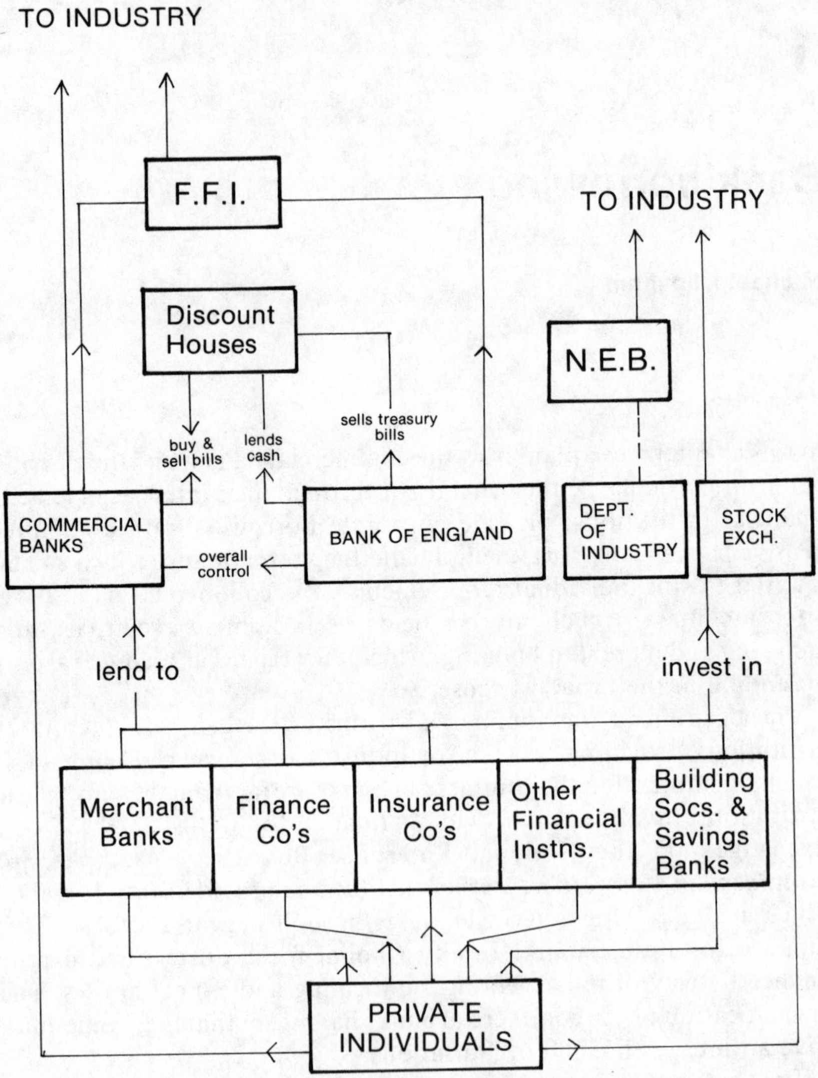

Fig. 11.1 Structure of institutions providing finance for industry

Having briefly put bank borrowing in perspective, we shall now turn to the question of how a company, or other business borrower, should identify a need for bank assistance. This will be followed by an examination of the relationship between banks and their corporate customers with regard to lending. The question of presenting a case to a banker will then be discussed in detail, together with the key criteria used by banks to evaluate propositions. Finally, the chapter ends with a review of the various facilities offered by the banks, either directly or through their subsidiary and affiliate companies.

IDENTIFYING THE NEED FOR BANK ASSISTANCE

If management is to obtain its objective and the company is to survive, competent management of working capital, to ensure liquidity and continuing solvency, is essential. To stay solvent, firms must budget their cash flows, control debtors, creditors and stocks, and avoid over-borrowing and over-investment. Cash flow forecasts are vital if the damaging impact of unforseen variations in working capital is to be avoided. Once an impending problem is identified, the question of how best to solve it can be dealt with in conjunction with financial advisers, accountant and bank manager.

In the long term, of course, profitability is of vital importance, since it is by achieving the required degree of profitability that replacement of plant and machinery becomes possible.

Traditionally the commercial banks have provided short term finance, in particular working capital, by way of overdraft, bridging and other short term self liquidating advances. However, they are now increasingly lending longer in response to customers' needs and competition from other institutions.

Even if a company uses simple financial planning and cash forcasting methods to identify its forthcoming requirements, it should consider three important questions before seeking either short or long term finance from outside sources.

How much is needed and when?

Underestimating cash requirements before a development programme reaches a profitable stage can be disastrous since banks are apt to be nervous about lending more than a previously agreed figure for a project. While it pays to arrange finance for conservatively more than estimated requirements, there are costs, since additional borrowing incurs unncessary interest. Even a flexible overdraft facility may attract fees related to the size of the agreed borrowing limit.

Obviously, ample time must be allowed for completing the formalities of obtaining finance well ahead of its requirements.

Will expansion be profitable?

Unless profits increase sufficiently to cover the costs of finance, including interest and a margin for risk, and provide cash flow for repayment of loans plus a reward for management effort, there is no point in raising capital for expansion.

Can the money be found internally?

All businesses should look within themselves for help before seeking outside funds. Management should think along the following lines:

Cash management

Do we bank funds received daily, if possible?
Are surplus funds placed on interest bearing accounts?
Does centralisation to reduce branch surpluses take place?
Do we maximise the use of the various money transmission services?
Have we enquired of the bank regarding payroll, direct debit, cheque reconciliation services, etc?

Debtors

Can we shorten the period of credit granted?
Can we amend any discount given?
Can we invoice more quickly, etc?
Have we considered block discounting or factoring?

Creditors

Can we negotiate longer credit – without incurring penalties?
Have we compared costs – e.g. discount v bank overdraft?

Stocks

Can we modify or reduce the level of stocks carried?
Are there slow moving lines which can be eliminated?
Can a better stock control system be introduced?

Do we maintain average age comparisons of the various items?
Could we reduce pilferage?
Remember, total storage costs can reach 30/40 per cent of average
stock value.

Shorten purchasing/manufacturing cycle

Is work in progress at an optimum? Could it be reduced by quicker
deliveries?
Can the length of production runs be improved?

Capital expenditure

Can we defer any capital projects not immediately connected
with productivity?
Have we considered hire purchase, leasing, sale and leaseback?
Can fixed asset requirements be modified?

Shareholders

Could dividends and payments to directors be reduced without
affecting confidence?
Could help come from existing shareholders?

Renegotiate – hardcore borrowing

Has some of the overdraft facility been used for capital expenditure? If so, this portion should be placed on term loan or other
long term finance. The effect will be greater control and an ability
ultimately to reduce borrowing.

If outside finance is required, the type will depend largely on the
period involved. However, in a period of changing rates of inflation
and interest rates the choice of the right financing 'package' can be
complex. In harmonising a successful mix of finance, the assistance
and guidance of the commercial banks can be very useful, since they
can provide a complete range of services available through local
managers and group companies.

TYPES OF FINANCE OFFERED BY THE COMMERCIAL BANKS

We shall now identify the more important forms of bank finance and
discuss the salient feature of each, the benefits that can be expected

from their employment, and where applicable, make some general observations regarding costs and suitability.

Overdrafts

Definition: an 'in and out' working capital facility for normal trading purposes with interest calculated on a daily balance basis.

The overdraft offers many advantages to the customer, including informal arrangements with the minimum of legal documentation, and there is no minimum sum. The overdraft facility is highly flexible, being normally renewable and even, possibly, unsecured. Against this, there are disadvantages in that, technically, an overdraft is repayable on demand and is subject to official credit restrictions.

The cost of an overdraft is usually a fixed percentage over and above the bank's advertised base rate, charged on the outstanding daily balance; and there may possibly be additional costs in the form of arrangement or management fees. However, an overdraft is still the cheapest form of 'external' finance.

Factoring

Definition: a facility by which the factor purchases all the trade debts of its clients as they arise, thus relieving the client of the need to administer a debtors' ledger and of the risk of bad debts.

Prepayments by the factor to the client of a substantial percentage of the value of the debts as soon as they are purchased frees the client from the need to finance the trade credit requirements of his customer.

It is important that the company seeking this service should sell standard products which do not require substantial after sales service and which are not subject to long term contracts which involve progress payments.

Block discounting

Definition: a source of finance arising from the purchase of contracts for the sale of goods (through hire purchase or credit sale) or rental of goods on a 'with recourse' basis.

The main criteria to be applied are that the business must sell or rent direct to the public and it must have built up business in at least one major field, for example TV sales, TV rental, car sales and contract hire, alarm systems. It is essential that the retailer finances his own credit or rental scheme, that credit agreements or contracts are available and that customers make payments to the retailer at regular intervals. The business may even be a finance company in its own right, but only a proportion of the face value of the block of agreements concerned, normally 70 per cent, is paid to the retailer.

Block discounting offers real advantages to the retailer in that it releases capital invested in rental stock or instalment credit finance for deployment elsewhere in the business, so facilitating increased turnover and profitability. Full advantage can be taken of trade discounts by subsequent prompt payments. Also, the retailer can pay for the block discounted, usually on a monthly basis. In addition, agreements are retained in the retailer's name, preserving the goodwill and business potential generated by personalised service. Yet another advantage is that it gives a reliable confidential credit source in addition to any banking facilities, enabling the retailer to provide flexible terms to his selective customers, to match his competitors' activities.

With regard to the cost, discount charges will depend on the volume of business, the type of merchandise handled, and the standing of the dealer. Charges are usually quoted as a flat rate calculated on the initial credit sum and added to the initial payment.

Support finance (stocking finance)

Definition: finance of stock-in-trade and demonstration merchandise (can be secured or unsecured).

The type of business most likely to benefit from stocking finance will be caravan dealers or motor car dealers. The main criteria are that stock must be readily saleable, that associated costs have to be met from the sale proceeds, and that title to the equipment is vested in the retailer.

Among the advantages which accrue to the bank's customer are that, for an assured term, the finance cannot be recalled or reduced on demand like an overdraft. It is a revolving loan up to an agreed limit, capital being repaid as and when stock is sold. Interest payments are monthly or quarterly depending upon requirements, and an early settlement of the agreement usually earns a generous rebate of charges. In addition, further advances up to the credit limit are available on demand.

Usually, the interest payable on this type of finance will be calculated on a day to day basis at a rate linked to finance house base rate.

Instalment finance (hire purchase)

Definition: a hiring agreement with an option to purchase. This is a means of obtaining the use of capital equipment over an agreed hire period at the end of which clear title passes to the user on the exercise of an option to purchase at a nominal sum.

The major advantages to the customer are that it facilitates the purchase of plant and machinery without immediate capital expenditure and therefore its effect on cash flow is predictable, thereby assisting budgeting. As beneficial owner the user can claim capital allowances, tax relief on the interest paid and even investment grants if the company is situated in a development area. At the same time the equipment has a chance to pay for itself out of the earnings which it generates and, of course, the title to it ultimately passes to the user. Unlike an overdraft, continuity of finance is assured, while the interest can be fixed or flexible. In addition the agreement length can be arranged to suit the earning capacity of the equipment and the period over which it is written off.

The cost of this service will depend upon the amount of the deposit, the term of the hire period (normally a maximum of 3 years, but exceptionally up to 5), and the frequency of the hire instalments. Rates vary considerably from company to company and the charges, usually expressed as a percentage rate, are applied to the amount of the initial advance.

Vehicle contract hire

Definition: a hiring agreement usually backed by a maintenance contract, with no option to purchase and requiring no initial deposit as such, monthly or quarterly rentals being paid in advance over a fixed period.

This type of financing is not suitable for a business already burdened with instalments and contract hire commitments. There must be a positive cash flow to meet all regular outgoings and the management must be seen to be capable of ensuring sufficient earnings are generated from assets employed. But for a business which can meet these requirements there are a number of very attractive advantages. This is a simple rental arrangement which leaves capital intact. The rentals are charged against revenue and are therefore eligible for tax relief. The contract period is variable according to the customer's choice to allow replacement of vehicles as required. A fixed monthly rental covers all costs and also covers regular maintenance of the hired vehicles, while any vehicles temporarily off the road can be substituted. The contract is not terminable at short notice like an overdraft, and it ensures un-interrupted use of the vehicle while the title remains with the financier.

The cost of this type of hire can usually be arranged to suit individual requirements of dealers and customers. The cost is the difference between the sale price of the vehicles and their purchase price, plus the hiring charge spread over the currency of the agreement.

Leasing

Definition: a contract between lessor and lessee for hire of a specific asset selected from a manufacturer or vendor, primarily industrial plant, machinery and equipment. The lessor retains ownership of the asset. The lessee has possession and use of the asset on payment of specified rentals over a period.

Among many advantages to the customer, leasing serves as a potential hedge against inflation and a variation clause can be incorporated to allow for changes in money rates. Leasing is available for almost any movable machinery, plant, equipment or commercial vehicle and immediate use of the asset is obtained on payment of the initial rental. The offer of leasing facilities to potential buyers can help to increase sales, both in the UK and abroad. A leasing agreement is not subject to changes in credit directives and it can be arranged flexibly making it possible to replace equipment as it becomes unsuitable or obsolescent.

Other points in favour of leasing are that the overall cost can be spread over five years, or even longer periods for large capital invest-ment programmes by substantial customers. Budgeting is made easier since the cost of the use of the asset can be assessed over a given period. The rentals, which may be paid monthly, quarterly, half-yearly or annually in advance, are chargeable as a revenue expense and fully allowable against taxable profits. Moreover, they can be self financing due to the increased earnings from the leased asset but the customer remains responsible for insurance, repair and maintenance.

Companies not currently paying tax can find leasing attractive since the tax benefits of capital allowances can be taken by the lessor and the resulting benefits made available to the lessee through lower rentals. Leasing is covered in greater detail in Chapter 12.

Medium term loans

Definition: Secured fixed term advances, usually up to seven years and exceptionally ten, for capital expenditure purposes, repayable by instalments at regular and predetermined intervals.

A medium term loan may facilitate the company's plans to acquire additional premises or extend existing ones, or to purchase new plant and machinery. It may be used to acquire other companies, or finance any form of general expansion other than for working capital purposes. It may even re-finance a hard core overdraft.

A medium term loan offers many advantages to the customer. It assures the borrower of the necessary finance on a contractual basis, thus insulating the business against possible future quantitative credit controls. By allowing a budgeted repayment programme in the company's cash flow, it provides the customer with a consistent and attainable means of reducing borrowing. The loan can be tailored to individual requirements, with total flexibility of repayments, including, if appropriate, an initial moratorium. The terms and conditions are clearly set out in the facility letter issued to the customer for acceptance.

Before agreeing to a medium term loan a bank will satisfy itself that the proposed finance will contribute to the earnings of the business through the asset acquired. It will also examine an analysis of the company's long term cash flow forecast, and usually advance on a secured basis.

The costs of the loan will vary, with rates of interest dependent upon the term. Other charges may include an arrangement fee, professional valuation fees, and a penalty clause for early repayment.

Long term loans

Definition: The provision of 10/20 year contractual finance for independent businesses, which, due to their limitation of size, have no direct access to the capital markets.

A long term loan may meet the company's capital needs for expansion better than short term finance. It provides for an agreed repayment programme which will not vary even if interest rates change and allows the company to have a capital moratorium period, until sufficient cash flow is generated to enable repayments to be made.

The advantages of a long term loan to the borrower are similar to those provided by the medium term loan, and the costs will vary depending upon the choice taken between either a fixed or floating rate of interest, and upon the actual length of the loan. Again, as for medium term loans, an arrangement fee and professional valuation fees may be charged, together with a penalty clause for early repayment.

Equity investment

Definition: Provision of finance by way of investment in the equity of a company which has a good potential for future profitable growth.

There are particular circumstances where investment by the bank in the equity of a company could prove to be the best method of providing finance. One likely reason for investment is to provide development finance; the introduction of new money against new shares, either to purchase productive assets, to provide additional trading finance, and/or to facilitate a takeover. Equity finance could be offered to newly-established companies formed by proven managers, who are skilled in the particular trade concerned, but who have inadequate capital. Alternatively, equity finance may be used to solve Capital Transfer Tax problems, where, by purchasing some shares, continuity of a business can be assured. It may be used either to assist a retiring shareholder director to provide for his retirement, or, indeed, to assist an inheriting shareholder, who has no interest in the business and wants to dispose of the shares. It may, perhaps, also be used where existing shareholders are drawing good income, but paying high personal rates of tax, and while wishing to remain in control of the business, would like to realise part of their shareholding for personal reasons. Another possible reason for equity investment is for a 'management buy-out' where a company wishes to sell a subsidiary to those who manage it, but are unable to find cash for the full cost of acquisition.

Several possible advantages accrue to the company as a result of bank-backed equity finance. It may improve the gearing of the company and give greater financial stability. By strengthening capital structure a company's credit worthiness can be enhanced. Conventional bank borrowing capacity may be enlarged, as the assets purchased through a capital injection may be used as additional security by direct or floating charges. Also, since no loan account repayments are incurred, funds may be liberated for working capital. A major advantage is that the owners retain control of the business, since any equity investment is on the basis of minority interest only. A company's image and trading reputation is often enhanced by going into 'partnership' with its bank, and in cases where a nominee director is appointed by the bank his calibre will often be higher than that which the company could otherwise afford.

Venture capital

Definition: Capital, plus expert management assistance, provided by a specialist investment capital company to the individuals or companies who want to exploit advanced techniques or ideas ('the project') by creating a new company or developing their existing company.

Typically, venture capital is sought when companies are unable to raise finance on the strength of the balance sheet or give adequate security in respect of a particular project.

The main criteria a bank will look for are that the project must have a novel or superior character, be protected by patent or 'lead' time, and there must be considerable market potential. While it is accepted that the management must stay with the company, they must expect some loss of control, be adaptable to rapid growth, and be prepared to expose themselves financially. In general the investing institution would require a stake of say between £25 000 and £500 000, representing a shareholding between 10 per cent and 40 per cent of issued capital.

Among the advantages which might accrue to the customer, are the experience in management, marketing and production of the investor, plus a better public image as a result of the association. Through the investing bank, access to all forms of finance and the recruitment of expertise on an international scale would be available. Potential international markets would be examined as part of the ongoing monitoring of the company's financial needs.

Export finance

This is a very important area of finance which can only be mentioned in passing and is beyond the scope of this chapter. Overdrafts, factoring, leasing and instalment finance have already been described, and all are available to the exporter.

In addition, several other methods of export finance are provided through the commercial banks. These include both the negotiation of, and advances against, foreign bills of exchange; foreign currency loans; documentary and acceptance credits; and the wide range of facilities available through the Export Credit Guarantee Department (ECGD). The services offered by the accepting, confirming and export houses supplement these options.

RELATIONS WITH A BANK

In lending, as in all creditor/debtor situations, confidence is central to the relationship. The borrower needs to be confident of obtaining ample lending facilities, at competitive interest rates, with manageable repayments and facilities that will not be withdrawn arbitrarily. The bank, as creditor, on the other hand, must feel assured that funds supplied will be deployed correctly and carefully so that, in due course, the borrowing is repaid.

Small businesses and first-time borrowers in particular, frequently do not understand the need to provide full details to a lending insitution. A borrower often fails to realize that lending organisations do not know his business affairs unless this knowledge is imparted. Adequate communication is essential to obtaining the confidence of banks or other lending bodies. The information imparted must be factual, precise and to the point; furthermore, where expectations and forecasts are offered, these should be as realistic as possible. Before making an approach to any bank, the applicant must be clear about at least three things; the amount of finance required and the period for which it is wanted; the purpose for which the finance is being sought; and the current financial position and future prospects of the business.

Especially for medium and long term finance when banks view the risk element more critically, a bank manager will also want to know the applicant's precise financial stake. The greater this is in relation to the bank's, the more convinced the lender will be of his customer's commitment to use the new funds prudently. This is one reason why banks often insist on the personal guarantees of the directors as security when a new and expensive project is put forward, since otherwise they could avoid personal liability and responsibility in the case of failure.

Many businessmen and directors feel reluctant to approach bank managers for financial assistance and, as a result, put off the 'evil day' until a crisis arises and the business is already heading for difficulties. An ill-prepared and rushed application at this time is obviously less likely to succeed. Although thorough preparation and presentation of a poor proposition will not appreciably alter its acceptability, the prospects for a good or marginal proposition could be damaged by inadequate forethought and bad presentation.

A number of practical considerations should be borne in mind by the business applicant when dealing with a bank:

1 *The character of the applicants* – directors, management, partners, etc. – is very important. A bank manager will not respond to obvious ploys designed to rush his decision making, to intimidate him or impress him through unsubstantiated or boastful claims. A small matter such as punctuality when an appointment is arranged is significant, as a banker will be influenced by first impressions. Furthermore, it should be remembered that he will seek affirmation of the view he is forming by checking any information he is given from outside sources (where appropriate) – for example, solicitors, surveyors – and will expect the customer's ready permission and co-operation to approach such people. The applicant's integrity will be doubted if the information given proves inaccurate or misleading. The banker will study the balance sheets of the company to see if these show an excessive life style by the directors, with large emoluments and drawings in relation to the performance of the business. He will also look for factors which could indicate extremes of optimism or prudence by examining the treatment of items such as tax, stock, work in progress and provisions.

2 *Applicants must not expect an on-the-spot decision* especially if the sum involved is large, since time will be required to evaluate the proposition. Specialists from other parts of the banking group may have to be contacted and their advice sought. For sums in excess of the branch manager's personal lending authority, the proposition will have to be referred to a more senior official or to head office before agreement can be given. In most cases, such referral would require an additional few days' time.

3 *Once the advance has been granted* most company directors expect their bank manager to show a continuing interest in the

company's affairs. However, mutual confidence and co-operation will be improved if the directors arrange to meet their bankers at regular intervals to discuss the company's problems and progress. This will be much appreciated by the banker and will help to cement the relationship, especially if the banker is occasionally invited to view the operation at the business premises.

PRESENTING A CASE FOR FINANCE TO A BANK

Research Report No. 5, *Committee of Enquiry on Small Firms*, explained that, 'in most cases . . . which they considered unfortunate not to have obtained finance, the reason was that . . . they failed to make out a good enough case to the supplying institution approached'. Thus let us now see how a company seeking finance from a commercial bank should prepare and present a proposition.

For the simplest bridging or seasonal overdraft facility, a banker will look particularly at management's experience, ability, drive, integrity, resilience in times of trouble and at the viability of the proposal. The longer term and' more complicated the requirement, the higher the degree of credit worthiness to be demonstrated. If equity finance is being sought, the bank or its subsidiary will delve into 'the man, the market, the margins, the management information systems and the money requirement'. Clearing bankers, as such, do not provide risk capital nor participate in equity profits. They expect acceptable security with suitable margins to be provided to safeguard repayments should forecast future profits not materialise. Apart from considerations of character, the banker regards liquidity ratios, together with details of creditors, debtors and stock turnovers, the past conduct of the account and the break-up value of the assets, as important to successful negotiations.

The banker must be convinced the customer is capable of implementing planned repayment schedules both as to capital and interest. This involves maintaining effective systems of financial planning and control incorporating a general business plan for, say, a five-year period, a detailed short term plan, capital and operational budgets, together with reporting systems and control mechanisms. These will prove invaluable when deciding what information to give the bank when submitting a proposal for finance. Many of the details suggested as appropriate in the following checklist will already be available if such systems are operating.

Proposals should be adequately documented

When a banker with whom the company already maintains an account is approached, much information will already be on file. When an entirely fresh approach is made, the following might form part of an overall presentation:

1 A short description of the company, its history, past achievements, current objectives and the strategy formulated in order to achieve these goals.

2 Memorandum and Articles of Association, together with a copy of the Certificate of Incorporation. The Memorandum is needed for the bank to assess the company's borrowing powers and ability to give security for loans. The Articles give details of the directors' powers.

    If the company is public, the bank will also require the company's trading certificate for inspection. If an account is not already open, then the bank will ultimately need a certified copy of the board of directors' resolution appointing the bank as the company's bankers and a mandate signed in conformity with the Memorandum and Articles.

3 A recent set of audited accounts.

4 Tabulations of detailed trading, profit and loss accounts and balance sheets, for five years (if possible).

5 An analysis of major influences on profit for the period tabulated.

6 If the company currently banks elsewhere, then a prospective new banker will almost certainly require:
    (a) Details of current facilities, both loans and overdrafts.
    (b) Details of any security given in support of the borrowing and any other charges or mortgages. Up to date valuations should be quoted where appropriate.
    (c) Three years' bank statements.

7 A full appraisal of the present and future market, including the activities of major competitors.

8 A detailed statement of the current order book and a comparison with the position in, perhaps, the two previous years.

9 What finance is now required, how much, for how long, and by

what means it will be repaid.

10 Detailed projections for the year ahead – cash flows, trading and profit and loss accounts and half-yearly balance sheets.

11 The current position regarding such matters as debtors and creditors, any amounts considered uncollectable, stock levels and cash balances.

12 Forecasts of the information detailed in No. 8 above for a further two years ahead.

13 Details of the assumptions on which information in Nos. 8 and 9 are prepared and an estimation of the degrees of 'guesswork' involved.

14 What security will be available if the proposition is accepted.

The presentation should enlarge upon pertinent matters in the documentation and aim to present a logical and well reasoned case to justify granting the appropriate finance on attractive terms. In achieving this, the presentation should refer to other matters which will be of interest to the banker and some of these are shown in the Appendix. This is by no means an exhaustive list and the individual applicant should use his common sense to decide which items are relevant and which are not, depending on the amount and type of finance required. It is included in order to illustrate the wide variety of information a banker may feel he needs from a business customer, depending on the circumstances.

Evaluation of the proposal

This may be regarded as a summary of the points already referred to in general terms in the text.

The proposal itself should reveal clearly:

1 Amount required.
2 Purpose of borrowing.
3 Length of commitment.
4 Source of repayment.

The bank will look particularly at:

1 Management – its experience, ability, drive, integrity etc.
2 Past conduct of the account.
3 Balance sheets, cash flow statements and other financial data, especially in relation to liquidity, establishing the viability of

the business as a going concern, and the likely position in the event of liquidation (i.e. the likely proceeds of various assets in forced sale, to meet liabilities, including bank borrowing).

4 Whether security is offered or required.

(1) and (2) are self explanatory, but closer consideration will now be given to (3) and (4).

Balance sheets

The first glance: the banker will form an initial impression by perusing the following points:

1 Date – Is the balance sheet up to date?
  In general, the older the information, the less relevant it is.
2 Audited/signed – the standing of the auditors is important and whether there are any reservations in their certification.
3 Whether interim or draft – Provision for tax and depreciation are particularly relevant.
4 Liabilities – Tax, secured creditors, contingent liabilities, debentures capable of re-issue, loans, are all of great interest.
5 Assets – Whether stock and work in progress seem reasonable for the type of business concerned.
6 Profit record – Directors' fees and salaries, dividends or drawings, bad debts, depreciation, non-trading income.

During this cursory inspection the banker will expect to pick out anything unusual: either exceptional items or special notes in the body of the accounts.

Going concern approach

This approach is a means of assessing the continuing viability of the business by the use of financial comparisons:

1 *Horizontal and vertical comparison* – This refers to extracting major fluctuations which may require investigation and/or explanation.
2 *Pre-tax return on net capital resources (percentage pre-tax profit)* – This is considered an important test of the success of a business and is thus of most interest to the bank where the safety aspect of the advance is concerned.
3 *Compare current assets with current liabilities* – Working capital

should be sufficient to finance the day to day transactions of the business. The working of the bank account is often a better guide to the liquidity of the business, since bank statements will tend to show the position over a period of time rather than at one particular point in time. The proposed loan must allow for sufficient working capital to finance increased turnover; where, for example, production is expected to expand as a result of purchasing new plant and machinery, the working capital requirement will undoubtedly increase.

4   *Net capital resources with total liabilities* – The proprietor's stake should provide sufficient reserve capacity to endure set-backs and obviate any risk of loss for the creditors.

5   *Net capital resources with net fixed assets* – Loans with a minimum term of 5 years are regarded as loan 'capital' and capital resources from the 'going concern' viewpoint.

6   *Stock with sales*

7   *Credit given* ⎱ These are very useful guides and are

8   *Credit received* ⎰ invariably calculated

9   *Relationship between bank advance and capital resources* – As a rough guide banks do not want to put more into a business than the proprietors or shareholders.

10   *Comparison of sales with bank account turnover* – This can highlight matters such as:

   (a)   An account at another bank
   (b)   Cash trade
   (c)   Inter-departmental sales
   (d)   Inter-company transactions
   (e)   Stock piling

Banks plot these relationships from available annual balance sheets to obtain trends.

Gone concern approach (i.e. 'break-up assessment')

The 'Gone concern' approach is a means of assessing the bank's position in the event of bankruptcy or liquidation. This is only one of the balance sheet tests, since banks are primarily concerned with the business of customers on a 'going concern' basis. It is an attempt to place a forced sale value on the assets, to deduct the preferential and secured creditors, and thus estimate a possible value for the bank's floating charge (if held) and any remaining distribution to the unsecured creditors.

Basically, the method of approach is as follows:

1   *Total liabilities*
    From these are deducted loans in the balance sheet postponed to the bank or capitalised since the balance sheet. In the main these will be loans from the directors.

2   *Additional considerations*
    (a)   Liabilities incurred or to be incurred since the balance sheet date.
    (b)   'Plus bank', i.e. the difference between the bank's proposed total lending and the balance sheet figure.
    (c)   Estimated risk for contingent liabilities, for example foreign credits, discounts/foreign bills negotiated, engagements, guarantees and so on.
    (d)   An estimate for tax, if omitted from interim accounts.

3   *Forced sale value of assets*
    The following are some of the more usual percentages which are used in calculating the break-up value of the assets shown in a balance sheet.

Sundry debtors	80%	
	85%	if covered by ECGD (Export Credits Guarantee Dept.)
	90%,	say, if Government contracts.
Hire Purchase debtors	60%	
Stock	50%	or sometmes higher (e.g. if raw materials).
Work in progress	60%	but only if value improved by production process.

Commercial and industrial property

Freehold	50%	of balance sheet value or manager's valuation with vacant possession, *or*
	60%	of recent professional valuation.
Long leasehold	33%	of manager's valuation or recent professional valuation.
Private property	66%	of manager's valuation or sale price.
Marketable investments	80%	(of current market value).

Plant and machinery	10%	
Office furniture, loose tools etc.	10%	
Vehicles	20%	
Loans to directors	nil	(unless evidence to the contrary).
Payments in advance	nil	

These percentages will vary according to the facts and circumstances of each balance sheet assessment and different banks will obviously use different percentages. No entry is made for cash or proceeds of sale of assets as these are included in the next stage.

4 *Cash position*

In the event of a bankruptcy or liquidation most cash will have been spent, either to meet the liabilities or to purchase assets.

For the purpose of the break-up, therefore, the bank summarises what has happened to the cash in a 'cash position' and then estimates and inserts the break-up value of the assets which were purchased.

Items included in the cash position may be:

(a) Cash.
(b) Proceeds of sale of assets.
(c) 'Plus bank'.
(d) Cash from additional capital raised or to be raised since balance sheet date or additional liabilities incurred, etc.

5 *Preferentials*

If the total liabilities are less than the total assets, the 'break-up' shows a surplus and a dividend of 100p in the £ is available for all creditors including the bank.

If liabilities exceed assets at break-up values, then the bank must subtract from both totals the total of all creditors whose claims in bankruptcy or liquidation would rank in priority to the bank i.e.:

(a) Secured creditors (Holding fixed mortgages)
(b) HP creditors
(c) Any floating charge ranking in priority to the bank, creditors who have been paid since the balance sheet date or will rank preferentially, e.g. tax, specific repayment loans, mortgages, debentures, and 50 per cent of trade creditors on the assumption that if the business gets into

difficulties trade credit will decrease.

6 *Dividend for unsecured creditors*
A dividend for unsecured creditors is then calculated from the resultant totals.

7 *Bank holding a floating charge*
The value attributed to this will be the break-up value of the assets after deduction of the preferentials.

8 *Bank's position*
This is a calculation and summary of the bank's total lending facilities and contingent liabilities compared with the likely proceeds (or divided if there is a shortfall) to be received by the realisation of security.

The need for security

The longer the commitment, the more difficult it is to forecast ahead, and so the greater the need for security, when banks are asked to finance fixed capital. Security is taken as an insurance in case things go wrong so as to minimise potential losses through bad debts.

The best security of all is the integrity, ability and continued solvency of the customer. The need for security is conditioned by the volume, quality and reliability of the financial information the customer can produce. The bank's ability to monitor the business regularly during the lifetime of a loan is to some extent an acceptable substitute for formal security. Security is usually taken where capital resources are not considered adequate in relation to the level of borrowing requested; the availability of security permits banks to lend more than otherwise would have been forthcoming. However, no amount of security would induce a bank to lend to a non-viable, uncreditworthy business.

1 *Forms of seurity*

All security is either:

Tangible – For example land, buildings, plant and machinery, ships, stocks and shares, and life policies.

or Intangible – For example floating charges and unsupported guarantees.

Security is also:

Direct – Where the security offered belongs solely

to the customer who is the borrower.

or Collateral — When a security belongs to and is deposited by a third party.

2 *Nature of security*

Broadly speaking the main forms of security acceptable to bankers are the following:

(a) Land.
(b) Life policies.
(c) Stocks and shares.
(d) Guarantees.

Generally, the banks protect their interest by means of legal mortgages or charge forms; these have many different formats.

3 *Attributes of a good security*

A good security is one with a good title, so that there can be no ambiguity as to ownership. It should be readily transferable, with a value which is both stable and easily assessable. Furthermore, it must be quickly marketable in case of need.

CONCLUSIONS

Twenty years ago the London clearing banks saw their function as collecting deposits, lending on short term and providing a money transmission service. The explosive growth in the structure of the banks since then has produced the modern banking group which today can rightly claim to satisfy any personal or corporate financial need.

In the latter part of this chapter we have seen something of the wide variety of financial services available to the bank's corporate customers and although several of these could hardly be regarded as 'traditional' banking services, the banks can now offer the businessman an opportunity to deal through one contact, his bank manager, for advice on all financial matters. Obviously, it is good business for a bank to provide a complete financial package to a corporate customer, but the expertise now available from within the ranks of the banking industry must be seen as a very attractive benefit to the businessman.

No matter how many ways the banks find to lend money, it is unlikely that the methods of assessment referred to will change significantly in the future. For this reason we have tried to provide an insight into the ways in which a bank looks at lending propositions it receives daily from its corporate customers who, collectively, represent the pulse of Britain's economy.

FURTHER READING

Bank of England and City Communications Centre, *Money for Business*, June 1978.

The London Clearing Banks – *Evidence by the Committee of London Clearing Bankers to the Committee to Review the Functioning of Financial Institutions*, November 1977.

Committee of Inquiry on Small Firms, *Research Report No. 5: Problems of Small Firms in Raising External Finance*, HMSO, 1971.

D. Thorpe, 'The package deal concept', *Investors Chronicle*, 14 September 1973.

G. Rice, 'Presenting a Loan proposal' *Accountancy*, November 1978.

APPENDIX – INFORMATION TO SUPPORT THE DOCUMENTATION

For the sake of simplicity, this has been categorised into broad functions, and is additional to the documentation referred to on page 262 et seq:

Personnel

Management structure	– ability, depth succession.
Organisation chart	
Key personnel other than management	
Breakdown of labour	– skilled and unskilled sex, turnover, availability.
Industrial relations record	– number of stoppages, reasons.
Union representation	
List of professional advisers	– solicitors, accountants, brokers.
Wage and salary bill	– when paid, method, average take-home pay.

Accounting

Management accounting dates   – draft accounts, return on assets, approach to depreciation, breakdown of manufacturing costs, especially between direct and indirect, costing methods; job, contract, batch standard, etc.

Hidden assets   – undervaluation of stocks, property, equity, etc. should be explored.

Control of liquidity   – including age debtor analysis, stockholding requirements, nature of stock control measures breakdown and creditors analysis.

Investment decisions criteria   – if one or more capital projects are mooted, then the pessimistic optimistic evaluation of each in terms of rate of return (DCF) or other criteria. Details of any recent valuation of assets.

Production

Method of production   – quality of plant and equipment
Product range
Research and development

Sales

Margin on sales
Relationship of sales mix to profit return
Product life
Exports   – history of activity in this field, details of agents employed, involvement with ECGD and other bodies. Current orders by amount and destination countries.

Market research	– brief details of any market surveys.
Marketing	
Pricing policy	
Photographs and sales literature	

Other

Inter-firm comparisons
Management consultancy projects
Names of principal shareholders
Full details of any subsidiary, parent or holding companies

Premises	– freehold/leasehold, mortgages, rent, rates.
Insurance	– buildings, stock, plant, employer's liability, life cover on key personnel etc.
Available security	– especially the possibility of utilising directors' personal assets and guarantees as collateral.

12

Leasing

Colin M Young

When a company makes an investment decision, this usually involves the productive use of a new asset. It may also, but not necessarily, require the ownership of the asset. Figure 12.1 lists a number of common methods of obtaining the use of an asset with declining degrees of 'ownership'.

Method	Description
Outright purchase	Purchase with firm's own funds
Unsecured loan	Purchase with borrowed funds not secured on equipment
Mortgage	Purchase with funds borrowed on security of equipment
Conditional sale	Purchase with title passing on completion of instalment payments
Hire purchase	Hire with option to purchase title at nominal price
Financial lease	Hire for economic life of asset – non cancellable
Operating lease	Medium term hire – cancellable
Hire	Short term rental

Fig. 12.1 Common methods of obtaining the use of an asset

For those methods ranging from outright purchase to hire purchase, the user of the asset eventually obtains title to the asset. For lease or hire agreements this is not the case. In fact, we may define a lease as 'a contract between lessor and lessee for the hire of a specific asset selected by the lessee. The lessor retains ownership of the asset. The lessee has possession and use of the asset on payment of specified rentals over a period'.

We should also make clear at this point what constitutes a financial lease: 'A financial lease is a contract involving payments over an obligatory period of specified sums sufficient in total to amortize the capital outlay of the lessor and give some profit'.

It is with the financial lease that this chapter primarily deals, although many of the points made apply equally to operating leases.

What makes leasing attractive?

Leasing provides a means of obtaining the long term use of an asset while the ownership of the asset remains with the lessor. It is the conditions of ownership that provide the basis for leasing. Investment incentives in the UK are provided in the form of allowances which enable the owner of an asset to offset the cost of the asset against taxable profits. Normally 100 per cent of the cost of the asset is allowed against profits in the year of purchase. If the investing company is not in a tax-paying position at the time of the investment, it cannot take immediate advantage of the allowance. Thus the value of the allownce to the investing company will be diminished. In these circumstances it may be possible to find a lessor that can take advantage of the capital allowances. The lessor will purchase the asset and lease it to the user at rentals that make leasing more attractive than purchase. Thus companies, who cannot claim capital allowances, may gain at least some advantage from investment incentives, by means of leasing.

This feature lies behind the rapid growth of leasing as a method of financing capital investment. At the time of writing leasing accounts for 12 per cent of all capital investments, and for about 25 per cent of all externally raised finance.

Who leases what

Leasing developed steadily from 1971 to 1975, but since then rapid growth has occurred. Table 12.1 shows the major categories of leased assets broken down by volume for the period 1977–81. Car leasing

Table 12.1
Leased assets broken down by type

Type of equipment	Amounts in £ million				
	1977	1978	1979	1980	1981
Plant & machinery	198	250	415	830	801
Ships & aircraft	108	158	298	349	355
Computers & office equipment	164	240	315	453	380
Commercial vehicles	114	154	225	291	225
Cars	57	343	468	267	222
Other	34	69	81	169	119
TOTAL	675	1214	1812	2359	2102

Source: Equipment Leasing Association

showed a particularly rapid growth in this period, although the rate of growth slowed after the 1979 Finance Act, which disallowed a 100 per cent first year allowance claim on cars.

The major users of lease financing in 1981 are shown in Table 12.2, broken down into types of user.

Table 12.2
Users of lease financing 1981

Type of user	Leased assets £ million	% of total
Manufacturing	711	33.8
Other industry	273	13.0
Transport	176	8.4
Agriculture	99	4.7
Distributive + other services	589	28.0
Local + central government	254	12.1

Source: Equipment Leasing Association

As might be expected the major providers of lease finance are leasing subsidiaries of major banks and finance houses.

Other reasons for leasing

Taxation was not the only reason for the growth in leasing in the 1970s. Many firms found leasing attractive because lease liabilities did not appear on the balance sheet and this was thought to provide a kind of hidden borrowing that increased the firm's overall debt capacity. At the beginning of the period leasing may have increased debt capacity, but the increasing awareness of leasing among banks and investing institutions has rendered any remaining advantage of this nature more illusory than real. The Accounting Standards Committee recommendations on accounting for leasing include full disclosure and so will bring to an end any 'off balance sheet' advantages if and when adopted.

One real advantage that has formed a major 'selling point' for leasing is the ease of arrangement and flexibility of lease finance. Leases can be written at short notice for a wide variety of assets. Leases can also be written easily to reflect the tax-paying situation of the lessee. Furthermore, and this applies particularly in the case of car fleet leasing, the lease deal may also include the day to day management of the asset and hence free the lessee to concentrate on his essential business. It is the ease of arrangement and flexibility of leasing that now provide its major non-tax advantages.

One last factor that played a major role in the growth of leasing in the mid-1970s was the unavailability of other forms of medium term finance. During that time lessors were virtually the only providers of finance for terms between three and ten years, and so filled a gap in the market between overdrafts provided by clearing banks and the kind of long term loans provided by insurance companies and pension funds. By the end of the 1970s, however, other forms of instalment credit had reappeared in the market, and leasing was no longer the only form of medium term finance available.

FINANCIAL BENEFITS OF LEASING – A SIMPLE EXAMPLE

Other advantages not withstanding, the attraction of leasing derives from the financial benefit that may be obtained. The primary investment incentive in the UK is the 100 per cent first year capital allowance on new plant and machinery. The entire cost of new equipment may be set off against taxable corporate profits for the year in which the asset is purchased. However, as mentioned earlier, a company with insufficient taxable profits will be unable to take the full allowance in the year of purchase. In these circumstances, when the benefit of the 100 per cent first year allowances is delayed (or in the case of a non-tax paying entity, lost altogether) the present (discounted) value of the investment incentive is reduced. It may be possible to recapture part of the reduced incentive by leasing from a lessor with taxable profits who can take advantage of the investment incentive and pass on at least part of the benefits through favourable rentals. The following example illustrates both the potential advantage of leasing and the method of valuing this advantage.

A company wishes to obtain the use of an asset costing £1 000. Under normal circumstances the company would buy the asset and obtain the 100 per cent capital allowance to set off against taxable profits in the year of purchase. At a rate of Corporation Tax of 52 per cent the allowance would result in a reduction in taxes of £520. Suppose, however, that the company's taxable profits are not large enough to allow it to take immediate advantage of the allowance and, in the first instance, for simplicity, suppose further that it will not be able to take advantage of the benefits in the foreseeable future. Then the asset will have cost £1 000 and the allowances will not have afforded any effective investment incentive.

Now suppose that as an alternative to purchasing the asset, the company finds a lessor who is prepared to purchase the asset and lease it back to the user company for 5 years at a rental of £235 per annum payable in advance. The question now is whether to purchase or lease the asset. To obtain the answer we discount the rentals at an appropriate rate and compare the value of the discounted stream of rentals with the purchase payment. If the present (discounted) value of the rentals is lower, then we should lease the asset. This leaves only the problem of selecting the correct rate at which to discount the rentals. The rate used is that which reflects the interest cost the company would face if it borrowed funds to purchase the equipment. We shall assume for the purpose of example that the rate is 14 per cent.

Table 12.3 shows the calculations for the lease versus purchase comparison.

Table 12.3
Lease versus purchase: non-tax-paying lessee

Date	Lease rental £	Discount factor (at 14%)	Present value £
31/12/81	−235.00	1.0000	−235.00
82	−235.00	0.8772	−206.14
83	−235.00	0.7695	−180.82
84	−235.00	0.6750	−158.62
85	−235.00	0.5921	−139.14

Present cost of lease = £919.72
Purchase cost saved = £1000.00
Net present benefit to lease = £80.28

The residual value of the asset at the end of the 5 year period has been ignored in this example. The treatment of residual values will be discussed later in the chapter.

The net present value of the lease is £80.28, which suggests that the user should lease rather than purchase the equipment. One should remember that the net present value represents a 'profit' established at the start of the lease equivalent to the diminution (in present day terms) of funds that need be committed to obtain the use of the asset by leasing as opposed to purchasing. In order to illustrate this point, consider two possible strategies available to the prospective user of the equipment. He may either purchase the equipment, giving an immediate outflow of £1 000, or he may arrange the lease. If he arranges the lease he can immediately invest a sum of money in interest bearing securities (for example, bank deposits) which, with the interest earned, will be just sufficient to discharge his liabilities under the lease. (See Table 12.4). One can see that the sum required to be invested at the start of the lease is £919.72 and that the difference between this and the alternative of paying £1 000 to purchase the asset is £80.28, the net present value of the lease.

We know that the lessee gains considerable benefit from the lease if he pays no taxes, but what of the lessor?

Table 12.4
Loan required to support lease payments

Data	Initial loan £	Lease payment £	Interest at 14% £	Loan outstanding £
30/12/81	919.72	−235.00		684.72
31/12/82		−235.00	95.86	545.58
31/12/83		−235.00	76.38	386.96
31/12/84		−235.00	54.17	206.13
31/12/85		−235.00	28.87	0.00

Consider the lease from the viewpoint of a lessor paying mainstream corporation tax at 52 per cent with a delay of twelve months from the tax year end. Further assume that the commencement date of the lease coincides with the lessor's tax year end.* From the lessor's point of view then the cash flows associated in the lease are as in Table 12.5.

Once more the rule for deciding whether or not the lease is attractive is to discount the cash flows associated with the lease at an appropriate

Table 12.5
Cash flows for the tax-paying lessor

Date	Lease payment £	Tax payable £	Purchase payment £	Tax effect of capital allowances £	Net cash flow £
31/12/81	235.00		−1 000.00		−765.00
31/12/82	235.00	−122.20		520.00	632.80
31/12/83	235.00	−122.20			112.80
31/12/84	235.00	−122.20			112.80
31/12/85	235.00	−122.20			112.80
31/12/86		−122.20			−122.20

*This assumption and that of the twelve month lag in the payment of tax, although made for simplicity, is not too unrealistic. The value of the lease to the lessor is increased by moving the commencement date towards the lessor's tax year end date. The delay in tax payment may be anything between 9 and 21 months under the UK corporate tax system.

rate. If the net present value obtained is positive then the lease is profitable to the lessor. The only remaining question is the appropriate discount rate. We know that we would lend money to the lessee at 14 per cent and that the contractual nature of the lease commitment is similar to that of a loan payment schedule. If equal returns are required from commitments of a similar nature, then the same rate should be used for the cash flows associated with the lease as would be appropriate on a loan to the lessee with a similar term to the lease and secured on an equivalent asset. However, 14 per cent is not the return on money – it is the pre-tax interest rate. If tax on interest is paid with a delay of 12 months, then the equivalent post-tax rate is 7.21 per cent and this is the rate which should be used to discount the cash flows. The net present value of the lease obtained at this after tax discount rate is £14.05 and hence the lease is also attractive to the lessor.

As in the case of the lessee, one can provide a more intuitive interpretation of the NPV of the lease. By purchasing the asset for £1 000 the lessor obtains the future cash flows attributable to the lease. Consider an alternative way in which he might have obtained those cash flows. Suppose the lessor had made a loan under the terms of which the sinking fund payments (interest and principal combined) were the same as the cash flows produced by the lease. Then we could directly compare the purchase price of the asset with the size of the initial loan, as both produce identical cash flows at every point in the future. Clearly, the preference will be for the alternative which involves the lower initial outlay. The loan schedule that is equivalent to the lease cash flows is shown in Table 12.6.

Table 12.6
Sinking fund equivalent of the lease

Date	Initial investment £	Interest at 14% £	Tax on interest £	Principal repayment £	Net cash flow £	Loan balance £
31/12/81	−1014.05			235.00	235.00	779.05
31/12/82		109.07		523.73	632.80	255.32
31/12/83		35.74	−56.71	133.77	112.80	121.55
31/12/84		17.02	−18.59	114.37	112.80	7.18
31/12/85		1.00	− 8.85	120.64	112.80	−113.47
31/12/86		−15.89	− 0.52	−105.79	−122.20	− 7.68
31/12/87		− 1.07	8.26	− 7.19	0.00	− 0.40
31/12/88		− .07	0.56	− 0.49	0.00	− 0.00

Thus, the NPV of the lease to the lessor is the difference between the purchase price of the asset (£1 000) and the amount he would have had to lend (£1 014.05) in order to obtain the same cash flows.

Leasing and the Inland Revenue

We have seen that this lease is beneficial to both the lessor and the permanently non-tax paying lessee. At this point it is interesting to consider the source of the benefits. Clearly, if the lessee and the lessor are both better off, some third party must be worse off. In this case the identity of the third party is obvious; it is the Inland Revenue. If we

Table 12.7
Leasing and the Inland Revenue

	Actual amount £	Present value to Inland Revenue £
Capital allowance	−520.00	−485.03
Tax on rentals	122.20	113.98
	122.20	106.31
	122.20	99.16
	122.20	92.49
	122.20	86.28
		498.22
Lessor tax on interest	− 49.84	− 43.37
	− 39.72	− 32.23
	− 28.17	− 21.32
	− 15.01	− 10.60
		−107.52
Total loss to Inland Revenue		− 94.33
Value of lease to lessee		80.28
Value of lease to lessor		14.05
Total present value gain		94.33

examine the participation of the Inland Revenue in the lease that we have been considering we find that there are three separate tax effects. First, the IR loses an amount of tax revenue equal to the capital allowance claimed by the lessor; second, it gains the tax paid by the lessor on rentals received; third, it loses tax on interest that would have been earned by the lessor had he lent his money rather than using it to finance the lease. The total of these gains and losses, discounted back to the start of the lease, is identical to the sum of the NPV's of the lease to lessee and lessor, as can be seen from Table 12.7.

One would be wrong to draw the conclusion that leasing is a tax avoidance exercise and is in some sense 'bad'. If we look at the basis of leasing we see that it is, in fact, a way of allowing a non-tax paying company to obtain some of the benefits of the government's investment incentive scheme that otherwise would be lost. Thus, rather than extracting £94.33 from the Inland Revenue by tax avoidance the lease we are considering allows a small part of the £520.00 investment incentive to be claimed.

THE TAX PAYING LESSEE

We have seen that when a lessee cannot claim capital allowances but a lessor can, leasing can be profitable to both the lessee and the lessor. Now, consider the case of a potential lessee who is fully tax paying (that is, he is in the same tax paying position as the lessor). Table 12.8 shows the cash flows attributable to our lease for this lessee.

Table 12.8
Cash flows for the tax-paying lessee

Date	Lease payment £	Tax relief £	Purchase payment £	Capital allowance £	Net cash flow £	Discount factor at 7.21%	Present value £
31/12/81	−235.00		1 000.00		765.00	1.0000	765.00
82	−235.00	122.20		−520.00	−632.80	0.9327	−590.24
83	−235.00	122.20			−112.80	0.8700	− 98.15
84	−235.00	122.20			−112.80	0.8115	− 91.54
85	−235.00	122.20			−122.80	0.7569	− 85.39
86		122.20			122.20	0.7060	86.27

Net present value = £−14.05

One can see that the cash flows are the same as those for the lessor (in Table 12.5) except that all the signs have been changed. Also, the rate at which these cash flows should be discounted is the same as that used for the lessor; that is, the effective after tax interest cost. This is because just as the lessor pays tax on interest received, so the lessee obtains tax relief on interest paid; and in both cases the effect of taxation is felt with an assumed twelve month delay. Thus the rate at which we discount the cash flows is 7.21 per cent, and we find that the NPV of the lease to the full tax paying lessee is £−14.05. This result should not be a surprise; we know that the basis of leasing lies in the lessee and lessor having different tax paying positions; when they are the same we would expect the lessor's gain to be the lessee's loss.

Now let us consider the more interesting, and more common, case of a lessee who is only temporarily non-tax paying. Table 12.9 shows the cash flows for a lessee who will not pay mainstream corporation tax for two years. As can be seen the capital allowance is not lost – it is merely postponed for two years. Similarly, the tax relief obtainable on rentals in the first two periods is not lost, but, rather, delayed. In the same way, when the effective after tax discount rate is calculated it is found that the delay in taking advantage of the interest tax savings in the first years has a small but significant effect on the discount rates used.

Table 12.9
Lessee non-tax-paying for two years

Date	Purchase payment £	Capital allowance £	Rental payment £	Tax on rental £	Discount factor £	Present value £
31/12/81	1 000.00		−235.00		1.0000	765.00
31/12/82			−235.00		0.9288	−218.27
31/12/83			−235.00		0.8663	−203.58
31/12/84		−520.00	−235.00	366.60	0.8081	−313.87
31/12/85			−235.00	122.20	0.7537	− 85.02
31/12/86				122.20	0.7030	85.90
NPV of lease						30.14

The fact that the lease is so much better for this lessee than for a fully tax paying lessee may surprise the reader. Why does the benefit increase so rapidly? A careful examination of Table 12.9 reveals the reason. The entire capital allowance of £520 on the purchase would have been delayed for two years at a present value cost of about £74; instead, just two of the five years' of tax relief on rentals have been delayed (one for only one year) at a present value cost of about £30. This gives a net increase in present value of about £44. Indeed, if the temporary non-tax paying period were extended to four years the effect would be even more dramatic. Lenthening the non-tax paying period beyond the end of the lease has a less dramatic effect. Table 12.10 illustrates the effects of different durations of non-tax paying on the value of the lease to the lessee.

Table 12.10
Significance of the duration of non-tax paying

Year end of first tax assessment	Present value
31/12/81	−14.05
31/12/82	10.90
31/12/83	30.16
31/12/84	43.67
31/12/85	51.54
31/12/86	53.91
Never	80.28

This explanation of the attractiveness of leasing to temporarily non-tax paying companies also provides the answer to another question: how does the level of interest rates affect the benefits derived from leasing? Of course, if the interest rate was zero, the delay in receiving capital allowances or in receiving tax relief on rentals paid would not affect the present value at all. Clearly, the level of interest rates is a key factor in making leasing attractive. Table 12.11 shows the benefits to both the fully tax-paying lessor and the two year tax-delayed lessee at different levels of interest rates for our example.

Table 12.11
Present value at different levels of interest rates

Interest rate % per annum	Present value to lessee	Present value to lessor	Total benefit (lessee + lessor)
	£	£	£
0	−84.00	84.00	0
5	−42.91	59.03	16.12
10	− 2.07	34.01	31.94
12	14.11	24.02	38.13
14	30.16	14.05	44.21
16	46.05	4.11	50.16
20	77.29	−15.64	61.65

Tables 12.10 and 12.11 taken together also provide an answer to another question: why was leasing so popular during the 1970s? During this period a large number of companies passed through a temporary non-tax paying position and a particularly high level of interest rates. Since each of these conditions serves to make leasing more profitable; it is not surprising that leasing should enjoy a boom in popularity when they prevail together.

CHOICE OF A SCHEDULE OF LEASE RENTALS

So far in the analysis we have considered a lease with a constant annual rental. We have shown that for a temporarily non-tax paying lessee the advantage of leasing derives from the fact that the delays in taking the tax relief on a rental schedule can be made shorter than the delay in claiming a capital allowance were the asset purchased. There are two simple ways of achieving this. Either the length of the lease can be increased, which will result in small annual payments, or a rising schedule of rentals can be used for the same five year period. (Ideally one would prefer not to start paying rentals until tax paying is resumed.) Tables 12.12 and 12.13 show, respectively, the advantage to be gained by increasing the length of the lease, and that gained by using a rising schedule of rentals. In both cases the lessor's advantage is held constant at £14.05, and the lessee is non-tax paying for two years.

By now, the reader should have realised that the example used has been deliberately simplified to aid exposition. Actual leases are considerably more complicated than those we have examined, but the principles of valuation remain the same. The exact timing of all cash flows within the year is important, as are the time lags involved in tax payments (or savings).

Table 12.12
Effect of length of lease on present value to lessee

Length of lease (years)	Annual rental £	P.V. to lessee £
5	235.00	30.16
7	179.09	35.61
10	137.75	39.61
15	106.60	42.65

Table 12.13
Effect of rising rental schedule on present value to lessee

Rental schedule (five year lease)					P.V. to lessee £
31/12/81	31/12/82	31/12/83	31/12/84	31/12/85	
82.14	164.27	246.41	328.34	410.68	42.54
0	304.70	304.70	304.70	304.70	43.79
0	421.25	421.25	421.25	421.25	53.02
0	0	0	654.89	654.89	53.02
0	0	0	0	1 357.12	53.02

An increasing number of leases, particularly the 'big ticket' ones, have variable rentals, with variations tied both to the corporate tax rate and some base rate of interest (usually either the London Inter-Bank Offer Rate or the Finance Houses Basis Rate). Leases of this type must be compared with a mixture of fixed and variable rate borrowing. (This analysis is beyond the scope of this chapter but is discussed at length in S. D. Hodges, *The Valuation of Variable Rate Leases*, working paper, London Business School, April, 1979.)

In the analysis of all leases it may be necessary to include cash grants, secondary rental payments and the residual value of the asset. Secondary rental payments provide a means of extending the period of the lease where the asset has useful life remaining at the end of the primary period. It is particularly important to be aware of secondary rentals, and to include them in the lease evaluation, in cases where the economic life of the asset is significantly longer than the primary period of the lease.

RESIDUAL VALUES

Most UK financial lease agreements contain a clause which stipulates that a specified proportion of the proceeds from the sale of the asset will be rebated to the lessee at the end of the lease. The proportion is generally between 90 and 99 per cent. If it is assumed that the proportion not rebated represents the transaction costs arising from the sale, then the value accruing to the lessee will be the same under leasing as it would have been under purchase. This assumption has made it possible to ignore residual value in the analysis. Otherwise, it would be necessary to include the residual value of the asset explicitly in the valuation calculations.

The future real value of the asset can be extremely difficult to forecast. If the asset is not likely to be subject to rapid technological obsolescence, one could assume it to be the present value of an identical secondhand asset of the appropriate age. This value, adjusted for the expected effects of inflation during the period of the lease, will provide an estimate of the residual value at the end of the lease. The resulting sum must then be discounted at an appropriate risk adjusted discount rate to obtain the required present value.

Where technological obsolescence is likely to be a problem one may have to introduce further adjustments in order to arrive at an expected value at the end of the lease. Clearly, the required risk adjustment for the discount rate will be considerably larger when the residual value is more uncertain.

OTHER EVALUATION METHODS

Although the present value method used in the previous analysis is recommended, several other valuation techniques are in common use. Of these the most common is the internal rate of return, or one of its derivatives. The internal rate of return (IRR) of a set of cash flows is the rate which, when used to discount the cash flows, gives a zero net present value. Intuitively it is an appealing decision criterion – if the IRR is lower than the cost of equivalent borrowing, then the deal is advantageous to the lessee, and we have a measure of the magnitude of the advantage in the margin between the rates. However, the use of the IRR involves a number of problems.

The major problem concerns the choice of whether to calculate the IRR pre- or post-tax. When calculating the present value of the cash flows in Table 12.5 for the lessor, we saw that it was possible to discount the cash flow at the post-tax cost of money. The point must be made, however, that this was only possible because each cash flow occurred on the same day of the year. Had the payments occurred on different days, it would have been necessary to calculate a separate post-tax rate for each cash flow. Calculation of a post-tax IRR faces the same problem. Thus, while a post-tax IRR can be calculated for the cash flows in Table 12.5 (it is 8.78 per cent per annum), in general, when cash flows occur on different days of the year, it would be difficult to interpret a post-tax rate calculated in this way.

The alternative of calculating a pre-tax IRR is a considerably more complicated procedure. The pre-tax IRR cannot be calculated directly. We must return to the idea of considering the sinking fund loan equivalent to the lease. We need to find the interest rate that must be applied in order that the lease can support a loan exactly equal to the purchase price of the asset. The solution can be arrived at by trial and error; and the sinking fund equivalent which gives a pre-tax IRR of 16.83 per cent, is shown in Table 12.14. One should note that an IRR greater than the return on equivalent lending is the acceptance criterion for the lessor.

Calculated in this way, the pre-tax IRR will give the same recommendations as the present value criterion. The pre-tax IRR has the drawback, however, that it cannot be used to compare alternative lease deals. Present value has the major advantage over other criteria, in the comparison of alternative lease proposals.

One further evaluation technique used commonly by lessors in the UK involves calculating the actuarial rate of return. This represents an attempt to estimate the rate at which profit can be taken out of the lease while the lessor has an investment in the lease. To this end the return on the investment in the lease is split into two parts. The major part represents the cost of money (in our example 14 per cent per annum) which may be required to meet the finance charge on the indebtedness

Table 12.14
Sinking fund equivalent for IRR

Date	Initial investment £	Interest at 16.83% £	Tax on interest £	Principal repayment £	Net cash flow £	Loan balance £
31/12/81	−1 000.00			235.00	235.00	765.00
31/12/82		128.75		504.05	632.80	260.95
31/12/83		63.92	−66.95	135.83	112.80	125.11
31/12/84		21.06	−22.80	118.58	112.80	10.53
31/12/85		1.77	−10.95	121.98	112.80	−111.48
31/12/86		− 18.76	− 0.92	−102.52	−122.20	− 8.92
31/12/87		− 1.50	9.75	− 8.25		− 0.65
31/12/88		− 0.11	0.78	− 0.67		0.00

the lessor established in order to write the lease. (Thus the lessor pays off a sinking fund loan at 14 per cent.) The second part of the return represents profit that the lessor may take out of the lease. For simplicity this is calculated net of tax and in each period is proportional to the level of the lessor's investment in the lease (as is the interest payment). No profit is allocated in the period when the lease generates surplus funds. Table 12.15 shows the sinking fund payments and the profit taken out of the lease period by period. The reinvestment rate used on surplus funds is 14 per cent, the same as the cost of money.

CONCLUSIONS

The main advantage of financial leases lies in their ability to bring forward the tax advantages offered by investment incentives which would not be immediately available otherwise. The size of the advantage depends crucially on the predicted tax-paying position of the lessee. We have also shown that the value of the lease could be affected by changing the duration of the lease or by using a schedule of rising rental payments.

The benefits of leasing must be divided between the lessee and the lessor. The division will depend on market conditions in the leasing industry. Prior to 1978 the bulk of the benefits went to the lessor because excess demand dominated the market. Since 1978, however,

Table 12.15
Sinking fund equivalent for actuarial return

Date	Sinking fund payment £	Interest at 14% £	Tax on interest £	Profit net of tax £	Capital repayment £	Invest-ment in lease £
31/12/81	−765.00				−765.00	765.00
31/12/82	632.80	107.10		10.40	515.30	249.70
31/12/83	112.80	34.96	−55.69	3.40	130.14	119.57
31/12/84	112.80	16.74	−18.18	1.63	112.61	6.95
31/12/85	112.80	0.97	− 8.70	0.09	120.44	−113.48
31/12/86	−122.20	−15.89	− 0.51		−105.81	− 7.68
31/12/87		− 1.07	8.26		− 7.19	− 0.49
31/12/88		− 0.07	0.56		− 0.49	0.00

Total profit = £15.52
Profit represents return of 1.36% per annum (net of tax) on funds invested in the lease

there has been excess supply of lease finance because the profits of financial institutions have exceeded the level of unclaimed capital allowances in manufacturing industry. This led to a situation where the bulk of the lessors were prepared to be more flexible in arranging lease terms to suit the lessee's tax-paying position. Obviously, the benefits available to the lessee depend on his ability to negotiate the terms that suit him best, and we have demonstrated the basic methodology for comparing alternative sets of terms for leases.

13

The UK new issue market

Elroy Dimson

At some stage, most companies need to issue equity to finance new investment. Many firms also wish to be able to issue marketable securities as a means of acquiring other businesses, and the owners of other companies wish to have the option of selling their shares at some future date. By obtaining a Stock Exchange listing, all these objectives can be achieved. While there are alternative means of attaining these objectives – for example, seeking a partner or selling out to a larger concern – any company of sufficient size is likely to give some thought to a flotation on the Stock Exchange. In this chapter, we therefore describe the UK new issue market and how a company can use it to go public.

We will try to answer six questions. First, what role does the Stock Exchange play in the new issue market? Second, why do companies seek a Stock Exchange listing? Third, what regulations govern companies that are going public? Fourth, what methods of issue can be used to obtain a listing? Fifth, how much does a flotation cost the company? And finally, what are the mechanics of a new issue; who is responsible for each step and when must each event take place?

The new issue market is often confusing to the layman. This is partly because people familiar with it make extensive use of technical terms, some of American origin. In the appendix, we therefore provide a glossary of the terminology used in relation to the new issue market.

THE ROLE OF THE STOCK EXCHANGE

The Stock Exchange fulfils two functions. These are the provision of a capital market where investors can be brought together with organisations which require new finance, and of a secondary market for existing financial assets which are already held by investors. This chapter is concerned with the first function. However, the primary capital market is inextricably linked to the existence of a secondary market, as investors are more prepared to acquire new securities if they know their investment will be readily marketable on the Stock Exchange. Thus, although a new issue market could exist in the absence of a stock market, in reality new issues are usually subject to the regulations of the Stock Exchange as well as the relevant statutory rules.

There are three ways in which the Stock Exchange may permit a company's securities to be traded in the stock market. Regular trading is allowed if the securities have an official listing on the Stock Exchange. A company can only acquire listing if, prior to its flotation and subsequently, it meets a series of stringent requirements laid down by the Exchange. At the other extreme, it is possible for unlisted securities to be traded on an occasional basis through the Stock Exchange's Rule 163. This rule permits members of the Exchange to negotiate transactions in such securities as shares in football clubs, certain mineral exploration stocks, and shares in companies which have not been scrutinised by the Stock Exchange. Every transaction in these securities requires prior consent by the Exchange.

Increased use of Rule 163 for trading in unlisted securities (supplemented by worries about the competing over-the-counter market operated by investment bankers M. J. H. Nightingale and the deliberations of the Wilson Committee) led to the creation of the new Unlisted Securities Market (USM) late in 1980. The USM offers a facility to companies that wish to have their shares traded on the stock market without prior approval for each deal, but do not wish to take on the full expense of obtaining listed status. The USM has enabled companies to turn to the stock market to raise sums as small as £100 000. At the time of writing, the typical company coming to the USM has raised about £350 000.

The Stock Exchange stipulates a minimum size for a company which seeks a listing for its shares and a maximum size for a company that wishes to be on the USM. As we mentioned earlier, the Stock Exchange subjects the affairs of the company to detailed scrutiny both before the issue and after it. For example, companies with no earnings history cannot obtain a listing, while a company which already has a listing may be suspended by the Stock Exchange if the nature of its business is altered radically.

The Stock Exchange exercises control over the procedures followed by the issuing company and the method it uses for offering securities to the public. The basic methods of making an issue have changed only in detail since the periods following the Companies Acts of 1929 and 1948. However, the degree of scrutiny applied to a new flotation has increased over the years and the following sections present the situation as it exists in the early 1980s.

REASONS FOR OBTAINING A LISTING

There are a number of reasons for obtaining a listing for the shares of a company. However, for the purposes of presenting the general background to a flotation, it is sufficient to classify four reasons for going public. These are:

1   The capital requirements of the firm.
2   The financial needs of the owners.
3   Improving the marketability of the shares.
4   Enhancing the prestige of the company.

We will consider each of these in turn.

Capital requirements of the firm

Companies which are unable to generate sufficient capital for expansion from retained earnings or by subscription from their owners must look to outside institutions for new funds. Loan capital is available in many forms and from many institutions. For instance, overdrafts, bill financing, trade credit, factoring, tax delays and deferrals, term loans, hire purchase, leasing, mortgages, sale and leaseback and loan stock all represent different sources, as well as different types, of external finance.

By contrast, external equity is normally obtainable from only two sources. Either the company may establish a link with a venture capital organisation, or it may create new shares which are sold to the public by means of obtaining a Stock Exchange listing. The main part of the UK venture capital business is conducted by a single organisation, the Industrial and Commercial Finance Corporation (ICFC). This company, and several of its competitors, are 'nursery' organisations and their funds tend to be invested in firms with a prospect of Stock Exchange or USM listing in the future. Both sources of equity therefore involve a firm in giving consideration to a public offering of shares.

The provision of a listing for a company will help it to meet its capital requirements in three ways. First, the firm can raise capital in order to finance current and impending capital expenditures. Secondly, it can reduce its level of gearing, using equity to repay overdrafts or long term loans which are nearing maturity. Thirdly, the firm will find that future financing is easier and cheaper for a quoted company than it is for a private company. Thus, listing gives strong financial advantages to a firm which is expanding rapidly.

Financial needs of the owners

A company which has been run as a family concern presents a number of financial problems to its owners, which they can overcome by going public. Often, the first motivation for obtaining a listing is the desire to consume some of the capital tied up in the business by selling some of the shares held by the family. A second factor may be a need to diversify the proprietors' investment portfolio out of the family business into a wider spread of assets. Thirdly, the owners may wish to alter their level of gearing, either because they will be able to borrow more against quoted securities than against unquoted securities, or because they wish to reduce their personal debt by selling some of their shares. A fourth reason for desiring a listing is the opportunity for speedy valuation and easy settlement of fiscal debts, such as Capital Transfer Tax. Finally, a listing conveys certain tax advantages to a company which is 'close', under the provisions of the Income and Corporation Taxes Act 1970, provided at least 35 per cent of the voting power is held by the public. This is because a close company is taxed at the relevant rates of income tax, rather than at the corporation tax rate, which does not currently exceed 52 per cent.

Though the financial requirements of the owners may provide a stong motive for going public, the distribution of a block of existing shares (known as a 'secondary' distribution) does not affect the company financially. However, most new issues are arranged to combine a secondary distribution with raising new capital for the company itself. Furthermore, some 'no new money' issues are made by companies that wish to raise fresh capital by means of a rights issue at some later date, once the share is listed. The distinction between 'new money' or 'primary' issues, which raise funds for the company, and 'no new money' or 'secondary' issues, which are sales of existing shares, is therefore blurred. Since the methods are the same for secondary and primary issues, we will not draw any further distinction between these two types of issue.

Improving the marketability of the shares

The third category of reasons for obtaining a listing is that of improving the marketability of the shares. From the company's point of view, it is the marketability of its shares that enables it to raise capital by means of a rights issue. Marketability also assists companies that want to undertake acquisitions of other businesses, as consideration can then be paid by means of the shares of the acquiring firm.

From the viewpoint of the proprietors of the new issue, marketability facilitates future consumption decisions. The facility to resolve fiscal problems without selling or liquidating the entire company also depends on the existence of a market in the shares. Finally, and most important, many investors are unwilling, and many institutions are not permitted, to hold unmarketable securities. The existence of a listing may therefore substantially increase the value of a company.

Enhancing the prestige of the company

The prestige of being a listed company is a supplementary, though relatively trivial, motive for going public. It is argued that a listing adds respectability to the business, and that mention in the financial press provides free advertising. Staff recruitment may be aided by this prestige and by the possibility of setting up an attractive share incentive scheme. The approval of the Stock Exchange and the dissemination of information is said to give confidence to the customers and employees of the firm.

There is, of course, another side to publicity, and this can be a potential disadvantage to a firm which goes public. The company may lose its family relationships with employees, and may be forced into disclosing sensitive or adverse information to a larger and more critical public. The proprietors of the firm may well lose control of the business, the directors' remuneration will be scrutinised publicly, and the proprietors may not wish to be exposed to the risk of being taken over. Another drawback to a public listing is that the value of the firm will be established for tax purposes at a higher level than if it were unlisted, in which case the worth would generally be based on an asset valuation. Finally, it will be seen that the costs of going public are usually very high. A private company does not decide lightly on obtaining a public listing.

REGULATIONS CONCERNING NEW ISSUES

At present, a company's application for an official listing is not considered by the Stock Exchange unless its expected market value is at least £500 000 and each security for which a listing is sought has an expected value of at least £200 000. From 1966 to 1973 the limits were £250 000 and £100 000 respectively, while there were no such requirements earlier than 1966.

At least 25 per cent of the equity must normally be made available to the public. In the case of the USM, this figure is reduced to 10 per cent. However, these requirements are interpreted with some discretion. For instance, Pilkington Brothers was floated on the Stock Exchange with only 15 per cent (£10 millions worth of shares) being offered to the public.

Unless it is a mineral exploration company or investment trust, the company must have a five year financial history. For the USM, however, this is reduced to three years, or less in certain circumstances. The company seeking an official listing must produce audited results for a financial period ending less than six months prior to prospectus publications, while much less onerous requirements are laid down for USM applicants. The current regulations for an official listing are laid down in the latest update of the so-called Yellow Book and in preliminary publications on the USM.

An application for a listing is required of a company that wants to be listed on the Stock Exchange in four circumstances:

1 If it has no previous listing on the Exchange.
2 If its previous listing has lapsed.
3 If it has been involved in 'shell' operations.
4 If the nature of its business has changed significantly.

If the proposed flotation involves the issue of an application form for shares or debentures for cash consideration, the Companies Act 1948 requires that the form be accompanied by a prospectus. However, if an issue is a wholly private placing, or a rights issue with no right of renunciation, the prospectus requirement is waived.

The Companies Act also imposes responsibility on those making an issue to ensure that accurate and sufficient information is published. In addition it regulates certain aspects of the issue procedure, ensuring, for example, that at least three days elapse between the appearance of the advertisement and the time the issue takes place.

The Stock Exchange supplements the statutory regulations in many ways. Even when the issue involves existing securities, if an official listing is desired the Exchange insists on a prospectus in the approved form. It requires a variety of information to be disclosed and documents to be supplied, including many items to a specified format. Finally, by means of the sanction of a withdrawal of the listing or a suspension of dealings, the Exchange ensures that it continues to receive up to date accounting information and company documents after the firm receives its quotation.

The Stock Exchange lays down rules governing the methods by which securities may be brought to the market, and these are described in the following section. It also co-operates with the Bank of England in exercising control over the timing of issues which raise £3 million or more. In such cases, it is necessary for the brokers who are sponsoring the issue to apply for a date known as 'Impact Day', which is the first day on which the size and terms of the issue may be known to the market.

METHODS OF MAKING A NEW ISSUE

A company may obtain a new listing by means of the following methods of issue:

1   An issue by prospectus (or public issue).
2   An offer for sale.
3   A placing.
4   An offer for sale by tender.
5   A public issue by tender.
6   A Stock Exchange introduction.
7   A transfer of listing from another stock exchange.

In addition, a company which already has a listing for its shares may obtain a listing for additional shares which are created as a result of:

8   An issue to existing shareholders (i.e. a rights issue or open offer).
9   The exercise of options, warrants or convertibles.
10 An issue of shares in connection with an acquisition.
11 An exchange or conversion of securities into other classes of security.
12 A capitalisation (or bonus or scrip) issue or a share split.
13 A placing or offer for sale (both of which can only be arranged in special circumstances).

Since the second group of issue methods do not enable a firm to go public (except in combination with a Stock Exchange introduction), and are largely described in Chapter 14, only methods 1 to 7 will be discussed here.

Before proceeding to explain the main methods of going public, however, it may be helpful to anticipate the thrust of the description by reference to Figure 13.1. The figure shows the types of companies which go public, their principal objectives in so going and the procedures which they can adopt. It also shows some of the inter-relationships between issue methods and some of their distinguishing features. The method by which shares are issued by listed companies is principally the rights offering, though in special circumstances listed companies may occasionally make use of the methods normally reserved for unseasoned issues.

Prospectus issues and offers for sale

The prospectus issue and offer for sale are almost identical methods of issue. In both cases, a fixed number of shares is offered to the public at a stated price. In the case of a prospectus issue (also known as a public issue) the offer is made directly by the company. In an offer for sale, however, the company sells its shares to an issuing house, which in turn offers the shares to the public at a slightly higher price. Thus, the company acts as principal in the case of a prospectus issue, frequently employing an issuing house to act as agent to the transaction. On the other hand, the issuing house is the principal in the case of an offer for sale.

These issues are made by means of a prospectus which includes an application form to subscribe. Except for an offering on the USM (which is unusual), the Stock Exchange requires the prospectus to be advertised in full in at least two London daily newspapers. In the case

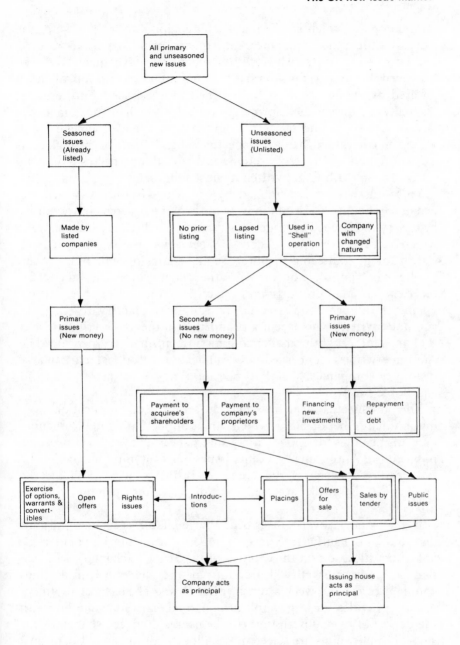

Fig. 13.1 The structure of the UK new issue market

of a company which is offering its share capital to the public for the very first time, the Companies Act requires the prospectus to state the minimum subscription which will enable the objectives of an issue to be achieved. If the issue fails to raise the minimum subscription, all funds offered by applicants must be returned by the issuer. Furthermore, virtually all unseasoned, primary issues (other than those made by investment trusts and property companies) are made by means of an offer for sale rather than a prospectus issue. Because of the high costs of failure and the statutory requirements, both prospectus issues and offers for sale are underwritten against failure.

The underwriting is arranged by the issue's sponsors, which are usually an issuing house but may be the broking firm which is acting as broker to the issue. The underwriters receive a disclosed commission, which over the recent past has been $1\frac{1}{2}$ per cent of the issue proceeds, in return for guaranteeing to purchase any shares not taken up by the public. The sponsor who provides the underwriting does not retain more than a small proportion of the underwriting as it reinsures itself against the failure of the issue. The reinsurance is placed with a range of sub-underwriters who accept a proportion of the underwriting risk in exchange for a slightly smaller commission, normally $1\frac{1}{4}$ per cent. The sub-underwriters concerned are financial institutions, particularly insurance companies, as well as pension funds, investment trusts and charitable funds.

The prospectus specifies the procedure for application, the minimum number of shares which can be applied for, and the opening and closing dates for application, usually several days after prospectus publication. Applicants for equity issues must submit a cheque for the full cost of the shares they require. If the issue is popular, the application lists will be closed immediately after opening, with the offer over-subscribed.

If the issue is over subscribed, the available securities must be distributed to a sufficiently large number of investors, and in marketable quantities, so that the Council of the Stock Exchange is satisfied that a ready market will develop in the shares when dealings commence, about a week after the offer closes. The basis of allotment usually provides for large applications to be scaled down in line with the degree of oversubscription (to the nearest hundred shares), while smaller applications are selected by ballot for allotment in full or on a partly scaled down basis. Usually, the degree of scaling down slightly favours smaller applications in order to spread ownership as widely as possible. Preferential allotments to employees and existing shareholders are limited to 10 per cent of the amount offered.

Placings

In a Stock Exchange placing the issuing house acquires the shares, as in an offer for sale. However, instead of inviting the public to subscribe for the issue the shares are 'placed' with clients of the issuing house and with jobbers. As in the case of an offer for sale, the issuing house is remunerated by the turn between the price it paid and the placing price, and it may also charge a fee.

This method of issue avoids the needs for the payment of underwriting commission and the expenses of administering the application and allotment procedure. The prospectus requirements are less onerous, and the prospectus need be advertised in only one newspaper with abridged details in a second paper. In the case of a USM placing, only an announcement of the placing need be advertised.

The Stock Exchange must give its approval to a placing, which it will not normally do for large companies. At present, a company of more than £4 million or so in value would probably be obliged to resort to an offer for sale, as might smaller issues offered by well known firms. The USM, in fact, refuses to accept placings of over £3 million. Since the dominant concern of the Exchange is the spread of shareholdings, the guideline for withholding permission for a placing is whether there would be significant demand for the share if issued by means of an offer for sale. With the same motives, the marketing arrangements should provide that at least 25 per cent of an equity placing (or more, if it is a popular issue) is offered to the market through being placed with jobbers, who may not retain more than 10 per cent.

Tender issues

Tender issues utilise a variant of the offer for sale or public issue methods. In a tender issue the offer price is not fixed, potential applicants being invited to tender for shares at the price they see fit, provided it is at or above a stated minimum price. The selling price for the shares is then determined from the bids received.

The tender method has been favoured when an issue is difficult to price. For this reason it has rarely been used by those companies which would otherwise make a public issue, namely investment trusts and property companies. Indeed, since 1962 there have been only a couple of public issues of equity by tender, those of Diners Club in 1964 and City & Gracechurch Investment Trust in 1969. All other tenders were offers for sale by tender, using an issuing house as principal to the issue.

Assuming the issue is not undersubscribed, applications are listed at each price level from the highest tender downwards. Taking each successive application in sequence from the list, there is a market clearing price at which the issue is fully subscribed. In principle all these applications could be accepted in full, but this might not ensure a reasonable spread of shareholdings. The Stock Exchange therefore encourages the issuing house to set a 'striking price' which is below the market clearing price, and to scale down applications accordingly. Regardless of the applicant's tender, applications are invariably (with one exception, Hurst and Sandler in 1963) allotted at the same striking price for all applicants.

The tender method has experienced short bursts of popularity since it was introduced for ordinary shares in June 1961. Though used in the UK in every year throughout the 1960s (especially 1963–4 and 1968) and in France until the present time, the tender method was not utilised throughout the 1970s. Its main advantage, namely taking the pricing and (most of) the allotment decision out of the hands of the issuing house, has been its downfall. While they acknowledge it to have a role in relation to issues which present extreme difficulties of pricing, neither the Stock Exchange nor the issuing houses have lent their support to tenders as a generally acceptable issue procedure. However, water company loan stock issues are required by the Water Act 1945 to be made by means of a tender issue (with discriminatory pricing, in this case). This experience, and the similarity of a tender to a conventional offer for sale, suggest that the tender method could easily be reintroduced to the new issue market. Indeed, two recent issues (Charterhouse Petroleum and Spring Grove in 1980) were offered for sale by the tender method.

Introductions and transfers of listing

Unlike the methods described so far, the primary objective of an introduction or transfer is not the sale of shares to the public. In many cases a reasonable distribution of shares already exists, and a listing is required in order to establish a market in the shares. Transfers of listing from provincial stock exchanges to the Stock Exchange in London were permitted until shortly after those exchanges were unified in 1973.

However, a prior flotation was required on the original exchange, and this was only a partial method of gaining a listing.

The introduction method, on the other hand, continues to be available to companies which are going public. Three categories of applications for listing are favoured for this method, namely:

1 Securities which are already listed on another exchange.
2 Large unlisted companies which can satisfy the Stock Exchange as to marketability.
3 Shares of a holding company which are issued in exchange for the shares of one or more listed companies.

Although the Companies Act does not demand a prospectus for an introduction, as no capital is being offered, the Stock Exchange requires one to be advertised and made available to participants in the introduction. This requirement is, however, waived in the case of a USM introduction of a company previously traded under Rule 163. As in a placing, many expenses, such as advertising the prospectus, are lower than in the case of an offer for sale. Since there is no commitment to sell a pre-specified number of shares, no underwriting is involved. The sponsors of the issue must be able to lay hands on sufficient shares to meet demand when trading commences, but this is a conventional, non-underwritten transaction.

The Stock Exchange will normally require a firm obtaining an introduction to have at least a hundred or so shareholders before a listing and will expect at least twice this number afterwards, to ensure a free market. As in the case of all other methods, the sponsors must demonstrate that the public will hold at least 25 per cent of the officially listed issue, or 10 per cent if it is seeking an introduction to the USM.

Finally, if a firm is obtaining an introduction but wishes to raise some new money at about the same time, two options are available. First, the shares to be introduced may be made subject to a prior rights issue to existing shareholders, at a price below the expected market price of the shares. Owing to the shares' impending introduction, existing shareholders will be especially likely to take up their rights in full. Alternatively, the introduction may follow a private placing, based on relatively good terms in view of the introduction. The rights issue procedure is more favourable to existing shareholders, who will generally receive a higher price for their shares when they are sold in the market, than if they are placed.

To summarise, the introduction method cannot, in itself, raise new money for a firm. The options explained in the preceding paragraph involve the sale of capital in companies as yet unquoted, and are comparatively unusual. The majority of introductions are of securities which already have a listing: in the past these were principally companies with a provincial listing or ones whose London listing had lapsed. Nowadays most introductions are either reintroductions following a suspension of listing, or involve securities listed on another market. However, a company which was set on an offer for sale is also occasionally permitted to undertake an introduction, if market conditions are especially adverse (e.g. Willis Faber in 1976).

Thus, shares which are introduced tend to have two characteristics. They are already listed (i.e. they are not really *new* shares), and they are securities which are already in existence (i.e. they do not raise new money). Introductions are therefore excluded from the remainder of our discussion.

ISSUE COSTS

The costs of obtaining a listing may be evaluated under four headings:

1 Administrative costs of the company.
2 Cash expenses associated with the issue.
3 Non-cash compensation of issue advisers.
4 Underpricing of the issue.

The first three items form the costs which are usually identified in discussion about the new issue market. The extent to which the shares are underpriced is, however, equally important and we will return to this matter at the end of the present section.

Administrative costs

The administrative costs faced by the company span several years, from the time when the directors first begin to contemplate going public. The firm may have formed a liaison with an institution offering private 'nursery' finance, and will certainly have invested considerable time in planning its development into a company with flotation potential. Prior to the issue the company will probably undertake capital re-organisations, company investigations, acquisitions of associated companies, preparation of documentation and negotiation with numerous parties to the issue. The time and effort expended by the issuer probably represent a major cost, which, though difficult to quantify, must not be forgotten.

Cash expenses

The cash expenses associated with the issue may be broken down into three parts. First, certain expenses are more or less fixed in magnitude, given the method of issue. Of these, advertising and printing costs are the most important. Secondly, other expenses are paid in the form of a fee which is set as a percentage of the size of the issue. Finally, some expenses will vary with the quantity of work generated by the issue, the relationship between the quantity of work and the size of issue being rather tenuous – for instance, small issues may still be heavily over-subscribed.

The work related expenses consist of the fees due to the two firms of accountants, the two firms of solicitors, the receiving bankers and any other advisers or temporary employees taken on for the issue. The size related expenses consist of the fees payable to the issuing house, brokers and subunderwriters, the allotment commission, the Stock Exchange listing fee and the capital duty. Some payments are made by the issuing house on behalf of the company, namely those made to the solicitors to the offer, the brokers and the subunderwriters.

The cash expenses vary not only with issue size but also with the method of issue. Offers for sale and tender issues are the most expensive methods. Issues by prospectus shift some of the costs onto the company itself, and the cash expenses are therefore marginally lower. Placings are exempt from a number of requirements and are definitely cheaper in terms of cash expenses, while introductions are cheaper still.

Non-cash compensation

In calculating the cash expenses, however, it becomes apparent that certain items of non-cash compensation received by the issue advisers are of equal importance. For example, the issuing house will be indifferent between charging a particular percentage fee on the issue and taking an equivalent 'turn' on the shares. If the issuer does not pay a fee, but sells the shares to the issuing house at less than the issue price, this non-cash cost is just as real as a cash expense and must therefore be included in any calculation of cost. This consideration is of particular

Type of expense	Issue by prospectus	Offer for sale	Sale by tender	Placing
Fixed expenses				
Advertising	Prospectus in at least two London newspapers. Abbreviated particulars in other paper(s), if desired.			Prospectus in one paper. Abridged particulars in another.
Printing	Prospectus for distribution to public, and letters of acceptance and allotment. Based on number of proofs and complexity of prospectus.			Only a few prospectuses for Extel service.
Work related				
Accountants	Based on the complexity of the issue. The auditors to the company and the reporting accountants are usually different firms.			
Solicitors	Based on the work to convert a private to a public company. The solicitors to the company and solicitors to the offer are usually different firms.			
Bankers	Based on number of applications submitted to the clearing bank's new issue department.			— — —
Miscellaneous	Frequently, the company will also utilise the services of management consultants during the period prior to issue, and a firm of public relations consultants near the time of an offer.			
Size related				
Issuing house	Percentage of the issue proceeds as a fee.	Percentage of the issue proceeds (in form of buy-sell spread) usually plus percentage fee.		
Stockbrokers	Percentage of issue proceeds (charged by issuing house, if one is used, and passed on to stockbrokers).			
Subunder-writers	Percentage of issue proceeds (charged by issuing house and passed on to subunderwriters).			— — —
Allotment commission	Payable to brokers and banks lodging successful applications for their clients.			— — —
Capital duty	Payable at the rate of one per cent on all new money raised. (Prior to the 1973 Finance Act payable at one half per cent on increases in the nominal share capital.)			
Listing fee	Payable to Stock Exchange according to the value of the shares to be listed rather than the size of the issue itself.			

Fig. 13.2 Conventional costs of issue

importance in the Unlisted Securities Market, where the issuing house may be remunerated by means of a buy-sell spread.

The 'conventional' costs (cash and non-cash expenses) associated with the major issue methods are summarised in Figure 13.2. As an indication of their magnitude in the case of an offer for sale, Figure 13.3 shows the average in a year with a large number of issues, 1972. In that year, the 29 offers in the £2.5 million range and the 15 offers over £5 million in size attracted costs of 4.6 per cent and 5.8 per cent, respectively. The remainder of the 118 issues suffered a much higher proportionate burden. These estimates of cost include the non-cash compensation of underwriters, the costs which are paid by the vendors of existing shares rather than by the company, and the cost of sub-underwriting. Since the last of these involves trading in a put option, rather than purely in a service, it is a rather different sort of 'cost' from the others, and it may be more reasonable to consider separately the 1 ¼

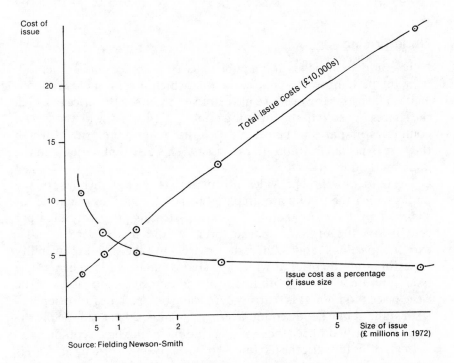

Source: Fielding Newson-Smith

Fig. 13.3   The costs of an offer for sale in 1972

per cent fee which is involved. (This point is discussed in Chapter 14.) The costs of issue shown in Figure 13.3 are now out of date. Over recent years, there has been an increase in the extent to which disclosure of information by companies going public is required by the Stock Exchange, by law and by the accounting bodies. This has been accompanied by drastic increases in newsprint costs and capital duty. As a result, the real costs of obtaining a listing have risen substantially. Indeed, this was one of the factors which prompted the creation of the USM.

Table 13.1 shows an estimate of the cost of an offer for sale at the present time, based on discussions with organisations which are active in this area of business. The trend noted by Vaughan, Grinyer and Birley (see reference at end) who found that 'between 1959 and 1974, costs as a percentage of issue size fell appreciably for offers for sale' has been reversed. Going public is now an expensive business.

Underpricing

If the company which is going public has a free choice of issue method, it might be tempted to choose the one which incurs the lowest conventional costs. However, we have not yet discussed the price at which the shares are sold to the investing public. With all issue methods, it is common for shares to be offered at a discount on the price at which they are expected to trade after the issue. This discount varies with the issue method used.

The tender method provides information to the issuing house on the prices which the public are prepared to pay for various quantities of shares. This makes it possible to issue at a striking price only a few per cent below the ultimate market price of the shares. At the other extreme, placings require the issue advisers to take sole responsibility for estimating the price at which the shares can be sold to clients. The issuing house will lose, both financially and in credibility, if it sets the issue price too high. It is scarcely surprising that placings are offered at a substantial market discount, averaging almost 20 per cent below the value established once stock market trading in the shares commences.

In an offer for sale, the likelihood of severely underpricing an issue is lessened. The company is likely to be larger and less risky and may therefore be easier to value. The pricing decision is more considered, is completed in consultation with the subunderwriting institutions, and is

Table 13.1
The current costs of an offer for sale

Type of expense	Basis for charging for expense	Typical costs of an offer for sale
Fixed expenses		| *£'000*
Advertising	Prospectus at £10 000 per page in two newspapers; say two pages	40
Printing	Depending on number of proofs, but say. . . .	15
Work related expenses		
Accountants	Reporting accountants' fee of £30–40 000 plus auditors' fees	50
Solicitors	Say £5 000 each	10
Bankers	Priced per sheet of paper handled, but say. . . .	5
Miscellaneous	Other advisers and temporary employees, say. . . .	10
Value added tax	VAT on fixed and work related expenses at the rate of fifteen per cent	20
Size related		*Per cent*
Issuing house	One per cent (less for large issues, more if substantial re-organisation required)	1
	One quarter per cent over-riding commission on underwriting	$\frac{1}{4}$
Stockbrokers	One quarter per cent plus extra if special work required	$\frac{1}{4}$
Subunderwriters	One and a quarter per cent plus one eighth per cent per week for periods in excess of three weeks	$1\frac{1}{4}$
Allotment commission	One eighth per cent on endorsed applications	$\frac{1}{8}$
Listing fee	According to a scale, but for an average issue, say. . . .	$\frac{1}{8}$
Value added tax	VAT on size related expenses at the rate of fifteen per cent	$\frac{1}{2}$
Capital duty	One per cent of new money raised	1
Total expenses	Fixed cost plus percentage of offer value	£150 thousand + $4\frac{1}{2}$ per cent

more in the public eye. Finally, a proportion of the fees are related to the capitalisation of the company at the offer price, and hence a higher offer price will generate larger fees for the issue advisers. Thus there is less temptation to underprice the shares. Nevertheless, it is in the general interests of the issuing house and subunderwriters for the offer to be made at a reasonable discount on the estimated market value of the shares, and in practice the market discount for offers for sale averages some 10 per cent.

Naturally, many factors other than the issue method have a bearing on the extent of underpricing. For example, it is relatively easy to value an investment trust; consequently, prospectus issues (which have been undertaken mainly by investment trusts) show very small market discounts. As a broad generalisation, however, we can say that the choice of issue method involves a tradeoff between the conventional costs of issue and the degree of underpricing. For very small issues, placings, which have the lowest conventional costs, are preferable; for large issues, offers for sale, which suffer less underpricing, are preferable; while for small to medium sized issues, the choice of method will be less clear-cut.

THE MECHANICS OF A FLOTATION

While the general preparations for becoming a public company may occupy a firm for years, the first formal step occurs when the directors give the go-ahead to a meeting with the issuing house to discuss the strategy and timing of a flotation. This sets off a chain of events which draws a wide range of financial advisers and institutions into contact with the company. These participants in the new issue are:

1 *Company*
   (a) Directors
   (b) Large shareholders
   (c) Management
2 *Issuing house*
3 *Stockbroker*
4 *Stock Exchange*
5 *Accountants*
   (a) Reporting accountants
   (b) Company auditors

6 *Solicitors*
   (a) Solicitors to the offer
   (b) Company solicitors
7 *Subunderwriters*
8 *Bankers*
   (a) Receiving bankers
   (b) Registrars
   (c) Clearing bank
9 *Public relations consultants*
   (a) Public relations consultants
   (b) Advertising agency
10 *Press*
   (a) News agencies and press
   (b) Extel
11 *Printers*
12 *Investing public*

If the issuing house is to lend its name to the new issue, it will require extensive details of the company's performance and prospects. It will therefore request a full financial history of the firm, together with information on its business, competitors, management, premises, labour force, expansion plans, and so on. A director of the issuing house will probably visit the company to obtain a closer impression of the business and its senior management, and if all the preliminary enquiries are favourable, the issuing house will instruct an independent firm of accountants to investigate the company. Only after a satisfactory accountants' report will the issuing house make its proposal to the firm.

The issuing house's proposal will outline the capital reorganisation required prior to obtaining a listing and will suggest the method and terms of issue. The capital reorganisation will involve some or all of the following adjustments to the firm's capital structure:

1 Eliminating inappropriate classes of equity (such as non-voting shares, founders' shares, deferred shares, etc.).
2 Repayment of certain loans.
3 Revaluation of fixed assets.
4 Acquisition of existing subsidiary companies.
5 Formation of a holding company.
6 Transfer of proprietor's shares to family trusts.

7 Waiver of dividend rights by large shareholders in high tax brackets.

Over the months leading up to the issue, the company will become committed to such aspects of the terms of issue as the earnings, dividends and asset value per share, and the accounting policies persued by the company will become obvious from the prospectus. The issuing house will give the company a broad idea of the aggregate value of the shares to be issued, and so the firm's capital structure will have to be reorganised by means of various share splits, scrip issues, and so on, so as to ensure that the price of each share is at a conventional level – probably within the range 50p to 150p.

Given the number of shares to be issued, the price at which the shares are marketed is the variable of greatest interest to the vendor. By comparing the earnings and dividend yield with firms in comparable industries, and by taking into account the prospects and riskiness of the business, the level of gearing and the prices at which shares have changed hands recently, the issuing house will estimate the market value of the shares. In order to ensure that all the shares are disposed of, the suggested issue price is then set at a discount below the estimated market value. In the case of a tender issue, where the public effectively set the price of the shares, the issuing house is confined to estimating the minimum price at which applications will be accepted.

If the issuing house's proposal is accepted, then a provisional timetable for the issue will be drawn up. Some of the key events of the issue, from initial meeting with the issuing house until well after the issue is complete, are shown in Figure 13.4. The timing of the early events is approximate, and the timetable has been designed to apply to placings as well as offers for sale (provided the application procedure is amended). The listing can be granted on a Friday or, as in this case (day minus 1), on a Wednesday. The impact day (day minus 8) will depend on the place of the issue in the Bank of England's 'queue'.

Much of the ensuing activity centres around meeting the regulations that affect the issue and the development of the prospectus (which is described shortly). The issuing house takes a coordinating role through this period until dealings in the shares have commenced. By two weeks before the offer, the prospectus is available in a final proof form, and the price of the shares will be set, subject to amendment before the printers start to produce the prospectuses.

At this stage the underwriting and subunderwriting agreements are

Day relative to offer	Key events	
-110	Directors and issuing house discuss strategy and timing.	
-100	Issuing house instructs reporting accountants and brokers.	
-70	Consider accountant's report	Meetings of directors, issuing house, brokers, accountants, auditors and solicitors
-60	First draft of prospectus to printers	
-50	Second proof to Stock Exchange	
-40	Discuss Stock Exchange Comments	
-30	Prepare application form and letters of allotment, acceptance and underwriting	
-20	Meeting to discuss further proofs of documents	
-14 (Thur)	FIX PRICE (subject to amendment) and prepare underwriting proofs	
-10 (Mon)	Finalise price and send proofs to printers	
-9 (Tues)	Post underwriting proofs and letter to sub underwriters	
-8 (Wed)	IMPACT DAY. Press conference	
-7 (Thurs)	Completion meeting of directors and all advisers	
-3 (Mon)	PROSPECTUS IN PAPERS. Final documents to Stock Exchange	
-1 (Wed)	Listing granted by Stock Exchange	
0 (Thurs)	APPLICATION LISTS OPEN (10 a.m.) and close	
+1 (Fri)	CHEQUES BANKED. Press announcement on basis of allotment	
+6 (Wed)	Allotment or acceptance letters posted	
+7 (Thurs)	DEALINGS BEGIN	
+28 (Thurs)	Last day for splitting	
+32 (Mon)	Last day for renunciation	
+60 (Mon)	Share certificates ready	

Fig. 13.4   Typical offer timetable

made firm. A week before the offer, the terms of the issue are made known to the market, and the resulting press conference generally prompts some mention of the issue in the financial press. A few days later the prospectus is published, giving investors some three days in which to apply for the issue.

The prospectus provides the information which must be made available to investors under the requirements of the Companies Act 1948 and the regulations of the Stock Exchange. The prospectus presents information under a sequence of headings following a set style; and the application form is also included in the case of an offer for sale, prospectus issue, or issue by tender. The main contents of the prospectus are:

1 *Background*
   (a) Statements of compliance with regulations.
   (b) Application instructions.*
   (c) Company's name and background.
   (d) Capital structure and voting rights.
   (e) Name and address of directors, professional advisers etc.
2 *History and nature of business*
3 *Management*
4 *Employees*
5 *Plant and premises*
6 *Working capital*
7 *Accountants' report*
   (a) Profits record (five years).
   (b) Balance sheet.
   (c) Intended acquisitions.
   (d) Dividends record (five years).
8 *Profits, prospects and dividends*
9 *General information*
   (a) Articles of association.
   (b) Contracts.
   (c) Recent capital changes and acquisitions.
   (d) Ownership and directors' interests.
   (e) Other statutory statements.
10 *Application form**
   (a) Time, date and place for applying.
   (b) Statutory declarations and letter of acquisition.
   (c) Conditions of application.

    (d)   Space for applicant's signature, name and address.

*Omitted if issue is a placing.

A more detailed description can be found in Stock Exchange's Yellow Book. In conjunction with press comment and other information available to them, investors use the contents of the prospectus to decide whether to apply for the issue, and for how many shares.

A week after the application lists open and close, the shares have normally been allotted and dealings begin. The company has obtained its listing, and only a few details regarding the issue itself are left to be done. So far as investors are concerned these include the periods during which 'splitting' and 'renunciation' are permitted. These are procedures for dividing an allotment of shares into several parts (if necessary), and selling them by renouncing title to the shares in favour of the buyer.

From the point of view of the financial participants (rather than professional advisers) involved in the issue, some key events should be noted from Figure 13.4. These financial events are shown in capital letters in the figure and the most important are:

1   Fixing the price (roughly two weeks before the offer).
2   Publicising the terms of the offer (one week before).
3   Closing of the application lists.
4   Commencement of dealings (one week after the offer).

The company's financial interests largely terminate at event 1, whereas the underwriters are at risk principally from event 1 to event 3. The applicants to the issue are involved with the shares from event 3 onwards. Finally, once event 4 occurs, investors and the market as a whole become involved with the company on a regular basis. They can look forward to news about the company's progress, about acquisitions and the financing of new investments, and hopefully to a consistently rising share price.

SUMMARY AND CONCLUSIONS

In this chapter, we have described the current structure of the UK new issue market. First, we looked at the role of the Stock Exchange in relation to new issues. We compared obtaining a Stock Exchange listing with alternatives such as a flotation on the Unlisted Securities Market and reviewed the controls imposed by the Stock Exchange.

We then went on to appraise four classes of reasons which might motivate a company to obtain a stock market listing. We stressed two groups of motives, those relating to the capital requirements of the firm and those reflecting the financial needs of the proprietors of the business. We also discussed the motives of improving the marketability of the shares and of enhancing the prestige of the company.

In the third section, we looked at the regulatory framework within which companies may seek a flotation. In the next section, we described the methods which are available for making a new issue. These are the offer for sale (and the related prospectus issue) method, the placing method, the tender issue, and the introduction. Each of these issue methods has its advantages and disadvantages, and each imposes different costs on the company which is going public.

The costs of issue were described in the fifth section. We identified four items of cost: the often overlooked administrative costs of issue, the cash expenses associated with the issue, non-cash compensation such as warrants to subscribe for further shares, and the important cost which is imposed through underpricing the new issue. Underpricing was found to be most severe for placings of shares in small companies. Finally, we turned to the mechanics of a flotation. We identified the tasks of the main participants in the issue, we examined a typical new issue timetable and we summarised the contents of the prospectus.

The UK new issue market has responded to the needs of the corporate sector over a long period of time. Especially with the advent of the Unlisted Securities Market, the Stock Exchange now provides a wide range of companies with ready access to the capital market. An understanding of how to use the new issue market is therefore likely to be important to an increasing number of businesses.

FURTHER READING

The steps which are involved in obtaining a stock exchange listing are described in M Richardson's *Going Public*, published by Business Books in 1976. So far as the regulations of the stock market are concerned, however, it is better to consult an updated copy of the Yellow Book, or *Admission of securities to Listing*, published by the Stock Exchange in 1979.

There have been a large number of academic studies of the new issue market in Britain and overseas. In *The Efficiency of the British New*

Issue Market for Ordinary Shares (Xerox Publishing Group, 1981), the author provides an extensive survey of this research, examines the question of how fairly the issue price is set and elaborates on other matters discussed in this chapter.

A useful study of the UK market is the one by C D Vaughan, P H Grinyer and S J Birley entitled *From Private to Public*. It was published by Woodhead Faulkner in 1977.

The most recent book on the subject is *Marketing Company Shares*, by David Fanning (Gower, 1982). This describes the principles and procedures involved in 'going public' and contains detailed analyses of nine cases.

APPENDIX: NEW ISSUE GLOSSARY

Advisory pricing. Pricing of a new issue by the issue advisors (under-writers, brokers etc.). Refers to the pricing method used in offers for *sale* and *placings*. Cf. *tender issues*.

Aftermarket. The market in which new issues are subsequently traded, i.e. the *secondary market*.

All-or-none. (US) Agreeent for the underwriter to attempt to sell all the issue at the offer price, subject to the issue being withdrawn if all the shares are not distributed. Thus, as in the case of a *best efforts* agreement, the underwriter is not at risk.

Allotment. The allocation of shares in a new issue to applicants. If the issue is *oversubscribed* large applications are usually *scaled down*, while a certain number of small applications, selected by ballot, are accepted in full. The allotment is notified in an allotment letter.

Application. An application on the official application form, which accompanies the *prospectus* for an issue, to buy a certain number of shares at the offer price. A cheque for the full cost of the shares must accompany the application.

Best efforts. (US) Agreement by the underwriter to sell only as much of the new issue at the offer price as he is able to, providing no *fixed commitment* to sell all the shares. Small or risky issues may be offered on this basis or on an *all-or-none* basis.

Close company. A company which has a tax status such that its income is taxed at the rate of its directors or members. Exemption is granted if shares carrying at least 35 per cent of voting power are held by the public and are dealt on the Stock Exchange.

Combination offering. See *mixed offering*.

Discount. (as in 'trading at a discount') The amount by which the market price of a share is below its issue price. Cf. *premium*.

Firm commitment, fixed commitment. (US) Agreement by the issue's underwriters to buy all the shares on offer from the vendor at a price below the offering price, accepting the risk of being unable to re-sell the shares (i.e. accepting the 'subunderwriting' risk, in the UK sense). The *market discount* includes the underwriting commission though there may be additional *non-cash compensation*. Cf. *best efforts* and *all-or-none*.

Flotation. New issue of previously unlisted shares.

Going public. Literally, becoming a *public company.* Generally used to describe gaining a stock exchange listing by means of a *flotation,* regardless of whether the company was previously public.

Impact day. The first day on which the size and terms of a new issue may be made known to the underwriters, placees and the market.

Introduction. A method of obtaining a listing for a share which is already of such an amount and so widely held that an adequate market will develop in the share once it is listed.

Introductory discount. The minimum *market discount* which is required to float an issue successfully.

Issue by tender. An invitation to the public to submit a tender for shares which are offered by the issuing company. See *tender issue.*

Issuing house. A specialist financial organisation which provides advice, *underwriting* and administrative services in connection with obtaining a *new listing.*

Market discouht. The difference between issue price and market value at the issue date, expressed as a percentage of the issue price or of the *net receipts* per share. Market value at the issue date is estimated from the price at which the issue is traded, corrected for market movements since the issue date.

Mixed offering. Offering of shares, some of which are newly created and some of which are already in existence. The new issue is a mixture of a *primary offering* and *secondary offering.*

Net receipts. The value of the issue at the issue price, minus administrative and other expenses.

New company. A company which is issuing shares to the public for the first time. A 'new company' might also be one whose previous quotation has lapsed, one which has been used for 'shell' operations, or one whose nature has been completely changed as a result of the issue. See *unseasoned issue.*

New issue market. The market for issuing financial securities to the public. The new issue market has no physical location, and consists of the institutions and investors involved in issuing the securities. The new issues may subsequently be traded in a *secondary market*. See *primary market*.

New listing. Provision of a stock exchange listing for shares which have not previously been quoted on that exchange. The shares may have been listed previously on another exchange.

New money. Money received by the company making a new issue, i.e. proceeds of the issue which arise from newly created shares. This figure can be calculated gross (i.e. number of new shares multiplied by price per share), net of all administrative expenses and/or redemptions of the company's existing securities, or net of purchases of any existing securities (e.g. Midland Bank Statistics, Bank of England Statistics). See *primary offering*.

Non-cash compensation. (US) Additional compensation for the underwriters of an issue, provided in the form of warrants to purchase shares after the issue is completed, etc.

Offer for sale. An offer to the public of securities already subscribed by an issuing house or broker.

Offer for sale by tender. An invitation to the public to submit a tender for shares which are offered by an issuing house or broker. See *tender issue*.

Old company. A company which already has a stock exchange quotation. See *seasoned issue*.

Overriding commission. A fee payable to the placing agents of the underwriting (including brokers and the issuing house's own investment department).

Oversubscription. An oversubscribed issue is one in which the number of shares applied for exceeds the number offered in an *offer for sale, prospectus issue* or *issue by tender*.

Over-the-counter (OTC) market. Organised market in unlisted securities. In the UK, this term usually refers to investment bankers M J H Nightingale's OTC market rather than the *Unlisted Securities Market* or dealings under the Stock Exchange's *Rule 163*.

Placing. Method of issue where the bulk of the shares are offered to the sponsor's own clients.

Premium. The amount by which the price at which a share is traded is above its issue price. Cf. *discount.*

Primary market. The market for issuing financial securities to the public, i.e. the *new issue market.* Frequently used to denote the market for issuing previously unlisted ordinary shares to the public.

Primary offering. Offering of newly created shares. *A new money* offering.

Prospectus. Document setting out the offer price and other particulars of an issue and fulfilling the requirements of the Stock Exchange and of the Companies Act 1948.

Provincial exchange. One of the UK stock exchanges which provided listings for companies, prior to the unification of the stock market in the UK in 1974. At this date, they became trading floors for the UK Stock Exchange.

Public issue or prospectus issue. An offer to the public by the issuing company itself of securities which are sold at the price stipulated in the *prospectus.*

Public company. A company, whose shares may be listed or unlisted, which has 50 or more shareholders other than employees.

Promotional offering. An offering by a company with no (or virtually no) certified earnings history.

Quotations department. The arm of the Stock Exchange responsible, among other things, for granting listings. This it does through the regular Wednesday and Friday meetings of the Committee on Quotations.

Registered offerings. (US) Public, interstate offerings over $500 000 (before 1971, $300 000) in value must be registered under the Securities Act 1933. Smaller issues fall under *Regulation A*, while interstate offerings come solely under state jurisdiction.

Regulation A offerings. (US) Interstate public offerings of shares which are exempt from the normal process required of *registered offerings.* Regulation A issues have a market value of under $500 000 (before 1971, $300 000).

Renunciation. Until a definitive share certificate is issued, (i.e. until one to two months after trading in a new issue starts), the holder of an *allotment* letter may sell his shares by renouncing his entitlement in favour of the buyer. All such dealings are free of stamp duty and registration fee.

Rights issue. An issue of shares to existing shareholders in proportion to their holdings, at an issue price which is generally below the current market price.

Rule 163. A special provision under the Regulations of the Stock Exchange, whereby dealings may take place in any security which has an official listing on another exchange, and also through Rule 163(2) in unlisted securities. In the case of the latter, prior approval is required for each transaction.

Scaling down. Large applications to an *oversubscribed* new issue are usually *allotted* in part only. They are usually scaled down by a factor which is slightly larger than the *times subscribed* and rounded to the nearest hundred shares, so as to facilitate a wide spread of shareholdings.

Seasoned issue. Issue of shares which already have a stock exchange quotation. Issue of shares by an *old company*.

Secondary market. The market for the purchase and sale of existing securities. The most important secondary market is the Stock Exchange.

Secondary offering. Offering of shares already in existence, (i.e. sale of shares owned by proprietors of the company). A *no new money* offering.

Sponsor (of an issue). Issuing house or stockbrokers who act as principal or as agent in the issue of shares to the public.

Stag. An individual who subscribes to a new issue, not with the intention of holding the shares he receives but anticipating that he will sell his *allotment* at a profit when dealings start.

Standby fee. (US) The *subunderwriting* commission paid to financial institutions, in return for their agreement to *take up* a specified proportion of any shares remaining as a result of *undersubscription*.

Striking price. The price at which shares are sold in a *tender issue*. It can be the minimum price (if there are insufficient *applications* in total), or the market clearance price (which will just clear the offering), or below the market clearance price (which will entail some *scaling down* of applications).

Subscription. See *times subscribed.*

Subunderwriting. The agreement by various financial institutions not directly associated with a new issue, to accept the risks taken on by the *underwriters* in return for a commission which is usually $\frac{1}{4}$ per cent below the underwriting fee of $1\frac{1}{2}$ per cent.

Take-up fee. (US) Fee payable (in addition to *standby fee*) on the proportion of an issue which is taken up by *subunderwriting* institutions.

Tender issue. Issue in which shares are offered to the public at a minimum price, and tenders are invited at or above the stipulated minimum. The shares are issued at a *striking price* which is set so as to enable the issuer to sell all the shares. Tender issues can be by means of the *offer for sale by tender* or *issue by tender.*

Times subscribed. The number of shares applied for in an *offer for sale, prospectus issue* or *issue by tender* divided by the number on offer. (In the case of tenders, it is necessary to state the price at which the times subscribed has been calculated.)

Turn. Percentage difference between the price per share at which the issuing house sells an issue and the price per share which is paid to the company which is going public.

Undersubscription. An undersubscribed issue is one in which the number of shares applied for is less than the number offered in an *offer for sale, prospectus issue* or *issue by tender.*

Underwriting. (UK) Agreement by the sponsors of an issue to take a specified proportion of any part of an offer which is not subscribed by the public. In return they receive an underwriting commission which is generally $1\frac{1}{2}$ per cent of the issue price. Most of the risk is laid off to *subunderwriters.* (US) The complete process of marketing shares in a new company to investors, including all the functions of the *sponsors* of the issue.

Unlisted Securities Market (USM). The Stock Exchange's organised market in unlisted securities.

Unseasoned issue. Issue of shares which have no previous listing on a stock exchange. Issue of shares by a *'new company'.*

Yellow Book. Nickname for the Stock Exchange book of listing regulations, entitled 'Admission of Securities to Listing'.

14

Equity rights issues

Paul Marsh

Rights issues are the method by which companies quoted on the Stock Exchange in the UK raise virtually all their new equity finance. An equity rights issue is an offer of shares for cash to existing shareholders (and possibly holders of other securities in the company) in proportion to their existing holdings. This chapter concerns the principal problems encountered by a company making a rights issue.

The topics covered are:

1 Issue methods for quoted companies raising money on the Stock Exchange
2 The choice between debt and equity
3 The rights issue method
4 The timing of external funding and rights issues
5 Rights issue procedures and timetable
6 Rights issue costs
7 Setting the terms and the underwriting decision
8 Market reaction to rights issues
9 Raising money at existing market prices
10 Summary and conclusions

ISSUE METHODS FOR QUOTED COMPANIES RAISING MONEY ON THE STOCK EXCHANGE

Essentially, four basic issue methods are open to quoted companies raising money on the Stock Exchange. They are:

1 Rights issues are offers of new securities for cash to existing

shareholders (and possibly holders of other securities in the company) in proportion to their existing holdings.

2 Open offers are offers of new securities for cash to existing shareholders (and possibly holders of other securities in the company) other than in proportion to their existing holdings.

3 Public issues are offers of new securities for cash, made to the general public either by the issuing company or by an issuing house or broker which has either subscribed for, or agreed to subscribe for, the securities of the company in question. Normally, the offer will be made at a fixed price, but occasionally it may be carried out by the tender method. The normal procedure in the case of tenders is that applicants are invited to submit a tender stating a price together with the number of shares they would accept at that price.

   With public issues, it is fairly common for preference in allotment to be extended to applications from existing security holders, particularly ordinary shareholders, although typically this applies to only a proportion of the total issue.

4 Placings are issues of new securities for cash whereby the new securities are 'placed' with both private and insitutional clients of the issuing house and with jobbers, rather than being offered to existing holders or to the public. It is a Stock Exchange regulation that at least 20 per cent of any placing must be available for purchase by the clients of other brokers through the medium of the market, that is through the jobbers. However, since January 1975, the Stock Exchange has been prepared to dispense with the latter requirement in the case of placings of additional shares of an existing class.

The choice between these four methods is largely dictated by the type of security being issued. For example, virtually all cash issues of equity or securities convertible into equity including options, warrants and convertible loan stocks are made via the rights issue method. Indeed, it is a Stock Exchange regulation that 'in the absence of circumstances which have been agreed by the Council to be exceptional', the rights issue method is the only one permissible for the issue of such securities unless shareholders' prior approval has been obtained in general meeting. Even with such approval, prior to January 1975, the Stock Exchange would not allow equity issues of more than £1 million or convertible stock issues for more than £5 million with an overriding limit that no issue could exceed 5 per cent of the existing listed equity capital.

In January 1975, the Council of the Stock Exchange announced that they had 'temporarily relaxed the current requirements governing issues of equity capital' because of 'existing market conditions', and would henceforth consider applications 'from existing listed companies for placings of additional shares or securities convertible into equity without limit as to the size of the issue'. During 1975, however, there were only ten new equity placings, raising a total of only some £10 million. The only other non-rights equity issue made by a quoted company was a public offer for sale by the Rank Organisation to raise some £28 million. In contrast, over the same period, there were more than 150 rights issues which raised a total of more than £1.2 billion. Figure 14.1 summarises the frequency of the various issue methods by the type of security involved.

The main reason for favouring the rights issue method is that it avoids any possibility of unfairness to existing shareholders. By giving all holders the opportunity to subscribe for new securities in proportion to their existing holdings, wealth transfers are prevented both between shareholders and also from existing to new shareholders, since shareholders can either take up their rights, or sell them at their market price. The same is not true for placings or offers since the securities are nearly always issued at a discount, thereby giving rise to a transfer of wealth from existing holders to the placees.

As we saw in the previous chapter, public issues (including offers for sale) and placings are also the principal methods used by previously unquoted companies when they go public (i.e. obtain a Stock Exchange listing).

THE CHOICE BETWEEN DEBT AND EQUITY

In 1958, Modigliani and Miller (1) made an important contribution to the theory of corporate capital structure by demonstrating that if interest on loans were not tax deductible, it would not matter whether companies raised debt or equity. They illustrated this by considering two companies with identical operating risks, one debt free and the other having some debt in its capital structure. They pointed out that:

1   An investor in the debt free firm who preferred greater risk could always replicate the position of an investor in the geared firm by

Type of Security / Issue Method	Rights Issue	Open Issue	Public Issue	Placing
Equity	Virtually all issues	Very infrequent	Very infrequent	Infrequent (very infrequent prior to January 1975)
Warrants		– – –	– – –	
Convertible loan stocks and convertible preference		Very infrequent	Very infrequent	
Loan stock and debentures	Very infrequent	Fairly common	Large issues only	Majority of issues – virtually all small issues
Preference	Very infrequent	Fairly common	Very infrequent – large issues only	Majority of small issues
Combined units	All issues	– – –	– – –	– – –

☐ requires shareholders' approval. Prior to January 1975 only equity issues less than £1m and convertible issues less than £5m permitted.

Fig. 14.1   Issue methods for quoted companies raising money on the Stock Exchange

increasing his holding in the debt free firm using money borrowed on his own account; that is, by gearing up for himself.

2   An investor in the geared firm who preferred less risk could achieve the same position as an investor in the debt free firm by selling part of his holding and investing the proceeds in the company's debt.

Thus, as investors can replicate companies' capital structure decisions on their own account, they should pay neither a premium nor a discount for the shares of geared companies. Hence, while debt financing leads to an increase in earnings per share, this increase is exactly offset by an increase in the rate at which the earnings are capitalised, the latter arising from the additional risk resulting from the use of debt.

Bringing taxes into the analysis leads us to the paradoxical conclusion that companies wishing to benefit their shareholders should gear up to as high a level of debt as is possible, since interest on debt is tax deductable, and this in a sense represents a government subsidy on debt financing. When the details of the imputation tax system and personal taxes are taken into account, the net tax advantage to corporate borrowing is reduced significantly, but remains positive. We are still left, therefore, with the intuitively unacceptable prescription of 100 per cent debt.

In practice, of course, companies employ only modest amounts of debt financing. The conflict between the theory and practice can probably be explained in terms of:

1 *Incomplete theory*. The theory may well neglect a number of important factors. A more recent theory by Miller (1977) (2) suggests that the net tax advantage is, in fact, zero in equilibrium. Miller's theory, however, fails to explain why debt ratios differ between companies and industries.

2 *Institutional factors*. Articles of association, and more importantly trust deeds of existing loans, typically set limits on the permitted debt/equty ratios and may also stipulate minimum interest cover requirements. In addition, the Inland Revenue may disallow tax deductability at high interest rates for companies which are very heavily geared.

3 *Bankruptcy consideration*. Higher gearing leads to increased bankruptcy risk. This will only affect shareholders who hold diversified portfolios insofar as there are costs to bankruptcy. However, management will tend to be cautious both to protect themselves and their employees, who generally hold less well-diversified portfolios by having a large part of their 'human capital' tied up in the firm's future.

Management may therefore select a target debt/equity ratio which takes account of these considerations and when new finance is required, choose between debt and equity on the basis of this guideline. In practice, companies will consider many other factors when choosing between debt and equity, including current capital market conditions as described later in this chapter.

THE RIGHTS ISSUE METHOD

This is best illustrated with a simple example. Consider a company that wants to raise £1 million via a rights issue. Suppose that there are 2 000 000 shares already in issue with a market price of £1 each, so that the company is valued at £2 million. The first column of Table 14.1 shows the effect of making a one for one issue (one new share offered for each share currently held) at 50p, while the second column shows that the £1 million could equally well be raised by a two for three issue at 75p.

A rights issue can be viewed as an issue of shares at the current market price combined with a scrip issue. Looked at this way, the terms above differ only in the size of the scrip issue involved. While the two different sets of terms lead to different share prices after the issue, this will not affect shareholders, since the value of the company will be the same in each case, as will be the fraction of the company which each shareholder owns.

Nevertheless, many finance directors, merchant bankers, brokers and press commentators still discus the 'attractiveness' of rights issue

Table 14.1
Rights issue terms

Details	Terms	
	1 for 1 at 50p	2 for 3 at 75p
Prior to issue		
Number of shares	2m	2m
Share price	£1	£1
Value of company	£2m	£2m
After ex-rights date		
Number of new shares	2m	$1\frac{1}{3}$m
New money raised	2m × 50p = £1m	$\frac{1}{3}$m × 75p = £1m
Value of company	£2m + £1m = £3m	£2m + £1m = £3m
Total number of shares	4m	$3\frac{1}{3}$m
Share price	£3m/4m = 75p	£3m/$3\frac{1}{3}$m = 90p
Price of the rights	75p – 50p = 25p	90p – 75p = 15p

terms, although very few of them would dream of applying the same terminology to scrip issues. Furthermore, they frequently argue that the larger the scrip element involved, the greater the dilution of earnings and dividends. One even sees the view put forward that the cost of the rights issue is the dividend yield calculated on the issue price, so that the lower the issue price is set, the higher the cost of the issue. This argument would presumably imply that scrip issues are infinitely expensive! This is clearly nonsense. Underwriting considerations apart, and excepting the fact that shares cannot be issued below per value, the terms of a rights issue and the level at which the issue price is set are irrelevant.

Finally, it is often argued that rights issues are unfair to shareholders who are unable to take up their rights, since this allows other shareholders or underwriters to 'get in' at a 'cheap' price. Again this view is misguided. Shareholders who are unable to take up their rights can sell them at a fair market price – 25p or 15p respectively in the examples given in Table 14.1. Even if such shareholders do not sell their rights, they seldom suffer financial loss, since in the majority of issues the rights will be sold on their behalf.

THE TIMING OF EXTERNAL FUNDING AND RIGHTS ISSUES

Stated simply, companies should raise external funds when the amount of money they require to finance profitable ventures (i.e. those with positive NPV's) exceeds the amount available from internal sources. For the corporate sector taken in aggregate, this has been the overall situation for at least the past 25 years.

Contrary to what one might at first suspect, there has been a clear general tendency, both in the USA and the UK, for companies to raise new external finance during, or shortly after, periods of buoyant sales. The usual explanation for this phenomenon is as follows:

After a company has been operating at a low level of capacity, any increase in sales is likely to result in a sharp improvement in profitability and therefore in retained earnings. Such an improvement will not generally be matched by an immediate increase in expenditure. Major investment in fixed plant is unlikely to be authorised as long as the company still has significant spare capacity and, even if it were authorised, there would be some delay before any payments were made. Furthermore, the initial effect of the pick-up in sales could lead to some involuntary temporary reduction in inventories. Thus, the net effect of the more buoyant conditions is an improvement in company liquidity, and it is only after the boom has persisted for a year or two that the pressure on funds is likely to be felt. In just the same way the initial result of any decline in sales will usually be a fall in retained earnings and a continued high level of investment in fixed plant and inventories. A more prolonged decline in sales will induce a reduction in investment expenditure to boost company liquidity. The net effect is that changes in company activity tend to precede changes in the raising of external funds.

Since both the total volume of external financing, and the level of the stock market are affected by economic prospects, it is not surprising to see an association between the two. After a rise in the market, companies are more prone to issue equity. Furthermore, there is also a tendency for equity issues to be made by companies whose shares have performed abnormally well in the period prior to the issue. A study of 997 UK rights issues between 1962–75, (3), revealed that over the year leading up to the issue, the shares of companies making rights issues experienced abnormal gains of over 30 per cent after adjusting for risk and market movements (see Table 14.2). However, there is no

Table 14.2
Summary of rights issue studies

Author	Country	Date of sample	Sample size	Type of returns	Preissue	Announ- cement	XR date	Post issue
Weller	USA	1956–7	81	Market adjusted capital gains	—	–3%	—	—
Boden- hammer	USA	1962–5	61	↓	—	–3%	–	–
Scholes	USA	1926–66	696	Abnormal returns	Unusual gains	—	–0.3%	Zero
Merrett/ Howe/ Newbould	UK	1963	110/ 95	Market adjusted capital gains	—	—	+1%	+3% (1 year)
Smith	USA	1926–75	853	Abnormal returns	+9%		–1.4%	1.4%
Marsh	UK	1962–75	997	↓	+33%	–½%	–¾%	+4% (2 year)

corresponding tendency in the UK for increases in debt issues to follow rises in bond prices (i.e. falls in interest rates), though several studies indicate a contrary experience in the USA.

This tendency for equity issues to follow share price rises is rather puzzling. Increases in share prices, after all, will have increased the equity base and should, if anything, encourage new debt issues. Why then do companies choose such times to reduce their gearing even further?

One possible explanation is that management's choice between debt and equity partly reflects its assessment of future share price movements, and that this, in turn, is influenced by recent share price movements. Such behaviour would be open to a number of criticisms. First, given the large body of evidence on stock market efficiency, it seems extremely unlikely that corporate management or their financial advisers will have any superior forecasting ability with regard to the future movement of share prices. This argument is borne out by the fact that there is absolutely no tendency for increases in the level of equity issues to be *followed* by any abnormal movements in share prices. Secondly, given the use of the rights issue method for virtually all equity issues by UK quoted companies, it is not obvious that existing shareholders would always benefit even if management could forecast future share prices. For example, if management's forecasting ability was limited to the residual movement in the price of their company's shares, existing holders would gain only if they failed to take up their entitlement *and* the shares were *overvalued* at the time of the issue. Similarly, if management's forecasting ability was limited to market movements, existing holders would gain if management correctly forecast a rise in share prices *relative* to other assets *and* if, as a result of the issue, their existing shareholders increase the proportion of their wealth held in equities (see Figures 14.2 to 14.4).

The second alternative explanation is that management's choice between debt and equity is based on incorrect notions of the cost of equity capital. It is still fairly widely believed, for example, that the cost of equity is either:

(a) the dividend yield, or
(b) the earnings yield.

In both cases, increases in the company's share price will lead to an apparent fall in the cost of equity, and for management who subscribe to this notion, equity appears much cheaper when the share price is

Existing shareholders	Loss or gain to existing shareholders if shares are:		
	Undervalued	Correctly valued	Overvalued
Take up rights	——	——	——
Don't take up	Loss	——	Gain

Fig. 14.2 Timing of rights issues

Shareholder action	Share values relative to other asset values	
	Fall	Rise
Takes up rights by (a) selling other shares (b) selling other assets (c) reducing consumption	—— Loss Loss	—— Gain Gain
Sells rights and (a) reinvests proceeds in other shares (b) reinvests proceeds in other assets (c) consumes proceeds	—— Gain Gain	—— Loss Loss

Fig. 14.3 Timing of rights issues and overall market movements

high. Again, while belief in these views may help to explain the observed financing behaviour, these concepts of the cost of equity are extremely misleading.

Neither of these alternative explanations of the strange 'cycles' in the choice of financing method are very impressive in terms of modern financial thinking. Nevertheless, discussions with both corporate management and their financial advisers indicate that a great deal of attention is paid to the careful timing of issues with respect to market conditions, and that considerations such as those above do play an

Dealings column headers: CR | XR | R | FP new

Date relative to XR date	Companies not requiring EGM	Companies requiring EGM
1 year	Management/Advisors review financing plans, possibly some hint or advance warning of issue	Management/Advisors review financing plans, possibly some hint or advance warning of issue
9 to 12 weeks	Decision taken to go ahead with issue	Decision taken to go ahead with issue
−6 to 8 weeks	Company/issuing house/brokers discuss various drafts of circular/terms/forecasts/timetable	Company/issuing house/brokers discuss various drafts of circular/terms/forecasts/timetable
−3 weeks	Holders registered date	Issue price/terms finalised; underwriting; sub-underwriting; issue announcement
−1 to 2 weeks	Issue price/terms finalised underwriting; sub-underwriting; issue announcement	Holders registered date: Notice of EGM and circular letter sent to shareholders
	Circular letter and provisional allotment letter sent to shareholders	
−1 to 2 days		EGM; provisional allotment letters posted
XR date	Latest date on which PAL's received; shares marked 'ex'	
+ 3 weeks	Last acceptance date: payment in full (or part)	
+ 3 weeks	Shares not taken up either sold (placed) for benefit, or allotted to applicants for excess shares.	
1–2 days	Cheques or allotment letter sent out	
+ 7 weeks	Last splitting date	
+ 7 weeks	Share certificates sent out	
2 days		

Fig. 14.4 Rights issue procedures and timetable

important role in explaining management's behaviour. It is difficult to escape from the conclusion, however, that much of this effort is misplaced, and that there is still a great deal of misunderstanding.

RIGHTS ISSUE COSTS

The following costs are incurred in the course of making a rights issue:

1 *Administrative costs*
   (a) Printing and postage of circulars and provisional allotment letters.
   (b) Costs of arranging Extraordinary General Meeting if necessary.
   (c) Costs of postage and printing of notices and proxy forms.
   (d) Fee to receiving bankers.
   (e) Stock Exchange listing fee.
2 *Tax*
   Capital duty (1 per cent).
3 *Professional fees*
   (a) Fee to broker.
   (b) Fee to solicitors.
   (c) Commission to advisers ($\frac{1}{2}$ per cent).
   (d) Fee to receiving bankers, (see above).
4 *Underwriting costs*
   Subunderwriting fee ($1\frac{1}{4}$ per cent) – not a true 'cost' – see below.

With the exception of the underwriting fee and capital duty, all the other costs decrease as a percentage of the money raised as the size of the issue increases. As a rough rule of thumb, the cost of a rights issue (excluding underwriting) has been about 2.4 + (0.7) ÷ (issue size in £million) per cent of the money raised.

SETTING THE TERMS AND THE UNDERWRITING DECISION

Purpose of underwriting

When companies make rights issues, the timing of events provides a period of approximately three weeks during which shareholders can decide whether to subscribe.

If the share price is above the issue price on the last acceptable date, the issue will be successful. However, if the share price falls below the issue price, the new shares will not be taken up since they could be bought more cheaply in the market, and the issue will fail unless it has been underwritten.

Underwriters therefore perform a useful service by taking on risk. Whether or not a company should underwrite will depend on the fee charged and the probability of the market price falling below the issue price. This, in turn, depends upon the terms of the issue, and the company could set the issue price low enough virtually to assure success. If this were done, the company should be prepared to pay only a trivial sum for underwriting and could effectively dispense with it altogether.

In recent years, however, over 90 per cent of rights issues have been underwritten. Normally, the merchant bank or broker advising the company on the issue acts as principal underwriter but passes on the major part of the risk of a failed issue to subunderwriters, who almost invariably charge a fixed fee of $1\frac{1}{4}$ per cent though, if the period from the date of underwriting to the last acceptance date exceeds thirty days, this fee is increased by $\frac{1}{8}$ per cent per week or part thereof. Note that while this fee is fixed, underwriters can still effectively vary the price they charge through the advice they give on the issue terms. The lower they advise the company to set the issue price, the higher the price the company will effectively pay for any underwriting.

Underwriting is thus the major single item of 'cost' in making rights issues, and for large issues, underwriters' fees can be substantial. ICI, for example, paid £2.8 million to the underwriters of its 1976 issue, and BP's massive 1981 rights issue cost not less than £12 million in underwriting fees.

The profitability of underwriting

A study of 671 underwritten UK rights issues between 1962 and 1975 showed that underwriters made an average return of 1.1 per cent per issue. (Marsh, 1977.) In only 35 cases (about 5 per cent) was any part of the issue left with the underwriters. The average loss in these 35 cases was 4 per cent, and the maximum loss over the whole period was only 13 per cent.

Valuing the worth of underwriting

While the figures above suggest that underwriters have done very well on average, at the expense of the issuing companies, this may be unfair to underwriters since the figures take no account of risk. However, it is possible to define a 'fair' return to underwriters, making due allowance for risk, when we recognise that underwriters are selling a put option.

A put option is nothing more than the option to sell shares (or any other assets) at a given price at some specified date or dates in the future.

The diagrams in Figure 14.5 show how a company underwriting a rights issue is in the same position as a purchaser of a put option. If the market price falls below the issue price by the last acceptance date, the shareholders will 'put' the failed issue onto the underwriters at the issue price. As the diagrams show, the closer the issue price to the market price, the higher the fee for underwriting should be.

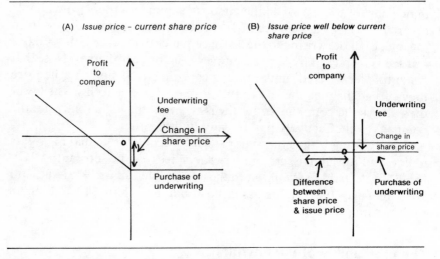

Fig. 14.5   Underwriting as a put option

A precise value for the underwriting put option can be calculated by using an ingenious option valuation model derived by Black and Scholes (1973) (4). They showed that the value of underwriting increases with the ratio of the issue price to the current share price, the length of the period over which the underwriters are at risk, the variability of the company's share price and the current short term interest rate. No other variables affect the underwriting value.

The precise valuation formula is rather complicated and is not given here. However, the items of information required in order to use this formula to value underwriting are very straightforward and an example is given in Table 14.3.

Table 14.3
Calculating the value of underwriting

Information required	Actual values for the Tube Investments rights issue made in April 1975
Share price on date underwriting arranged	236 p (⟶229 ex rights)
Issue price	190 p
Duration of underwriting agreement	22 trading days
Standard deviation of returns on the share	40 % per year
Short term interest rate (Treasury Bill rate)	9¼ %
Underwriting value (as % issue price) = 0.11 %	

Historical returns to underwriters

The Black and Scholes valuation formula was applied to 539 underwritten UK rights issues between 1962 and 1975 to determine whether underwriters made excess returns; that is, returns over and above the risk adjusted 'fair' value.

The average excess return to subunderwriting was approximately 0.7 per cent. As can be seen from Figure 14.6, the distribution of the excess returns was very skewed with a median value of 1.11 per cent. In other words, in the majority of cases, underwriting appeared grossly overpriced. Underwriting values were greater than the fee paid in only 14 per cent of cases.

Conclusions on underwriting

It may be unfair to conclude too readily that underwriters overcharge companies for their services. The relationship between company and financial adviser is not limited to underwriting rights issues, and it is possible that merchant bankers undercharge for other services or advice.

However, the evidence strongly suggests that companies should be

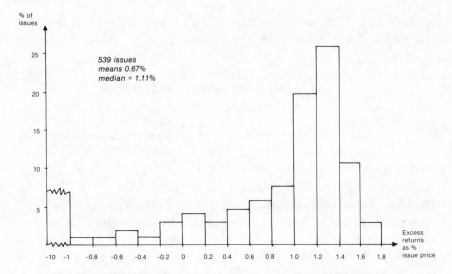

Fig. 14.6   Distribution of excess returns to subunderwriting

cautious, and not accept too readily the issue terms suggested by the principal underwriter. The company can use the Black & Scholes formula to assess the value of underwriting at the terms suggested. If the company cannot get a reasonably 'priced' underwriting arrangement, it should consider whether to set the issue price lower and dispense with underwriting.

MARKET REACTION TO RIGHTS ISSUES

A study of 997 UK rights issues between 1962 and 1975 found that on average, the announcement of a rights issue prompted only a negligible decline of less than $\frac{1}{2}$ per cent in the company's share price (see Table 14.2), suggesting that companies' financing needs cause little surprise or concern to the market. However, the way in which *individual* companies' share prices react to the news of an issue depends, of course, on the information accompanying and conveyed by the announcement. This information may concern:

1   *The company's existing business.* Rights issue announcements are frequently timed to coincide with the announcement of the annual or interim results, and are often accompanied by other

news items on the company's existing business. Even in the absence of explicit announcements, the market may interpret the rights issue as indicating unforeseen problems in the company's existing business, or previous underestimation of financing requirements.

2 *Management's assessment of prospects.* Rights issues are frequently accompanied by earnings forecasts, and almost invariably by forecasts of future dividends. The market's reaction to the news of the issue will therefore depend partly on whether these forecasts come as a pleasant or unpleasant surprise. In fact, the study referred to above found, roughly speaking, a 1 per cent increase in the share price for every 15 per cent increase in the forecast dividend.

3 *Uses of the new money.* If the finance to be raised is for investment in new projects or acquisitions, the market's reaction to the issue will depend upon its assessment of the NPV of the new projects, and this, in turn, will depend upon its view of the quality of the company's management. If the new money is to be used to repay debt, the market's reaction could be unfavourable if this heralded an unanticipated reduction in the company's target debt/equity ratio. These common sense views are again borne out by the empirical evidence which found that the share prices of companies announcing rights issues to finance new investment rose by 2.1 per cent from the day before the announcement to one month later. Companies announcing issues for the purposes of reducing gearing, however, experienced an average fall of $\frac{1}{2}$ per cent in share price. Similarly, companies with a good track record, both in terms of share price and accounting measures of performance experienced share price rises of 1.8 per cent over the month of the announcement, while companies with a relatively poor or indifferent record experienced an average decline of 0.6 per cent.

4 *Capital structure.* If an equity issue is announced when an issue of debt was expected, the market may take this to imply a downward revision in the target debt/equity ratio, and this may lead to a fall in the share price. This is again borne out by the evidence in that there is a difference of approximately 2 per cent in the market's reaction to the rights issue announcement, depending on whether or not the market was expecting an equity or a debt issue.

Thus while there is, on average, little share price movement on the announcements of rights issues, the market's reaction can differ quite widely from one company to another. Furthermore, it is difficult to disentangle price movements due to the rights issue from those due to the accompanying announcements of other information.

RAISING EQUITY AT EXISTING MARKET PRICES

A view widely held by both professional investors and by finance directors is that, because it increases the supply of a company's shares, a rights issue will have a depressing effect upon the company's share price. This effect is usually referred to as 'price pressure', and belief in its existence is implicitly based on the assumption that the demand curve for a company's ahres is not perfectly elastic but slopes downward.

Price pressure implies temporary price depression and cheap buying opportunities, and hence is inconsistent with stock market efficiency. The alternative view consistent with market efficiency is that the demand for a particular company's shares is perfectly elastic so that increases in the supply of its shares alone will not lead to a decline in the share price.

According to this view, the company selling shares is in a position precisely analogous to that of the wheat farmer in the standard economics textbook example who is able to sell large additional quantities of wheat at existing market prices, and in so doing, has essentially no effect on the world price of grain.

In both cases, the high elasticity of demand stems from the existence of very close substitutes, in one case this being the produce of other farms, and in the other, the existence of alternative risky assets. Since shares are valued purely on the basis of their risk and expected return, one share will prove a very close substitute for another.

Unless the additional supply of what or shares is large relative to the total supply of grain or risky assets, respectively, its effect on market prices should be negligible. The largest rights issue ever made on the London Stock Exchange was by BP who raised £624 million in June 1981. At the time of this issue, the new money raised was less than 0.2 per cent of the total value of London quoted equities, and thus was very small in relation to the total supply of risky assets, especially if the definition of the latter is extended to include fixed interest securities, property, commodities, works of art and so on.

Which of these two views is correct can be determined by examining the evidence. If price pressure exists, companies making rights issues should experience an abnormal price decline on the ex rights date, and this price decline should be greater the larger the issue. As can be seen from Table 14.2, the mean abnormal return for the one-week period over the Xr date for 997 UK rights issues made between 1962 and 1975 was between $-\frac{1}{2}$ per cent and $-\frac{3}{4}$ per cent. Although this could be taken as weak evidence of price pressure, the effect is very small, and could, of course, be explained by other factors.

However, further investigation showed that there as no relationship between the abnormal price movements at the time of the issue and the issue size, regardless of whether the latter was taken as the absolute size of the issue or the size of the issue expressed as a percentage of the issuing company's market capitalisation. Figure 14.7 shows the scatter diagram of abnormal returns against issue size for the relative size case. It is worth noting that the estimated elasticities of demand, while not

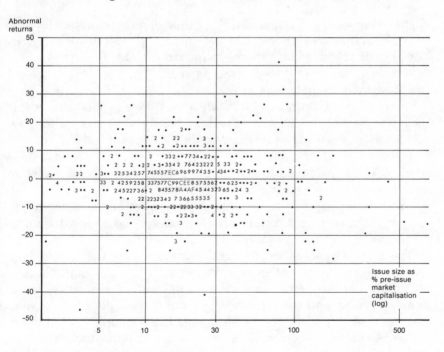

Fig. 14.7 Abnormal returns and relative issue size

remotely significant statistically, were approximately +650 and –300 for the absolute and relative size cases, respectively. Thus, contrary to the predictions of the price pressure hypothesis, the demand curves are almost horizontal in both cases, and in the case of absolute issue size, the slope of the demand curve is not even in the predicted direction. To put these figures in perspective, the estimated relationship for the relative size case implies that a company increasing the size of its rights issue from 10 per cent to 20 per cent of the value of its existing equity will induce a price fall of less than 0.2 per cent, while a further increase from 20 per cent to 100 per cent will result in an additional fall of only $\frac{1}{2}$ per cent. On the basis of this evidence, the price pressure hypothesis can be firmly rejected. Companies *can* raise money at existing market prices.

SUMMARY AND CONCLUSIONS

Rights issues are a fair and equitable method of raising equity. The cost of equity is the return shareholders require for the risk involved and is not the dividend yield or the reciprocal of the P/E ratio. The Government tax subsidy on interest payments is the only factor which might make debt preferable to equity.

Companies should raise equity when they have profitable uses for the money; except in this sense, the timing of rights issues appears very much less relevant than some city traditions suggest.

The issue terms are irrelevant except from the point of view of underwriting. The apparent earnings and dividend 'dilution' resulting from setting a lower issue price does not matter.

Underwriters appear to earn large excess returns at companies' expense, and finance directors need not accept too readily the issue terms suggested by the underwriter.

The news of rights issues produces, on average, only a slight price fall, and appears to cause neither surprise nor concern. The market reacts efficiently to the new information contained in the rights issue announcement, and the incidence of a rights issue does not provide investors any opportunity to make abnormal gains. The evidence indicates that price pressure does not exist and that the stock market is a highly liquid market in which companies can raise equity at existing market prices.

REFERENCES

(1) F Modigliani and M H Miller, 'The Cost of Capital, Corpora-
     tion Finance and the Theory of Investment', *American
     Economic Review*, 48, pp.261–277, June 1958.
(2) Merton Miller, 'Debt and Taxes', Presidential Address at the
     Annual Meeting of the American Finance Association, *Journal
     of Finance*, 32, pp.261–275, May 1977.
(3) Paul Marsh, 'An Analysis of Equity Rights Issues on the
     London Stock Exchange', Unpublished doctoral dissertation,
     London Business School, 1977.
(4) F Black and M Scholes, 'The Pricing of Options and Corporate
     Liabilities', *Journal of Political Economy*, 81, pp.637–654,
     May–June 1973.

PART V
THE EXTERNAL
ENVIRONMENT

OVERVIEW

A company must be aware of the financial environment in which it operates. This environment consists of its shareholders and bankers, the tax and regulatory authorities and other companies.

Shareholders and bankers supply capital, and the company needs to maintain good relationships with them to ensure an adequate flow of investment funds. Maintaining these relationships entails publishing relevant up-to-date information so that investors can value their company, decide whether to subscribe new funds and monitor the use of assets.

The ultimate sanction that the capital market can apply is a company takeover and the replacement of senior management. Thus, mergers and acquisitions form important aspects of the financial environment, both for companies seeking to grow by this method and for those wishing to avoid being taken over.

The tax regime under which the company operates has a large impact on the cash flows resulting from financial decisions. Effective use of the tax laws to minimise the cash drain on the company requires that the tax impact of all decisions be understood and incorporated into the decision making process.

These three aspects of the financial environment: presentation of information in accounts, mergers and taxation are covered by this section. Chapter 15 by George Thomson explains the regulations concerning disclosure in company accounts. These requirements form the basis for external financial reporting, but there may be good reason to disclose more than the minimum required. The kinds of extra information that are likely to prove most helpful, and the agreements for providing such details are explored and explained. So is the recent requirement to present inflation-adjusted accounting information, which is the major change in this area in recent years.

Since investors use company accounts for three major purposes: valuation, portfolio decisions, and monitoring asset use, the information provided must be appropriate to these ends. Valuation and portfolio decisions require more than just raw accounting information. Somehow, information on the company's position in its product markets, strategic plans and operating performance, has to be communicated, in addition to the dry numerical data.

This additional requirement is achieved by a mixture of formal and informal contacts with the investment community, of which the published accounts are merely the tip of the iceberg. Given the high cost of raising funds when relationships with investors are poor, and the threat of takeover if the situation deteriorates too much, effort spent on keeping investors informed is an important part of good financial management.

Although investors can refuse to provide companies with new funds when asked, many concerns manage to operate for long periods of time by using retained earnings and not making rights issues. Such companies are not immune to external financial markets, however, since their share prices may fall to such a level that it becomes attractive for another company to purchase a majority of the shares and gain control of the assets. The other side of this coin is that a company with a very high share rating resulting from able management can gain control of more assets by merger or acquisition.

In Chapter 16 Julian Franks analyses in detail the various motivations that are put forward for mergers and acquisitions: managerial skills, economics of scale, new product opportunities and valuation differences. In addition to these operational motivations, several purely financial incentives are sometimes suggested. Dr Franks shows that some of these may not be such powerful reasons for merging as is often stated. In particular, diversification through merger is not likely to benefit shareholders much, since they can diversify their own portfolios.

Even when there is a legitimate reason for merging, care must be taken that the premium paid does not exceed the synergistic benefits of the merger. Dr. Franks describes the various techniques that are applied in analysing acquisition opportunities. Finally, he examines the profitability record of past mergers, to indicate whether they have achieved the expected gains, and, if so, how these gains have been split between acquirors and acquirees.

The final chapter of Part Five, Chapter 17, by Raymond Ashton, covers the taxation of corporations in the UK. Almost all financial decisions have an impact on the amount of tax paid, and this must be included in the financial evaluation of the decisions. For instance, the hundred per cent initial allowance on certain kinds of industrial capital expenditure means that profitable companies reduce their effective initial cost to only 48 per cent of the cost of these assets. The other 52 per cent comes from a reduction in the corporation tax payment for that year. Similarly, the tax deductability of interest payments means that the value of projects that are financed partially by debt is increased by the value of this tax saving as discussed in Chapter 2.

Clearly, an understanding of the way that corporations are taxed is essential to good financial management. Dr. Ashton describes in detail the way that the tax system operates with respect to corporations. The most important aspect is the definition and taxation of corporate income, including the effects of allowances, grants and charges on income. Part of this corporation tax liability is offset by Advance Corporation Tax on dividends and this is also explained in detail.

The UK corporate tax system involves delays in payments which depend on the year end of the company concerned. Such delays are very valuable when interest rates are high, and Dr. Ashton shows how to work out the timing of the payments. Finally, he describes three additional features of the corporate tax system which can have a major impact on some companies; overseas tax, stock relief and value added tax.

Many corporations do not pay corporation tax, and it might be argued that such companies can ignore the tax impact of their decisions. This is fallacious, since companies which have unused tax loses are wasting opportunities to save money. The most common ways of taking advantage of unused tax losses are merging with or acquiring a profit-making company, sale and leaseback of assets from profit-making companies, or reduction of interest payments through retiring debt.

In these and other ways, understanding the financial environment is crucial to good financial decisions. These three aspects: taxation, mergers and financial reporting cover relationships with the tax authorities and the financial markets, the two most important external financial influences on companies. Mismanagement in these areas can be hazardous to the separate existence of a company, but good external relations ensure a continued flow of capital to support the growth and development of a soundly based and progressive organisation.

15

Presentation of external financial reports

George R Thomson*

This chapter is concerned with the requirements to be met by UK limited companies in corporate external financial reporting, that is, publication of financial information for use by people outside the business. These requirements are discharged by the inclusion of accounts and related information in the company's published annual report. This information is subject to audit, and it is the task of the auditors to report on whether or not the requirements have been met.

Financial reporting requirements for companies stem from three sources:

1 The law, principally the Companies Acts 1948, 1967, 1980 and 1981, together with the Directives of the European Economic Community as and when these are reflected in UK law.
2 Financial accounting standards laid down by the Accounting Standards Committee of the UK accountancy bodies as Statements of Standard Accounting Practice (SSAPs).
3 For companies whose securities are listed in the UK Stock Exchanges, the rules of the Stock Exchange.

Requirements may fall into either or both of the following categories:
1 Disclosure requirements: that is, what information elements should be provided.
2 Measurement standards: that is, the methods whereby the amounts reported under particular headings should be determined.

*For the second edition this chapter was comprehensively updated by Simon Archer.

The law and the Stock Exchange rules are concerned with disclosure, with the proviso that the amounts reported should provide a 'true and fair view' of the company's financial position and results. Specification of measurement standards is left to the Accounting Standards Committee. In addition to its concern for accounting measurement, however, the Accounting Standards Committee also includes further disclosure requirements in its SSAPs.

Financial reports or 'accounts' required for external users include two financial statements and accompanying notes, a balance sheet and a profit and loss account, plus a third statement required under SSAP No.10, namely a statement of sources and application of funds, or funds statement. In addition, the Stock Exchange rules for listed companies require:

1 A statement giving reasons for any departures from prescribed SSAPs.
2 A geographical analysis of sales turnover.
3 Details of shareholdings of more than 5 per cent in other companies.
4 A statement giving details of directors' shareholdings in the company.
5 A similar statement of directors' interests in company contracts.
6 Details of dividends waived by directors or other shareholders.

The role and implications of the SSAPs call for particular comment. In the first place they do not have the force of law. Neither is compliance mandatory for listed companies under the Stock Exchange rules; however, as already noted, if a listed company fails to comply with an SSAP, it is required to publish a statement giving the reasons for non-compliance. Finally, it is up to the company's auditors to decide whether the failure to comply with one or more SSAPs means that the accounts fail to provide a 'true and fair view' of financial position and results; for if so, it is their duty to word their audit opinion accordingly.

Naturally, the view of the Accounting Standards Committee and of the UK accountancy bodies is that, with very rare exceptions, failure to comply with either a disclosure requirement or a measurement standard laid down in an SSAP means that a 'true and fair view' has not been published. This would seem to imply that failure to comply with an SSAP is tantamount to failure to comply with the law which requires that a 'true and fair view' be provided. However, this proposition has not been established by the courts.

Nor do SSAPs cover all aspects of financial reporting, although coverage is increasing as new SSAPs are added. In fact, companies have considerable discretion as to how they report their financial position and results. The requirement to provide a 'true and fair view' is inherently subjective. We return to these issues later in this chapter.

A further point which must be made regarding SSAPs concerns current cost accounting. The existing law considers financial reporting requirements in terms of the hitherto generally accepted 'historical cost' accounting conventions. In 1980, however, the Accounting Standards Committee laid down SSAP No. 16 which requires all companies, excluding smaller firms and a few designated kinds of business, to produce financial reports – a balance sheet, a profit and loss account and accompanying notes – based on a set of 'current cost' conventions, in addition to those produced on the 'historical cost' basis. No 'current cost' funds statement is required. More will be said about these requirements later in this chapter.

OBJECTIVES

In deciding its presentation of existing financial reports, management has to consider appropriate objectives. The minimum objective is to show proprietors how their funds have been used and what profits have been made. This can be said to have been achieved by presenting a balance sheet, profit and loss account and funds statement, which show 'a true and fair view' of the state of the company's affairs. 'The true and fair view' implies an appropriate classification and grouping of the various items involved and the consistent application of generally accepted accounting principles. The law also requires that annual accounts show figures for the preceding year as well as the most recent year. Consistency is insisted upon by a further legal requirement for disclosure of any material changes in the accounting treatment and a statement of how such changes have affected the latest and the previous years' figures.

A manager who is also a controlling shareholder, with only a few unsophisticated relatives as minority holders, may be right in judging that presentation should end at this point. Before doing so he should take other considerations into account. Is the business likely to need outside cash, either through borrowing or through an extension of the shareholding? Is it likely to acquire another business or be acquired by one? Will death duties or other reasons make it desirable to sell existing shares, either privately or through a stock market flotation?

In any of these (and in numbers of other) cases, the accounts will be scrutinised by sophisticated outsiders. They will want to know the answer to a number of points which are not covered by minimum statutory requirements. They will almost certainly wish to see accounts for some years previously. Indeed, it is a legal prospectus requirement that at least five years' figures must be produced by a company seeking to raise money in the market. Application for a stock market quotation normally has to be supported by ten years' figures.

Bearing these factors in mind, it is obvious that the objectives of a presentation of annual accounts should take note of many things beyond the immediate objective of producing a single year's figures economically and with the least fuss possible. Financial management should regard presentation as an important element in promoting the general image of a company. Presentation is concerned with good public relations. Properly done it confers many benefits.

The main benefits can be listed as follows. First, against any given economic background, to make it easier and cheaper to borrow money or to attract new capital either from existing or new investors. Secondly, to make it cheaper and easier to expand by acquisitions or to get better terms from a merger. Thirdly, to make it easier to resist an unwanted takeover bid. Many other, less tangible, benefits accrue even down to helping individual salesmen to sell a company's product.

Financial managers of the majority of big stock market quoted companies are aware of these factors and would regard it as failure on their part not to carry the point with any higher managerial executive.

Technically, the accounts are only being presented to shareholders, as in the case of the individual controlling head of a family business mentioned above. The latter may only have to publish for circulation to one or two people. The big public company will have many thousands of shareholders all of whom have to be circulated. The essential objectives of presentation are the same.

In the nature of things the big publicly quoted company will be more complex than the small family business. Statutory requirements insist on a greater degree of disclosure, and other organisations, such as a stock exchange, require further disclosures.

What is scarcely germane in modern circumstances is the number of shareholders. For weal or woe it is simply a fact that a greater proportion of thousands of shareholders in a quoted company is no more likely to be sufficiently interested, or knowledgeable, in the study of accounts than the one or two members of a family business. And, because it requires a vastly greater effort to communicate with and herd together a multitude than a taxi-cab load, the theoretical concept that a business is owned by a democracy of proprietors (shareholders) seldom has any relevance in practice.

Only short-sighted managers would take the view that, because this is so, shareholders should not be told more than is necessary. Institutional investors (the insurance companies, investment trusts, unit trusts, pension funds, etc.) are invariably large shareholders who can exercise considerable influence. The financial press is a powerful force in guiding investment thinking and is very much the champion of the private investor.

Both of these forces will be highly critical if they suspect that relevant information is being withheld unnecessarily and their criticisms will be echoed throughout the investment world.

The degree of disclosure

Obviously, a prime objective of presentation should be for accounts not to lay themselves open to suspicions and criticisms which can blight a company's financial standing for years after the original causes have been put to rights. It follows that careful attention should be given to the degree of disclosure.

The general principle should be that disclosure of significant information should not be avoided unless it can be shown that it would damage a company's interests. The most thorny aspect of this is non-disclosure on the grounds that the information would be of value to competitors.

In a few cases, usually concerning consolidation of overseas subsidiaries' accounts, Board of Trade absolution from full disclosure can be given. In others, permission can be obtained from the Council of the Stock Exchange not to give such items as a full breakdown of turnover. Exemptions like these confer the highest guarantee that the case for disclosure is unarguable. Where such exemptions have been given the fact should be stated clearly.

In all other cases the best criteria to be followed is for a financial manager to ask himself: 'Could I justify non-disclosure to an intelligent third party such as an investment manager of an institution or a city editor?'

The majority of companies recognise today that the tide of political, trade union and investment opinion in favour of the fullest reasonable disclosure continues to flood ever more strongly. It is almost a quaint thought that, until the 1967 Companies Act insisted upon it, many companies refused to disclose their total sales on the plea that this would be damaging. Obscurantism on this scale, or even the suspicion of it to a far lesser degree, wins no marks. Today it merely arouses suspicion, which is the mortal enemy of confidence. Moreover, following the 1981 Companies Act the profit and loss account must now provide an analysis of expenses.

Only one degree less dangerous to a company's image is when non-disclosure continues to flood ever more strongly. It is almost a quaint editor (for the sake of convenience this character will serve as an archetype for any influential person whose opinions count in deciding a company's financial rating) that disclosures of a certain figure would be giving aid and succour to a main competition if the city editor can pick up a telephone and discover that the competition is well aware of the figure concerned.

Even if such tales, and there are many, do not get into print, they are enjoyed as jokes among the financial coterie.

In all this it should be remembered that the normal professional inquisitor of accounts is a reasonable chap who has a wide experience of the problems involved in their presentation. He will understand, for instance, a reluctance to split an overall figure on research and development down to a level at which the precise spending on development of a potential product, which cannot be marketable for several years, will give valuable information to the competition.

What he will want to know is how, overall, research and development has been treated in the accounts. If it is being written off profits as it is incurred, published profits will be conservative. If it is being capitalised (in other words, being put into the balance sheet as an asset), there will be a day of reckoning if the project fails to become commercial.

The majority of larger companies today have interests in different areas of a single industry and, in many cases, in totally different industries. In the case of quoted companies, the accounts are expected to give a clear indication of the division of profits and turnover between these different interests.

Even when such treatment is not mandatory it is often desirable. A financial analyst tends to use comparative statistics as measures of managerial efficiency. Where he is not fully in the picture his judgements may be quite unfair but, none the less, damaging.

Example

Two companies are both in the food supply industry. Company A shows a profit of £1 million from sales of £25 million. Company B shows the same profit from sales on only £14 million. The analyst may jump to the hasty conclusion that Company B is more efficient.

Company B, however, gets all of its sales from retailing. Company A sells only £5 million retail on which it earns £500 000. The remaining £20 million of sales comes from wholesaling, which involves big turnover and small margins. A profit of £500 000, or 2½ per cent, from this source is quite acceptable.

Given the additional information, the analyst will realise that he is not comparing like with like and will revise his first judgement. Of course, it can be argued that he would have revised his first judgement anyway through other statistics such as the return on capital employed. But there is no virtue in letting him puzzle out the position for himself when a simple line of explanation makes everything clear.

Explanatory notes

Disclosure usually involves a short explanatory text to elaborate the bare figures. To attempt to do this directly against every item would call for elaboration in the profit and loss account, the balance sheet and funds flow statement and would give a muddled and unpleasing result.

The presentation of accounts, like the presentation of goods, should aim at aesthetic appeal. The typographical layout deserves as much consideration as that bestowed by a newspaper editor on the appearance of his front page. Maximum simplicity and clarity are the keynotes. For this reason it is normally desirable to confine each account to a single page.

Further disclosure should take the form of notes which should be numbered clearly against each relevant item. For ease of readership, those appertaining to profits should be on the page or pages immediately following the profit and loss account. Similarly, those to do with assets and liabilities should follow immediately after the balance sheet.

Because of the complexity of legislation, accountancy procedures, stock market requirements, international complications and the differing nature of businesses, it is impracticable in a chapter of this scope to give an example of every accountancy figure which may call for an explanatory note. The items which most frequently do so are listed under their appropriate headings in what follows. The Companies Act 1981 specifies standard formats and line items for the profit and loss account and the balance sheet, as well as the information which, if not disclosed on the face of these statements, must appear in the accompanying notes. The examples given in the following tables reflect the requirements of the Act.

Table 15.1
Profit and loss account, following Format 1 of the Companies Act, 1981

GENERAL TRADING LTD

Profit and loss account for the year ending 31 March 1982

	Notes	1982 £000	1981 £000
Turnover	1	2400	provide
Cost of sales		1900	compara-
			tive figures
Gross profit		500	
Distribution and administrative costs	2	330	
Operating profit		170	
Interest payable	3	10	
Profit on ordinary activities, before taxation	1	160	
Taxation	4	70	
Profit for year		90	
Dividends	5	50	
Retained profit for year		40	

NB. An alternative format (Format 2) is allowed under the Companies Act 1981, reflecting Continental European disclosure practice. It is expected that most British companies will prefer Format 1, which resembles US disclosure practice.

PROFIT AND LOSS ACCOUNT

It is assumed that the reader is familiar with the way in which the profit and loss account classifies items (1). An example is shown in Table 15.1. Certain items which call for additional disclosure in the form of notes are:

Turnover and profit

Note 1. Turnover should be analysed into different business categories such as printing, engineering, leisure activities etc., with disclosure of proportionate profits before taxation in each subdivision.

Another subdivision required is a geographical analysis of sales turnover and profits before taxation.

Distribution and administrative costs

Note 2. The split between distribution and administration must be given.

Note 3. Interest payable. This should be analysed according to the type and term of indebtedness, e.g. bank loans and overdrafts repayable in total within 5 years, other loans repayable in total within 5 years, other loans not repayable in total within 5 years.

Taxation

Note 4. The note should show the basis of corporation tax on profit from ordinary activities, so that the relationship of the two figures can be understood.

A high tax figure can result from a number of factors. A company may derive considerable income from trading overseas in areas of high taxation. Depreciation may have been applied in excess of that allowed by the Inland Revenue. The Revenue may have caught up on tax under-charged in previous years.

A low tax figure can result from the opposite of any of the factors in the last paragraph, or it may result from losses made in previous years. In the latter case it is desirable to indicate the extent of the remaining relief to be expected from this source.

Note 5. Dividends. These should be analysed into preference and ordinary, interim and final, the amounts per share being shown.

BALANCE SHEET

There are two methods of presenting a balance sheet which are acceptable under the 1981 Companies Act.

Net asset format (Format 1)

The method which has been gaining ground in recent years is the *net asset* format.

In this case the same figures are shown in a single column vertical tabular form. First come fixed assets and net current assets. The latter figure is derived from an inset table listing current assets and liabilities with the latter being deducted from the former to show net current assets. Below appear non-current liabilities followed by capital and reserves, these figures being totalled to produce a figure of total long-term funds employed.

Although the same figures are used in both presentations the resulting balance sheet total in the account format is lower to the extent of the current liabilities figure.

In the net asset method it is becoming increasingly common to use a form of presentation which shows no details in the face of the statement. All detail is supplied in the form of notes.

An example of Format 1 is shown in Table 15.2, with detail indicated in note form.

Account format (Format 2)

The older account format consists of opposing columns. On the left is itemised the share capital followed by reserves (which together comprise shareholders funds). Then come long term liabilities, followed by current liabilities.

The right hand column details fixed assets followed by current assets.

Fixed assets

Note 6. Fixed assets as defined in the Companies Act 1981 include intangible assets (e.g. goodwill, patents) and long term investments as well as tangible fixed assets. The Act specifies the minimum breakdown to be given, either on the face of the balance sheet or in the notes (see the Appendix). In the case of General Trading Ltd, all the fixed assets are tangible. The note should show, for each subdivision: gross cost or valuation and accumulated depreciation at the beginning of the year, and at the end of the year; and the total amounts of additions, disposals, revaluations, depreciation charges and any other items needed to explain the change during the year.

Notes 7, 8, 9 and 10. Current assets, current liabilities and non-current liabilities. The Companies Act 1981 specifies the minimum breakdown to be given of the various components, either on the face of the balance sheet, or in the notes (see the Appendix).

Table 15.2
Balance sheet, following Format 1 of the Companies Act, 1981

GENERAL TRADING LTD

Balance sheet, 31 March 1982

	Notes	£000	1982 £000	£000	1981 £000
Fixed assets	6		800	provide	
Current assets				compa-	
Stocks	7	400		rative	
Debtors	8	350		figures	
Cash at bank and in hand		150			
		900			
Current liabilities – creditors due within one year					
Trade creditors		180			
Sundry creditors	9	120			
		300			
Net current assets			600		
Total assets less current liabilities (net assets employed)			1400		
Non-current liabilities – creditors due after more than one year	10		200		
Capital and reserves					
Called-up share capital	11	1000			
Profit and loss account	12	200	1200		
			1400		

Notes 11 and 12. Called-up share capital and reserves. The notes should show:

- the number of shares authorised and their nominal value
- the number of shares issued and paid up, and their nominal value
- the reserves, divided into *revaluation reserve, other reserves,* and *profit and loss account* (retained profits). A breakdown of other reserves is required (see the Appendix).

Notes on accounts generally

Where the affairs of a company are complicated, which is invariably the case with large holding companies, there is a danger that the notes to accounts will be so numerous and so lengthy that sheer mass will defeat the object of illuminating the figures.

This problem can be minimised by devoting a page immediately preceding the accounts to a description of the accounting policies being pursued. The disclosure of accounting policies on significant items is required by SSAP No. 2 and hence by the Stock Exchange rules.

It is important to remember that notes on the accounts form part of the accounts themselves and, like the balance sheet and profit and loss account, are subject to the reports of independent auditors.

FUNDS STATEMENT

The purpose of a funds statement, or statement of sources and applications of funds, is 'to identify the movements in assets, liabilities and capital which have taken place during the year and the resultant effect on net liquid funds', (SSAP No. 10, para 1). Since publication of such a statement is required under the SSAP in question, it is also a normal requirement under the Stock Exchange rules.

The form of the funds statement, and, to a lesser extent, its content, are matters about which there is less general agreement than in the case of the balance sheet and profit and loss account. Nor is any minimum content laid down by law. SSAP No. 10 does not prescribe a particular format, but provides an Appendix giving an example which is reproduced below. (Other alternative presentations are also given in the Appendix to SSAP No. 10.)

Table 15.3
Sources and application of funds

GROUPS LIMITED: Statement of source and application of funds
(based on the accounts of the group and showing the acquisition of a subsidiary as a separate item)

	This year £'000	This year £'000	This year £'000	Last year £'000	Last year £'000	Last year £'000
Source of funds						
Profit before tax and extraordinary items, less minority interests			2,025			2,610
Extraordinary items			450			(170)
			2,476			2,440
Adjustments for items not involving the movement of funds:						
Minority interests in the retained profits of the year			25			30
Depreciation			345			295
Profits retained in associated companies			(40)			—
Total generated from operations			2,805			2,765
Funds from other sources						
Shares issued in part consideration of the acquisition of subsidiary*			290			—
Capital raised under executive option scheme			100			80
			3,195			2,845
Application of funds						
Dividends paid		(650)			(650)	
Tax paid		(770)			(970)	
Purchase of fixed assets		(370)			(736)	
Purchase of Subsidiary Ltd*		(351)			—	
Debentures redeemed		(890)			—	
			(3,030)			(2,356)
			165			489
Increase/decrease in working capital						
Increase in stocks		80			166	
Increase in debtors		70			122	
Decrease in creditors – excluding taxation and proposed dividends		115			17	
Movement in net liquid funds:						
Increase (decrease) in cash balance	(35)			10		
Increase (decrease) in short term investments	(65)			174		
		(100)			184	
			165			489

Analysis of the acquisition of Subsidiary Limited

Net assets acquired		Discharged by	
Fixed assets	290	Shares issued	290
Goodwill	30	Cash paid	60
Stocks	40		
Debtors	30		
Creditors	(40)		
	350		350

DIRECTORS' REPORT

This does not, strictly speaking, form part of the accounts of a company, but it is an important element in presentation. Indeed, the report and the accompanying chairman's statement, which most companies issue each year, are likely to be more widely read than the accounts themselves.

Contents

Because of this it is usual to give a brief summary, in the simplest form, of results for the year. Any major changes in the company's structure should be listed, such as acquisitions or disposals of assets, and it is desirable to give reasons for these.

Unless covered separately in the chairman's statement, the report is expected to review operations during the year, give an indication of trading to date in the current year and some comments about future prospects.

The report offers great scope for presentation. The growth of a company can be shown by simple charts and graphs of such items as sales and pre-tax profits over a number of years. Many reports show a ten-year record of important extracts from the accounts. Where these include earnings and dividends per share it is important that adjustments should be made for scrip issues and rights issues.

Well presented graphs, diagrams and statistical surveys are undoubtedly a desirable feature of a report. The sophisticated analyst is grateful to them for the toil which they save him. The unsophisticated small shareholder finds them meaningful in a way in which the actual accounts never could be; they help to make him feel more truly a real member of the company.

The bulk of a directors' report normally consists of volunteered information. In addition, certain information, not all of it of an accounting nature, must be shown if not shown elsewhere. For instance, the report must show the directors' individual shareholdings at the beginning and the end of the accounting year. It may be that a substantial reduction is shown in the holding of a director. He may have given shares to his children, or he may have sold them in order to make safer provisions for death duties or for some compelling business reason.

In such a case it is obviously desirable that an explanation should be given. Equally, it is undesirable that the fact should appear to be tucked away in some obscure corner or in unduly small type. Such treatment would be sure to arouse suspicion.

CURRENT COST ACCOUNTS

The 'current cost' set of accounting conventions, contained in SSAP No. 16, differs from the hitherto generally accepted 'historical cost' set of conventions in two main respects:

1 Assets are stated at their *value to the business*, on a current cost basis. This is generally the current replacement cost of *equivalent service* (or *operating*) *capability*, except in the relatively rare case where both the net realisable value and the expected value in use are lower, in which case the greater of the two latter will be used.
2 Profit is calculated as the surplus out of revenue after making provision for maintaining the *operating capability* of the business, as represented by the value to the business of its net assets at the time the revenue is recognised.

This second point identifies the main motivation for the efforts which led to the introduction of SSAP No. 16 – the feeling that a profit which was not a surplus after making provision for maintenance of operating capability was not a 'real' profit. These issues are further discussed in the Accounting Standards Committee's Guidance Notes to SSAP No. 16.

The following categories of company are not required to comply with SSAP No. 16:

1 Those which do not have any class or share or loan capital listed on the Stock Exchange and satisfy at least two of the following three criteria:
(a) They have a turnover of less than £5 million per annum.
(b) Their balance sheet total on an historical cost basis at the beginning of the relevant accounting period was less than £2.5 million, the balance sheet total being calculated as follows:
Fixed assets (net book value) other than investments
Investments
Current assets including prepayments and accrued income (before deduction of current liabilities).

(c)   Their average number of UK employees (UK companies) or Irish employees (Republic of Ireland companies) is less than 250.

2   Wholly owned subsidiaries of companies where the parent is registered in the UK or the Republic of Ireland except where the parent is excepted under (3) below.

3   (a)   Authorised insurers.

(b)   Property investment and dealing companies, with the exception of companies which hold the properties of another company within the group which is not excepted from SSAP No. 16.

(c)   Investment trust companies, unit trust and other similar long term investment businesses.

The information required to be disclosed under SSAP No. 16 is:

1   A current cost profit and loss account.
2   A current cost balance sheet.
3   Notes which describe the bases and methods adopted particularly in relation to:

(a)   The value to the business of fixed assets and the depreciation thereon.

(b)   The value to the business of stock and work in progress and the cost of sales adjustment (difference between historical and current cost of goods sold).

(c)   The monetary working capital adjustment (see below).

(d)   The gearing adjustment (see below).

(e)   The bases of translating foreign currencies and dealing with translation differences arising.

(f)   Other material adjustments to the historical cost information.

(g)   The corresponding amounts (SSAP No. 16 para, 58).

The monetary working capital adjustment is a measure of the effect of specific price changes on the monetary amount of trade credit given less trade credit received (trade debtors less trade creditors and, where applicable, short term bank borrowings). Under SSAP 16, this amount is required to be deducted (or where trade creditors, etc., exceed trade debtors, added) in arriving at current cost profit.

The gearing adjustment is that fraction of the cost of sales and monetary working capital adjustments and the depreciation adjustment (difference between historical and current cost depreciation) which corresponds to the proportion of net operating assets financed by borrowings. According to SSAP No. 16, this amount is not part of the provision which needs to be made for maintaining the operating capability of the shareholders' interest in the business. It should therefore be added back to the current cost profit from operations in arriving at the current cost profit attributable to

Table 15.4
Example of current cost profit and loss account

Y LIMITED AND SUBSIDIARIES
Group current cost profit and loss account
for the year ended 31 December 1981

1980		1981
£000		£000
18 000	Turnover	20 000
2 420	Profit before and taxation on the historical cost basis	2 900
1 320	Less: Current cost operating adjustments (Note 2)	1 510
1 100	*Current cost operating profit*	1 390
180	Interest payable less receivable	200
920		1 190
610	Taxation	730
310	Current cost profit after interest and taxation	460
170	Gearing adjustment	166
480	*Current cost profit attributable to shareholders*	626
400	Dividends	430
80	Retained current cost profit of the year	196
16.0p	Current cost earnings per share	20.9p
5.2%	Operating profit return on the average of the net operating assets	6.0%

Statement of retained profits/reserves

£000		£000
80	Retained current cost profit of the year	196
1 850	Movements on current cost reserve (Note 4)	2 054
NIL	Movements on other reserves	NIL
1 930		2 250
14 150	Retained profits/reserves at the beginning of the year	16 080
16 080	Retained profits/reserves at the end of the year	18 330

shareholders.

Examples of a current cost profit and loss account and balance sheet, as provided in the Appendix to SSAP No 16, are given in Tables 15.4 and 15.5.

It follows from what was said earlier that, to comply with the Stock Exchange requirements, a company which does not fall into one of the categories exempt from SSAP No. 16 must either comply with that Standard or publish a statement giving its reasons for non-compliance.

Table 15.5
Example of current cost balance sheet

Y LIMITED AND SUBSIDIARIES
Summarised group current cost balance sheet
as at 31 December 1981

1980			1981	
£000	£000		£000	£000
		Assets employed:		
	18 130	Fixed assets (Note 3)		19 530
		Net current assets:		
3 200		Stock	4 000	
700		Monetary working capital	800	
3 900		Total working capital	4 800	
(400)		Proposed dividends	(430)	
(600)		Other current liabilities (Net)	(570)	
	2 900			3 800
	21 030			22 330
		Financed by:		
		Share capital and reserves:		
3 000		Share capital	3 000	
12 350		Current cost reserve (Note 4)	14 404	
3 730		Other reserves and retained profit . . .	3 926	
	19 080			21 330
	1 950	Loan capital		2 000
	21 030			23 330

CONCLUSIONS

The presentation of accounts should take into consideration the various categories of people who will be reading them, the diverse interests of these categories and their relative importance. The broad categories are shareholders, small and large, the financial press, employees, potential investors, creditors, customers and the government.

The wider the potential readership, the more desirable it is to make disclosures well in excess of statutory or stock market requirements.

The result should be a successful financial public relations operation which enhances the company's image in commercial and investment circles.

REFERENCE

(1) The subject is dealt with comprehensively in *The Meaning of Company Accounts* by Walter Reid and D R Myddelton (Gower, 1982).

APPENDIX: REPORTING REQUIREMENTS OF THE 1981 COMPANIES ACT

Profit and loss account – Format 1

1   Turnover
2   Cost of sales
3   Gross profit or loss
4   Distribution costs
5   Administrative expenses
6   Other operating income
7   Income from shares in group companies
8   Income from shares in related companies
9   Income from other fixed asset investments
10 Other interest receivable and similar income
11 Amounts written off investments
12 Interest payable and similar charges
13 Tax on profit or loss on ordinary activities
14 Profit or loss on ordinary activities after taxation
15 Extraordinary income
16 Extraordinary charges
17 Extraordinary profit or loss
18 Tax on extraordinary profit or loss

19   Other taxes not shown under the above items
20   Profit or loss for the financial year

Balance sheet – Format 1

A   Called up share capital not paid

B   Fixed assets
    I   Intangible assets
         1   Development costs
         2   Concessions, patents, licences, trade marks and similar rights and assets
         3   Goodwill
         4   Payments on account
    II   Tangible assets
         1   Land and buildings
         2   Plant and machinery
         3   Fixtures, fittings, tools and equipment
         4   Payments on account and assets in course of construction
    III   Investments
         1   Shares in group companies
         2   Loans to group companies
         3   Shares in related companies
         4   Loans to related companies
         5   Other investments other than loans
         6   Other loans
         7   Own shares

C   Current assets
    I   Stocks
         1   Raw materials and consumables
         2   Work in progress
         3   Finished goods and goods for resale
         4   Payments on account
    II   Debtors
         1   Trade debtors
         2   Amounts owed by group companies
         3   Amounts owed by related companies
         4   Other debtors

     5 Called up share capital not paid
     6 Prepayments and accrued income

  III Investments
     1 Shares in group companies
     2 Own shares
     3 Other investments

  IV Cash at bank and in hand

D Prepayments and accrued income

E Creditors: amounts falling due within one year
     1 Debenture loans
     2 Bank loans and overdrafts
     3 Payments received on account
     4 Trade creditors
     5 Bills of exchange payable
     6 Amounts owed to group companies
     7 Amounts owed to related companies
     8 Other creditors including taxation and social security
     9 Accruals and deferred income

F Net current assets (liabilities)

G Total assets less current liabilities

H Creditors: amounts falling due after more than one year
     1 Debenture loans
     2 Bank loans and overdrafts
     3 Payments received on account
     4 Trade creditors
     5 Bills of exchange payable
     6 Amounts owed to group companies
     7 Amounts owed to related companies
     8 Other creditors including taxation and social security
     9 Accruals and deferred income

I Provisions for liabilities and charges
     1 Pensions and similar obligations
     2 Taxation, including deferred taxation
     3 Other provisions

J Accruals and deferred income

K Capital and reserves
    I   Called up share capital
    II   Share premium account
    III   Revaluation reserve
    IV   Other reserves
        1 Capital redemption reserve
        2 Reserve for own shares
        3 Reserves provided for by the articles of association
        4 Other reserves
    V   Profit and loss account

16

Acquisitions and mergers

J R Franks

Every year large numbers of companies combine into new corporate organisations. A formal combination is called a merger when it results from a friendly arrangement between the managements of two or more companies of roughly equal size or strength. A holding company may be set up and stockholders advised to exchange their existing stocks for those of the holding company. Alternatively, one of the two merging companies may play the role of the holding company and offer an exchange of ordinary shares, cash or some combination of securities and cash as payment for the other company. This latter arrangement is often called an acquisition or a takeover, especially when the merger has not been agreed between the two managements. Why, one may ask, should companies merge in a competitive economy? Why should it be worth one company paying a bid premium in excess of otherwise normal market prices to acquire the assets of another company? In this chapter we examine the economic and financial rationale for merging. We also provide a framework for valuing a company for acquisition purposes and point out the problems arising from the use of alternative valuation methods.

ECONOMIC BENEFITS OF MERGING

One should be clear about the difference between a merger and a capital investment. A merger does not increase productive capacity but simply records the transfer of title or ownership over a set of assets from one party to another, while a capital investment actually adds to the real assets of the firm. The former is on its own simply a financial transaction, and it is this aspect that should lead managers to be careful when valuing a potential acquisition. After all, if you are paying a substantial bid premium, the only way to justify the premium is to increase the profitability of the assets over and above that expected under existing management. As a result, it is difficult to see how a merger can be successful unless the acquiring firm has some plan for improving the profits of the acquired or acquiring firm as a result of the merger.

The purchase of managerial and technical skills

Acquirers often make a bid because they wish to acquire unique managerial and technical skills in the acquired company and use these skills to improve their own profitability. Before undertaking an expensive takeover bid for this purpose, management first must consider alternative means to the same end. A less costly alternative may be to make handsome job offers to key individuals either in the potential takeover company or in other companies. The premium paid to individuals with unique skills might be less than the premium which must be paid in the market for a company which includes these skills within its ranks.

The alternative of hiring individuals may not always be practicable, however, when the unique managerial and technical skills are embodied within a large team or organisation. Also the acquiring company may have no way of determining from the outside what subtle combination of elements within the team may make it effective. Hiring sufficient numbers of the team to be assured of the 'critical mass' may not be possible. While a friendly merger could provide a rapid means of obtaining an excellent managerial and technical team intact, one should be sceptical in the case of a contested takeover as to whether a management team will maintain its effectiveness if it is hostile to the acquiring management at the outset.

Changes in economies of scale

One of the more obvious incentives to merge is the economies of scale which might arise from the merger. For example, let us assume a new plant has been developed that will reduce the unit costs of making a barrel of beer by 20 per cent. The first question is: 'should we replace existing plant with the new plant?' That change will only be worthwhile if the reduction in the operating costs, discounted to present value, is greater than the capital investment required for the new plant.

Even if it is profitable to scrap the existing plant, the present market share of the firm may be less than the minimum capacity of the new plant. Thus a merger may be necessary to capture the extra market share required to obtain the new economies of scale. Mergers of small breweries in the UK and Germany in the 1960s were justified on this basis. When it is not economic to scrap existing facilities, market growth will seldom be sufficient to justify immediate investment in large new plant if the market is divided between many firms. Companies with the larger market shares can often obtain the benefits of scale more rapidly by installing additional new plant.

In Figure 16.1 we have a simple diagram that illustrates how this incentive to merge may arise. There are three firms, A, B and C. For historical reasons firm A has the much larger share of the market with sales totalling 50 units. A new plant with much lower operating costs is

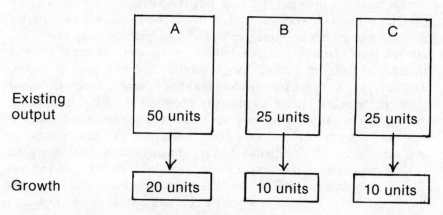

Fig. 16.1   Growth and the incentive to merge

available, but it is not profitable to replace the existing plant with the new plant in the near future. An increase in market demand from 100 units to 140 units is allocated to each firm on the basis of past market shares. The increase in demand for firm A is large enough to justify an investment in the new plant; however this is not so for the other two concerns. Firms B and C must either build an outdated plant (with higher unit costs) to cope with the new demand or lose the opportunities for growth and a maintained market share. An alternative is for B and C to enter a joint venture to exploit their combined growth or agree to a full scale merger. The third possibility is for B and C to persuade firm A to acquire them.

Exploiting a new product

A firm may wish to produce a new product but may require additional facilities (production, marketing, etc.) to make it in quantity. Construction of new facilities takes time, and it may be more profitable to acquire the existing facilities of another company. If these existing facilities are unused, then they should cost no more than the depreciated cost of similar new facilities. If the existing facilities are being used, it may still be profitable to buy them and switch their production to the new product.

Time may be as important a reason as cost for acquiring another company's facilities. Since a product's comparative advantage over similar products does not last long, it is often essential to exploit a new product as quickly as posible. Delays involved in building new facilities may be too costly in strategic terms. Competition may erode the advantage of the new product, reduce its potential market share and thereby reduce its prospective revenues and net present value. Similarly, a firm with a new product may not have an established brand name in the market place. Frequently, products which lack established brand names sell at a lower price than well known products. The reason is that consumers are either unaware of the new product or require a lower price to change their purchasing habits. The lower price must compensate the consumer for the possibility that the product will not live up to its claims or that the guarantees (or warranties) may prove costly for the purchaser to exercise. The costs of establishing a brand name and the resulting delay in exploiting the new product may make it worthwhile to buy another company's brand name.

Market power

Monopoly is one of the reasons frequently given for merging. The reason is that competition inevitably leads to lower prices and lower profits. Although it is undeniable that maintaining or increasing a company's market share can justify a merger, there are still some qualifications to be made. The first is that the merger may be contested by the Monopolies Commission. A challenge by the Commission can prevent a merger or at the very least delay its consummation. Secondly, high profits will attract new entrants into the industry and encourage the development of close substitutes; thus, the market protection afforded by a merger may only be temporary.

Valuation differences

Some mergers have been justified because the acquiring management believes the assets of the acquirer are undervalued in the stock market. Such an undervaluation may be due to one of three reasons:

1 The assumption that the stock market is generally 'undervalued' and the acquirer knows better than everybody else. Such an attitude does not provide a convincing justification since shareholders are just as capable of perceiving an undervalued market as managers.
2 The acquired company's stock is really a 'good buy' at the current price. Again, we do not find this argument convincing because managers can always buy some shares in the 'undervalued' firm without trying to obtain control and without paying the large bid premium that is usually required for control.
3 The assets of the firm are priced below their replacement cost. This argument is clearly justified if and only if the acquiring firm can exploit the assets and obtain a net present value from their use. In 1978 the second-hand value of ships was substantially below their replacement cost; however, the reason was that the prices merely reflected the low profitability of operating the ships. Only if a firm could operate the ships more profitably than other companies would it be profitable to buy other company's ships. Clearly, as more and more companies find it profitable to buy ships in the second-hand market, so prices will rise. Until prices exceed replacement cost, few new ships will be built.

The stock market may not always reflect the value of a firm's assets. Since it costs money to obtain information, neither the market nor the management of the acquisition may be aware of a profitable alternative use of assets envisioned by the management of an acquiring company. A merger may not be the best way of improving this situation, however. The acquiring company could merely make speculative purchases of a company's shares and then provide the vital information lacking to existing management and to the stock market. If it is unlikely that the existing management will be willing or able to take economic decisions on the basis of the new information, then a takeover could be justified.

FINANCIAL BENEFITS OF MERGING

Merging and diversification

Theory suggests that diversification for the purposes of risk reduction can only be justified from a shareholder's viewpoint if default or bankruptcy would entail substantial costs. In the absence of such costs, the argument is that shareholders can always achieve such risk reduction for themselves by investing in a diversified portfolio of equities on their own account, or by investing in unit trusts. However, there are a number of reasons why managers of the firm may take a different view.

From a shareholder's view the costs of bankruptcy lie primarily in the legal costs of reorganisation. There are, however, costs to other parties; for example, to managers. A bankruptcy may not only deprive a manager of his salaried job but may also undermine his value in the job market when he seeks alternative employment. Since information is imperfectly disemminated, the bankruptcy may reflect unfairly on the perceived competence of individual managers involved. The risk is not easily diversified by managers whose main wealth is human capital: that is, in their ability to earn a high salary. In these circumstances a wise manager may reject some takeover projects which would be profitable to diversified shareholders. An alternative strategy would be to diversify the assets of the firm.

One should not imagine that the self interest of managers in this regard is wholly at odds with the interests of shareholders. Managers and other employees in risky, undiversified companies will tend to demand higher salaries or other benefits to compensate for the risks entailed in working for such concerns. The resulting additional labour costs must be borne by the owners or the shareholders. Furthermore, managers who are exposed to unnecessary risks to their job security are more likely to bias investment decisions towards lower risk situations. This bias is seldom in the interest of diversified shareholders. If it is not too costly, both shareholders' and employees' interests may be served by some degree of company diversification. Diversification also provides a means of preserving goodwill.

Only if the company stays in existence can it seize future opportunities to make profitable investments. Diversification helps to remove the risk of losing the value of such growth. Furthermore, as argued elsewhere in the chapter, diversification may actually increase the portfolio of growth opportunities available to the merger partners.

Once managers and employees are protected in these ways, management can identify more closely with the interests of diversified shareholders when making investment decisions. When company diversification is too costly, shareholders often grant options to managers to purchase the company's shares at a fixed price. This provides a financial incentive for management to take decisions which favourably affect shareholders' wealth. The effectiveness of this method is limited by the fact that it does not eliminate the manager's vulnerability to the unique risks of capital projects. Share options in the company of employment increase an already large stake which managers have in the fortunes of that one enterprise. There is some obvious scope here for devising imaginative compensation schemes to bring executive incentives more closely into line with the interests of diversified shareholders.

Risk reduction and lower borrowing costs

When two firms merge the risk of the combined earnings stream may be reduced as a result of the diversification effect. But, even when this is so, the question remains whether the value of the two merged firms is greater than the sum of their individual parts. It might be argued that if the merged firm's earnings are less risky, borrowing becomes cheaper; the lower borrowing costs provide an incentive to merge. In our analysis, we must distinguish carefully between the effect of a merger upon outstanding debt and the effect of a merger on the terms for raising additional debt. We shall discuss raising additional debt first.

A merger of two companies reduces the risk of the combined earnings stream below the risk of the individual companies pre-merger, if the two earnings streams are imperfectly correlated. As a consequence, the merged firms are able to borrow at a lower interest rate than before the merger. The reason that the risk has been reduced is that when one of the firms would otherwise have defaulted, the surplus of the other firm is applied to the deficiencies of the first (this is known as the 'coinsurance effect'). Thus, the merger of the two firms reduces the risk of default only because the shareholders give up some of the protection of limited liability; for without the merger the surplus of one firm would not be applied to the debts of the other when it defaulted.

It is easier to understand this problem when one considers an individual who controls a business which has the protection of limited liability. Currently his firm is borrowing from a bank at 3 per cent over the bank's base interest rate. The owner is wealthy, owning a large house and some stocks and bonds besides the stock in his company. The bank suggests to the owner that if he would only guarantee the loans of his company, the bank would gladly reduce the interest rate on the outstanding loans. Is the bank being generous? The answer is No! It is asking the owner to permit his personal assets to be applied to any deficiencies of the company, should default occur. It is asking the owner to give up the protection of limited liability. Put another way, it is asking for a merger of his personal assets and the assets of the firm. Consequently, a merger may reduce the risk of the earnings stream and the cost of borrowing, but this will not increase the value of the firm since the lower interest rate charged by the bank merely reflects the less risky claim it now holds. However, if there are default costs, (such as legal costs attendant on liquidation) then a merger will reduce the probability of default and therefore reduce the expected value of the default costs. The reduction in expected default costs would provide an incentive to merge. This said, the probability of default is usually small and the costs of default are also small (about one per cent of the value of the assets according to Warner, 1977). Thus the expected benefits to merging from this source may not be significant.

Now consider the effect of a merger on the value of the equity when there is existing debt outstanding in the two firms. If the earnings of the two firms are imperfectly correlated, the coinsurance effect of the merger will reduce the probability of default to the combined debtholders. Debtholders will gain since previously agreed interest payments were based upon a higher probability of default. The shareholders suffer a corresponding loss equal to the gain of the debtholders. If the firms had not merged, a default by one firm would not have affected the other firm's shareholders. Thus, shareholders must lose as a result of the coinsurance of debt. After the merger the value of limited liability as an option to default is reduced by virtue of a lower probability of default.

Unused debt capacity

It is often claimed that if a firm does not utilise its debt capacity, it will prove a valuable asset to any would-be bidder. However, Franks and Broyles (1979) have shown that the advantages to debt financing are probably not very large and certainly not sufficient to justify bid premiums of 15 per cent to 20 per cent plus the costs of transacting the bid. Secondly, the acquiring firm does not need to acquire control over the assets to obtain some advantage from the unused debt capacity. The acquiring firm needs only to buy the shares of the inadequately geared company and borrow, using the purchased shares as collateral for the loan. Thus, unused debt capacity does not provide very much incentive for a merger. [See Franks and Pringle (1981) for a more detailed review of these points.]

Tax losses and unused capital allowances

A company that has made losses in the past is able to carry such losses forward and offset them against future taxable profits in order to reduce tax liabilities. For example, the (American) Anaconda Company made losses totalling hundreds of millions of dollars in 1971 as a result of the nationalisation of its assets in Chile. Such losses could be offset against future profits in order to reduce tax liabilities. However, Anaconda might have tried to seek a merger with another company which had sufficiently large taxable profits to absorb the tax losses immediately. The benefit would derive from obtaining the reduction in tax liabilities much earlier than the company could hope to do without the merger.

A second tax reason for merging arises if a company is investing large sums in capital equipment and so qualifies for capital allowances that cannot be absorbed by taxable profits when they occur. A merger with a profitable company can absorb the unused tax allowances at an earlier date than would otherwise be possible, as in the case of accumulated tax losses. As we saw in chapter 12, when a company is investing heavily on capital account, leasing can provide an alternative method to merging for the purpose of accelerating the benefit of tax shields.

ACQUISITION VALUATION - FOUR QUESTIONS

In any acquisition valuation four important questions must be answered:

1 What is the value of the company as it is presently constituted? In answering this question we shall look first at the market value of the company's securities and make some adjustment for any 'bid prospects' already impounded in the share price. For companies whose securities are not traded we shall look for the market values of individual assets. When markets in the assets do not exist, we must estimate values by alternative means.

2 What is the source and value of the merger benefits? In the previous section we have outlined some of the benefits to merging, both economic and financial. The present value of the expected merger benefits establishes the maximum premium that can be paid in excess of the value of the acquisition as it is currently constituted. It is important to deduct from these merger benefits the professional and administrative costs of acquiring the company, including a charge for managerial time.

3 What are the alternatives to merging? The potential acquirer should establish the other methods (if any) of capturing the benefits of the merger. For example, a new capital investment may prove a viable alternative. The difference between the net present values of the merger benefits and of the best alternative provides the maximum bid premium which can be given to the acquiree's shareholders.

4 What price will be adequate to gain control of the acquiree? The answers to the first three questions must provide a price that management and its advisors consider is acceptable to the acquiree's shareholders. It is important to establish this framework prior to the bid, since an aborted bid is expensive both in management time and in direct costs such as legal fees and advertising.

VALUING A QUOTED COMPANY

In a competitive stock market the price of a security reflects the underlying worth of the assets plus the present value of expected growth opportunities. If we can accept this proposition, then the maximum price that should be paid for a company is its existing market value plus the present value of any benefits that may accrue from merging which have not already been anticipated by the market.

If the merger is to be profitable to the acquirer, the maximum premium that can be paid above the current market price must be no more than the difference between the value of the merger benefits expected by the acquirer and the value of the merger benefits already anticipated by the market. Of course, if there are alternatives to the merger, then the maximum bid premium should also be reduced by the net present value of the most attractive alternative.

The valuation of the premium is easier and provides a more interesting exercise than the attempt to value the entire company. There are however, some difficulties attached. The current market price may already reflect part of the benefits of this particular merger or of another possible merger. The evidence strongly suggests that the market anticipates a merger prior to its announcement. Thus, if one finds that the share price of the acquiree has risen more than the market (or has fallen less than the market) after adjusting for risk, then one should suspect that the current market price reflects some of the bid prospects.

An easy method of computing the price 'ex bid prospects' is to subtract any abnormal returns over the period when a merger rumour may have been circulating. This computation is accomplished by estimating the returns that would have been realised if the security had moved with the market. Roughly speaking, this means that if the market has risen by, for example, 5 per cent over the 3 months prior to the merger announcement and if the security were twice as risky as the market, then we would expect the security to rise by 10 per cent. If the actual increase were 15 per cent, then we would say that there are abnormal returns of 5 per cent. We would assume that the abnormal returns of 5 per cent were related to the merger and subtract these returns from the current share price to obtain the value of the company 'ex bid prospects'. Let us examine an example.

A company is about to announce a bid for another company. The share price of potential acquisition (Table 16.1) is currently 97p. The management has estimated the present value of the merger benefits at 25p per share. What is the maximum price the acquirer should pay? If the market expects the bid, and the share price reflects part of the premium to be paid the premium must be taken into account in deciding the maximum bid terms.

Over the six months prior to the announcement date, the share price of the acquisition has risen 20 per cent, after adjustment for changes in the total number of shares, while the market has risen only 5 per cent. We would have expected the security to rise twice as fast as the market,

Table 16.1
Estimate of abnormal gains from share price movements

	Dates relative to announcement date		
	−6 months	−3 months	0 months
Financial Times index	500	512	525
Expected price of acquisition (pence)	80	85	89
Price of potential acquisition (pence)	80	88	97
Abnormal return (pence)	0	4	9

Risk, beta, of acquisition = 2.0.

Beta is a coefficient of systematic risk which measures the tendency of price changes for a share to move with changes in the market index. Thus the value of beta for the average equity is 1.00. Beta values are obtainable for quoted companies from the London Business School's Risk Measurement Service

or 10 per cent, because the estimate of its beta value is 2.0. The difference between what we would expect, given the movements in the market, and the actual returns constitutes the abnormal gain. Thus, since the security has risen by 17p against the 8p we would have expected, the abnormal gain is 9p.

If the merger is expected to be profitable for the acquirer's shareholders, the bid price must not exceed the current price plus the difference between the expected merger benefits per share and the past abnormal return per share. The maximum bid price is therefore 113p [97p + (25 − 9)p]. Of course such abnormal returns may reflect circumstances other than bid rumours: for example, unexpectedly good earnings results. Judgement must therefore be exercised in adjusting market prices to their ex bid prospect value.

TRADITIONAL METHODS OF ASSET VALUATION

In the past there has been a great deal of confusion regarding acquisition valuation methods. In this section, we shall review the more familiar methods. Initially, let us confine ourselves to quoted companies.

Earnings per share

The most familiar valuation method is based on an analysis of the earnings per share of the acquirer with and without the acquisition. Let us consider the following example taken from Franks and Broyles (1979). Table 16.2 shows the financial details of two companies: company A is the acquirer and Z is the potential acquisition. Table 16.3 shows the earnings and the earnings per share expected by the market for each company. We assume that A purchases Z on the basis of two shares of A (valued at £5) for every three shares of Z held (valued at £3.90). Thus A is paying a bid premium of 28 per cent.

Table 16.2
Financial data

	Company A	Company Z
Current earnings after tax (£)	1.0 million	2.41 million
Number of shares outstanding	10 million	18.5 million
Earnings per share	0.10	0.13
Market per share (£)	2.50	1.30
P/E ratio	25	10
Expected annual growth rate in earnings in the absence of a merger (%)	15	0

If we now calculate the earnings per share of the combined company (AZ) over a period of years and compare them with the earnings per share of A, what do we find? Initially the combined EPS exceeds the EPS of A alone by an amount totalling 5.3 pence. Is this good news? The answer is, 'not necessarily', and for two reasons. First, the growth expectations for AZ are lower than for A alone. The effect of growth differences can be seen by following the EPS forecasts. In the fifth year, the EPS of A is expected to be 20.1p and that of AZ only 19.8p. In the sixth year, the EPS of A is expected to be almost 2p greater than that of AZ.

Table 16.3
Earnings of A and Z before and after the merger

Years	0	1	2	3	4	5	6
(a) Earnings (£m)							
A at 15%	1.0	1.15	1.32	1.52	1.75	2.01	2.31
Z at 0%	2.41	2.41	2.41	2.41	2.41	2.41	2.41
AZ	3.41	3.56	3.73	3.93	4.16	4.42	4.72
(b) Earnings per share (pence)							
A at 15%	10	11.5	13.2	15.2	17.5	20.1	23.1
Z at 0%	13	13	13	13	13	13	13
AZ	15.3	16.0	16.7	17.6	18.7	19.8	21.2

Number of shares outstanding: A, pre-merger, 10 million; Z, pre-merger, 18.5 million; AZ, 22.3 million.

This example suggests that focusing attention on current earnings per share is misleading. Shares are valued for their growth opportunities. Putting it another way, why are shareholders prepared to pay only 10 times the EPS of company Z but 25 times the EPS of company A? It can only be because A's earnings are in some sense more valuable. We have already provided one reason, that of future growth prospects. Another possibility could be that the earnings of A are less risky compared with those of Z. Risk will be perceived in terms of the variability of future earnings. It has been suggested that the incremental loss or gain in EPS of the combined company compared with that of the acquirer on his own should be discounted at an appropriate rate. If the present value of the earnings addition is greater than the present value of earnings dilution, then the acquisition at that price might be considered acceptable.

There are a number of objections to this analysis. First, there is evidence that share prices reflect cash flows rather than reported earnings. Second, the value of a quoted company is measured by the price traded on the Stock Exchange. If the company's analysts try to value the combined company, they are in danger of using different forecasts from those used by other market analysts. The previous analysis does not separate the value of the company without the bid prospects from the value of the merger benefits. In valuing a quoted company the important question is, what value should be placed on the acquirer's ability to extract benefits from the acquisition which are not already impounded in the present market price? The answer can only be obtained from a detailed analysis of what the acquirer is intending to do after the merger.

The valuation of shares of traded companies is relatively straightforward because we assume that the price of the share represents the value of the company's assets and existing growth opportunities. We do not have such data for unquoted companies and consequently we would propose a variety of methods of arriving at the value for their assets.

Written-down replacement values

The written-down replacement cost (WDRC) method has been increasingly discussed as an alternative to valuations based upon historic cost accounting. It is based upon the following formula:

$$\text{WDRC} = \begin{matrix}\text{Current cost} \\ \text{of asset}\end{matrix} \times \left[\frac{1 - \text{Age of existing asset}}{\text{Economic life of asset}} \right]$$

where 'current cost' represents the price of an equivalent asset if it were purchased now. Replacement cost accounting is an improvement on historic cost accounting for two reasons. First, in an inflationary period asset values are constantly rising; replacement cost accounting captures this increase in price. Secondly, if specific assets are being used in a highly profitable way, the primary producers of the assets will probably be able to charge higher prices in consequence. Similarly, if the industry using the capital assets is finding business difficult and profits are low, asset values are likely to be weak, otherwise asset replacement will not take place. Thus replacement cost accounting can capture some of the changes in both positive and negative economic values which accrue with changing business conditions.

However, there are still a number of limitations to this method. First, somewhat arbitrary depreciation methods must be used for existing assets and their economic lives must still be estimated. Secondly, current prices of new assets charged by primary producers will still be below their economic values if firms are replacing assets (at positive net present values); or replacement may not even take place if replacement costs are above economic values. Finally, it may be difficult to obtain the prices of new assets which are similar to existing ones; for instance, where there is rapid technological change, prices of new (replacement) assets will reflect different levels of operating efficiency compared with similar assets in existing use.

In summary, replacement costs should be expected to provide superior estimates of asset values compared with historic cost accounting. Such numbers provide useful estimates of value for firms which are comparing the cost of acquiring a company with the alternative of buying new assets from primary producers. However, the analyst should be aware of the pitfalls in order to know how valuable his data really is.

Market value of the assets

If the individual assets of the company are traded in a second-hand market, recent prices may provide a good estimate of their value. However, the second-hand market may be relatively inactive. Also, the price of the asset may reflect a use value other than that currently applicable. For example, a building may be worth far more as an office block than as a factory.

If the firm is using the asset as a factory the question is: 'What is the cost of converting it to the alternative use?' Other assets, such as patents or specialised machinery, may only have a value in one particular use. Also, even if approximate values can be obtained for all the assets of the firm, some price may still have to be paid for growth potential.

Present value of future cash flow

One obvious valuation method is to forecast the future net cash flows of an asset and discount them at some risk-adjusted rate of return. The rate chosen should reflect the prevailing risk free rate of interest plus some premium for the risk associated with post-merger activity; (see Chapter 2 for a method of arriving at a discount rate). This may be an essential step even if a company's shares are traded on a stock exchange, because, in order to find the value of the merger benefits, the difference between the pre-merger and post-merger value of the assets must also be determined, and that difference may often only be found by forecasting and discounting future cash flows.

CONCLUSIONS

In this chapter, we have stressed the need to justify mergers in terms of potential economic benefits. In examining these benefits it is important to compare them with alternatives to mergers. A merger is frequently costly in terms of legal costs, management time and the bid premium which is paid by the acquirer to the acquiree. The benefits might be obtained at a lower cost by, for example, direct investment in real assets. We have also described in some detail the financial advantages shareholders may expect from a merger. While some can be significant, others seem minor if not worthless, for example unused debt capacity and the coinsurance effect. Finally, we have briefly described methods of valuing quoted and unquoted companies and the bid premium.

FURTHER READING

J R Franks, 'An Investigation into the Distribution of Gains from Merging', PhD Thesis 1979, London Business School.
J R Franks and J J Pringle, 'Debt Financing, Corporate Financial

Intermediaries and Firm Valuation', *Journal of Finance*, June, 1982.

J R Franks and J E Broyles, *Modern Managerial Finance*, Wiley 1979.

R C Stapleton 'The Acquisition Decision as a Capital Budgeting Problem', *Journal of Business Finance and Accounting*, No 2, 1975.

R C Stapleton, 'Merger Bargaining and Financing Strategy', *The Manchester School*, June 1971, pp. 131–144.

G Warner, 'Bankruptcy Costs: Some Evidence', *Journal of Finance*, May 1977, 32, pp.337–348.

17

Taxation of corporations in the UK

Raymond K Ashton

An understanding of the corporate tax system is a prerequisite to a full understanding and appreciation of those entries in the financial accounts labelled 'taxation', and the impact of taxes on project profitability. The treatment of deferred taxation can dramatically affect such ratios as earnings per share, return on shareholders' funds and 'gearing'. This chapter sets out the main provisions of the UK tax system as it affects companies.

THE STATUTORY PROVISIONS

The taxation of income, capital and value added (VAT) is governed by the provisions of the Income and Consolidated Taxes Act 1970 and subsequent Finance Acts. The levying provisions relating to expenditure taxes, such as VAT, excise and stamp duties, are contained in individual Acts and Standing Orders.

Direct and indirect taxation

Taxes are usually categorised as either direct or indirect. Those based on the receipt of income or capital are termed direct, whereas those levied on expenditure are termed indirect.

Principal direct taxes are:

1 Income tax.
2 Corporation tax.
3 Capital gains tax.

Principal indirect taxes are:

1   Customs duties.
2   Excise taxes.
3   VAT.
4   Stamp duties.

The relative importance of individual taxes

The total UK revenue from the various taxes and their relative importance can be seen from Table 17.1.

About 40 per cent of all government tax revenue derives from individual income taxes, 7 per cent from corporation tax (including advance corporation tax) and 18 per cent from VAT. Various customs and excise duties account for most of the remainder.

Who pays the different taxes?

Direct tax is assessed on individuals and corporations. Individuals include the self-employed, partnerships and those persons in full time employment. They pay income tax, capital gains tax, capital transfer tax, stamp duties, development land tax, value added tax. Corporations pay corporation tax, petroleum revenue tax, development land tax, VAT, excise duties and stamp duties.

Taxes which have been repealed but are included in Table 17.1 are surtax (last assessments relate to 1972/1973) and estate duty (last assessments relate to the period prior to 26/3/74). These are retained because prior year assessments are still outstanding.

The 'Schedules' within the tax system

The income of both corporations and self-employed individuals (including partnerships) is calculated by reference to a number of Schedules which make up the Consolidated Taxes Act. These categorise income according to source. Their coverage and related cases are set out below.

Schedule A –   Income from land and buildings, including rents and certain premiums for leases.

Schedule B –   The 'assessable value' of woodlands managed on a commercial basis. ('Assessable value' is one-third of the woodland's annual value.)

Schedule C –   Income from 'gilt edged securities' payable in the UK as well as certain overseas public revenue dividends, paid through a banker or other person in the UK.

Table 17.1
Taxation and miscellaneous receipts

£ million

	1981–82	1982–83 forecast
	Estimated outturn	
Taxation		
Inland Revenue—		
Income tax	28,504	30,775
Corporation tax	4,800	4,850
Petroleum revenue tax	2,380	2,290
Supplementary petroleum duty	2,050	2,040
Capital gains tax	540	600
Development land tax	35	40
Estate duty	16	10
Capital transfer tax	470	465
Stamp duties	800	810
Special tax on banking deposits	355	—
Total Inland Revenue	*39,950*	*41,880*
Customs and Excise—		
Value added tax	12,300	14,750
Oil	4,550	5,100
Tobacco	3,325	3,525
Spirits, beer, wine, cider and perry	3,000	3,275
Betting and gaming	500	550
Car tax	525	600
Other excise duties	20	20
EC own resources		
Customs duties, etc.	920	1,060
Agricultural levies	210	270
Total Customs and Excise	*25,350*	*29,150*
Vehicle excise duties	1,629	1,854
National insurance surcharge	3,594	3,443
Total taxation	70,523	76,327
Miscellaneous Receipts		
Broadcast receiving licences	603	754
Interest and dividends	260	321
Gas levy	383	512
Other	4,519	4,981
Total	**76,288**	**82,895**

Schedule D – This is divided into the following 'cases':

Case I   – Trade

Case II   – Professions or vocations (applicable to individuals only)

Case III   – Interest received, annuities and other annual payments (from UK sources)

Case IV   – Overseas income from shares

Case V   – Overseas income from trading and loan interest

Case VI   – Miscellaneous income, includes insurance commission and any other income not falling within any of the other cases of Schedule D

Schedule E – Wages and salaries from employments (including directorships) are taxed under Schedule E, which is made up of three cases: most individuals are Case I

Case I   – This covers employees resident in the UK, irrespective of whether the employment is based in the UK or overseas.

Case II   – Work done in the UK by a non-resident

Case III   – Work done wholly abroad by a UK resident domiciled abroad, whose salary is remitted here during the course of an overseas employment, but excludes income taxed under Case I or II

Schedule F – Dividends paid by companies and certain other distributions.

Financial and fiscal years

The taxation of corporations is levied by reference to financial years, while individuals are taxed by reference to fiscal years.

Financial Year – This runs from 1 April in one year to 31 March in the next. The financial year 1982 refers to the period from 1 April 1982 to 31 March 1983.

Fiscal year   – This runs from 6 April one year to 5 April the next. Fiscal year 1982/83 refers to the period from 6 April 1982 to 5 April 1983.

The Chancellor, in his Budget speech, announces the rate of corporation tax for the previous financial year and the rates of personal tax etc., for the forthcoming year. Thus, in March 1982 he announced the Corporation tax rate for the financial year 1981 and the personal tax rates and allowances for the fiscal year 1982/83.

Companies whose financial year does not end on 31 March normally have to calculate their tax liability on a provisional basis, for at least part of the year.

Example

A company with its financial year ending on 30 June 1982 will make its tax provision as follows:

> 1 July 1981 – 31 March 1982 at the rate declared in the Budget speech in March 1982.
> 1 April 1982 – 30 June 1982 at the rate declared in March 1982, which will then be amended if necessary to the rate announced in March 1983. Any additional liability is generally charged against unappropriated profits.

CORPORATION TAX

A corporation may be assessed to tax, under a number of headings. Tax is chargeable on:

1   trading profits.
2   investment income.
3   net chargeable gains (capital gains tax).

Relief from tax may be given for:

1   capital allowances (balancing charges and allowances).
2   charges on income (e.g. debenture stock interest).

We shall now deal with each of these items.

Trading profits

Trading income for corporation tax purposes is calculated by reference to the rules of Schedule D Case I. These rules are a mixture of statute and case law. The Courts have agreed that companies' profits, based on normal accounting principles, are acceptable for tax purposes, unless statute or case law rules to the contrary.

As a result, a company's tax computation is based on its accounting profits. These are then adjusted for any income items which are not taxable and any disallowable expenses. The most important of the former are dividends received from other UK companies, while depreciation represents the major disallowable item. Also, as we shall see later, the government gives specified capital allowances.

The criteria for determining whether any particular expense item is allowed for tax purposes are:

(a) Is the expense disallowed by statute; for example, entertaining UK customers?

(b) Has the expense been incurred 'wholly and exclusively' for the purpose of the business?

Unless the expense qualifies on both counts it will not be allowed for tax purposes. Obviously, some items will give rise to contention. Examples are bad debt provisions and repairs; in the latter case the Inland Revenue might seek to 'capitalise' a proportion of the expenditure.

The general presumption, however, is that accounting profits are taxable profits, subject to the specific adjustments referred to above. A proforma corporation tax assessment is shown in Table 17.2.

Table 17.2
Proforma corporation tax assessment

	£
Taxable income (i.e. adjusted accounting profit)	X
Deduct: Capital allowances, given in lieu of depreciation	X
	X
Less: Charges on income, this includes deeds of covenant and more importantly, loan stock interest	X
	X
Add: Net chargeable gains – capital gains minus capital losses	X
Taxable profit	X

Investment income

As stated above, dividends received from other UK corporations are not subject to further tax, as they have been paid from profits on which corporation tax has already been charged. Other forms of investment income, such as interest and dividends received from overseas companies, are taxed in full.

Capital allowances and cash grants

This section covers both the allowances a company can claim and the liabilities it can incur, on the acquisition or disposal of a capital asset.

Capital expenditure allowances

Before calculating the allowances, expenditure must be classified into one or more of the following categories:

(a) Plant and machinery.
(b) Motor cars.
(c) Factories and warehouses.
(d) Insulation of factories and warehouses.
(e) Patents, R and D expenditure and agricultural buildings.

The courts have been very permissive in their interpretation of what constitutes plant and machinery. As a result, office furniture and equipment and vans and lorries are treated as plant and machinery. The significance of this will become evident below.

Since the 1960s there have been a number of changes in the allowances given to companies in respect of capital expenditure and the allowance for plant and machinery and industrial buildings. As in most countries in the world, the tax relief for capital expenditure is restricted to the historic cost of the asset and so no account is taken of inflation. The main features of the current system are set out below.

(a) *Plant and machinery.* An allowance known as the first year allowance (FYA) can be claimed in the year the plant is acquired. The current (1982/83) rate is 100 per cent, and so, in practice, most companies write off the full cost of their plant and machinery acquisitions against the profits of the year in which they purchase the plant and machinery. Where, for some reason, the 100 per cent FYA allowance is not claimed, a 25 per cent writing down allowance can be claimed in year two and until the asset is written off, but not in year one. The WDA is computed on a reducing balance basis.

Where the plant and machinery was acquired before October 1970, the allowances were less generous and the system of granting relief was slightly different. However, most companies still own plant and machinery acquired before October 1970. This expenditure ranks for a 25 per cent WDA, calculated on a reducing balance basis. In practice, for most companies, this allowance is relatively unimportant.

(b) *Motor cars.* Where the cost of the motor car is £8 000 or less, a company can claim a writing down allowance of 25 per cent on a reducing balance basis. Where the cost of the car is in excess of £8 000, the maximum allowance that can be claimed is £2 000 in any one year and cumulatively £8 000.

(c) *Factories and warehouses.* In the year of acquisition, expenditure on this asset ranks for an initial allowance of 75 per cent, also a WDA of 4 per cent on cost is allowed until the full cost of the asset is written off. This means that a factory is now written off completely after seven years.

(d) *Insulation of factories and warehouses.* The full cost can be written off in the year the expenditure is incurred.

(e) *Patents, R and D expenditure and agricultural buildings.* Special rates apply to these assets but they are of specialised importance only.

Balancing allowances and charges

Where a company sells an asset, the proceeds are normally taxable. The proceeds of sale are deducted from the expenditure on plant and machinery acquired before October 1970, irrespective of whether the plant was acquired pre- or post-October 1970.

Example

During the year ended 31 December 1981, X Ltd incurred capital expenditure on plant and machinery of £100 000, and sold plant and machinery acquired post-October 1970 for £16 000. The original cost of the plant sold was £50 000 and the unamortised balance of expenditure on plant and machinery acquired prior to October 1970 was £40 000.

Table 17.3
Example of balancing allowances

	Allowances	Post-October 1970 expenditure £'000	Pre-October 1970 expenditure £'000
Balance b/fwd		—	40
Additions/(sales)		100	(16)
FYA – 100%	100	100	24
WDA – 25%	6		6
	106	—	18

The company can therefore offset £106 000 against its trading profits for the year ending 31 December 1981, leaving expenditure of £18 000 to carry forward. Where the disposal proceeds are greater than the pooled balance brought forward, the residual balance will be taxed as a balancing charge.

Balancing allowances will now only occur where either a company ceases to trade, or where a particular activity is discontinued and the related assets are sold. In these cases the balancing allowance on each asset category will be the difference between the written down value for tax purposes and the disposal proceeds.

Investment grants

Investment grants were introduced in 1966 and were in the form of cash grants given to firms who invested in new plant and machinery and new industrial buildings. The grants were calculated as a percentage of the asset's acquisition cost and were usually between 20 per cent and 25 per cent.

The Industry Act 1972 reintroduced investment grants (now renamed regional development grants) for expenditure on new plant and machinery, and industrial buildings in regions designated as development, or intermediate development areas. The Department of Trade and Industry can provide a map of designated areas, together with a schedule of the allowances etc., available to firms interested in setting up in these areas.

With regional development grants up to 20 per cent, the net cost per £100 of investing in plant and machinery in a special development area is:

	£	£
Cost		100
Tax relief £100 at 52%	52	
Grant	20	72
Net cost		28

Net chargeable gains

Net chargeable gains are capital gains minus any capital losses. They are calculated by applying the rules of capital gains tax. For assets acquired after 6 April 1965, the calculation is relatively simple. From the proceeds of disposal, the original cost and any other allowable expenditure is deducted. If the result is a 'surplus' on disposal, the amount is assessable to corporation tax. A loss can be offset against:

(a) Current or future capital gains.
(b) Current trading profits.

For assets acquired before 6 April, 1965, two calculations are involved:

1 As above, disposal proceeds are compared with original cost and any other allowable expenditure.
2 Disposal proceeds are compared with the asset's value at 6 April 1965, together with any allowable expenditure incurred on the asset since that date.

If a gain results from both these calculations, the lower gain is included in the corporation tax assessment. If both figures show a loss, the lower loss will be available for relief, as outlined above. Where these calculations show a gain by one method and a loss by another, no liability will arise and no loss relief will be given.

Taxation of capital gains is a relatively recent innovation. A comprehensive capital gains tax was first introduced in 1965. Until the financial year 1973, net chargeable gains were taxed at corporation tax rates.

The present system charges both income and gains at a uniform rate, but allows capital gains to be taxed at a lower effective rate, by requiring only a fraction of the gains to be charged. For the financial years 1973 to 1982 inclusive, the fraction is $^{30}/_{52}$, so that the effective tax rate on capital gains is 30 per cent.

Charges on income

These are defined in the Act as annual payments and include deeds of covenant, debenture interest and royalties. For most companies the most important of these is debenture interest. It should be pointed out that only the interest actually paid is allowable, which could mean that some of the interest charged in the accounts will not be allowable until a later year.

HOW THE SYSTEM WORKS

Rates

The current rate of corporation tax is 52 per cent. Small companies pay tax on their profits at 40 per cent. The question is then: 'What is a small company?' This is defined by reference to profits. For the financial year 1982 companies will pay tax at 40 per cent if their taxable profits are less than, or equal to, £90 000. There is also a tapering relief, where a company's profits are greater than £90 000 and less than £225 000. The effect of this relief is to increase the average rate of corporation tax gradually, so that at £225 000 the 52 per cent rate is reached.

Example

It is easier to explain the system by reference to an example. Suppose a company whose accounting period is co-terminus with the financial year, has been earning profits of £200 million for a number of years and that during the year to 31 March 1982 it paid a dividend of £70 million; the profit and loss account for that year would be as follows:

Table 17.4
Example of corporation tax effects

	£ million Year to 31 March 1982
Taxable profits	200
Corporation tax (52%)	104
	96
Dividend	70
Profits after tax	26

On the dividends the company must pay Advance Corporation Tax (ACT). The ACT is an advance on the company's corporation tax liability for the accounting period in which the dividend is paid. This advance is related to the amount of the dividend, as the profits for the year in which the dividend is paid are not known when the distribution is made. To date, the advance has been some fraction of the dividend paid, although there is no reason why it should not be a multiple, as in some other countries. The current rate of ACT is 30/70ths.

Any ACT paid during an accounting period can be offset against the corporation tax payable on the profits of that accounting period. This will become clearer by looking at the example.

How much ACT will be paid on the dividends?

	£ million 1981/82
Rate of ACT	3/7ths
Dividend	70
ACT	30

How much tax will be paid on the profits for the same period?

The ACT paid can be offset against the tax payable for the period thus:

	Yr to 31 March 1982 *£ million*
Corporation tax	104
Less ACT	30
	74

The residual amount of £74 million is known as *mainstream corporation tax*.

ACT paid during an accounting period can be offset against the corporation tax payable on the profits of the accounting period in which the related dividend is paid. The amount which can be offset is restricted to the lower of:

(a)   ACT paid on the distribution; or
(b)   30 per cent of income chargeable to corporation tax, excluding capital gains.

It is important to note that the level of dividends paid does not affect the company's total corporation tax bill; as we shall see, it only alters the date that bill must be paid.

If the company cannot fully offset the ACT paid:

1   Unrelieved ACT can be carried back for up to two years, in the following order:
   (a)   Against the corporation tax payable on the preceding year's profits.
   (b)   Any residual balance, against the corporation tax payable on the profits of the year prior to the preceding year.

(The restriction referred to above also applies to the two years. This relief must be claimed within two years of the end of the accounting period in which the unrelieved ACT arose.)

2   Any ACT unrelieved by a claim under [1] can be carried forward and relieved in future accounting periods without time limit.

Shareholders are given a tax credit on the dividend they receive, equal to the amount of ACT which has been paid on that dividend. For a standard rate taxpayer, this means there is no additional tax liability. The following example, which is based on the figures in Table 17.4, shows how the calculations work out:

Income of shareholders	*1978/79* *£*	*1981/82* *£*
Dividend	67	70
Tax credit	33	30
Gross income	100	100

The tax credit is equal to tax at the standard rate on effective gross income so that there is no further tax liability for the standard rate payer.

Where a taxpayer's marginal rate of tax is less than the standard rate, he can reclaim the difference from the Inland Revenue; in the opposite case, the IR will raise an additional assessment on the taxpayer. To date the rate of ACT has been such that it has given the taxpayer a tax credit equivalent to the tax which would have been payable on the gross equivalent income.

Payment of tax

ACT is accounted for on a quarterly basis and corresponds to the usual quarterly periods, that is 31 March, 30 June, 30 September and 31 December. Where a company's accounting period does not end on one of these dates it has to make an extra return: this extra return will cover a period of less than three months so that the first return in the new accounting period will also be for a period of less than three months.

Companies formed after 31 March 1976 pay mainstream corporation tax nine months after the end of the accounting period. The position is more complicated for companies formed before that date.

Until 1965/66 companies paid tax by reference to fiscal years. The assessment for a particular fiscal year was based on the accounting period ending in the preceding year of assessment. The accounting period for 31 December 1964 would be the basis period for the 1965/66 assessment because the period ended in the preceding fiscal year (1964/65). All companies paid taxes on 1 January in the year of assessment, e.g. the 1965/66 liability would have been payable on 1 January 1966. For companies incorporated before April 1965, the new system came into operation after the end of the 1965/66 fiscal year. It was decided that these companies should retain the credit period they had been given previously. For example, in the above case this would be one year and one day. The credit period clearly depended on the date of the accounting period and, as we shall see, the most advantageous accounting period from a tax planning point of view, was any time after 6 April; in practice the Revenue would only accept accounting periods ending at a month end, for example 30 April.

Companies therefore discharged their tax liabilities some time after earning the profits on which they paid tax. This period varied from nine months, in the case of companies with accounting periods ending in March, to 20 months in the case of those with periods ending in April.

Suppose X Ltd ended its accounting period on 30 June 1964. This period ends in the fiscal year 1964/65 and so would form the basis of assessment for the fiscal year 1965/66, since companies paid tax on the accounting profits ending in the preceding year of assessment. Tax would be payable on 1 January 1966 and the period of credit between earning the profits and paying tax would be eighteen months, i.e. June 1964–January 1966.

Many people have difficulty understanding this rule. An easy way to remember the rule is as follows:

Accounting period date	*Payment of tax*
1 January – 31 March	The following 1 January
1 April – 31 December	Go to the following 1 January and then add one year.

From a tax planning point of view, the most advantageous time to end an accounting period would have been 6 April 1964, as the interval between earning the profits and payment of tax on those profits would have been nearly twenty-one months.

Implications for financial reports

Post-1966 companies only show the current tax charge in their accounts.

For pre-1966 companies the situation is more complex: those with accounting periods ending January, February and March will show one tax charge, all other companies will show two charges.

In order of importance, the most popular accounting dates are: 31 December, 31 March and 30 September.

Companies in some sectors report their results very close to each other. For example, a number of banks end their accounting periods in February, while September is a popular date for brewers.

Illustration of a corporation tax computation

In the following example C Ltd makes up its accounts to 31 December each year. Table 17.5 shows results for the year to 31 December, 1975, when ACT and standard rate tax were 35%.

Table 17.5
A corporation tax computation

	£'000	
	£'000	
Trading profits before capital allowances	100.0	
Charges on income (only £5 000 paid)	10.0	
Dividends paid	35.0	
Chargeable gains	10.4	
Capital allowances	15.0	

	£'000	Notes
Schedule D Case I	100.0	1
Deduct capital allowances	15.0	2
	85.0	
Add chargeable gains	6.0	3
	91.0	
Less charges on income	5.0	4
Net taxable profit	86.0	
Corporation tax at 52% on 86.0	44.7	
Less relief for ACT paid	15.0	5
Net mainstream tax liability	29.7	

Notes

1 It was assumed that the trading profit figure had been adjusted for tax purposes, i.e. non-deductable items had been added back and vice versa.

2 Capital allowances are deducted from trading profits before adding chargeable gains.

3 The original £10 400 represents the net chargeable gains over the period; only $^{30}/_{52}$ of this figure is brought into the computation, because the effective rate of capital gains tax is 30 per cent, not 52 per cent.

4 Of the £10 000 charged in the accounts, only £5 000 was paid and so the remaining £5 000 has to be carried forward.

5 Relief for ACT: restricted to the lower of:
(a) ACT paid or (b) of profit after charges, but before capital gains.
(a) ACT paid $£32.5 \times \dfrac{35}{65} = £17.5$.
(b) 35% of profits after charges = 35% of £(85–5) = £28.

OVERSEAS TAX

This section discusses the treatment of overseas income received by a UK resident company. Attention will be focused on two main issues: relief for overseas tax paid and how ACT restricts the availability of this relief.

In principle all foreign income of a UK resident company is subject to corporation tax. Income, in this context, includes profits from foreign business, dividends, interest, royalties, receipts from foreign subsidiaries, associates and portfolio investments. In many cases this income will have suffered tax at source and to avoid double taxation a tax credit is given.

The general rule is that relief for foreign taxes paid is restricted to the lower of:

(a) foreign taxes paid

(b) the amount of UK corporation tax payable on the foreign income.

In cases where the rate of overseas tax is greater than UK corporation tax, relief will be restricted to the latter and in the opposite situation relief will be restricted to the former. Prior to 1965, relief was given in full for overseas taxes paid, whatever the rate. The post-1965 restriction increased the cost of investing abroad and it was hoped that this would stimulate UK investment at the expense of investment overseas.

Where companies have both UK and overseas income from which dividends and ACT are paid, the Finance Act 1972 states that ACT relief must be taken before claiming any relief for overseas tax paid. The steps involved in calculating this relief are as follows:

1 Calculate the UK corporation tax liability on each source of income.
2 Allocate ACT paid, subject to the restrictions noted above against each tax liability. This is calculated in two stages:
   (a) The maximum amount of ACT is allocated to UK income.
   (b) Any unrelieved ACT must then be offset against the UK tax liability on the overseas income. The resultant net figure is the maximum amount of relief available in respect of the tax paid overseas.

Example

X Ltd has overseas profits of £4 000 and UK profits of £1 000. Overseas tax of £2 400 has been paid (at 60 per cent), together with dividends of £1 000 and ACT (3/7ths) of £600. The example below compares the maximum amount of double tax relief available and shows an extract of the profit and loss account after the claim has been made.

1 Calculation of relief for overseas tax paid

Source	Income	UK tax	ACT paid	Net	Relief for overseas tax paid
UK	1 000	520	300	200	—
Overseas	4 000	2 080	300	1 780	1 780

2 Profit and loss extract

		£	£
Overseas profits			4 000
UK profits			1 000
			5 000
Less: UK corporation tax		2 600	
Less: Relief for overseas tax		1 780	
		820	
	Overseas tax	2 400	3 220
			1 780
Less: Dividends			1 400
			380

3 The irrecoverable tax (£300) is referred to as surplus ACT, since this is the cause of the additional restriction on the amount of available relief.

STOCK RELIEF

In this section we discuss briefly why stock relief was introduced, how it is calculated, and then outline the current position.

During the second half of 1974 companies were finding it very difficult to replace stocks of raw material and finance work in progress, owing to the sharp increase in raw materials prices and wages rates. The escalation in the price of materials resulted from the commodity boom in late 1973 and early 1974. The increase in wage rates reflected the inflationary settlements in the aftermath of the miners' strike.

The government's original intention was that the relief would defer tax temporarily and last two years at the most. As we shall see, for most practical purposes this measure will be permanent. If this is the case most businesses will have achieved a permanent tax saving rather than just a deferral of tax.

To ease the pressure on company liquidity, in November 1974 the Chancellor of the Exchequer announced a stock relief measure, which would apply to accounting periods ending in the year to 31 March 1974. The magnitude of this measure had the effect of greatly reducing companies' tax liabilities for that year. Given that the tax on those profits would have been payable in most cases on 1 January 1975, the relief was of immediate benefit.

The relief was computed as follows:

Closing stock	a
Less Opening stock	b
	$\overline{x}$
Less 10% of trading profit before	y
capital allowances and loss relief	$\overline{x - y}$

Companies deducted (x–y) from their trading profit to arrive at the figure on which corporation tax was charged. It should be pointed out that stock relief, as originally announced, was only a *deferral* of tax and *not* a *permanent* tax saving.

The provisions relating to stock relief were first incorporated in the Finance Act (1) 1975. Since then there have been eight Finance Acts, Finance Act (2) 1975, 1976, 1977, 1978, 1979, 1980, 1981 and 1982.

Finance Act 1975 (2) continued the relief for another year and also extended its coverage in two important ways:

(a) In the case of companies, stock relief was extended to all companies, irrespective of the value of their stock. Originally, the relief was only given where the value of the company's stocks exceeded £25 000.

(b) To compensate those businesses not previously eligible for stock relief, a bonus was given in the form of additional stock relief.

Finance Act 1976. The clawback, in the form of 10 per cent of trading profits, was amended. In future the clawback was to be 15 per cent (rather than 10 per cent) of trading profits after deducting capital allowances and losses, rather than after adding back capital allowances and losses as before.

Finance Act 1977. The relief was to continue in its existing form.

Finance Act 1978. The Chancellor in his Budget speech announced that the existing scheme would continue until 1979/80 and indefinitely thereafter, unless an acceptable scheme of inflation accounting had been accepted for tax purposes. If by April 1979 no permanent scheme seemed likely, the relief given in the first two years of the scheme was to be written off. Provisions were also announced for writing off relief allowed in later years.

Finance Act 1979. The government honoured the promise of the previous administration to continue stock relief in its present form and introduced legislation to prevent accumulation of large deferred tax liabilities relating to unrecovered stock relief. In relation to the latter, legislation was passed which had the effect of:

(a) writing off the potential tax liability in respect of stock relief allowed for accounting periods ending in the financial years 1973 and 1974; *and*

(b) writing off stock relief which has not been clawed back within a six-year period.

The example in Table 17.6 below shows how the legislation affects companies.

Table 17.6
How a company can benefit from stock relief

Accounting period	Stock relief	Financial Year
Year ended 31 December 1973	400	1973
1974	200	1974
1975	300	1975
1976	400	1976
1978	600	1977
1978	400	1978
1979	250	1979
1980	350	1980

The effect of the legislation was that stock relief granted for the financial years 1973 and 1974 (400 and 200) was written off in the first accounting period after 31 March 1979, i.e., 31 December 1979. Thereafter, unrecovered relief for subsequent accounting periods will be written off after six years. This means that the relief granted for the accounting period ending 31 December 1975 will not be written off until 31 December 1982.

The maximum amount of clawback that can be recovered is limited to the amount of unrecovered relief. That is, the stock levels of periods that have been written off are ignored. This means that the opening stock value for the purposes of computing the maximum amount of clawback is the value of the stock at the beginning of the period which immediately follows the accounting period in which the stock relief has been written off.

Finance Act 1980. It was announced that until an acceptable system of inflation accounting is introduced, stock relief would continue in its present form. In addition, where stock levels fall by more than 5 per cent of the opening value of the stock at the beginning of the accounting period, the clawback can be deferred to the next accounting period. If the level falls again in the second year no further deferrment is possible. The relief will also be restricted if the clawback is in excess of £100 000 and the stockholding is financed by creditors, i.e., if creditors are greater than debtors.

Finance Act 1981. In November 1980 the government announced that a new form of stock relief would be introduced in the Finance Act 1981. The new relief took effect from the date it was announced, in the form of an index linked stock adjustment. A general index, based on a number of indices for various categories of stock, is applied to opening stock. The relief is computed by multiplying the opening stock by the change in the general index during the accounting period. An example of how this relief works is set out below.

	£m	*All Stocks Index*	
Opening stock	10		
Closing stock	2	1 January 1981	100
Taxable profits	5	31 December	110

Stock relief = Opening stock × $\dfrac{\text{Change in the index during the period}}{\text{Opening index}}$

$$= 10\,000\,000 \times \frac{(110 - 100)}{100}$$
$$= 10\,000\,000 \times 0.10$$
$$= \text{£1 million.}$$

Taxable profits after stock relief: £5 million – £1 million = £4 million. The other points to note about this form of relief are:

(a) A reduction in stock *values* during the year do not affect the relief claimed for that year.

(b) The first £2 000 of stock is ignored: only the excess is brought into the computation.

(c) There is no clawback of the relief unless the business ceases to trade or there is a reduction in the scale of business which amounts to a cessation.

(d)   Tax losses attributable to stock relief can only be carried forward and offset against future trading profits for 6 years.

For the purposes of the relief trading stock includes property of any
description sold in the ordinary course of a trade and any materials
used in the manufacture of such property. It includes work in progress
but excludes:

(a)   securities such as stocks and shares;
(b)   land, other than land ordinarily sold in the course of the trade
only after being developed by the company or, by another
company in the group;
(c)   goods let on hire purchase.

Payments on account are deducted from the value of stock and
special provisions cover company reconstructions, successions and the
avoidance of tax by means of increasing stock value.

In summary, this relief represents a close approximation of the effect
of inflation on stock.

Finance Act 1982 There were no changes in stock relief in the 1982
Finance Act.

LOSSES

So far the chapter has assumed that only profits have been made: this
section will cover the treatment of losses. Losses can be used by
individual companies, and where the company is a member of a group
they can be used to relieve the profits of other members of the group.
Both aspects will be covered.

Basic relief

This is allowed as follows:

1   Against trading profits of future periods, without any time limit.
2   Against other profits of the accounting period in which the loss
was incurred; these include chargeable gains, but charges on
income cannot be used in these circumstances to increase the
trading loss and must be carried forward. In a later year these
charges can be relieved against trading profits.
3   Any balance which remains after (2) can be relieved against the
total profits of the preceding accounting period. Total profits for

this purpose are defined as trading and other income, including net chargeable gains but *before* charges on income.

It should be noted that a claim under (3) can only be made after a claim under (2), but a claim under (2) does not have to be accompanied by a claim under (3).

To be able to claim relief under (2) and (3), the company must be able to satisfy the Inland Revenue that the trade was being carried on with a reasonable expectation of profit.

Group relief

Group relief is available to members of a group. For this purpose companies are members of a group if one is the subsidiary of the other, or both are subsidiaries of a third company. A subsidiary is a company whose share capital is at least 75 per cent owned by a parent company (or 51 per cent in some cases).

This means that losses made by one company within a group can be offset against the profits of another. Before deducting any group relief, the claimant company must deduct from its total profits chargeable to corporation tax any losses brought forward, capital allowances and charges on income.

Consortia

Group relief is also available within consortia. The most common type of arrangement is where the surrendering company is a trading company whose share capital is owned by five or fewer companies.

If the company owned by the consortium makes trading losses, these can be surrendered to the owners of the consortium in proportion to their shareholding in the consortium.

A few years ago Barclays Bank organised a consortium to buy the rolling stock of British Rail. This was then leased back to British Rail. The losses attributable to the capital allowances were shared among the members of the consortium.

VAT

This section briefly covers the main provisions of value added tax and its effect on companies' cash flows.

The main provisions

VAT came into operation on 1 April 1973 and is administered by the Customs and Excise. It is collected at each stage of the production process, or supply of service. For VAT purposes, goods are classed either as inputs or outputs. Input tax will be suffered when a registered trader buys goods or services. Output tax is charged by a registered trader on goods or services supplied to customers. VAT returns are made up on a quarterly basis and if the input tax suffered exceeds the output tax, the taxable person is entitled to a refund. In the reverse case a payment must be made to the Customs and Excise office.

When VAT was first introduced the rate was 10 per cent on sales; subsequently, this was reduced to 8 per cent in July 1974. Since then there have been a number of changes, mainly affecting particular goods or categories of goods. For instance, the rate on petrol was increased to 25 per cent in November 1974 and this rate was also extended to a number of other goods in the 1975 Budget. In the 1976 Budget, the 25 per cent rate on petrol and on certain other goods was reduced to $12\frac{1}{2}$ per cent, although in the case of petrol, there was a duty increase to compensate for the reduction in VAT. The Finance Act 1979 standardised VAT at 15 per cent.

Certain types of goods, though taxable, have a zero VAT rate. Obviously this makes it easy for the government to increase the rate in future. Food, water, books, newspapers, fuel and power are among the most important of the zero-rated goods.

Some goods and services are exempt from VAT; they include land, health, education, insurance and banking. Where a person supplies exempt goods or services he need not register for VAT, but if he does not, he cannot reclaim a refund on his input tax; if he does register he can reclaim the input tax.

Who is liable to VAT? Anyone who supplies taxable goods or services in excess of £17 000 per annum (the original limit was £5 000).

SUMMARY

The system of corporate taxation has implications for the cash flow of companies and for their reported results. Payments of corporation tax depend on corporate profits net of various allowances and stock relief. Other tax payments result from VAT, ACT and capital gains tax. The difference between tax paid and tax accrued in the income statement results in a liability in the balance sheet.

Financial managers need not understand the immense detail of the tax system, but they should be aware of the general tax impact of decisions that they make. For instance, capital investment that attracts a one hundred percent first year allowance results in a large tax deferment for tax-paying companies. Companies that are not paying taxes receive this benefit only when they resume tax paying. In those cases it may pay them to acquire the use of the asset through leasing, as discussed in Chapter 12.

Companies that are not currently paying taxes but are making dividend payments must make payments of ACT which can be offset against corporation tax only when they resume tax paying. These dividends thus have a higher tax cost than for corporations paying corporation tax.

The features of the tax system described in this chapter have important implications for almost all financial decisions by corporations. Although the detailed management of the tax position can be left to tax experts, managers must understand the general features of the tax system to be able to make profitable decisions.

Bibliography

General

The following books provide a comprehensive discussion of corporate finance in a UK context:

J. R. Franks and J. E. Broyles, *Modern Managerial Finance*, (Wiley, 1979)

J. A. Samuels and F. M. Wilkes, *Management of Company Finance*, (Nelson, 1982)

J. F. Weston and E. F. Brigham, *Essentials of Managerial Finance*, (Holt, Reinhart and Winston, UK Edition, 1979)

A superb textbook which is more slanted to the US audience is:

R. A. Brealey and S. C. Myers, *Principles of Corporate Finance*, (McGraw-Hill, 1981)

Two books giving a useful treatment of financial accounting and management accounting respectively are:

W. Reid and D. R. Myddelton, *The Meaning of Company Accounts*, (Gower, 1982)

J. Sizer, *An Insight into Management Accounting*, (Pitman, 2nd edition, 1979)

Use of Funds

The four books on corporate finance in the general section above all give thorough treatments of capital project appraisal.

A more detailed treatment of capital budgeting and capital project appraisal is given in:

H. Bierman Jr. and S. Smidt, *The Capital Budgeting Decision: Economic Analysis of Investment Projects*, (5th edition, Macmillan, 1980)

A thorough treatment of the impact of inflation (apart from tax implications) is given by:

B. V. Carsberg and A. Hope, *Business Investment Decisions under Inflation* (Institute of Chartered Accountants, 1976)

An extended treatment of working capital management is:

G. P. E. Clarkson and B. J. Elliott, *Managing Money and Finance*, (2nd edition, Gower 1972)

The following book examines comprehensively the areas of money and exchange risk management:

A. R. Prindl, *Foreign Exchange Risk* (Wiley, 1976)

Financial control

Two books covering the general topic of planning and control are:

J. Dermer, *Management Planning and Control Systems* (Irwin, 1977)

R. V. Anthony and J. Dearden, *Management Control Systems*, (Irwin 1976)

The first of these books is mainly concerned with the overall design of information systems for organisational planning and control, while the second deals with accounting aspects.

A comprehensive basic textbook on costing and internal pricing is:

C. E. Horngren, *Cost Accounting: A Managerial Emphasis*, (Prentice-Hall, 1981)

A useful treatment of techniques of preparation, production and analysis of accounts as given in the Reid/Myddelton book in the general section above.

Raising funds

General discussions of the methods which investors use to appraise investments are given in:

W. F. Sharpe, *Investments*, (Prentice-Hall, 1978)

P. Richards, *United Kingdom and European Share Price Behaviour: The Evidence* (Kogan Page, 1978)

A discussion of financial statement analysis from the investor's point of view is:

G. Holmes and A. Sugden, *Interpreting Company Reports and Accounts* (Woodhead-Faulkner, 1979)

A thorough treatment of leasing in the UK is provided by:

T. M. Clark, *Leasing*, (McGraw-Hill, 1978)

An elementary introduction to the UK stock market is contained in:

Investors Chronicle, *Beginners Please*, (Throgmorton Publications, 1973)

More detailed references on going public are provided at the end of Chapter 13.

A general description of UK financial institutions is given in:

J. Revell, *The British Financial System*, (Macmillan, 1980)

The external environment

A good discussion of the issues in mergers and acquisitions is given in the books by Samuels and Wilkes and by Franks and Broyles referred to above. These books also review the general implications of taxation for corporate financial decisions.

Index

Accounting Standards Committee 353, 354, 355, 367
Accounting Standards Steering Committee
The Corporate Report 10
Acquisitions and mergers 375–92
  acquisition value – four questions 383–4
  economic benefits of merging 375–80
    changes in economies of scale 376–8
    exploiting new product 378
    market power 378–9
    purchase of managerial and technical skills 376
    valuation differences 379–80
  financial benefits of merging 380–3
    merging and diversification 380–1
    risk reduction and lower borrowing costs 381–2
    tax losses and unused capital allowances 383
    unused debt capacity 382–3
  traditional methods of asset valuation 386–91
    earnings per share 387–9
    market value of assets 389–90
    present value of future cash flow 390
    written-down replacement values 390–1
  valuing quoted company 384–61
Anaconda Co. 383
Argyris, C.
  Personality and Organisation 133
Archer, Simon 118, 169, 349, 353
Ashton, Raymond K. 350, 351, 393
Assets
  methods of obtaining use of 273
  valuation of 386–91
Association of Corporate Treasurers 13
Auditing, *see* Internal auditing

Bank borrowing 247–72
  appendix – information to support documentation 270–2
    accounting 271
    personnel 270
    production 271
    sales 271–2
  identifying need for 249–51
    question of amount needed and when 249–50
    question of internal financing 250–1
    question of profitability in expansion 250

presenting case for finance to bank
261–9
  balance sheets 264–8
    going concern approach by
      bank to 264–5
    gone concern approach by
      bank to 265–8
  evaluation of proposal 263–4
  need for adequate documenta-
    tion 262–3, 270–1
  need for security 268–9
    attributes of good security 269
    forms of security 268
    nature of security 269
relations with bank 259–61
  practical considerations 260–1
types of finance offered 252–9
  block discounting 252–3
  equity investment 257–8
  export finance 258–9
  factoring 252
  instalment finance (hire pur-
    chase) 254
  leasing 255–6
  long term loans 256–7
  medium term loans 256
  overdrafts 252
  support finance (stocking
    finance) 253–4
  vehicle contract hire 254–5
  venture capital 258
Bank of England 297
Barclays Bank 416
Borrowing, see Bank borrowing
British Petroleum
  rights issue of 1981 342
  underwriting costs 337
British Rail 416
Broyles, J. E. 19, 21
  See also Franks, J.R. and Broyles,
    J.E.
Budgetary control, see Budgets
Budgets 147–67
  budgetary control 146, 157–9, 167
    advantages and disadvantages
      147–8

installing the system 163–7
  budget committees 165–6
  budget manual 165
  budget period 164–5
  information codes 167
  timing of feedback 158–9
centres 149–50
compiling 150–7
  balance sheet 155, 157
  capital expenditure budget 154
  cash budget 155
  operating and service depart-
    ment budgets 153–4
  personnel budgets 153
  production costs budget 152–3
  profit and loss account 154, 156
  sales budget 151
computer use 162
defining 148–9
flexible 159–62
zero-base budgeting 162–3

Calvert, H.W. 118, 169
Capital project planning 21–47
  cash flow discipline 27–9
  computational resources 37–8
  data 38–40
    missing data – reverse economics
      38–9
    uncertain and erroneous 39–40
  defined 21
  essential elements 21
  goals 22
  probability analysis 42–4
  re-appraisal 46–7
  required rate of return standards
    and cost of capital 22–6
    cost of capital 22, 23–4
    effect of debt on required returns
      25–6
    required rates of return 24–5
  risk 44
  sensitivity analysis 40–2
    example 41–2

testing viability 26–7
  modern techniques 27
  traditional techniques 26–7
use of concept of internal rates of
    return (IRR) 30–3
use of concept of net present value
    (NPV) 29–30
  mid-year discounting 33–4
  NPV and expected value: deci-
    sion trees 36–7
  optimisation of mutually exclu-
    sive alternatives 34–6
use of discussion forum for
    problems 44–6
  tactics 45–6
Charterhouse Petroleum 302
City and Gracechurch Investment
    Trust 302
Clarkson, Geoffrey P.E. 19, 67
Clipsham, Michael 223, 247
Committee of Enquiry on Small
    Firms 261
Companies Acts
  1929 293
  1948 293, 296, 297, 300, 303, 353
  1967 353, 358
  1981 353, 358, 360, 362–4
Cooper, Ian 19, 21, 49
Corporate taxation, see Taxation of
    corporations in the UK
Costing 169–92
  break even graphs 184–90
    limiting factor 189–90
    'profit' or 'contribution' chart
      188–9, 190
    profit/volume (P/V) ratio
      186–7, 190
  cost control through variance
    analysis 175–82
    direct materials 176–7
    labour 178
    overheads 178–81
    presentation 182
  marginal 182–4
  question of making or buying in
    190–1
    opportunity costs 191

standard 170–5
  direct labour 173–4
  direct materials 173
  historical 172
  ideal 172
  normal or expected 172
  overheads 174–5
  revision of standards 172–3
treatment of fixed production ex-
    penses for financial state-
    ments preparation 191–2

Daniel, D.R.
  'Management Information Crisis'
    137
Dean, Joel 3
Decision trees 36–7
Dimson, Elroy 224, 291
Diners Club 302
Discounted Cash Flow 3
Driver, B.J.W. 197n

Equipment Leasing Association 275
Equity Capital for Industry 247
Equity rights issues 325–44
  choice between debt and equity
    328–30
  costs 336
  issue methods 325–8
  market reaction 340–2
  method 330–1
  raising equity at existing market
    prices 342–4
  setting terms and underwriting
    decision 336–40
  timing of external funding and
    rights issues 331–6
  underwriting 336–40
    historical returns to under-
      writers 339
    profitability 337
    purpose 336–7
    valuing worth of 337–9
European Economic Community
    (EEC)
  directives on financial reporting
    353

Export finance 258–9
External financial report presentation, *see* Presentation of external financial reports

Factoring 252
Finance Acts 393
  1972 410
  1975 and 1976 412
  1977 and 1978 413
  1979 275, 413, 417
  1980 and 1981 414
Finance for Industry 247
Finance function 3–14
  conceptual framework 6–8
    capital market opportunity costs 7
    efficient markets hypothesis 6–7
    required reward for risk 7–8
  financial management 8–10
    debt/equity ratio 8–9, 10
    debt structure 9, 10
    dividend policy 9–10
  historical perspective 3–4
  objectives of financial management 4–6
    maximising company value 6
    profit maximisation 4–5
  organisation 11–13
    Controller 12, 13
    Finance Director 12, 13
    Treasurer 12–13
  reporting and control 10–11
Financial control 117–18
  review of Part III on 118–19
  smoothing 117–18
Financial decisions
  effect of inflation 49–65
Financial environment 349–51
  review of Part V on 349–51
Forecasting financial requirements 227–45
  dynamic aspect 243–4
  inflation 242–3
  international aspects 244–5

long term cash forecasts 240–2
  format 240–2
  objective 240
monthly cash forecast and control 228–31
  capital expenditure 229
  interest 229
  investment income 229
  loans or financing received 229
  purchases, salaries and overheads 229
  receipts/payments – overseas subsidiaries 229
  tax 231
  trade debtors 229
short term cash control 239
short term cash forecast 231–7
  capital expenditure 235–6
  dividends 237
  interest 236
  investment income 234
  loans/financing arranged 234
  other overheads 235
  other payments 237
  other receipts 234
  receipts from debtors 234
  repayment of loans 237
  salaries and costs of employment 235
  stock purchases 234–5
  tax 236
source and application of funds 237–8
timing of cash plans 227–8
Franks, J.R. 350, 373
Franks, J.R. and Broyles, J.E. 8, 24, 383, 387
Franks, J.R. and Pringle, J.J. 383
Funds
  cash flows 17–18
  effect of inflation 19
  interest 18, 19
  review of Part II on 19–20
  review of Part IV on raising 221–5
  structure of institutions providing 248

use of company's 17
See also Bank borrowing

Henry, P.J. 197n
Hire purchase 254
Hodges, S.D.
  The Valuation of Variable Rate Leases 286
Hunt, P., Williams, C.M. and Donaldson, G. 4
Hurst and Sandler Co. 302

Imperial Chemical Industries (ICI) underwriting costs 337
Income and Consolidated Taxes Act 1970 393
Industrial and Commercial Finance Corporation 293
Industry Act 1972 402
Inflation and financial decisions 49–65
  computing interest rates 52
  effect of inflation on cost of funds 51
  effect of lags in cash flows 56–7
  forecasting for long and short term projects 55–6
  forecasting in real and money units 49–51
  forecasting prices 54–5
  impact on profitability 62–4
  relation between profits and cash flows 57–9
  relative price changes 52–3
  taxes 60–1, 64
    impact of stock relief 60, 61
  working in money terms or real terms 62
Inland Revenue 361, 398, 406, 407
  leasing and 281–2
Institute of Cost and Management Accountants
  defined budget centre 149
  defines budget centre 149
Institute of Internal Auditors 199
  Code of Ethics 214

Statement of Responsibilities of Internal Auditors 213
Internal auditing 197–218
  Appendix 1 – responsibilities of internal auditors 213–14
    independence 214
    nature 213
    objectives and scope 213
    responsibility and authority 213–14
  Appendix 2 – allocation of risks to auditable units 215–16
  Appendix 3 – example of 5-year internal audit plan 216–18
  audit of computing systems 209–12
    of computing department 211
    of operational systems 211–12
    of systems under development (pre-audit) 211
  audit programs 203–5
    auditing of financial controls 203
    operational auditing 203–5
  audit review 205–7
    audit in depth 206–7
    sampling methods 207
  benefits v. costs 212
  off-line controls 197–8
  on-line controls 197
  organisation 198
  planning 200–3
    audit plan 200–2
    budget 202
    calculation of staff numbers 202
    management agreement and stewardship 202–3
  reporting 207–9
  staffing 199–200
  terms of reference 198–9
Internal pricing 192–6
  transfers between cost centres 193
  transfers between profit centres 194–5
  two part and three part transfer price systems 195–6
Internal Rates of Return 27

in leasing 288–9
use of concept 30–3
International money management
  91–113
defined 91
domestic cash management 92–5
  collection process 92–4
    customer payment methods
      93–4
    guidelines 94
    order and invoice systems 93
  disbursements 95
  local treasury management 94
international cash management
      95–100
  acceleration of export proceeds
    96–8
  dollar interception 97
  interception in other curren-
    cies 98
  intercompany transfers 99
  value compensations 99
  netting 100
  retained foreign currency
    accounts 98–9
  accumulation accounts 99
  transfer of funds 95–6
international liquidity manage-
    ment 100–13
  export financing vehicles 110
  external hedges 111–13
    summary 113
  foreign exchange exposure
    103–7
    computer application 107
    decision responsibility 106–7
    defined 103–4
    exchange risk management
      104–5
    hedging 107
    identifying exposed positions
      105–6
    projection of possible losses
      106
    setting strategy 106
  internal techniques affecting

  future positions 108–10
  internal techniques affecting
    outstanding positions
    107–8
  intercompany term adjust-
    ment 108
  pre-payment of third-party
    commitments 107–8
  need for centralisation 101–2
  reinvoicing vehicles 110
  utilisation of funds interna-
    tionally 102
  vehicle companies 102–3

Leaper, Alan R. 118, 147
Leasing 273–90
  assets most subject to 274–5
  attractions of 274, 276
  choice of schedule of lease rentals
    285–90
  financial benefits – example
    276–82
    capital allowance 276–7
    leases v. purchase 277–8
    leasing and Inland Revenue
      281–2
    tax paying lessee 282–5
London Clearing Banks 269

Managing working capital, see
    Working capital
Mansbridge, R.L. 223, 227
Marsh, Paul 225, 325, 337
Mergers, see Acquisitions and
    mergers
Merrett, A.J. and Sykes, A. 3
Miller, Merton H. 221, 222
  See also Modigliani, Franco and
    Miller, Merton H.
Modigliani, Franco and Miller,
    Merton H. 221
  on choice between debt and equity
    328–9
Monopolies Commission 379

National Enterprise Board 247
Net Present Value, 4, 27, 341
  use of concept 29–30, 33–7
New issue market 291–324
  glossary 318–24
  issue costs 304–10
    administrative 304–5
    cash expenses 305
    conventional 306
    non-cash compensation 305, 307–8
    offer for sale 307, 309
    underpricing 308–10
  mechanics of flotation 310–15
    offer timetable 313
    prospectus 314–15
  methods of making new issue 297–304
    introductions and transfers of listing 302–4
    placings 301
    prospectus issues and offers for sale 298, 300–1
    tender issues 301–2
  reasons for obtaining Stock Exchange listing 293–6
    capital requirements 293–4
    enhancing company prestige 295–6
    financial needs of owners 294–5
    improving share marketability 295
  regulations 296–7
  role of Stock Exchange 291–3
    control 293
    listing 292
  structure 299
Nightingale, M.J.H., Co. 292

Overdrafts 252

Pilkington Brothers 296
Presentation of external financial reports 353–71
  balance sheet 361–4
    account format 362
    net asset format 362–4
    notes on accounts 364
  current cost accounts 367–70
  directors' reports 366–7
  funds statement 364–5
  law covering 353
  objectives 355–60
    degree of disclosure 357–9
    example 359
    explanatory notes 359–60
  profit and loss account 360, 361
    expenses 361
    sales 361
    tax 361
  requirements 353–5
  standard-setting bodies 353
Prindl, Andreas R. 20, 91

Rank Organisation 327
Ratzer, Peter 3
Reporting and responsibilities 121–46
  criteria for information usefulness 136–41
    management information needs 136–7, 138
    structured approach to reporting 139–41
    uses of financial information 137, 139
  internal financial reporting and management control 141–4
    cybernetic systems 143–4
    definition and distinctions 141–2
    feedback and effective systems 142–3
    management control systems 142
  keys to control 128–30
    accountability and controllability 129–30
    interpretation 129
    selectivity 129
    what to measure 128

organisational and behavioural
implications 130–6
impact of control on individuals
132–3
responsibility accounting 130
weaknesses of budgetary control
134–6
staffing, and operating management control system 144–6
accounting department 144–5
budget committee 145–6
management control/systems
committee 146
systems design in managerial
accounting 121–8
accounting control systems considered 127–8
control as perspective for
accounting systems 125–6
cycle of control 121–2
distinctions in accounting
systems 126–7
operating principles 122–5
Runton, Tessa Ryder 19, 21, 222

Scholefield, Harry H. 119, 197
Shares, *see* Equity rights issues, New
issue market
Solomon, Ezra
questions for financial management 14
*The Theory of Financial Manage-
ment* 14
Somers, A.J. 197n
Spring Grove Co. 302
Statements of Standard Accounting
Practice (SSAPs) 353, 354,
355, 364, 367–70 *passim*
Stock Exchange 247, 301, 302, 303,
311, 316, 342, 367, 389
Council 300, 327, 357
raising money on 325–8
reasons for obtaining listing on
293–6
regulations on new issues 296–7,
314

role 291–3
rules on financial reporting 353,
354
Yellow Book 296, 315

Taxation of corporations in the UK
393–417
Advance Corporation Tax (ACT)
404, 405, 406, 409, 410, 411
corporation tax 398–403
balancing allowances and
charges 401
capital allowances and cash
grants 399–400
charges on income 403
investment grants 402–3
net chargeable gains 402–3
on investment income 399
on trading profits 398–9
losses 415–17
basic relief 415–16
consortia 416–17
group relief 416
overseas tax 409–11
statutory provisions 393–7
direct and indirect taxation
393–4
financial and fiscal years 397
payers of different taxes 395–6
relative importance of individual
taxes 394–5
'schedules' within tax system
396–7
stock relief 411–15
system in action 403–9
corporation tax computation
408–9
implications for financial
reports 408
payment of tax 406–8
rates 403–6
VAT 417
Thomson, George R. 349, 353

Underwriting 336–40
Unlisted Securities Market (USM)
    292, 296, 298, 307, 308, 316

Value Added Tax (VAT) 417
Vaughan, C.D., Grinyer, P.H. and
    Birley, S.J. 317

Warner, G. 382
Water Act 1945 302
Willis Faber Co. 304
Wilson Committee 292
Wilson, Richard M.S. 118, 121
Working capital 67–90
  borrowing on 70–1, 85–6, 88
  current assets 67
  current liabilities 67–8
  defined 67
  flow of funds 76–80
  flows
    example 73–4
    timing 74–6

liquid assets 70
  ratio 71
long and short term management
    72–3
managing creditors 89–90
  question of discounts 89
  taxes 90
managing debtors 83–6
  borrowing on debtors 85–6
  buying debtors 86
  factoring debtors 84–5
  financing debtors 84
  net cash value 83–4
managing stocks 86–8
  types of stock finance 88
product cash cycle 80–1
  example of cash flows of new
    product 81–3
ratios 68–71

Young, Colin M. 224, 273